ENCYCLOPEDIA *of* DISCOVERY

Nature

Consulting Editors

Dr. Roger Carolin

David Ellyard

George Else and specialist staff

Dr. Allen E. Greer

David H. Levy

Dr. Susan Lumpkin

Dr. George McKay

Dr. Angela Milner

Dr. Eldridge M. Moores

Dr. Marie Rose

Dr. John Seidensticker

Dr. Frank H. Talbot

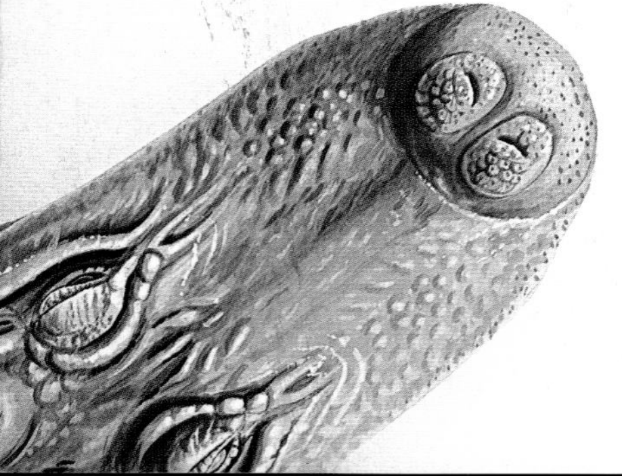

ENCYCLOPEDIA *of* DISCOVERY

Nature

FOG CITY PRESS

Published by Fog City Press
814 Montgomery Street
San Francisco, CA 94133

Copyright © 2002 Weldon Owen Pty Ltd
Reprinted 2003 (twice)

Chief Executive Officer John Owen
President Terry Newell
Publisher Lynn Humphries
Managing Editor Janine Flew
Coordinating Designer Helen Perks
Editorial Coordinator Jennifer Losco
Production Manager Caroline Webber
Production Coordinator James Blackman
Sales Manager Emily Jahn
Vice President International Sales Stuart Laurence

ISBN 1 876778 93 8

Color reproduction by Colourscan Co Pte Ltd
Printed by SNP Leefung Printers Limited
Printed in China

A Weldon Owen Production

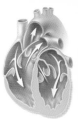

Project Managing Editor Rosemary McDonald
Project Editors Helen Bateman, Ann B. Bingaman,
Helen Cooney, Jean Coppendale, Kathy Gerrard,
Selena Quintrell Hand
Text David Burnie, Carson Creagh, Lesley Dow,
Linsay Knight, David H. Levy, Dr. Susan Lumpkin,
Sally Morgan, Steve Parker
Educational Consultants Richard L. Needham,
Deborah A. Powell
Text Editors Ann B. Bingaman, Lynn Cole,
Claire Craig, Emma Marks
Project Art Director Sue Burk
Designers Sylvie Abecassis, Karen Clarke, Nicole Court,
Kathy Gammon, Robyn Latimer, Michéle Lichtenberger,
Giulietta Pellascio, Sue Rawkins, Melissa Wilton
Assistant Designers Janet Marando, Kylie Mulquin,
Angela Pelizzari, Megan Smith
Visual Research Coordinators Jenny Mills, Esther Beaton
Photo and Visual Research Peter Barker, Karen Burgess,
Annette Crueger, Carel Fillmer, Sue Liu, Dimity MacDonald,
Amanda Parsonage, Amanda Weir

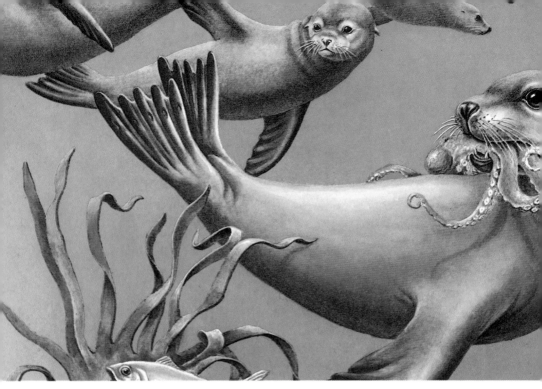

Contents

Plants and Animals

Planet Earth

Introduction

Encyclopedia of Discovery: Nature is a dynamic, fact-filled book that brings to life a multitude of subjects relating to the natural world. Here, in one compact volume, is detailed information about the world's amazing diversity of living things. Learn about the lives and habits of plants and animals both familiar and exotic, domestic and dangerous. Discover, too, the intricate and amazing workings of the human body.

The volume also presents information about earthquakes and volcanoes, stars and planets, tornadoes and floods—all the fascinating phenomena that play a vital part in the world in which we live, on land, in the sea, and right out to the farthest reaches of the universe.

Nature comprises 11 chapters, each structured as a series of self-contained double-page spreads dealing with one aspect of the subject. Simple, direct language and detailed, atmospheric illustrations and photographs will engage young readers and encourage them to discover for themselves the world around them.

Plants
and
Animals

Incredible Plants

Why are plants so important to animals and people?

How do plants make their own food?

Which plants grew when dinosaurs were alive?

Contents

• UNDERSTANDING PLANTS •

• THE PLANT KINGDOM •

• WHERE PLANTS LIVE •

• PLANTS AND HUMANS •

Introducing Plants

Plants are the key to the survival of all other living things. Plants provide much of the oxygen that animals and humans breathe, as well as much of the food they eat. Scientists who study plants, called botanists, have found and described more than 350,000 types of plants, but there are more. Plants come in all sizes and shapes. Some are so tiny you cannot see them without a microscope, but some are so tall you can scarcely see the top of them without a telescope. Many plants have brilliantly colored flowers and others have no flowers at all. Plants look different because they live in very different environments—on land or in water, thick forests or open plains, freezing mountains or hot deserts. Over millions of years, they have adapted to suit their own environment.

MICROSCOPIC VIEW
This tiny, single-celled diatom is one of the simplest plants. Its ancestors grew during the time of the dinosaurs. It could take up to 50 diatoms to cover the period at the end of this sentence.

ALL SHAPES AND SIZES
Plants grow in almost every environment in the world. Their size, shape and the way they grow are designed so that they can get the essential water and energy they need to survive, wherever they grow.

PLANT CELL

All living things are made up of microscopic cells and each cell has its own special function or purpose. Most cells contain a nucleus (the genetic control center) and a number of mitochondria that convert sugars into energy. They float in a liquid jelly called cytoplasm. Only plant cells, however, have chloroplasts. These contain chlorophyll, which is used in making the plant's food supply. Plant cells are also the only cells that have firm walls made of cellulose.

Group of plant cells

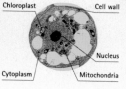

Single plant cell

Chloroplast

Cell wall

Nucleus

Cytoplasm

Mitochondria

PLANT PROFILE
Plants make their own food and have hard cell walls made of cellulose. They never stop growing and are usually rooted to one place.

DID YOU KNOW?

Most plants keep on growing until they die. Other living creatures stop growing when they reach maturity or become adults. Humans usually stop growing in their late teens or early twenties. Can you imagine how tall you would be at 80 if you kept on growing?

Plant Parts

ATTRACTING INSECTS
Rose petals may look smooth, but under a microscope you can see special light-reflecting cells that make the petals colorful and attractive to insects.

Unlike single-celled green algae (left), most plants have hundreds, thousands or even millions of cells. Plant cells are highly organized, and each part of a plant has its own specialized group of cells. Flowering plants have four parts: roots, stems, leaves and flowers. The roots, stems and leaves all contain xylem, the specialized transporting tissue that carries water and mineral salts, and phloem, which carries the nutrients (food) the plant makes. Each part of the plant has a different task. The roots anchor the plant and draw up water and mineral salts from the soil. The stem holds the plant up towards the light and transports water, mineral salts and other nutrients to the rest of the plant. The leaves make food for the whole plant and provide most of the breathing holes. The flowers contain the reproductive organs. The plant can survive only if the four parts do the jobs they are designed to do efficiently.

Xylem

Phloem

STEM SUPPORT
The xylem in the stem transports water and mineral salts up to the leaves and flowers. The phloem transports nutrients up or down to wherever they are needed.

GROUND HUGGING
Mosses have a less efficient transport system than flowering plants and do not grow tall. They form a blanket close to their water supply.

GROWING UP AND UP
To support the extra weight of a growing plant, some stems become woody while others become thicker but remain soft (left). Some plants grow tendrils to cling to something stronger if the plant is too heavy.

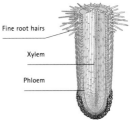

Fine root hairs

Xylem

Phloem

GATHERING SUPPLIES
Fine hairs on the tip of the root absorb water and mineral salts from the soil. These flow up the xylem like milk up a straw. Nutrients that provide energy travel down to the roots through the phloem.

Stigmas

Stamen

Ovary

MIX AND MATCH
This rose contains both male and female reproductive organs. The female organ contains the stigma (on a style or stalk above the ovary). This receives pollen from a male stamen, usually from another flower.

DID YOU KNOW?
As a tree gets older, the roots grow bigger. The roots of large trees, which need a lot of water and a firm anchor, can grow strong enough to destroy a drainpipe, pierce a pavement or raise bumps in the road above them.

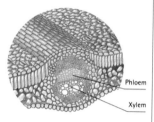

Phloem

Xylem

MAKING SUPPLIES
Cells in the middle layer of the leaf manufacture sugars—the plant's nutrients or food supply. This layer also contains xylem and phloem, the transport systems.

SEARCHING FOR WATER
There are two basic sorts of roots—tap roots and fibrous roots. All other roots are variations of these. A tap root, which grows straight down to reach water deep in the soil, is a single main root with smaller roots branching off it. Fibrous roots have no main root and spread out (rather than down) to gather water from the top layers of soil. Plants that grow in unfamiliar environments are often forced to adapt their roots to suit their surroundings. Aerial roots, for example, are adapted fibrous roots. They gather moisture from the air and mineral salts from the surface of the tree on which they grow.

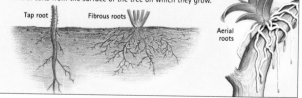

Tap root   **Fibrous roots**

Aerial roots

Discover more in Helping Nature

Plant Processes

Animals must go out and find food, but most plants stand still and make their own. Their food-making process is called photosynthesis and it uses four ingredients: daylight (*photos* in Greek), chlorophyll to absorb or trap the light, water and mineral salts from the soil, and carbon dioxide from the air. Chlorophyll is found only in the green part of plants. This is usually the leaves, but in some plants, like the cactus (above), most of the chlorophyll is found in the stem. From these ingredients, the plant manufactures sugars and, in the process, gives off oxygen. Some of this oxygen is used by the plant in another process called respiration. In dark and daylight hours, this process converts the sugars into the energy the plant needs to live and grow. Most of the oxygen, however, returns to the air and is the source of the vital oxygen that we breathe.

Carbon dioxide
Carbon dioxide from the air enters the leaves through the stomata.

Oxygen and water
Oxygen, a by-product of photosynthesis, and excess water are released into the air.

THE RECYCLING PLANT
The leaves absorb sunlight and "breathe in" carbon dioxide. The roots absorb water and mineral salts, which the xylem transports to the leaves. The chlorophyll now has all it needs to make the sugars, which the phloem transports around the plant.

UPSIDE-DOWN LEAVES
The stomata in most plants are on the underside of the leaves. In these lily pads the stomata are on the upper side, facing the air, because this is their source of carbon dioxide (for photosynthesis).

SAVING WATER
As water is lost through the leaves in a process called transpiration, some trees shed their leaves in the coldest or driest season. The tree survives on stored food and the leaves fertilize the soil around the roots.

DID YOU KNOW?
As seaweeds produce food through photosynthesis, they need green chlorophyll. In red and brown seaweeds, the green chlorophyll is hidden by the stronger colors of "assistant" pigments. These help the chlorophyll to absorb the sunlight passing through water.

Growing flower
The flower needs energy from the plant's sugars to grow.

Chlorophyll
Green chlorophyll in the leaf cells absorbs sunlight.

Phloem
Phloem cells transport the sugars from the leaves to other parts of the plant.

Water
Rainwater lands on the soil where the roots collect it.

Xylem
Xylem cells transport water and mineral salts from the roots to the leaves.

Mineral salts
Phosphates, nitrates and other mineral salts are absorbed by the roots.

OVERGROWTH

Plants grow more rapidly in tropical rainforests than in almost any other natural environment. The hours of sunshine and the rainfall are high in these rainforests and provide ideal conditions for photosynthesis.

OPENINGS TO THE OUTSIDE WORLD

Open stomata in leaves allow the carbon dioxide needed for photosynthesis to enter the leaf and the oxygen created during photosynthesis to exit. Not all of the water carried to the leaves from the roots is used in photosynthesis and any extra water evaporates through the stomata in a process called transpiration. Water evaporates through the open stomata during the day, but much less water is lost when the stomata are closed at night or in very dry weather.

Open stoma   Closed stoma

Discover more in Life in the Desert

21

New Life

Plants use a number of methods to reproduce, and some use more than one. In asexual reproduction, a single-celled plant can divide to create new plants that are identical to each other and to the parent plant. More complex plants, such as flowering plants, cone-bearing plants and ferns, tend to reproduce sexually. In sexual reproduction, male and female cells are needed to create the new plant, which inherits some genes from both parents and is not identical to either parent. The male cells in the pollen must reach and fertilize the female cells in the ovule, inside the ovary. Since plants are usually fixed in one spot, the male cell relies on insects, birds, mammals, wind or water to perform this task. In plants that have seeds this process is called pollination. The fertilized female cell develops into an embryo that is contained inside a seed.

FOOD FOR THE HIVE
Bees brush pollen from the male stamen of a plant, such as a peach blossom, into a "basket" on their back legs. Some of the pollen sticks to them. If they brush against the ripe female stigma on another peach blossom, some of this pollen fertilizes the ovary, which grows into a fruit (far right).

THE PROTECTING POD
The ovary in the female peaflower grows into a pod, which protects the fertilized seeds. The flower dies but the seeds continue to grow. We eat the sweet seeds of the garden pea (right).

Stigma
Stamen
Style
Ovule

Pollination
Yellow pollen containing the male sperm is released from the male stamen and carried to a female stigma.

A new plant
When the ripe fruit drops to the ground, the seed can germinate and begin to form a new plant.

THE CIRCLE OF LIFE
Sexual reproduction in plants is not easy. The life of a peach tree, for example, will begin only if pollen reaches a ripe female stigma on another peach tree.

Fertilization
The pollen develops a tube that grows down the style to the ovule. The sperm fertilizes the female cell. The ovule starts to develop into a seed inside the ovary.

Ripening fruit
The ovary grows into a fleshy fruit with the seed inside the peach stone.

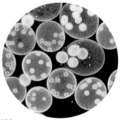

CHOICES

This colony of volvox (simple single-celled algae) can reproduce asexually by releasing new colonies into the water (as shown), or sexually by releasing male sperm and female ova.

NAKED SEEDS

Each scale on this female cone protects two seeds without ovaries. They are fertilized by pollen from a smaller male cone. When the scales open, the winged seeds fall gently to the ground.

REPRODUCING WITHOUT SEEDS

Some plants can grow, or propagate, identical plants from their stems or roots. They can also provide water and food for the new plant until its own roots and leaves grow. Many ferns have underground horizontal stems, called rhizomes, which divide and produce identical plants. Daffodil bulbs split and grow new bulbs on the side of the parent bulb. Strawberries send out horizontal stems or runners above the ground. A new strawberry plant grows where the part of the runner with small leaves, called the node, reaches the ground.

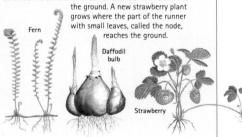

Fern

Daffodil bulb

Strawberry

TWO STAGES

Fern spores, on the underside of fronds, drop to the ground and grow into a new plant that produces male and female gametes, or sex cells. If these cells unite, a new spore-producing fern will grow.

Discover more in Plants with Spores

Germination and Growth

Once a plant seed is fertilized, it needs to find a suitable patch of ground, where the light, moisture and temperature are right, in order to grow. Directly underneath the parent tree, which would shade it from the light and whose bigger roots would compete for water, is not an ideal position. Plants use various methods to make sure their seeds reach good growing ground. Some plants scatter their own seeds and others rely on wind, water or animals. Not all of these seeds start growing immediately, and some never begin to grow at all. Inside the seed casing is a supply of food that allows the seed to wait for days, months or even years until conditions are right for germination. Then the first tiny shoot and root break through the seed case. After an initial period of growth, which in some plants may last days and in others years, the plant matures and can reproduce.

GONE WITH THE WIND
The fruits of the thistle have a parachute of hairs. They are light enough for the wind to carry them long distances. With luck, some will find the right environment in which to germinate.

HOOKED
Check your clothes and the dog's fur next time you go for a walk. Some seeds, like the goosegrass, have tiny hooks that latch on to animals or humans and are moved to a new location.

THE BUOYANT COCONUT
The coconuts that fall from palm trees are often carried by water to a suitable growing environment. A new coconut palm may grow and produce its own fruits.

HARDWORKING HELPERS
The gathering instincts of ants are very useful for plants. Ants collect seeds for food and move them from one place to another. Some of the uneaten seeds will germinate in fertile soil.

BUILT TO FLY
Like tiny whirling helicopters, maple seeds spin in the wind and land gently. If not eaten by animals and birds, the seeds may take root and start to grow.

DID YOU KNOW?

Some fruits explode to scatter their seeds away from the shade of the parent plant. Squirting cucumbers, dwarf mistletoe and Himalayan balsam shoot out seeds at up to 46 ft (14 m) per second.

Washed ashore
A coconut, with the seed inside, floats on water and can travel many miles from its parent tree before it reaches land.

CATCHING THE LIGHT

Leaves and sunlight are needed to make food for the new plant to grow. Leaves may grow singly off the stem, in pairs from the same point (node) on the stem, or in groups. But if you look at them from above, the way the sun shines on them, the leaves are all at different angles from each other in a spiral shape. Each leaf has some of its surface facing the sun and is not shaded by the leaf above it.

SWALLOWED WHOLE

Fruit bats, birds and other animals eat many seeds without killing them. The seeds travel in the animal's gut inside their seed casings, which can survive digestive juices. Then they are passed out—still whole—in the animal's droppings.

When the time is ripe
The embryo is dormant in the seed but when conditions are suitable, it feeds on the coconut milk and sends out the first stem and root.

Breaking out
As the roots take in water and the stem grows stronger, the outer shell breaks open.

The second generation
The coconut tree will drop its own fruits. These will be washed out to sea and begin their own long voyage to germination.

Carboniferous: 362–290 million years ago
Giant horsetails, club mosses, ferns and cordaitales, as well as giant amphibians and dragonflies, appeared.

Permian: 290–245 million years ago
Seed-bearing gingkoes and conifers thrived. Mammal-like reptiles appeared.

Triassic: 245–208 million years ago
Cycads flourished, cordaitales became extinct. Meat-eating dinosaurs appeared.

• THE PLANT KINGDOM •

Plant Beginnings

The Earth's crust is 4,600 million years old, but for more than 1,000 million years only non-living things, such as rocks and water, could exist because of the poisonous gases in the atmosphere and the fierce heat of the sun. The first true plants grew in the nutrient-rich oceans about 550 million years ago and the first land plants appeared 400 million years ago. As these primitive land plants did not have a water-transport system, they grew near lakes. They were the ancestors of the spore-bearing plants—the giant club mosses, horsetails and ferns (fossilized fern above left) that formed huge forests during the Carboniferous Period. Seed-bearing plants, such as conifers, which appeared 350 million years ago, and flowering plants, which appeared only 135 million years ago, contributed to dinosaurs' food and oxygen supplies. Unlike the dinosaurs, however, plants did not become extinct when many animal species did, 65 million years ago.

Swampy Carboniferous
Giant club mosses (1), giant horsetails (2) and cordaitales (3) grew as tall as houses.

Cooler Permian
Gingkoes (4) and conifers (5) shared the world with other early plants.

Drier Triassic
Cycads (6) flourished.

Cooler and wetter Jurassic
New species of conifers, such as swamp cypress (7) and monkey puzzle (8), appeared in the lush, ferny undergrowth (9).

Flowering Cretaceous
Flowering plants, such as bulrushes (10), magnolia bushes (11) and willow trees (12) appeared.

Palaeocene
Flowering plants began to rule the plant kingdom.

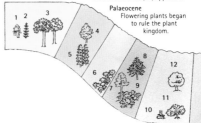

PLANTS ON LAND

Over millions of years, different plants—spore-bearing plants, cone-bearing plants and flowering plants—have dominated the Earth. Climate affected plant and animal life. The plants shown here grew in a cold climate in the Northern Hemisphere.

LIVING FOSSILS

These stromatolites in Western Australia are spongy structures created by layers of blue-green algae and mud that are shaped by waves and currents. They are usually found only as fossils, some of which date back 3,500 million years.

A Slimy Survivor

The next time you see dark slime in a fish tank or slip on some on a wet path, you should be amazed rather than annoyed. The slime is made up of chains of single-celled blue-green algae or cyanobacteria. Like bacteria, they have no roots, stems or leaves but, like plants, they produce oxygen during photosynthesis. Blue-green algae

are the earliest known life forms and have survived for 3,500 million years in watery environments as extreme as Arctic pack ice and boiling hot springs.

Jurassic: 208–145 million years ago
New species of conifer appeared. Long-necked dinosaurs, plated dinosaurs and flying reptiles appeared.

Cretaceous: 145–65 million years ago
Flowering plants, including trees, appeared. Horned dinosaurs and snakes appeared.

Palaeocene: 65–56 million years ago
Flowering plants dominated. Dinosaurs disappeared and small mammals appeared.

The First Plants

A lgae, the world's first plants, are even more different from each other than roses are from palm trees. Among the 25,000 species there are single-celled green slime, freshwater weed and huge brown or red seaweed. But they do have some things in common. They grow only where there is water, and this includes the underside of whales, snowfields and desert soils. They have no true roots, stems or leaves but they do have green chlorophyll and manufacture their food supplies by photosynthesis. Algae have no seeds and reproduce by dividing or breaking off cells, by releasing spores from spore cases in their fronds or, sexually, by releasing male and female cells. All of these methods require water and, when the first green algal colonies reached land, their methods of reproduction gradually adapted to a less reliable water supply. Algae now share the world with their more complex seed-bearing descendants.

CHAMPION GROWER
Giant kelp grows extremely quickly—up to 12 in (30 cm) a day! As tall as rainforest trees, giant kelp forms dense canopies or ocean forests. These provide shelter, food and oxygen for sea creatures.

POISONOUS EXPLOSION
Millions of blue-green algae together can form a huge colored tide that you can see from space. This algal tide, or bloom, suffocates or poisons the fish that usually feed on algae.

GREEN SLIME
Seen under a microscope, pond spirogyra has long chains of identical cells. It can reproduce asexually, when the long chains break into pieces that form new plants, or sexually, when cells from different chains fuse.

LIVING TOGETHER

Lichen is not a single, independently growing plant but is the result of close cooperation between an alga and a fungus (below left). The alga provides the food, and the fungus wrapped around it provides shelter and minerals. Lichens grow very slowly—0.04 in (1 mm) a year—but can live for up to 4,000 years. They are the hardiest of all plants and can survive on rocks in sunbaked deserts, high in the Himalayas or in the freezing Arctic.

Fungus and alga

Rainforest lichen

Food-producing fronds
The waving fronds provide the kelp's food through photosynthesis and release their spores into the water in spring.

Buoyant bladders
Filled with gas, the giant kelp's bladders hold the fronds afloat, nearer to the surface and the sunlight.

MAKING AIR
These bubbles show that algae produce oxygen during photosynthesis. Other sea dwellers need this oxygen to live. Since oceans cover a large part of the Earth's surface, algae are also a major source of the oxygen we breathe.

Hanging on
The holdfast clings to the ocean bedrock and, like the rest of the plant, absorbs water and mineral salts from the sea.

Plants with Spores

Ferns, mosses, liverworts and hornworts produce spores in order to reproduce. A spore is a tiny specialized cell that is able to grow into an organism. These plants are more primitive and reproduce less efficiently than plants that produce seeds. Mosses, liverworts and hornworts are descended from algae. They have no true roots, stems or transport systems. They form low-growing mats in damp places to get water directly from their environment. The 20,000 and more species of moss and liverwort have not evolved into other kinds of plants and have no descendants. Ferns, club mosses and horsetails have adapted better to life on land. They can grow tall and get a better share of the light because they developed roots, stems and transport systems for water and nutrients. Millions of years ago, their larger ancestors were the most dominant plants on Earth. Today, however, it is the turn of seed-producing plants to dominate the plant kingdom.

A FERN SELECTION
Elkhorn (top) and crow's-nest ferns grow on trees without harming them. Rasp fern (bottom) reproduces rapidly from its horizontal stems. Tree ferns (far right) can grow as tall as palm trees but the delicate maidenhair below them stays close to the ground.

Breaking out
When the spore case opens, the spores scatter in the wind.

Asexual spores
Spores have no sex cells and form in spore cases (sporangia) on the underside of the fern's fronds.

THREE GENERATIONS
Ferns have a unique life cycle. The first generation produces asexual spores, the second generation produces sex cells, or gametes, and these grow into a third generation of spore producers.

Gametes
The spore grows into a tiny plant called a gametophyte because it has male and female sex cells, or gametes.

A new spore producer
The male cell needs at least a film of water to swim to and join the female cell before a new spore-producing fern can grow.

COPY CONE
Club mosses are related to ferns, not mosses. They have special spore-carrying leaves that grow in tight spirals. These leaves protect the spore cases and look like cones.

WATER CATCHER

Mosses and liverworts need water to survive and to produce the next generation, but they have no roots to trap water and no xylem to transport it inside the plant. They must use other means to trap water. This *Frullania* liverwort, which grows on trees in a dry environment, has an ingenious water-trapping system. Small "flasks" form on the primitive "leaves" and catch water running down the tree trunk. The water can then trickle to other parts of the plant.

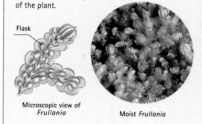

Flask

Microscopic view of *Frullania*

Moist *Frullania*

MOSS SPORES
The spearlike stalk with its spore capsule grows on a moss parent plant until it ripens. The hood falls off and the spore capsule releases its tiny spores through "teeth" at the top of the capsule.

THE GREATEST SOAKER
Sphagnum moss can soak up 20 times its own weight in water. This soggy carpet grows in acid water with few bacteria so it is sterile enough to be used as an emergency bandage. When sphagnum moss is dried and partly decomposed, it forms peat—a household fuel in some countries.

SURVIVORS
The horestail's whorls of green branches and hollow stem work together to produce the plant's food. The leaves, which are the brownish-black scales pressed tightly against the stem, are not food producers. Horsetail spores, grouped into cones, grow on separate stems.

Conifers and Their Relatives

Seed-bearing plants evolved 50 million years after the first land plants. Their seeds grew inside cones, not inside fruits. Today the largest group of cone bearers are the conifers—pines, spruces, firs, cypresses and their relatives. Most have hard, woody male and female cones, although a few species have fleshy cones. The tough-skinned leaves of many conifers are like green needles or like scales pressed flat against the branch. They are called evergreen trees because they do not shed their leaves all at the same time. Conifers grow fast in forests in cool, temperate climates. Their wood is soft and easy to work with so they are planted in commercial forests, often in places where they would not grow naturally. Cone-bearing cycads, gingkoes, yews and the unusual desert welwitschia are distantly related to the true conifers.

TWO CONES
Male and female cones can grow on the same or a different tree. The pollen needed for fertilizing the female cell is inside each scale of the smaller male cone.

Gingko
Female gingko trees have fleshy, foul-smelling cones and fan-shaped leaves.

Yew
Yew leaves are narrow and flat. Female yew seeds are a fleshy red.

Scots pine
Scots pines have egg-shaped cones and paired, blue-green leaves.

Arizona cypress
Dark green overlapping leaves cover each cypress twig, like scales. The cones are small and round.

Cycad
Cycad cones are the largest cones in the world. They grow in a crown of spiky fronds.

Plum Pine
Plum pines have berry-like cones with a fleshy seed stalk sticking out.

A burst of yellow dust
In spring, the male pine cone releases millions of pollen grains. A few days later, the male cone drops off the tree. Its job is finished.

Sticky cone
The pollen lands on a sticky female cone. A pollen tube starts to grow and, up to a year later, the sperm finally fertilizes the ovule.

CONIFER CYCLE
Conifers do not require water to reproduce. They rely on wind to carry pollen from the male cone to seeds in the female cone.

Swelling cone
The female cone grows to four times its size as the seeds grow inside. Two years later when the seeds are mature, the cone opens to release them.

Germination
If the seed finds a spot with enough warmth, moisture and light, it germinates and a new conifer grows.

Spreading seeds
Each seed has a wing and can take off in the wind. It also has food for germination inside a tough, outer casing.

ODD ONE OUT
In spring and summer, larches have green leaves. These leaves change color in autumn and drop off in winter, which is unusual for a conifer.

INSIDE A TREE TRUNK

The outer bark of a tree is made up of dead phloem cells but the inner bark is spongy and living. New cells grow between the phloem, or bark layer, on the outside and xylem, or wood layer, on the inside. This is why a tree trunk gets wider every year. The xylem rings—one for each year of growth—tell how old the tree is. The V shapes in these rings show where branches grew.

Wood

V shapes

Bark

Growth ring

TALLEST REDWOODS

The redwoods of California (*Sequoia sempervirens*), shown here, are the tallest trees in the world. The giant redwood (*Sequoiadendron giganteum*) is slightly shorter but it is the world's largest and heaviest tree.

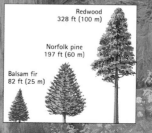

Redwood
328 ft (100 m)

Norfolk pine
197 ft (60 m)

Balsam fir
82 ft (25 m)

Flowering Plants

Flowering plants are the most recent and the most dominant plants in the plant kingdom. There are more than a quarter of a million species of flowering plant, such as garden flowers, wildflowers, vegetables, grasses, trees and shrubs (with fruits not cones), vines and some water plants. Whether the flowers are large or small, beautiful or plain, they all contain the plant's reproductive structures or sex cells. The color and scent of some flowers attract birds or insects. The visitors feed mostly on the nectar or sugary water inside, then flit from flower to flower and carry the male pollen to the female stigma. Grasses and other plants with less obvious or attractive flowers rely on the wind to carry their pollen. Because the wind scatters the pollen, rather than taking it directly from flower to flower, these plants release millions of pollen grains. At least some of this pollen will reach the female stigma.

A STORM OF POLLEN
Grasses have small, unscented flowers arranged in spikelets at the end of the stem. In summer the wind scatters millions of grass pollen grains. They can cause hay fever, but without the pollen we would have no wheat, oats, barley, rice or corn to eat.

PERFECT PARTNERS
Birds are attracted to red flowers. The streamertail's small head and beak allow it to search for nectar in the pendant firebird's flower. The bird picks up pollen as it feeds.

LOOK AT ME!
Size, shape, scent and color attract insects to showy flowers. They also attract gardeners and botanists who try to improve on nature. Some of the flowers shown here are hybrids that can be produced naturally or artificially by cross-pollination.

34

New Genes

The male pumpkin flower (below), which withers and dies after it has released its pollen, grows on the same vine as the female flower (below). The male can pollinate a female sister flower and this is called self-pollination. The new plant is very similar to the parent plant, but cannot survive environmental changes as well as plants with genes from two separate parents. To avoid self-pollination, male and female flowers on the same plant often mature at different times. In some species, male and female flowers grow on separate plants and this ensures cross-pollination.

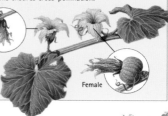

Male

Female

NECTAR HUNT

Many trees, especially those in the Southern Hemisphere, have brightly colored flowers. Insects find their way easily to the nectar at the center of the Judas tree flower. On the way to the nectar, they pick up or brush off pollen.

STRANGE BUT TRUE

The *Amorphophallus titanum* grows to a height of 12 ft (3.7 m) in the rainforests of Indonesia. The internal cluster of flowers opens for a few days and smells like rotten fish mixed with burnt sugar. Flies love the smell and come to lay their eggs. They also act as pollinators.

Discover more in New Life

The Life of Flowering Plants

Some flowering plants live, grow, disperse their seeds and die all within one spring and summer. These plants are called annuals. In spring an annual germinates from a seed, in summer it flowers and produces seeds inside a fruit, in autumn it withers and dies. But it does leave behind its seeds, which lie dormant over winter and germinate when spring arrives. Other flowering plants, including many trees, continue to live and grow year after year. These plants are called perennials. In temperate climates, where there are four seasons, perennials rest and stop growing in the cold of autumn and winter. Trees may drop their leaves during this rest period. Some plants, like the sweet potato (above left), survive the rest period on food stored in bulbs or stem tubers below the ground. Plants in tropical monsoon climates, where there is no autumn or winter, grow and reproduce when it is wet, but rest when it is dry.

A BRIEF BLOOM
During the few weeks of the very short Arctic summer, the sun never sets. With enough light, water from melting snow and some warmth, plants quickly flower and disperse their seeds before the cold, dark Arctic days return.

FOUR SEASONS
A London plane tree has four very different stages in its yearly cycle. This tree grows tall and strong, even in city streets, and is tough enough to resist pollution.

Spring
The numerous yellow male and red female flowers hang in separate, globular clusters on the same tree. Once fertilized, the female flower begins to grow fruit.

Summer
During summer, the clusters of tightly packed green fruits grow larger and protect the seeds inside.

WET AND DRY SEASONS

Temperate areas of the world have four seasons each year. Tropical monsoon areas have only two seasons—the wet season and the dry season. For plants growing in these areas, the wet season is the same as spring and summer when most of the growing takes place, the flowers bloom and the seeds disperse. In the dry season, the plants rest and some even drop their leaves to reduce the amount of water they lose. Just as plants in temperate regions have adapted to survive the cold winter months, these baobabs in Australia have adapted to survive the months when water is in short supply and fire is a constant danger.

FOOD STORES

The daffodil bulb stores food to use when it rests between growing and reproducing. Like an onion, the bulb is a series of concentric rings. These are the swollen bases of the leaves from the last season. In spring, new stems and leaves appear above the ground.

EVERGREEN COLOR

An evergreen grows new leaves before losing the old ones. In winter, when many other plants are leafless, the leaves and red berries of the holly provide a splash of color.

Autumn
As the leaves begin to change color, the hairy fruits also change from green to brown. They are dispersed by the wind.

Winter
The leaves and their stalks drop off the branches. The sticky buds on the end of the bare twigs protect the young leaves, which emerge in the spring.

Discover more in Forest Views

37

Plant Imposters

Fungi do not really belong in the plant kingdom. The 70,000 species of fungi, which include mushrooms, molds, mildews and rust on plants, have no roots, stems or leaves and no chlorophyll to make their own food. They feed on other plants and animals—dead or alive. Most fungi are made up of branching threadlike cells called hyphae, which break down living or dead cells into substances they can digest. They can digest almost anything, including the cellulose of plant cell walls. Their own cell walls are made of much stronger material, otherwise they might eat themselves. Fungi do not need light to produce food and often grow in the dark. Sometimes only the fruiting body appears above the surface in which the fungus is growing. When the fruiting body of a fungus releases its spores, the wind carries billions of them through the air.

COSTLY PARASITE
Rust is a parasitic fungus that can grow and feed on wheat. It damages the leaves, which produce sugars, and the wheat crop is much smaller or ruined.

Underneath the cap
Spores form on gills underneath the cap. In just a few days, the spores shoot out of the gills and the fruiting body dies.

Stalk of threads
Hundreds of hyphae, compacted together, make up the column or stalk of the mushroom.

A PUFF OF SPORES
Puffballs produce spores inside the hollow ball of the fungus. As the outside of the ball becomes hard and rigid, any knock causes the ball to vibrate and puff out spores.

Thread network
The long threads of hyphae consume dead or decaying plant parts underground. The more they feed, the more they spread.

LOOK BEFORE YOU EAT
Mushrooms are fungi that form fruiting bodies. Some of these are good to eat and others are deadly poisonous. But it is very difficult to tell which is which. Poisonous mushrooms, often called toadstools, can look more attractive than mushrooms that are safe to eat.

Ghost fungi

Cup fungi

Bracket fungi

Conical slimy cap

STRANGE BUT TRUE

This mushroom grows and glows on the forest floor of tropical rainforests. Scientists are not certain why the fungus glows in the dark. Perhaps the green light attracts nocturnal animals to help distribute the mushroom's spores.

SPACE INVADER

Parasites are fungi that feed and grow on live animals and plants. This fungus invaded the spider's body and slowly ate it.

Scarlet flycap

Parasol mushroom

Forest fungi

Angel of death

MOLDY WONDER DRUG

If you leave bread, an apple or an orange in your schoolbag for a few days, a fungus, or mold, called penicillium may grow on it. You certainly would not want to eat the lunch once you found it but, in fact, penicillium saves millions of lives every year. Penicillin, an antibiotic extracted from penicillium (grown in a laboratory rather than in your schoolbag), cures many bacterial diseases. Penicillium also gives some cheeses their blue veins—and their strong taste and smell.

SNIFFING FOR TREASURE

One of the world's most rare and expensive foods is a fungus. The fruiting part of a truffle grows underground and is sniffed out by pigs.

Lady's veil

Aspen Bolete

How Plants Survive

Plants, animals and humans cannot live and grow without water, minerals and food. They must also have some way of defending themselves from danger. Unlike animals and humans, however, plants cannot move around to find what they need, nor can they run from danger. Instead plants have evolved and adapted to their environment by growing special structures or developing unusual means for survival. Some plants have special roots or hairs to get the vital water they need from places other than the soil. Parasite plants have special roots that allow them to get all, or most of, their food and water from another plant. Carnivorous plants have special leaves or hairs to trap insects, which provide the plants with extra minerals. Many plants have prickers, thorns and poisons to protect themselves from sucking insects, pecking birds or chomping animals.

THE WORLD'S LARGEST FLOWER
Rafflesia, a parasite, spends most of its life living inside a rainforest vine. For a short time, it breaks through the stem, flowers and attracts flies as pollinators. Then it dies.

CLOSE TO THE LIGHT
Tropical orchids can germinate and spend all their lives high in trees. They produce their own food and absorb water from the damp air through special dangling aerial roots.

DID YOU KNOW?
The deadly nightshade plant produces a poison called atropine. Women in Renaissance Europe dropped atropine into their eyes to enlarge the pupils and make them look more beautiful. That is why the plant has another name, belladonna, which means "beautiful lady" in Italian. Atropine from belladonna is still used in eye surgery today.

Poisonous Protection

Many plants produce poisons in their leaves, flowers, sap, fruits, or seed coats. Buttercup flowers, castor-oil beans and the sap of some canes are all poisonous. Uncooked cashew nuts have a poison that blisters the mouth. Often one part of the plant may be poisonous to deter predators while other parts are harmless to attract potential pollinators. Insects avoid the poisonous leaves of some tomato plants, but other animals eat the fruits of tomato plants and disperse their seeds.

SUCKING ROOTS
Parasites have special roots that attach to and pierce the roots or stem of the host plant. The parasite then absorbs sugar, water and mineral salts directly from the host.

Sweet smells
The color of the pitcher and the smell of nectar attracts an unsuspecting insect to the lid.

False flower
The pitcher looks like a beautiful flower but it is really a large leaf tip.

A closer look
To reach the nectar the insect has to leave the safety of the lid and land on the slippery mouth of the pitcher.

A BARBED WARNING
Roses have thorns, or barbed growths, attached to their stems. The thorns snag painfully on animals that get too close and warn them to keep away.

Tumbling down
Losing its foothold, the insect falls into the pitcher. Special downward-pointing hairs keep it from climbing or flying back up.

Trapped
The insect drowns in the pool of digestive juices at the bottom. The plant absorbs the minerals from the insect leaving only its shell.

MINERAL SUPPLEMENTS
Pitcher plants grow in wet, boggy soil that does not provide all the minerals they need. To get extra minerals, they trap and digest insects, such as wasps.

DEW TRAP
Hairs on the sundew's leaves produce a sticky, digestive liquid. Insects think it is water, but stick fast when they land. The liquid then digests them.

Discover more in Germination and Growth

COLOR BLAZE
A mixed forest in autumn is ablaze with the green leaves of evergreen trees and the brown, yellow, orange and red leaves of deciduous trees.

SPRING FLOWERS
Decaying leaves from trees add nutrients to the soil. In spring, before new leaves have grown on the trees, there is plenty of light for flowers to grow.

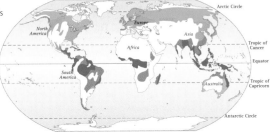

• WHERE PLANTS LIVE •

Forest Views

Forests in Canada or Russia are different from the forests in France, India, Indonesia or Australia. Climate and soil influence the kind of trees that grow in a forest, and the trees determine what grows on the forest floor beneath them. In cold, northern latitudes, evergreen conifers grow in boreal forests (named after Boreas, the Greek god of the north wind), but few plants grow on these dark forest floors. In temperate regions of the world, spring flowers grow on the floor of deciduous forests, where the trees shed their leaves in winter. Mixed forests of different kinds of conifers and flowering trees grow in some parts of the world. In tropical rainforests, growth occurs almost throughout the year, but in tropical monsoon forests, where there is a wet and a dry season, trees and plants on the forest floor grow mainly in the wet season. In the eucalypt forests of Australia, a variety of vegetation grows on the forest floor.

BANDS OF FOREST
Regions on the same latitude, above or below the equator, tend to have similar climates. This is why most types of forests grow in bands running east to west across many countries.

- Boreal forests: northern parts of North America, Europe and Russia
- Deciduous forests: eastern USA, most of Europe, eastern China and Japan
- Mixed forests: western USA, southern Chile and parts of Argentina and New Zealand
- Tropical rainforests: South America, Central Africa, Southeast Asia and northeast Australia
- Tropical monsoon forests: South America, India, northern Australia and parts of Southeast Asia and Africa
- Eucalypt forests: Australia

KEEPING OUT THE COLD

The needle shape and waxy outer coating of conifer leaves allow them to tolerate the cold and shrug off snow. Evergreen conifers allow little light to reach the forest floor. Dwarf evergreen shrubs, mosses and lichens are all that you will see there.

NEW LIFE

A forest fire burns the leaves of tall trees and clears the undergrowth. Dormant seeds now have enough light and space to germinate in soil that is rich in nutrients from the ash.

EUCALYPT FORESTS

The Australian continent drifted and became separated from the rest of the world around 50 million years ago. With no competition from species that dominated other parts of the world, unusual animals and plants were able to flourish in Australia. The dominant trees are the 500 species of eucalypt or gum tree that grow in forests in both temperate and tropical regions of Australia. Like conifers they are evergreens but their leaves hang down and allow light to reach the forest floor.

Discover more in Plant Industries

Life in the Desert

Lack of water and intense daytime heat are the main problems for plants that grow in the desert. The roots of most desert plants go deep or spread out widely in search of every drop of water. Rain may fall in the desert only once every few years, so storing this precious water is vital. Plants store water in swollen roots, in succulent (juicy) leaves or in stems with ridges that can expand to hold it. But water is still lost, mainly through the leaves and other green parts. Some plants drop their leaves or grow spines instead of leaves. Many desert plants have a waxy coating on their leaves with stomata buried in pits rather than on the surface of the leaf. Succulent plants have a special photosynthesis system that can operate without the stomata being open in dry periods. But some plants avoid these problems altogether. They spend most of their lives as dormant seeds and complete their very short life cycle only when rainfall is good.

Sunblocking spines
The tufted spines on the chain-fruit cholla reflect and scatter the fierce rays of the sun.

IN THE MIDDAY SUN
The tall green stem of the giant saguaro cactus makes the plant's food supply. The stomata are closed to cut down water loss. The saguaro cactus provides a home for woodpeckers while a ground-squirrel gets water from the beaver-tail cactus.

A BRILLIANT BURST
Desert annuals grow, flower, fruit and disperse their seeds in a few short weeks after rain. Their seeds often have a chemical coating that prevents germination, sometimes for many years. Only a really good shower of rain washes this coating away. When it does, the desert blooms.

A SLOW LIFE
The saguaro grows very slowly. Branches begin to grow from quite high up the stem when the plant is "middle-aged."

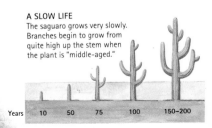

| Years | 10 | 50 | 75 | 100 | 150–200 |

44

NEVER-ENDING LEAVES

The bizarre welwitschia, a distant cone-bearing relative of the conifers, grows in the drought-ridden Namib Desert of Africa. Two leaves grow like long straps from the flat cushion of the stem and continue growing throughout the plant's very long life. Wind, and the sand it stirs up, may tatter the leaves of the welwitschia, which in a 2,000-year-old plant may be 26 ft (8 m) long. The leaves trap moisture from the early morning dew and fog, and channel it down to the swollen tap root.

WATER SEARCH
The mesquite tree (above left) sends its roots down deep to tap into the water table far below. The cactus (above right) sends its roots out horizontally in search of every drop of surface water.

LIVING STONES
The two round, fat leaves of the stone plant look like stones, because stones do not attract grazing animals. Most of the plant remains underground, hidden from the fierce sun.

IN THE COOL OF THE NIGHT
As the sun sets, the stomata in the cacti open to balance the gases in the plants that are generated by their special photosynthesis system. A nocturnal bat goes from flower to flower and is the saguaro's main pollinator.

Facing away
The flat pads of beaver-tail cacti face the warmth of the late afternoon and early morning sun. When the sun is high, they face sideways to avoid the intense heat.

SURVIVAL TECHNIQUES
The succulent leaves and the soft fiber inside the trunk of the quiver tree store water. The white-powdered branches and pale trunk reflect the sun's rays and stop the tree from overheating.

Grasslands

A DIET OF GRASS
The giant red kangaroo of Australia is the world's largest marsupial. It eats types of grass that sheep and cattle do not eat. But in times of drought, when the grass is not growing, all these animals compete for food.

Grasslands occur in areas that get more rain than deserts but not as much rain as forests. They have few trees, and some have no trees at all. Grasses are hardier than trees and lose less water in dry winds than taller plants. The horizontal stems of some grasses prevent wet areas from eroding. As a weapon against competitors, many grasses secrete a chemical that reduces the nutrients available for other plants. Grasses are enormously varied. Some grow in tussocks and others grow in mats (like lawns). Some are perennials and others are annuals. Many grow only to knee height but some, like sugar cane, grow tall. Grasses are flowering plants that reproduce sexually. Many can also reproduce from horizontal stems above the ground (stolons) or just below the ground (rhizomes). These stems are often hollow with solid joints or nodes from which new grass plants sometimes sprout.

AFRICAN SAVANNA
Savanna animals graze on different types and ages of grass. Grass continues to grow when the upper part of the leaf is eaten because the growing cells are at the base of the grass leaf rather than the tip.

Large animals of the grasslands have no place to hide. They rely on speed rather than hiding places to escape danger. But for many birds the grasslands are a safe haven with plenty of building material. Weaver birds use grass to weave complex nests on the ground or in one of the few trees (above). One tree may hold as many as 400 nests. The social weaver bird, however, builds one huge nest with a roof of grass and sticks. This nest has a separate chamber for each pair of birds that live there.

DID YOU KNOW?

A female elephant who has just given birth eats 440 lb (200 kg) of grass, leaves and fruits a day. She bulldozes and uproots trees to get her rations.

Grasslands

FROM BUFFALOS TO TRACTORS

In North America, some of the natural grasslands where buffalo once fed are now planted with wheat, a grass food crop.

GRASSLANDS

The American prairies, the African savannas, the steppes of Asia and the pampas of South America are large areas of grasslands. The only continent that does not have grassland is Antarctica.

North America

Europe

Asia

Africa

South America

Australia

Discover more in Flowering Plants

AN ALPINE FLOWER
Edelweiss grows in cracks in
rocks. Its waxy leaves reduce
water loss and its leaf hairs help
to prevent heat loss. The large
flowers attract pollinating insects
when they flower briefly.

• WHERE PLANTS LIVE •

Extreme Lives

It is difficult for plants to live in the cold temperatures,
chilling winds and low rainfall of the polar regions and
high mountain tops. In Antarctica, only one flowering
plant (a grass), and lichens, mosses and algae can survive
the severe conditions. But in the Arctic tundra, and on high
mountains around the world, some plants have adapted
to the extreme conditions. As you climb higher or travel
nearer to the North Pole, the temperature drops. Stands of
conifers give way to occasional, stunted, ground-hugging
tree species until you reach an area known as the tree
line. Beyond this, life is impossible for trees. For the
low-growing plants above or beyond the tree line, the
growing season is short. As rainfall is low, many have
waxy leaves to cut down water loss. Many also have
hairy stems and leaves to prevent the loss of water and
heat. The hairs also protect the plant from damaging
ultraviolet rays, which are stronger at high altitudes than
in any other environment. Some plants even have special
cell sap to prevent the plant's cells from freezing solid.

THAWING OUT
In the Arctic tundra,
the soil is permanently
frozen. When snow and
ice melt, the water
cannot penetrate
the frozen soil,
so it gathers on
top. Some plants
have adapted to this
stagnant water.

STRANGE BUT TRUE

The Arctic buttercup's white flower and shape reflect and focus the sun's rays into the center of the flower. This little pool of heat attracts insect pollinators. After pollination, the flower darkens to reduce reflection and absorbs the warmth for the growing ovary.

GIANT OF THE ANDES
This giant woody-stemmed herb, the puya, lives for up to 150 years. The prickly rosette folds upwards around the stem to keep the plant warm during the cold mountain nights.

ODD-SHAPED STRAGGLERS

Between the last of the tall straight trees and the low-growing plants beyond the tree line, a few straggling trees survive. They are often stunted dwarves, twisted into strange shapes by fierce winds. The branches of some grow only on the side of the tree that is away from chilling winds and blasting snow. Some tree species grow along the ground instead of up from it. They reach only a few inches in height but their stretched-out length can equal the height of a medium-sized lowland relative.

HUDDLED TOGETHER
This cushion plant in the mountains of Tasmania, Australia, is not one, but many plants. Huddling tightly together creates a warmer and more humid environment, and the hard cushion of leaves keeps out the worst of the cold, drying wind.

ARCTIC TUNDRA
At the tree line, the trees are bare on the windblown side. Low-growing flowering plants, grasses, mosses and lichens survive better near ground level, where the temperature is warmer and the wind less chilling. In summer there is water and warmth for a short growing season.

By the Sea

There are many different coastal environments, and different plants, where the land meets the sea. If you stand at the high-tide mark on a sandy beach and look towards the sea, you will notice that plants do not grow on the wet sand between high and low tide. The waves would soon uproot any plants that grew there. However, on rocks exposed between high and low tide, you will see algae growing. If you turn and look towards the land, you are looking at grasses—the "front line" of the land-plant community. Their long underground stems and strong tufts bind the sand and stop it from blowing away in the wind. Behind the grasses, the dunes become more stable as the roots of salt-resistant and wind-resistant plants take a firm hold. Beyond these low-growing plants, forests of trees grow in the sandy soil. In estuaries, where land and river meet the sea, there is no clearly defined beach. Tropical mangroves or temperate salt marshes thrive here.

SURVIVING STILL
On exposed rocks or rock platforms, lichens keep on growing, slowly, year after year. These hardy survivors can cope with being splashed by the coldest of seas and salt spray.

WHERE RIVER MEETS SEA
Grasses and shrubs bind the sediments brought down by the river to the estuary. Many salt marsh plants have succulent leaves, which store fresh water.

WINDBLOWN SAND
On an Australian beach, hardy plants resistant to salt spray help to stabilize shifting sands. The plants closest to the water trap the sand, and the taller canopies in the dunes reduce the wind.

SAILING FRUIT
The sea and the wind transport the buoyant fruit of the screw-pine to islands or coastal land great distances away from the parent plant.

Foredunes
Animals eat the fruits of coastal pigface, a creeping herb. Its stems run along or just below the semi-stable sand.

Above the sea
Blue-green algae, which are almost black, cling to rocks that are splashed by waves.

Splash zone

Intertidal zone

Between high and low tide
On rocks that are underwater at high tide but exposed to the air at low tide, you will see brown, ribbonlike wracks and bright green seaweeds.

Below the sea
Here you will see the red seaweeds or huge brown kelp that spend most of their live covered by the sea and become exposed only if the tide is very low

COLOR ZONES
On rocky shorelines, at low tide, you can see different types of colored algae. Each has a particular preference for one zone of the sea. Tidepools contain the greatest number of species in one place.

Subtidal zone

FROM BARE SAND TO FOREST

The seeds of grasses and herbs, carried by the wind or birds, germinate in the bare sand of a coral island. As their roots bind the sand, low-growing plants and a ring of shrubs begin to grow in the more stable sand behind them and away from the sea. Within this protective ring, trees take root and what was once bare sand becomes green forest. But if seas wash over the island or animals trample the plants, the island will return to an earlier stage of plant development or become bare sand once again.

High canopy
The canopy of the coastal banksia trees deflects and reduces the strong sea breezes.

High dunes
Coastal wattle grows along the ground, acting as wind and sand barriers.

Close to the sea
Beach spinifex is an efficient sand binder. The female fruiting head cartwheels on its spines along the sand, dispersing seeds as it goes.

SALT WATER
Mangroves cope with high salt levels by excreting excess salt through special leaf cells or by sending the salt to dying leaves, which then drop off.

51

Freshwater Worlds

Many different freshwater plants grow in the running water of streams and rivers or the still, calmer waters of ponds and lakes. They live at various depths, as long as the light they need for photosynthesis can reach them. Some freshwater plants float freely on top of the water, with hairlike roots that do not anchor the plant but do absorb nutrients from the water. Others spend their lives submerged underwater. Free-floating and submerged plants usually have soft green stems. Spaces between their cells are filled with water and gas. These hold them up towards the light as effectively as stiff stems. Emergent, or "wet-feet", plants however, have stiff stems, which hold part of the plant above the water while the roots and lower part remain under water. Nearly all water plants can flower and reproduce sexually. Most have inconspicuous flowers and rely on wind or water to pollinate. Life is not always easy for water plants. Their environment is prone to disturbances such as changing water levels and pollution.

A FREE-FLOATING TAKEOVER
The water hyacinth, a native of Central America, has been introduced to many waterways around the world. It is carried by wind and water, and spreads rapidly, often becoming a pest. It can push other plants out and take over the waterway.

FOOD CHAIN
Microscopic plants, called phytoplankton (left), provide food for small crustaceans and insects, called zooplankton. When a carnivorous fish eats the zooplankton it gets some of the plant's energy. The fish's waste provides nutrients for other plants.

Duckweed
The smallest of flowering plants, this is a favorite snack for ducks. Hairlike roots balance the plant and draw nutrients from the water.

Water nymph
You cannot see the water nymph, which flowers underwater, but you can see its bubbles of oxygen at the water's surface during photosynthesis.

HOLDING ON
The fast-flowing water in rivers can uproot plants and rip leaves to shreds. This tropical plant can survive in such waters because it has strong holdfasts and its fine leaves last only a few weeks. The short, thick leaf bases then continue the plant's photosynthesis.

Bulrushes
This emergent plant is closely related to grasses. Its flowers are small and its stiff stem holds it above the water.

Weeping willow
The willow can tolerate soggy soil. The leaves that it sheds add nutrients to the mud in the pond.

Water milfoil
The leaves under the water help to balance the plant. The broad leaves above the water collect light.

Algae
On stones, in or above the water, slimy algae take hold.

Water lily
The lily's soft stems carry oxygen from the air down to the roots. The flower attracts insect pollinators.

LIFE IN A VILLAGE POND

Plants on the bank, in the shallows, or in deep but sunlit water provide food and shelter for many animals. Plant and animal waste ends up at the bottom of the pond, where scavengers and fungi break it down into usable nutrients.

FROM WATER TO WETLAND

Over thousands of years, lakes can change into wetland, an environment halfway between land and water. Rivers running into the lake deposit sediment, or silt. The lake bed rises and the water depth drops. Land plants take root on the silt at the shoreline. Water plants move towards the center of the lake. More silt and plant debris build up. Peat forms under the marsh, on which more land plants and water-tolerant trees take root. What was a habitat for water plants is now wetland, dominated by land plants.

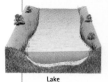

Lake

Marsh

Swamp or wetland

53

PLANT CROPS
On one-fifth of the world's cultivated
land, fully mechanized farms produce
539 million tons (550 million tonnes) of
wheat each year. We eat most of it, but
one-fifth is used to feed farm animals.

SPOONFULS OF SUGAR
More than half of the world's sugar comes from the
thick, jointed stems of sugar cane, which is a tropical
grass. The cane is cut just above ground level, leaving
the stem to sprout new shoots for next year's crop.

PLANT PROTEIN
Nuts are rich in protein and fats. They
provided a nutritious alternative to
meat in the Stone Age and are
now eaten by vegetarians for
the same reason. Hundreds
of species of trees and
shrubs produce nuts, but
not all of them are
true nuts and only
20–30 species are
cultivated on
nut farms.

• PLANTS AND HUMANS •

Food Plants

The first humans were nomads. They were constantly on the move, gathering wild plants and hunting wild animals for food. Some nomads realized that if they cultivated plants, as food for themselves and for the animals they herded, they could remain settled in one place. Since they had no form of transportation—apart from feet—the fruits, vegetables and grasses or grains they cultivated were those that grew wild within walking distance. Wild wheat and barley crops were grown in the Middle East, rice was cultivated in China and wild maize (Indian corn) in Central and South America. As trade around the world increased during the sixteenth century, plant crops became trade goods that were taken from one part of the world to another. With growing populations to feed, farmers began to grow greater quantities of crops to feed themselves and to sell to others. Today, wherever you live in the world, you can eat grains, fruits, vegetables and nuts whose plant ancestors grew wild in another far corner of the world.

54

TEA LEAVES

When tea was introduced to the rest of the world from China, it was considered an exotic, fashionable drink. Today, it is drunk by many people. Only the young leaf tips are picked, then fermented, dried and crushed.

WILD FOODS

Most of the food we eat today has been grown on farms, but food plants still grow in the wild, just as they did in Stone Age times. Fruits, berries, leaves and nuts can be picked. Tubers, bulbs and roots can be dug up and eaten.

TERRACES OF RICE

For more than 5,000 years, rice has been planted in China and Southeast Asia in water-filled paddy fields or terraces cut into the hillside. Rice is the main grain of more than half the world's population.

FRUITS AND VEGETABLES

A fruit is the seed-bearing part of a plant; other edible parts are vegetables.

A strawberry is a fruit with many ovaries, each with a single seed.

An orange is the fruit of an evergreen tree.

A carrot is an orange-colored tap root.

A potato is the thickened end of an underground stem, or rhizome, called a tuber.

A tomato is a fruit originally from the Americas.

An onion is an underground bulb that stores the plant's sugars.

A pumpkin is a fruit grown on a vine. The seeds are also eaten.

Ginger is an underground stem, or rhizome.

A lettuce is a bunch of leaves, usually eaten raw.

Asparagus is a green stem with reduced leaves, or bracts.

Discover more in Introducing Plants

Medicines from Plants

ANCIENT REMEDY
Science has now proved what ancient people believed. The bulbs, or cloves, of garlic can help to cure bronchitis and colds as well as lowering cholesterol levels and blood pressure.

Plants have always been a major source of medicines. By trial and error, early humans discovered that many plants could cure diseases, heal wounds or reduce pain. Among the early herbalists were some pioneers of medicine and pharmacology who studied the effects of certain plants on their patients. They recorded their discoveries in books called "herbals" so that their knowledge could be shared with others. This knowledge is still used by pharmaceutical companies to develop drugs that contain plant ingredients or synthetic substitutes. Traditional plant medicines can now be investigated and analyzed in laboratories. The questions that herbalists of previous times could not answer can now be answered. What is the main chemical ingredient of the plant part being used? How does it work on the human body? And, most importantly, what is the correct dosage that will cure the disease without killing the patient?

A MEASURED AMOUNT
In the Middle Ages, apothecaries were the equivalent of today's drug stores or pharmacies. Their medicines were mainly dried plants or herbs, not pills. The dosage was measured out very precisely, but people were still unsure how much it took to cure, or kill.

REGULAR HEARTBEAT
Foxglove leaves contain digitalin, a drug that keeps millions of heart patients alive today. There is no manufactured substitute for digitalin, which is powdered and used to regulate heartbeat.

TRADITIONAL CURE
In many parts of Asia, shops sell prepared herbal syrups and dried herbs, which the patient mixes in water before drinking. Many of these herbal remedies have been used for centuries.

DID YOU KNOW?
Ipecacuanha, which comes from the rhizomes and roots of a Brazilian native plant, is used in traditional villages and in modern homes. If someone accidentally swallows something poisonous, ipecac syrup makes them vomit and get rid of the poison.

Chemical Detective Work

For centuries, herbal medicines made from willow bark reduced fever and eased the pain and inflammation of aching joints and muscles. Although nineteenth-century chemists extracted the active element, called salicin, from the bark, it had unpleasant side effects such as nausea and ringing in the ears. In 1899, a chemist who was anxious to find a drug that would help his father's rheumatoid arthritis made a substance similar to salicin, but with fewer side effects. The drug, one of the most commonly used today, is known as aspirin.

PLANT GUM
Australian Aborigines use the red gum, or kino, from the bloodwood tree as a skin ointment. The kino helps to heal wounds, sores and rashes. Mixed with water and gargled, it also helps to cure a sore throat.

HERBAL MEDICINE
A village doctor in Asia grinds seeds to make herbal medicine. In many countries, especially those where doctors and hospitals are not available to everyone, some medicines are still made from plants. Scientists analyze their healing properties and develop synthetic substitutes.

ADDICTIVE PAINKILLER
A cut seed pod from an unripe opium poppy leaks a milky sap. The dried sap is opium, which contains the powerful painkillers morphine and codeine.

Plant Industries

SAILING SHIPS
The forests of western Europe were plundered in the 1500s when galleons were built from hardwoods such as oak. The cleared forests became farming or grazing lands.

CORK STRIPS
Cork comes from the dead outer bark of the cork oak tree. The live inner bark grows a new layer of cork bark, which can be stripped again in eight to ten years.

A MANAGED FOREST
About one-quarter of the world's forests are not natural forests. Conifers, which grow rapidly, are planted in managed forests. As trees in one section are felled, seedlings are planted in other sections so the forest is constantly renewed.

Many domestic items that we use every day come from the raw materials of plants. Sisal rope, as shown above, is made from a large herb. In earlier times, when populations were small and needs were simple, people built shelters from plant materials. They gathered plant fibers, which they spun and made into clothing. They made wooden bows and axe handles, and wove rope from the stems of flax plants. They gathered their own fuels, such as wood, coal and peat. All this changed during the Industrial Revolution when the first factories, growing urban populations and the development of transportation increased the demand for wood, coal, cotton, rubber and other plant materials. Large numbers of people harvested and processed these materials and new plant industries were born. By the 1800s, the forests in the industrialized countries of Europe were almost gone. Plant industries must be managed carefully today to ensure they do not destroy the plant resources of tomorrow.

Second thinning
After 20-30 years, more of the trees are removed.

Planting
Seedlings are planted close together so branches remain small and most of the growth is in the trunk.

Clear felling
The tree trunks are removed, but the branches and pine needles are left on the ground.

PULPED WOOD

Almost 40 per cent of the timber cut each year ends up in pulp mills. Here the bark is stripped off and the wood is ground into small chips that are chemically "cooked," dried and pressed into sheets. From these sheets, paper mills manufacture paper and cardboard.

NO WASTE
In some sawmills, computers are used to determine the maximum amount of usable wood. They generate a cutting pattern and program the mechanized saws for cutting.

NATURAL PLANT FIBERS

For centuries, people have worn clothes made of cotton and linen, which are natural plant fibers. Cotton comes from the white fibers that surround the seeds of the cotton plant (shown here). After the seed capsules are picked, the seeds and husks are removed, the longer fibers are spun into yarn and the shorter fibers are used for cotton wool. Linen, one of the strongest natural fibers, comes from the stem of the flax plant, which is soaked until partly decomposed. The fibers are then rolled or scraped off.

Ready for planting
A chopper roller mulches plant material into the ground before it is plowed.

First thinning
After 10–15 years, some trees are removed and used for fence posts or pulpwood.

Mature trees
The remaining trees reach maturity in 50–60 years.

STRANGE BUT TRUE

The Mayans of South America made their own shoes by dipping their feet into bowls of white sap from the trunks of rubber trees. They sat with their feet up for a few hours until the sap dried into soft, rubber shoes that were a perfect fit.

Discover more in Conifers and Their Relatives

59

Helping Nature

MADE IN A TEST TUBE
A cutting from an adult plant, placed in a test tube containing a gel with growth hormones, will grow into a new plant called a clone. The clone is identical in size, shape and quality to the original plant.

Food and textile plants today are the result of thousands of years of experimentation and research. Many of their original wild ancestors are now extinct. In their place we have cultivated plants that give higher yields or produce two crops each year, have better quality seeds or fruits, and are more able to resist disease or pests. The New Stone Age farmers started this process by selecting and planting seeds from the strongest and healthiest plants for the next year's crop. With the aid of the modern science of genetics, scientists can now cross-fertilize plants. The resulting plant often has the best features of each parent and is a genetic improvement on both. In another technique, called cloning, large numbers of identical plants can be produced from a small amount of plant tissue, even from a single cell of an adult plant. The technique of grafting, a form of vegetative propagation where part of one plant is attached to and grows on another closely related plant, has been used for 2,000 years.

Savoy cabbage
One very large bud grows at the end of the stem.

Broccoli
Many flower clusters grow at the top of the stem.

HUMAN CONTROLS
Inside a greenhouse, out-of-season fruits and vegetables, or plants that would normally grow only in warmer countries, thrive. The hours of light can also be altered to increase photosynthetic activity. This often speeds up the plants' growth and the development of flowers and fruits.

Successful graft

Grafted vine

Stock vine

GRAFTING
A vine that produces good grapes can be grafted onto, and nourished by, a disease-resistant parent, or stock, vine. A cut is made in the stem of the stock vine and a grafted plant twig with buds is inserted and bound.

Brussels sprouts
An enormous number of buds or sprouts grow from the sides of the stem.

SOIL SUBSTITUTE
Plants can be grown in water that is rich in minerals, a method called hydroponics. Tomatoes, cucumbers, lettuces, spinach and strawberries thrive in this environment.

STRONG OFFSPRING

Many of the fruits, vegetables and grain we eat are hybrids. They are created by cross-fertilizing two related, purebred parents. Hybrids are more resistant to diseases and pests and produce more food for us than self-pollinating plants, which produce weak offspring after a few generations. Seeds from a hybrid, however, will not produce another good quality hybrid. Only seeds created by cross-fertilizing purebred parents will produce a good quality hybrid.

Cross-fertilization

Purebred parent A
The male flower is cut off the plant. This prevents the plant from pollinating itself.

Purebred parent B
Pollen is collected in a bag and used to pollinate parent A.

Seed for hybrid

Self-pollination

Hybrid
Bigger than parents and produces more grain.

What we eat
Cob produced by the hybrid.

Cauliflower
One slow-growing, dense cluster of immature flowers grows within the leaves.

Kohlrabi
The stem is swollen and enlarged.

Cotton fibers

Rayon fibers

MAKING FIBER

Rayon, the first fiber made by humans, is produced from the cellulose of wood pulp and short cotton fibers. It is made into fabric that does not crease.

CULTIVATING PARTS

All these vegetables are cultivated varieties of the wild cabbage (above). They are developed by selecting plants with certain overdeveloped parts and passing this feature on to the next generation.

DID YOU KNOW?

If you throw away an apple core with its seeds, it just might produce an apple tree, but the apples that grow would probably be small, hard and sour. The apples we eat are from hybrids, and seeds from hybrids rarely produce good fruit.

Discover more in Plant Parts

61

PLANT DENSITY

Plants are necessary for life on Earth. By comparing present and future chlorophyll maps we can monitor plant density. On this map areas of highest chlorophyll are dark green on land and red to yellow in the sea. Pale yellow (on land) and pink (in the sea) indicate lowest densities.

STORING FOR THE FUTURE

Wild plants, cultivated plants and scientifically developed plant varieties are kept for the future. Seeds are stored in airtight packages or frozen in liquid nitrogen. Plants that do not have seeds, such as potatoes, can be stored as cuttings in laboratories, as shown here.

• PLANTS AND HUMANS •

Future Plants

Plants in the future, with the aid of genetic engineering, are likely to produce larger quantities or more nutritious foods and be better able to resist pests and diseases. New medicines may also come from future plants. As plant fossil fuels such as coal and oil run out, plants may provide alternative, safer and less polluting sources of energy. Plants may even hold the secrets for measuring and solving environmental pollution. But to use plants in the future we must avoid repeating the mistakes of the past. Many plant species have become extinct since the Stone Age, as land was cleared and wild plants were discarded in favor of large cultivated crops of only one species. What knowledge we might have gained from these plants is lost forever. Today, scientists can preserve a greater variety of plant species and genes. These are crucial for our future needs and research.

FUTURE PESTICIDES

Toxic pesticides, sprayed on crops, can badly affect animals and humans. Scientists have implanted a gene, from a bacterium that kills pest caterpillars, into experimental cotton plants. The leaves now produce the plant's own pesticide, which is not toxic to animals or to humans.

DID YOU KNOW?

Cars in some parts of America fill up their tanks with an alcohol called ethanol that is mixed with gasoline. Ethanol is produced by distilling fermented sugar from sugar cane and may become more widely used in the future.

VACCINE SEARCH

In the future, plant vaccines may stop the spread of new and fatal diseases. A common virus from cowpea plants has now been "mixed" with the HIV virus. An AIDS vaccine, produced from virus particles on the leaves, has been tested successfully on mice.

NATURAL HABITAT

Traditional farmers cultivate their crops, such as yams, where wild crops still grow. They provide a natural gene bank with greater genetic variety because genes flow between wild plants and their cultivated relatives.

BIODIVERSITY

Fields of grains, fruit orchards and managed forests are not natural environments. Only one species of plant grows, and any other species is either weeded out or has little opportunity to grow. In a natural environment, many different plant species share the same habitat and attract different wildlife. This natural variety of plant and animal species is called biodiversity. Other plants are now grown around cultivated crops to provide windbreaks, prevent soil erosion and attract—or distract—wildlife that would otherwise eat the crops. Biodiversity may be the way of the future.

POLLUTION INDICATORS

Lichens (above) are extremely sensitive to air pollution, especially sulfur dioxide. The lack of lichens in and around cities is a fairly reliable indicator of high pollution levels. Too many duckweeds or blue-green algae usually indicate water pollution.

Discover more in Food Plants

What Tree is That?

All trees have some things in common. They are perennial, which means they live and grow for many years, and they use seeds to reproduce. The trunks of trees, except those of palms, grow thicker and stronger every year. But it is the differences among trees that help us to identify them. Conifers, most of which have evergreen needle-shaped leaves, have no flowers and grow seeds inside cones. Broad-leaved trees are mostly deciduous, and all of them flower and grow seeds inside fruits. Within these two major groups, there are many types of tree. The shape of the tree, the patterns on the bark, the leaves, the cones, and the seeds (or flowers and fruits) can all be used to identify a tree or the genus to which it belongs. On these pages are 14 common trees, which are typical of their genera.

Moreton Bay Fig
(*Ficus macrophylla*)

FIGS
The flowers are hidden inside the fig, which resembles a ball with an opening at the top. Rings around the twigs are formed when the leaf sheaths, which protect the bud, break off.

English Oak
(*Quercus robur*)

OAKS
The fruits of the 600 species of oak tree are called acorns. Each fruit grows singly inside a special, easily recognizable cup.

American Elm
(*Ulmus americana*)

ELMS
Elm leaves are not symmetrical. One side of the leaf is longer or straighter than the other. The seeds have two broad wings.

Common
Beech
(*Fagus
sylvatica*)

BEECHES
Male flowers grow in catkins. Female flowers grow in groups of 1–3 inside a woody structure, which opens to release the triangular nuts.

Silver Birch
(*Betula pendula*)

BIRCHES
Birches have condensed spikes of separate male and female flowers, known as catkins. Fruiting female catkins look like small cones.

Sugar Maple
(*Acer saccharum*)

MAPLES
Maple leaves have distinct lobes or divisions. Seeds have two wings that break into single wings as they fall.

64

Atlas Cedar
(Cedrus atlantica)

Monterey Pine
(Pinus radiata)

Balsam Fir
(Abies balsamea)

CEDARS
Needle-like leaves grow in clusters of up to 20 on dwarf shoots but are not held together by a sheath like pine needles. The cones break up after the seeds are shed.

PINES
Pine needles grow in groups of 2–5, held together by a sheath at the base of a dwarf shoot. Each pine branch has a number of needle-bearing, dwarf shoots.

FIRS
Fir cones stand upright on the branches and break up after shedding their seeds. Flattened leaves grow directly from branches, not on dwarf shoots.

Coastal She-oak
(Casuarina equisetifolia)

Southern Blue Gum
(Eucalyptus bicostata)

CASUARINAS
A flowering tree with unique leaves that are fused to small branches except for the leaftips (left), which resemble whorls of colorless or brown teeth.

GUM TREES
Different species of gum tree or eucalypt have distinctive bark patterns. Each flower has a lid that comes off to allow insects, birds or mammals to reach the nectar or pollen.

Senegal Date Palm
(Phoenix reclinata)

Lawson Cypress
(Chamaecyparis lawsoniana)

Batswing Coral-tree
(Erythrina vespertilio)

FEATHER-LEAVED PALMS
Each leaf is like a feather, made up of a number of segments that grow along a single main vein. The trees have no bark.

FALSE CYPRESSES
Small scalelike leaves grow in pairs, opposite each other, on green side branches. Female cones become soft as they mature.

CORAL TREES
These trees have prickly bark. Flowers have one large, folded red petal and several smaller, less obvious petals.

Insects and Spiders

How does an insect breathe underwater?

Why are head lice difficult to dislodge?

Which spider throws a silk net over its prey?

Contents

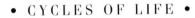

The Great Success Story

TAKING OFF
Insects were the first animals that were able to fly. Cockchafers use their wings to escape danger. This male may also fly far in search of a mate.

Insects are among the most successful creatures in the living world. They first appeared more than 400 million years ago, and fossilized specimens, such as the dragonfly at left, show that some have changed little over this time. More than a million species of insect have been identified, which means that they outnumber all other animal species put together. Even more await discovery, and some scientists think that the total number of species may be as high as 10 million. There are several reasons for these tremendous numbers, but the most important is size. Because insects are so small, individuals need only tiny amounts of food. They eat many different things, including wood, leaves, blood and other insects, and they live in a great range of habitats. The survival of insects is also helped by the ability of some to fly, and by their ability to endure tough conditions. Some desert insects can cope with temperatures above 104˚F (40˚C), and many insect eggs can survive temperatures much colder than a freezer.

UNDERWATER INSECTS
Although insects are common in fresh water, hardly any are found in the sea. This diving beetle is one of many insects that live in fresh water.

LIVING TOGETHER
Many insects gather in groups for part of their lives. This swarm of hungry locusts may have more than a billion individuals, who can munch through huge quantities of food.

THE INSECT ARMY
Scientists divide insects into about 30 different groups, called orders. Insects from some of the most important orders are shown here. .

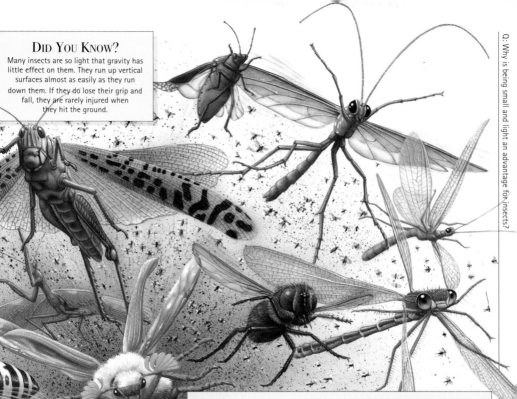

DID YOU KNOW?

Many insects are so light that gravity has little effect on them. They run up vertical surfaces almost as easily as they run down them. If they do lose their grip and fall, they are rarely injured when they hit the ground.

SMALL LIVING SPACES

The way insects are built means that their bodies need to be small and light, or they would become too heavy to move. As shown on this graph, most insect species are less than 1 in (25 mm) long. However, even long insects can still be very light. The goliath beetle weighs no more than 3¹/₂ ounces (100 g). Insects have turned being small into an advantage by exploiting places that are too cramped for larger animals. These places include the space between the upper and lower surfaces of leaves, and the tiny gaps among particles of soil.

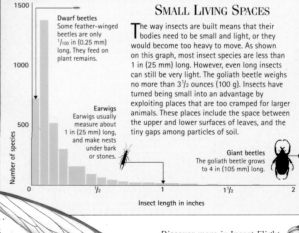

Dwarf beetles
Some feather-winged beetles are only ¹/₁₀₀ in (0.25 mm) long. They feed on plant remains.

Earwigs
Earwigs usually measure about 1 in (25 mm) long, and make nests under bark or stones.

Giant beetles
The goliath beetle grows to 4 in (105 mm) long.

Number of species — Insect length in inches

Discover more in Insect Flight

What is an Insect?

Insects belong to a group of animals called arthropods. All arthropods have a protective, hard body case, or exoskeleton. It covers the whole body, and is made up of separate plates that meet at flexible joints. An arthropod's muscles are attached to the inside of its exoskeleton, and they pull against the plates to make the body move. An insect's body is divided into three basic parts—head, thorax and abdomen. In adult insects, the head carries a pair of antennae, the eyes and a set of mouthparts. The thorax carries three pairs of legs and, usually, two pairs of wings. The abdomen contains the insect's digestive system, the organs used for reproduction and the sting organs—if the insect can sting. An insect's exoskeleton is made of a substance called chitin, which is like a natural plastic. It is usually covered with waxy substances that help prevent the insect from drying out.

Ocellus
Three simple eyes, or ocelli, detect the amount of light in the bee's surroundings.

Head
This consists of several interlocking plates and is one of the strongest parts of the body.

Mouthparts
Jaws, or mandibles, handle food and guide it into the insect's mouth.

Eye
Adult insects have compound eyes made up of many small eyes packed together.

Thorax
This contains powerful muscles that operate the wings and legs.

Antenna
Antennae are delicate sensory organs that help the insect feel, smell, taste and hear.

Centipede

Scorpion

Tick

Crab

PLATED BODIES
As well as insects, arthropods include arachnids (spiders, mites, ticks and scorpions), crustaceans (crabs and lobsters), centipedes and millipedes.

Spider

DID YOU KNOW?
A flea can jump 100 times its own height. Before a jump, it uses its muscles to squeeze special rubber-like pads in its thorax. When it releases the pads, they spring back into shape and catapult the flea into the air.

REPEATING PATTERN
An insect's body is made up of plates arranged in segments. These segments are easy to see on the abdomen of this cockroach.

Wing
Insect wings are supported by thickened veins. The pattern of veins varies in different insects.

PRIMITIVE INSECT
A silverfish does not have wings or ocelli. Its flattened body allows it to wriggle into small crevices, even between the pages of a book.

Abdomen
More flexible than the head or thorax, this expands when the insect feeds.

Leg
In some insects, the three pairs of legs are very different in size. They are all attached to the thorax.

Foot
Hooks, pads and suckers on the feet allow insects to cling onto surfaces or to catch food.

A TYPICAL INSECT
A worker honeybee is a typical flying insect, with two pairs of wings and six legs. Its body is divided into three basic parts: the head, thorax and abdomen.

NEW SKINS

Our skeleton grows in step with the rest of our body, but once an insect's exoskeleton has hardened, it cannot become any larger. In order to grow, the insect has to molt, or shed, its "skin," and replace it with a new one. During molting, the old exoskeleton splits open and the insect crawls out. The insect then takes in air or water, so that its body expands before the new exoskeleton becomes hard. Some insects molt more than 25 times, while others molt just twice. Once an insect becomes an adult, it usually stops molting and does not grow any more.

Discover more in Getting Started

73

A Closer View

Inside an insect's body, many different systems are at work. Each one plays a part in keeping the animal alive and in allowing it to breed. One of the largest, the digestive system, provides the insect with fuel from its food. It is based around the gut, or alimentary canal, which runs the whole length of the body. When an insect eats, food is stored in a bulging part of the canal, called the crop. It then travels into the midgut, where it is broken down and absorbed. Leftover waste moves on to the anus and is expelled. The insect's circulatory system uses blood to carry digested food, but not oxygen, around the body. The blood is pumped forwards by a heart arranged along a muscular tube, but it flows back again through the body spaces among the body organs. The nervous system and the brain ensure that all the other systems work together. They collect signals from the sense organs, and carry messages from one part of the body to another.

Sensing the surroundings
A honeybee's exoskeleton is covered with tiny hairs that detect the slightest air current. Each hair sends signals to the brain.

Trachea

Control center
An insect's brain collects signals from the eyes and other sense organs, and coordinates its body. It is connected to the nerve cord.

Power plant
The muscles in the thorax power the bee's wings and legs. Like all the bee's muscles, they are bathed in blood.

Mini–brain
Swellings, called ganglia, are arranged at intervals along the nerve cord. These control sections of the body.

Liquid meals
The bee uses its tongue like a drinking straw to suck up sugary nectar from flowers.

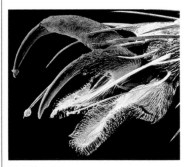

GETTING A GRIP
Each fly's foot has a pair of claws and bristly pads. The claws allow the fly to grip rough surfaces, while the bristly pads help it to cling onto smooth surfaces.

INSIDE A BEE
This illustration shows major body systems of the worker honeybee. The digestive system is colored cream, the respiratory system white, the nervous system gray and the circulatory system green.

Air intakes
Openings, called spiracles, let air into the bee's internal air tubes (tracheae). Each spiracle has hairs to keep out dust and water.

Hooked together
A honeybee has two pairs of wings. The larger front wings are joined to the smaller back wings by a row of hooks. The two pairs of wings beat together.

Strong wings
The wings are made of chitin, the same material as the rest of the exoskeleton. In some insects, the wings are covered in tiny hairs.

FLEXIBLE LEGS
Like all arthropods, an insect's leg has flexible joints that allow the leg to bend. This is the leg joint of a human head louse.

Midgut refueling
Food is digested and absorbed here. Insects that eat solid food have a muscular pouch (gizzard) where food is ground up before being digested.

Heart

Poison sac

Crop

Nerve cord

Shake a leg
This set of muscles in the bee's leg pulls on a long tendon to move the claws.

Sting

FINE TRACHEAE

Like all animals, insects need to breathe—take in oxygen and get rid of carbon dioxide. Because their blood does not carry oxygen, and they do not have lungs, insects breathe with the help of tiny air tubes called tracheae. The openings of these tubes, called spiracles, are located on the sides of the thorax and abdomen. Each trachea divides into many branches that eventually become so fine they go inside cells. When an insect molts, it sheds the linings of its tracheae through its spiracles. This caterpillar is undergoing this remarkable process.

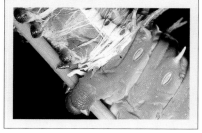

DID YOU KNOW?

All insects are protected by body cases, but in larvae (grubs), the case is often quite thin. These lily beetle larvae shield themselves from their enemies with a protective coat made from their own droppings.

DEADLY WEAPON
A honeybee's sting is like a sharp rod with hooks on it. Once embedded in the skin, the sting releases its poison. Here, the sting (top) is compared to a needle.

Discover more in Insect Senses

SENSORY SKILLS
The shape of antennae varies
among insects, and sometimes
even between males and females
of the same species.

Night-time feeder
A long-horned
beetle's long antennae
are used for feeling its
way in the dark.

Seeking a mate
In flight, a male
cockchafer's
antennae open
out to detect the
scent of a female.

Damp skin spots
The human louse
uses its antennae
to sense damp
parts of a body
where it feeds
on blood.

Air detector
Each butterfly antenna
is a slender shaft
ending with a small
knob. The shafts are
covered with hairs
that detect air currents.

Hot spots
A female mosquito's
feathery antennae
sense heat from
warm-blooded animals.
This enables her to
find food in the dark.

Feathery sniffer
A male emperor
moth can smell a
female more than
2 miles (3 km) away.

• STAYING ALIVE •

Insect Senses

To survive, an insect has to know about the world around it. It must be able to find food, track down a mate and, most important of all, detect its enemies before they have a chance to attack. Like many other animals, insects have five main senses—sight, hearing, smell, touch and taste. Each type of insect specializes in using some of these senses more than others. Because dragonflies and horseflies fly during the day, they have large eyes that help them find their victims. Most moths, on the other hand, fly at night. Instead of using sight, they find their food and partners by smell. As well as using senses to find out about the world, insects also have senses that monitor their own bodies. These tell them which way up they are flying, how their wings and legs are positioned, and whether they are speeding up or slowing down. For flying insects, these senses are particularly important.

Human's view

Bee's view

SEEING THE INVISIBLE
Many insects see wavelengths of light that are invisible to us. Above right is how a bee may view a flower. It gives more detail than a human view and guides the bee to the nectar.

Simple eyes
Known as ocelli, these small eyes on the top of the head sense the difference between sunlight and shade.

SMALL EYES
The more eyelets an insect has, the more clearly it sees. This wingless worker ant lives in the dark and has small compound eyes, which contain only a few hundred eyelets.

EARS ON THE BODY

Insects often use their antennae to hear, but they also have other ways of detecting different sounds and vibrations.

Ears on legs
Bush crickets have ears on their front legs. Each ear is a thin oval membrane that moves when the air vibrates.

Feeling the ground
Ants sense vibrations through their legs. They often respond to these vibrations by preparing to attack an enemy.

Ears on the abdomen
Grasshoppers and locusts have ears on their abdomen. They are particularly sensitive to the calls made by their own species.

Leg bristles
A cockroach uses special bristles to sense the vibrations made by something moving towards it.

Wings as ears
The thin and delicate wings of a lacewing pick up vibrations in the air and sense movements.

Feeling the heat
A horsefly's antennae are sensitive to heat, and are used to locate areas of exposed skin on a warm-blooded animal.

Making up a picture
The horsefly's compound eyes each contain several thousand eyelets. The fly's brain combines the signals from the eyelets to make up an image of the surroundings.

LOOKING FOR BLOOD
Female horseflies feed on blood, and they rely mainly on vision to track down a meal. Like most insects, they have compound eyes, which are made of many smaller eyes, called eyelets, packed tightly together.

Taste bud | Hair

Smell sensor

MULTIPURPOSE ANTENNAE
This magnified picture shows the surface of a wasp's antenna. These antennae carry taste buds for sensing food, sensors that smell the air, and hairs that respond to touch.

Discover more in Insect Flight

77

LIVING DRILL
The hazelnut weevil has a long, slender "snout" with tiny jaws at the tip. Using its jaws like a drill, the weevil chews holes in hazelnuts.

Food and Feeding

Individually, insects are quite choosy about what they eat, but together they devour a vast range of different foods. Many insects feed on plants or on small animals, but some survive on more unusual food, including rotting wood, blood, horns or even wool. To tackle each of these foods, insects have a complicated set of specially shaped mouthparts. A praying mantis, for example, has sharp jaws, or mandibles, that stab and cut up its captives, while its other mouthparts help to hold the food and pass it towards the mouth. A grasshopper has similar mouthparts, but its main jaws are much stronger and blunter, and so are ideal for crushing the plant material it prefers. The mouthparts of insects that feed on liquids often look very different than those of insects that live on solid foods. A mosquito has a long stylet that works like a syringe, while a butterfly or moth has a long tongue, or proboscis, which acts like a drinking straw. As this butterfly (above left) demonstrates, the tongue conveniently coils up when not in use.

MIDAIR REFUELING
With its tongue uncoiled, a hawk moth drinks nectar from deep inside a flower. Some hawk moths have tongues that are more than 6 in (15 cm) long.

CHANGING TASTES
Larvae and adult insects often eat very different foods. An adult potter wasp feeds on nectar whereas its larva (left top) feeds on caterpillars.

INSECT MOUTHPARTS

Insect mouthparts are like tools in a toolkit. They are specially shaped to gather particular food and allow it to be swallowed.

Spongy pads
Houseflies use a spongy pad to pour saliva over their food. After the food has dissolved, it is sucked up.

Piercing mouthparts
Female mosquitoes use their needle-like mouthparts to stab through the skin and suck up blood. Males sip only plant juices.

Powerful jaws
Many ants have strong jaws for gripping and cutting up small animals. Some can slice through human skin.

FAST FOOD
A locust chops through a tasty leaf quickly. Its mouthparts, called palps, explore the leaf as it eats.

DID YOU KNOW?

This darkling beetle lives in Africa's Namib Desert, where the only moisture comes from mist rolling in from the sea. To get water, the beetle points its abdomen into the wind, and collects the moisture that condenses on its body.

MOPPING UP
Before it can eat, a housefly must pour saliva over its food. The saliva often dries to form small spots that can be seen after the fly has moved on.

PATIENT KILLER
A praying mantis surprises its victims by striking out with its front legs. The legs snap shut and help grip the prey with sharp spines. The mantis often begins to feed even while its catch is still struggling to escape.

FEROCIOUS TWIG
Most caterpillars eat plants for food, but this looper moth caterpillar catches other insects. Camouflaged to look like a twig, it attacks small flies when they land nearby.

DEADLY DASH
After cockroaches, tiger beetles are among the fastest sprinters of the insect world. Moving at more than $1^1/_2$ ft (0.5 m) per second, this tiger beetle is chasing some ants. The beetle's large jaws will quickly snatch and crush the ants.

Predators and Parasites

One third of all insects feed on other animals, either as predators or parasites. Predators catch their prey by hunting it actively, or lying in wait until food comes within reach. Some of the most spectacular hunters feed in the air. Dragonflies, for example, swoop down and snatch up other flying insects with their long legs. On the ground, active hunters include fast-moving beetles, as well as many ants and wasps. Some wasps specialize in hunting spiders, which they sting—sometimes after a fierce battle. Insects that hunt by stealth, or lying in wait, are usually harder to spot. These include mantises and bugs, which are often superbly camouflaged to match their background. A few of these stationary hunters build special traps to catch their food. Antlion larvae dig steep-sided pits in loose soil and wait for ants to tumble in. Insects that are parasites live on or inside another animal, called the host, and feed on its body or blood. The host animal can sometimes be harmed or killed.

EASY PICKINGS
Hunting is sometimes easy work. Because aphids move very slowly, they cannot escape hungry ladybugs.

UNDERWATER ATTACK
Only a few insects are large enough to kill vertebrates (animals with backbones). This diving beetle has managed to catch a salamander.

DEATH OF A BEE
Assassin bugs use their sharp beak to stab their victims and then suck out the body fluids. This one has caught a honeybee by lying in wait inside a flower.

80

CLEANING UP

Instead of hunting live animals, burying beetles feed on dead bodies. They bury carcasses, then feed themselves and their larvae on the remains.

DINING IN

Parasitic insects use living animals as fresh food. Many lay their eggs on the larvae of other insects, or inject eggs through the skin of the victim. When the eggs hatch, these larvae feed on their host. They start with the less essential parts of the host's body, so that it survives for as long as possible. Eventually, they burst out through the host's skin and turn into adults. This hawk moth caterpillar has been feasted on by parasitic wasps, and is covered with their empty cocoons.

DID YOU KNOW?

The larvae of fungus gnats, found in caves in New Zealand, catch flying insects by glowing in the dark. Each larva produces a thread of sticky mucus that traps insects as they fly towards the glowing light. The larva then eats the insect and the trap.

Insects and Plants

When insects first appeared on Earth, they found a world brimming with plants. Over millions of years, insects and plants evolved side by side. During this time, some insects became deadly enemies of plants, but others became valuable partners in the struggle for survival. Insects use plants for many things, but the most important of all is for food. Different insects eat all parts of plants, from roots and stems to leaves and flowers. Most of them eat living plants, but some help to break down plants once they are dead. By doing this, insects help to recycle important nutrients so that other plants can use them. Insects also live on or in plants, and they often damage plants when they set up home. Despite this insect attack, plants are not completely defenseless. Many use sticky hairs or chemicals to keep insects away, and some even catch insects and digest them. However, not all visitors are unwelcome. When bees feed at flowers, they carry pollen from plant to plant. This helps plants to pollinate and spread to new areas.

FLYING COURIER
Bees, butterflies, moths and wasps are all common visitors to flowers. These insects become dusted with pollen while they feed on the sugary nectar of the flowers.

GETTING A GRIP
Caterpillars have to hang on tight while they feed. They do this with special "legs" that end in sucker-like pads. They lose these legs when they become moths or butterflies.

BREAKING OUT
Seeds are packed with stores of food that help young plants to survive. This weevil climbing out of a grain of wheat has just finished eating some of these nutrients.

SLOW GROWTH
The larva of a stag beetle spends its entire early life hidden inside rotting wood. Because wood is not very nutritious, it takes the larva a long time to mature.

STRANGE BUT TRUE
The caterpillars of one Mexican moth grow inside the beans of a small bush. If a bean falls onto warm, sunny ground, the caterpillar inside jerks its body to make the bean "jump" into the shade. Each bean can move up to 2 in (5 cm) in a single hop.

LEAFY FEAST

Eating side by side, beetle larvae chew away at a leaf. Insects kill some plants, but enough plants are always left to allow both plants and insects to survive.

BUILDING WITH LEAVES

Female leafcutter bees clip out pieces of leaf with their jaws, and take the pieces back to their nests. They use them to make tube-shaped cells for larvae.

PLANTS THAT EAT INSECTS

In order to grow, plants need substances called mineral nutrients. They usually get these from the ground, but some plants that live where nutrients are scarce also get them from the bodies of insects. This sundew has trapped a fly in its sticky hairs, and will soon digest its prey. Other carnivorous plants catch insects in fluid-filled traps, or with leaves that suddenly snap shut.

Insect Defense

For insects, the world is full of danger. They are under constant threat of being eaten, and their enemies include not only birds, lizards and spiders, but also other insects. Many insects defend themselves by hurrying away at the first sign of trouble. Others stay still and well hidden. They hide in soil or rotting wood, or make themselves look like the objects around them. Some insects imitate thorns, sticks, leaves and even animal droppings, and they are often invisible until they move. Another line of defense works in a completely different way. Instead of hiding, some insects are brightly colored and easy to see, like the caterpillar on the left. But their colors warn predators that they are unpleasant or even dangerous to eat. Insects like this, however, are not always what they seem. Some harmless insects imitate those that have a bad taste, and others look just like those with a dangerous sting. If all these defenses fail, some insects stand their ground and attack. With their armored bodies, sharp jaws and toxic chemicals, they often live to fight another day.

Mottled beauty
With wings spread out, the moth blends into the tree bark.

Bark bug
This has a flat, patterned body like the surface of tree bark.

Leaf insect
The flattened body and forewings mimic a single leaf

Stick insect
Slow movements help a stick insect to look like part of a plant.

Sword-grass butterfly caterpillar
The caterpillar's slender green body is well hidden among blades of grass.

BATTLE POSTURE
This wood ant prepares for battle by thrusting its abdomen upwards. When an attacker comes closer, the ant squirts it with a stream of acid from the tip of its abdomen.

SICKLY SCENT
When some insects, such as this bush cricket, are threatened, they ooze droplets of a liquid that has a repulsive smell. Attackers usually stay away.

Comma butterfly
Ragged brown wings imitate the color and shape of dead leaves.

Long-headed grasshopper
The grasshopper's pointed head gives it a sticklike outline.

BLENDING IN
Insects are experts in the art of camouflage. This scene shows how 13 different insects use camouflage to avoid being spotted.

STARING EYES
Many moths have two large spots on their back wings. When disturbed, they reveal the spots, which look like two eyes set in a menacing face.

DEFENSE PLANS
There is no such thing as one completely successful defense plan. Many insects have several ways to defend themselves. If one method is not successful, they will try another. The puss moth caterpillar relies initially on camouflage, but if an attacker sees it, the caterpillar moves onto the next plan. This involves inflating its head, and producing a pair of "horns" to frighten its attacker. If the caterpillar is still in danger, it squirts a spray of acid at its attacker, from a gland just beneath the head.

Emerald moth caterpillar
The body projections make this caterpillar look like a twig with buds.

Swallowtail butterfly larva
The texture and shape of the larva's body look like bird droppings.

Bush cricket
The veined front wings are pressed together to look like an upright leaf.

Flower mantis
This mantis is the same color as the flower. It is disguised as it waits to catch prey.

Angle shades moth
The wings look like a newly fallen leaf.

KICKING BACK
The giant weta from New Zealand raises its powerful back legs to show that it can fight back. These legs have large spines.

Cryptic grasshopper
The round outline and mottled colors imitate a small pebble.

DANGEROUS MOMENT
Male insects are often smaller than females, and some have to be careful when they mate. Unless he is careful, this male mantis will end up as a meal for his partner.

FOOD FOR THE YOUNG
Insects often use their sense of smell to find good places for their eggs. This dead mouse has attracted blowflies that are ready to lay eggs.

Getting Started

Animals begin life in two different ways. Some develop inside their mother's body until they are ready to be born. Others, including most insects, develop from eggs outside their mother's body. Before a female insect can lay her eggs, she normally has to mate. Once this has happened, she chooses a place for her eggs, making sure that each one is near a source of suitable food. In most cases, she then abandons them, and makes no attempt to look after her young. However, not all insects start life this way. A few female insects can reproduce without needing to mate. Some insects give birth to live young, such as aphids who give birth to nymphs, and tsetse flies who give birth to larvae. A few insects are careful parents and take care of their eggs. Female earwigs lay small clutches of eggs and look after them by licking them clean. Many bugs carry their eggs on their backs, and guard their young after they hatch.

A QUEEN'S LIFE
In an ant colony, only one individual—the queen—lays eggs. The eggs are carried away by worker ants, who tend and feed the young after they hatch. Most termites also reproduce this way.

DID YOU KNOW?
Insects that give birth to live young have fast-growing families. Within a few days, a female leaf beetle or aphid can be surrounded by dozens of offspring. Unlike insects that start life as eggs, each one can feed right away.

EGGS ON THE MOVE
A female giant water bug glues her eggs onto the back of a male. While carrying the eggs, the male is unable to use his wings.

INSECT EGGS

Horsefly eggs

Insect eggs are remarkable objects. Because they are so small, it is often difficult to see them without a microscope. A few insects drop their eggs from the air, but most glue them firmly to something that will provide food for their young. Insect eggs are sometimes laid singly, but many are laid in clusters, with hundreds or even thousands of eggs side by side. A few insects make special structures to help their eggs survive. Cockroaches lay batches of eggs in special cases; green lacewings lay their eggs on slender stalks, which makes the eggs difficult for predators to reach. Some eggs hatch soon after they are laid, but others stay inactive during months of cold or dry weather, when all the adults may die.

Eucalyptus tip bug eggs

Cockroach egg case

Green lacewing eggs

A GOOD START
This female ichneumon wasp drills into a tree branch. She stings the larva of a wood wasp and deposits an egg through the tube, or ovipositor, onto the larva. When this egg hatches, it will feed on its unlucky host.

From Nymph to Adult

After an insect has hatched out of its egg, it starts to feed and grow. However, as well as growing, it often changes shape. This is called metamorphosis. In some insects, the changes are only slight, so the young insect looks much like the adult form. In others, the changes are so great that the young and adult look completely different. Insects that change only slightly include dragonflies, grasshoppers, earwigs, cockroaches, true bugs and praying mantises. Their young are called nymphs. A nymph does not have wings, although it does have small wing buds, and it is usually a different color from its parents. It often lives in a different habitat and feeds on different food. Most nymphs will molt several times. Each time a nymph sheds its skin, its body gets bigger and its wing buds become longer. Eventually, the nymph is ready for its final molt. It breaks out of its old skin, and emerges as an adult insect with working wings. It can then fly away to find a mate.

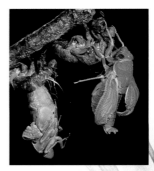

FINAL MOLT
After many years feeding underground as nymphs, these cicadas are shedding their skins for the last time. Their crumpled wings will soon expand and dry.

MANTIS MARCH
These newly hatched praying mantis nymphs look like miniature versions of their parents. They have well-developed legs, but their wing buds are still very small.

UNDERWATER NYMPHS
Adult dragonflies live in the air, but their nymphs develop under the water. Each nymph lives in water for up to five years before it hauls itself up a plant stem, sheds its skin for the last time, and emerges as an adult, able to fly.

Laying eggs
This dragonfly inserts her eggs into a water plant. Some species let the eggs fall to the bottom of ponds.

On the move
Dragonfly eggs can take several weeks to hatch. Each tiny nymph chews its way out of its egg case.

NYMPH TO ADULT
Like their parents (far right), nymphs have six legs. Their bodies change in proportion as they grow, but they keep the same overall shape.

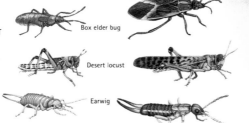

Box elder bug

Desert locust

Earwig

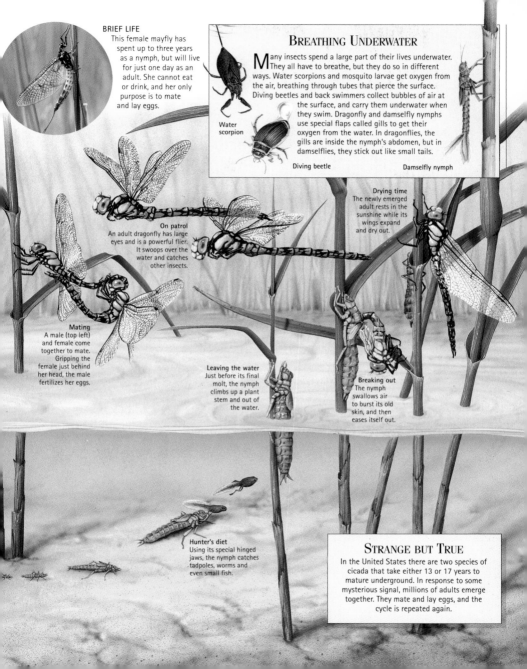

BRIEF LIFE
This female mayfly has spent up to three years as a nymph, but will live for just one day as an adult. She cannot eat or drink, and her only purpose is to mate and lay eggs.

BREATHING UNDERWATER

Many insects spend a large part of their lives underwater. They all have to breathe, but they do so in different ways. Water scorpions and mosquito larvae get oxygen from the air, breathing through tubes that pierce the surface. Diving beetles and back swimmers collect bubbles of air at the surface, and carry them underwater when they swim. Dragonfly and damselfly nymphs use special flaps called gills to get their oxygen from the water. In dragonflies, the gills are inside the nymph's abdomen, but in damselflies, they stick out like small tails.

Water scorpion

Diving beetle

Damselfly nymph

On patrol
An adult dragonfly has large eyes and is a powerful flier. It swoops over the water and catches other insects.

Drying time
The newly emerged adult rests in the sunshine while its wings expand and dry out.

Mating
A male (top left) and female come together to mate. Gripping the female just behind her head, the male fertilizes her eggs.

Leaving the water
Just before its final molt, the nymph climbs up a plant stem and out of the water.

Breaking out
The nymph swallows air to burst its old skin, and then eases itself out.

Hunter's diet
Using its special hinged jaws, the nymph catches tadpoles, worms and even small fish.

STRANGE BUT TRUE

In the United States there are two species of cicada that take either 13 or 17 years to mature underground. In response to some mysterious signal, millions of adults emerge together. They mate and lay eggs, and the cycle is repeated again.

A CHANGE OF LIFE
The atlas moth has four stages in its life cycle—egg, larva, pupa and adult. Larvae put all their energy into feeding, while adults mate and lay eggs.

Mating
A female's scent attracts a male, and the moths mate.

Laying eggs
The female moth searches for suitable food plants and glues her eggs to the leaves.

The next stage
A larva, or caterpillar, hatches from an egg. It grows bigger with several molts.

DID YOU KNOW?

Most larvae feed for many hours every day, and they put on weight very quickly. Just before they turn into pupae, fully grown larvae are often heavier than the adult insects of the same species.

LEGLESS LARVAE
Mosquito larvae live in water and feed on microscopic animals. They swim by wriggling their bodies, and breathe through short tubes.

• CYCLES OF LIFE •

A Complete Change

Many young insects look quite unlike their parents. They do not have wings, and some do not even have legs. They often spend all their time on, or in, the things they eat. Young insects such as these are called larvae, and they include maggots, grubs and caterpillars. Compared to adult insects, they have soft bodies. Larvae protect themselves by tasting horrible, by being difficult to swallow, or by hiding away. A typical larva feeds for several weeks, shedding its skin several times while growing. When mature, its appetite suddenly vanishes, it stops moving and it becomes a pupa. The pupa has a tough outer case, and is sometimes protected by a silk cocoon. Inside the case, the larva's body changes dramatically. It is broken down and reassembled, so that it gradually turns into an adult insect. When this change, or metamorphosis, is complete, the case splits open and the adult insect, with wings, breaks out. It is now ready to reproduce.

90

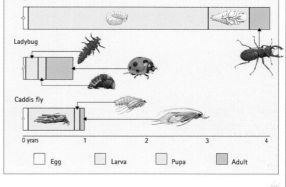

Pupating
The caterpillar fastens itself in position with threads of silk.

Airborne
When its wing veins have hardened, the moth flies off.

Opening up
After breaking open the pupal case, the adult moth pumps blood into its wings.

NATURAL SILK
Each silk moth cocoon is made of a single silk thread more than $^1/2$ mile (1 km) long. As soon as a moth emerges from its cocoon, it mates.

PAMPERED UPBRINGING
Honeybee larvae mature inside wax cells, and worker bees bring food to them. These bees are turning into pupae, and will soon emerge as adults.

TIME FOR A CHANGE

Insects that change completely when they mature have four stages in their life cycles. Each stage usually lasts for a different length of time and these times vary from species to species. The stag beetle is a relatively slow developer, and spends many months as a larva hidden in wood, feeding only on rotting vegetation. The ladybug develops more quickly, and spends over half its life as an adult. The northern caddis fly spends most of its life as a larva. It lives in ponds and quiet waters in a specially constructed case.

Stag beetle

Ladybug

Caddis fly

0 years	1	2	3	4

☐ Egg   ☐ Larva   ☐ Pupa   ☐ Adult

Discover more in The Great Success Story

91

Insect Flight

WINGS COMPARED
In most insects, the front
and back wings look
different. Insect wings are
supported by branching veins,
and are sometimes covered
with tiny hairs or scales.

Pleated back wings
The back wings of a
mantis fold up like
fans when not in use.

Insects were the first animals to fly. Today they share the air with birds and bats, but they are still the most numerous fliers in the animal world. Some insects fly on their own. Others, such as midges and locusts, gather in swarms. A swarm can contain just a few dozen insects, or more than a billion. Flying allows insects to escape from danger, and makes it easier for them to find mates. It is also a perfect way to reach food. Bees and butterflies fly among flowers, and hawk moths often hover in front of them. Dragonflies use flight to attack other insects in the air. They are the fastest fliers in the insect world, and can reach speeds of more than 31 miles (50 km) per hour. Most insects have two pairs of wings, made of the same material that covers the rest of their bodies. The wings are powered by muscles in the thorax. These muscles either flap the wings directly, or make the thorax move and this causes the wings to flap.

DID YOU KNOW?

Insects such as thrips and aphids are too small and slow to make much headway on their own. Instead, they are carried by the wind, blowing them from one place to another far away.

VERTICAL TAKEOFF
Butterflies rest with their
wings together. At takeoff, the
wings peel apart, and the air
sucks the butterfly upwards
and away from danger.

REFUELING STOP
Flight is a fast and
efficient way of
getting about, but it
uses a lot of energy.
Many insects, such
as bees, drink sugary
nectar from flowers
to give them energy.

LONG-DISTANCE TRAVELERS

Although insects are small animals, some of them travel huge distances in search of food or warmth. Dragonflies, locusts and moths often migrate, but the star travelers of the insect world are butterflies. In spring, North American monarch butterflies (left) set off northwards from Mexico. Many travel more than 1,500 miles (2,400 km). Painted lady butterflies set out from North Africa, and often make even longer journeys. Some of them manage to cross the Arctic Circle in Scandinavia, making a total distance of more than 1,800 miles (2,900 km).

Single pair of wings
Instead of back wings, true flies have tiny knobs called halteres.

Plumed wings
Thrips and plume moths have wings that look like tiny feathers.

Hooked wings
A wasp's back and front wings are connected to each other by tiny hooks.

Double pair of wings
A dragonfly's front and back wings beat in opposite directions.

ASSISTED TAKEOFF
Weak fliers, such as this scorpion fly, often jump into the air from a high point. This assists them in gaining lift during takeoff.

FLY AWAY LADYBUG
Like all beetles, a ladybug has hardened front wings that do not beat up and down. They provide lift that helps the ladybug stay in the air.

Takeoff!
The front wings swing outwards, and when the back wings are beating fast enough, the ladybug takes off.

Making ready
Before it can fly, a ladybug opens its front wings and unfolds its back wings.

Grounded
A ladybug's back wings are normally packed away under its hard front wings.

LOOPING WALK
Some caterpillars move by holding the ground tight with their front legs, and pulling their body into a loop. They stretch forwards to straighten the loop, and then start the process again.

• AN INSECT'S WORLD •

Moving Around

Many people find insects alarming because of their sudden movements. Insects are not always fast, but because they weigh so little, most of them can stop and start far more suddenly than we can. The way an insect moves depends on where it lives. On land, the slowest movers are legless larvae. They have to wriggle to get around. Adult insects normally move using their legs, and they either walk or run, or jump into the air. The champion jumpers of the insect world are grasshoppers and crickets, but jumping insects also include fleas, froghoppers and some beetles. Tiny, wingless insects called springtails also jump, but instead of using their legs, they launch themselves by flicking a special "tail." Legs are useful in water, and insects have evolved a variety of leg shapes to suit watery ways of life. Water boatmen and diving beetles have legs like oars, and row their way through the water. Pond-skaters live on top of the water, and have long and slender legs that spread their weight over the surface.

HEAD-BANGER
A click beetle escapes danger by lying on its back and keeping perfectly still (above left). If attacked its head suddenly snaps upwards, hurling it out of harm's way and back onto its feet.

WALKING IN THREES
Insects walk by moving three legs at a time—one on one side, and two on the other. This makes their bodies zigzag as they move along.

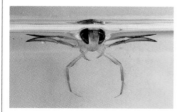

ROWING ALONG
The lesser water boatman has flattened back legs fringed with hairs. It uses these to push itself along. This species swims right side up, but some water boatmen swim upside down.

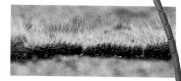

HEAD TO TAIL
Processionary moth caterpillars travel in long lines when they leave their nests to feed. If they are touched, their long hairs can cause a painful rash.

WALKING ON WATER
Water has a thin "skin" that is held together by a force called surface tension. Pond-skaters are light enough to walk on the skin without falling through.

Power-packed legs
Muscles in the upper part of the legs provide most of the power for the jump.

Springy knees
A springlike mechanism in the knees increases the force of the jump.

MIGHTY KICK
Grasshoppers jump to avoid predators and to launch themselves into flight. Their powerful back legs flick backwards to push them into the air.

THE RIGHT LEGS FOR THE JOB

A close look at an insect's legs often helps to show where it lives and how it gets around. Insects that live on the ground often have claws to grip rough surfaces, or flat pads if they live on sand. Beetles that live on smooth leaves have broad feet with brushlike hairs, but those that live on hairy leaves have tiny claws to help them grip individual hairs. Many water insects have hairs along their legs. On a pond-skater, these hairs repel water and prevent the insect from sinking.

Water insect

Ground insect

Discover more in True Bugs

Making Contact

I n every insect's life, there are times when it has to make contact with other members of its species. It may need to warn of danger, to attract a mate, or to prove that it is not an enemy but a friend. Many insects communicate by sight, and they often use bright colors or patterns to identify themselves. After dark, most insects are hard to see, but fireflies are easy to spot. They make their own light, and flash coded signals to one another through the dark. For crickets, cicadas and some smaller insects, sound provides a way to contact a mate. Unlike sight, sound works during the day and night, and allows an insect to stay hidden while it broadcasts its call. Insects often use touch and taste to communicate when they meet, but they can also make contact by smell. Some of their scents waft a long way through the air, while others mark the ground to show where they have been.

Male firefly

LIGHTS IN THE NIGHT
Fireflies are small beetles that make contact using a pale-greenish light. The males flash as they fly overhead and the females—which are often wingless—flash back from the ground.

The Honeybee Dance

W hen a worker honeybee finds a good food source, it returns to the hive to pass on the news. It tells the other honeybees the distance and location of the food through a special figure eight dance. If the food is far away from the hive, the honeybee does a waggle in the middle of the figure eight (as shown below). The speed of the waggle tells the honeybees how far they must fly to find the food. The angle of the waggle shows the honeybees where the food is in relation to the sun.

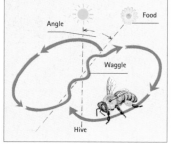

Food

Angle

Waggle

Hive

SCENTED MOTH
The male tiger moth attracts females by a scent called a pheromone, which is released into the air by two glands in the abdomen. These fold away when not in use.

SOUND SIGNALS
A grasshopper calls by scraping its back legs against the hard edges of its front wings. This causes the wings to vibrate and make a sound. This process is called stridulation.

TOUCH AND TASTE
When two ants meet, they touch each other briefly with their antennae. This tells them if they are from the same nest, and passes on the taste of any food they have found.

DID YOU KNOW?

The male mole cricket attracts mates with one of the loudest calls in the insect world. The cricket makes his call by rubbing his front wings together, and his Y-shaped burrow amplifies the sound. In still air, it can be heard more than 1/2 mile (800 m) away.

Butterflies and Moths

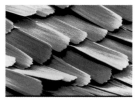

Butterflies are the most eye-catching members of the insect world, while moths are often quite dull. Yet despite their differences in color, these insects are closely related and have many features in common.

Butterflies and moths spend the first part of their lives as caterpillars. They change shape during a resting stage as a pupa (left), and emerge as adults with wings covered with tiny scales. Unlike caterpillars, an adult butterfly or moth eats liquid food, such as nectar or rotting fruit. It does this with a sucking tube called a proboscis, which coils up when the insect is not using it. Butterflies fly by day, but most moths fly at dusk or after dark, and spend the day hidden on leaves or trees. There are more than 150,000 species of butterfly and moth. The largest have wingspans of more than 10 in (25 cm), but the smallest, called pygmy moths, are not much bigger than a fingernail.

I SPY
Most moths use camouflage to protect them during the day. When this moth from Borneo rests on a tree, it seems to disappear.

Hercules moth caterpillar

Orchard butterfly caterpillar

SURVIVAL KIT
Caterpillars have many enemies, so they defend themselves with poisonous chemicals, irritating hairs, and inflatable "horns" that release an unpleasant smell.

Silk moth caterpillar

FLY-BY-NIGHTS

Many night-time insects are attracted to bright lights. They flutter around street lights, and often gather outside windows after dark. Scientists are not certain why light attracts insects in this way, although with moths, it may be that the light disrupts their navigation system. Moths probably fly in straight lines by using a distant light, such as the moon, like a fixed point on a compass. When a moth does this with a nearby light, the system does not work, because the position of the "fixed" point changes as soon as the moth flies past. As a result, the moth spirals around the light, and eventually flies into it.

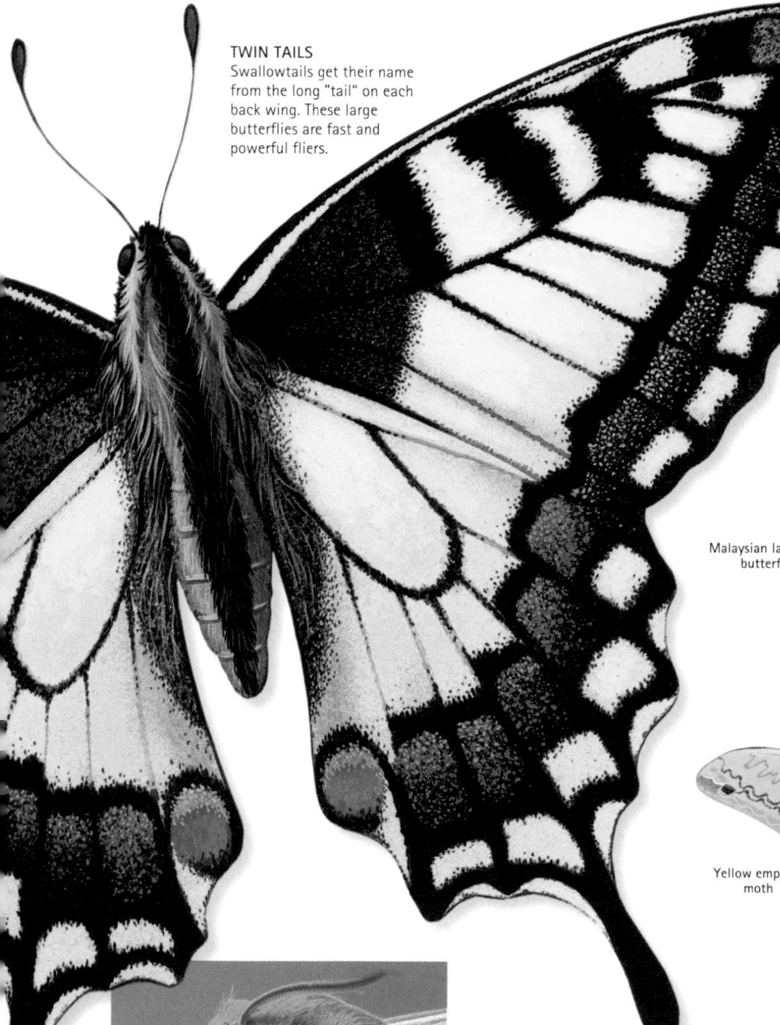

TWIN TAILS
Swallowtails get their name from the long "tail" on each back wing. These large butterflies are fast and powerful fliers.

Q: What are some of the differences between moths and butterflies?

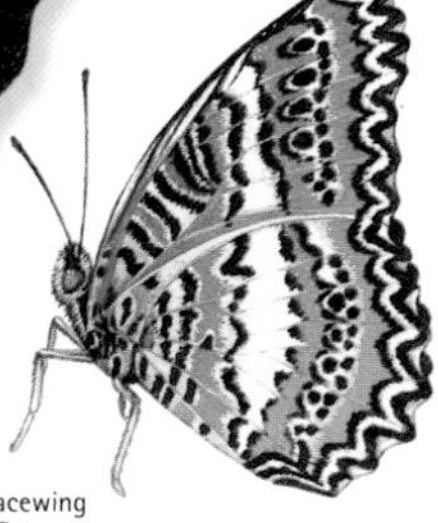

Malaysian lacewing butterfly

TIME OUT
Butterflies usually rest with their wings upright, although they often spread them when they bask in the sunshine. Moths usually rest with their wings held flat.

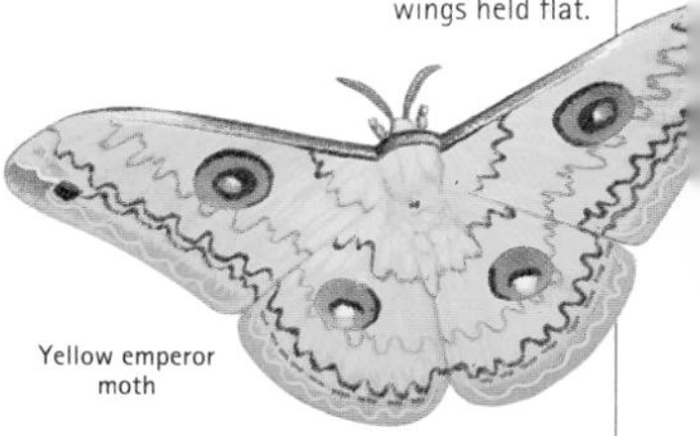

Yellow emperor moth

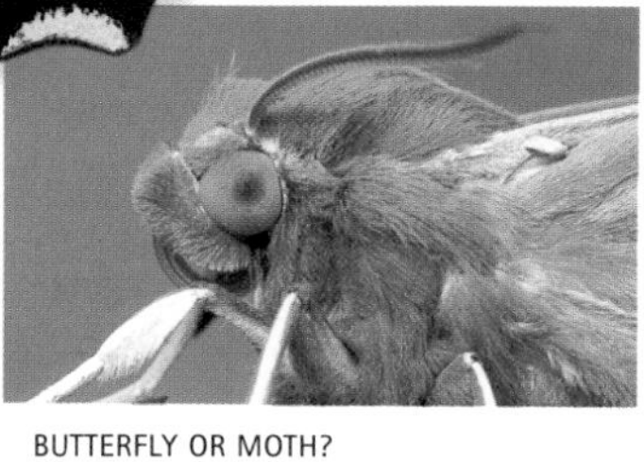

BUTTERFLY OR MOTH?
Moths do not have a knob on the end of each antenna like most butterflies do. This elephant hawk moth has feathery antennae.

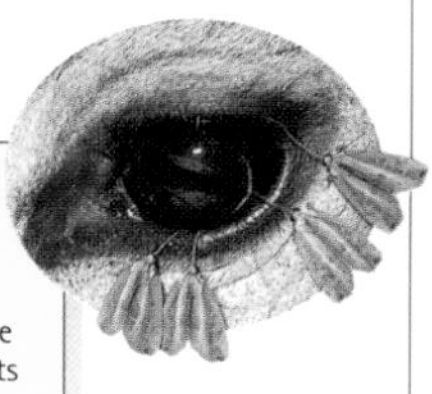

Strange but True

Tear moths, from Southeast Asia, feed on the tears of large animals, such as cattle and buffaloes. Settling close to the eye, the moth drinks the tears through its long proboscis. Although they can be annoying, the moths do little harm.

Discover more in A Complete Change

• THE BIG ORDERS •

Bees, Wasps and Ants

Most insects live alone, coming together only to mate, but social insects have a very different way of life. They live in family groups and share the work necessary to survive. Social insects include all ants and termites, and many species of bee and wasp. These insects usually build nests in which they raise their young and store food. Some nests contain fewer than a dozen insects, but others can house more than a million. Inside each nest, one insect—the queen—normally lays eggs, and all the other insects are her offspring. Workers look after the eggs, find food and raise the young, and in ant and termite colonies, soldiers defend the nest against attack. Every year, some of the males and queens fly away and mate. After mating, the male dies and the queen starts building a new nest. She is soon surrounded by a growing family of her own.

PAINFUL JAB
This wasp can sting repeatedly, but once a honeybee stings, it dies. Because a honeybee sting has a barbed tip, some of its organs are torn out when it flies off.

SOLITARY BEE
Not all bees live together. Most live a solitary life, such as this digger bee, digging its way to an underground nest.

Pollen stores

Drone
Drones are male bees that develop from unfertilized eggs. Their only job is to mate with new queens.

Empty cell

Drone cell
Drone pupae need larger cells than worker pupae.

Queen cell
Larvae selected to become queens are fed only royal jelly and are raised in special cells.

Open larva cell
This cell contains a newly hatched larva. Larvae are first fed royal jelly, and later pollen and honey.

MAMMOTH LOAD
Leafcutter ants bite off pieces of plants, and carry them underground. Instead of eating these plant pieces, they eat the fungi that break the plants down.

DID YOU KNOW?

Bumblebees survive as far north as the polar tundra, where the summers are cool and short. Their large bodies are covered with a layer of insulating hairs, and they insulate their nests to keep their larvae warm.

HIVE OF ACTIVITY
Honeybees collect nectar and pollen from flowers, and take them back to their nests made of wax. The bees use the wax cells for raising young and storing pollen and honey.

SAFETY IN NUMBERS
South American army ants march across the forest floor, preying on any small animals in their path.

LIVING FOOD STORES

Honey ants live in dry places, where flowers bloom for just a few weeks each year. To survive the long dry season, they store food and water in a remarkable way. Some of the workers collect sugary nectar and feed it to workers that remain underground. The abdomens of these workers swell up like balloons as they fill with nectar. Enough is stored to provide the whole nest with food and water in times of drought, until the rains return and flowers bloom once more.

Honey stores
The nectar is capped with wax and the bees change it into honey.

Nectar stores

Worker
Workers are females that cannot breed. Royal jelly is produced from glands in their head.

Queen bee
A queen can live for five years, and lays up to 1,500 eggs each day.

Capped pupae cells
These capped yellow cells contain pupae, which will soon emerge as adult worker bees.

QUESTION OF SIZE

Male stalk-eyed flies use their strange eyestalks to measure each other's size. The largest male wins the right to mate with females.

Flies

Flies are the aviation experts of the insect world. Unlike almost all other flying insects, they have only a single pair of wings, which gives them great speed and agility in the air. They also have excellent eyesight, and a pair of special stabilizers, called halteres. These keep them balanced while on the move. Altogether, there are 120,000 known species of fly. They include not only the flies that sometimes find their way indoors, but also midges and mosquitoes, brightly colored hover flies, and many other insects that buzz noisily through the air. Although all flies eat liquid food, they do so in different ways. Some mop up fluids from flowers and fruit, or from rotting remains. Others settle on skin and use their sharp mouthparts to collect a meal of blood. Flies begin life as legless larvae, which often live inside decomposing food.

LITTLE AND LARGE

The fruit fly (left) starts life as an egg, and matures in rotting fruit. The flesh fly facing it is born live, and lives in rotting meat.

BALANCING ACT

Flies have special balancing organs called halteres, which are the modified remnants of back wings. When a crane fly lands, its halteres are easy to see.

Haltere

UPSIDE DOWN

How do houseflies land on ceilings? By using high-speed photography, scientists have learned that they do it front-feet first. When a fly is about to land, it flies the right way up, but lifts its front legs above its body. The pads on its feet secrete an adhesive fluid, and the claws on its feet catch hold of the ceiling. The fly's body then flips upside down. Its other four legs make contact with the surface, and the fly is fastened securely. This complicated maneuver takes just a fraction of a second, and is much too fast for the human eye to see.

BLOOD SUCKERS

The African tsetse fly feeds on the blood of mammals, including humans. Like many blood-sucking flies, it can spread diseases as it feeds.

LAYING EGGS
Within the space of a few seconds, a female blowfly leaves a batch of eggs on some rotting remains. Her eggs will produce blind, legless larvae called maggots.

AN AERIAL COURTSHIP
Hover flies can fly forwards, backwards and sideways, and are among the few insects that are able to hover for long periods. Here, a male courts a female by hovering above her.

UP, UP AND AWAY
Like their close relatives the mosquitoes, many midges spend the first part of life in pools and puddles. These newly emerged adult midges will soon take to the air.

STRANGE BUT TRUE

Before they mate, male dance flies present their partners with a tasty insect wrapped in silk. This gift keeps the female occupied during mating, and reduces the chance that she will attack the male. But some males cheat, and when their females unwrap the silk, they discover that there is nothing inside!

Discover more in A Closer View

True Bugs

People often use the word "bug" to mean any kind of insect, but true bugs are insects with mouthparts that pierce and suck. There are about 82,000 species of true bug, and while most live on land, some of the biggest and most ferocious live in lakes and ponds. Bugs use their piercing mouthparts to eat very different kinds of food. Some, including many water bugs, attack other animals. After stabbing them with their mouthparts, they suck out the nutritious fluids. Other bugs, including aphids, shield bugs and cicadas, live on plants and drink sugar-rich sap. Bugs hatch from eggs as nymphs, which are similar in shape to their parents. They molt up to six times before they become adults, and during this process, they often change color. Australian harlequin bugs (above) are bright orange when adult, but orange and steely blue as nymphs.

SMELLY PREY
When threatened, stink bugs produce pungent chemicals from glands near their back legs. Many, including this specimen from Borneo, are brightly colored to warn off birds.

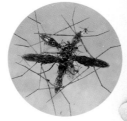

WALKING ON WATER
Pond-skaters are bugs with long legs that live on the water's surface. Here, several of them are feeding on a dead insect.

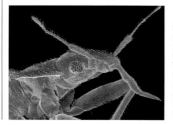

SLEEP WALKERS
Bedbugs use their piercing mouthparts to feed on human blood. They are active at night, but hide away in bedding and clothes during the day. Because of modern insecticides, they are becoming less common.

SNEAK ATTACK
The back swimmer swims upside down under the water, using its long back legs as oars. It pounces on insects that fall into the water and stabs them.

PIERCING MOUTHPARTS

A bug's mouthparts are very long and form an organ called a rostrum. The rostrum contains a central tube with a sharp-tipped stylet on either side. Inside the tube are two hollow channels that carry liquids up or down. To feed, the bug pierces an animal or plant with its stylets, and then pushes the tube into the wound. It pumps saliva down one of the channels and sucks up liquid food through the other. This cicada shown above is sucking plant sap. In many bugs, the rostrum folds away against the body when not in use.

BUG FARM
When aphids feed, they produce droplets of a sugary fluid called honeydew. Ants use this as food, and in return, they protect the aphids from their enemies.

LIVING THORNS
These treehopper bugs from Florida are disguised as thorns. If predators do find them, their shape makes them hard to eat.

Discover more in Food and Feeding

105

Insect Impact

Insects can both help and harm people. Without the ceaseless work of bees and other insects, many flowers would not be pollinated, and many of the plants we grow would not produce food. Without honeybees, there would be no honey, and without predatory insects, there would be many more pests. However, many of those pests are actually insects themselves. Caterpillars, bugs and beetles attack our crops, and in some parts of the world, swarms of locusts (a single locust is shown above) sometimes descend on fields, stripping them bare in less than an hour. Weevils bore their way through stored grain, beetles and termites tunnel through wood in houses and furniture, and some insects attack farm animals. Insects also harm us more directly. Some sting, but the most dangerous by far are those that carry diseases. Houseflies and cockroaches spread germs when they walk over our food, while mosquitoes, flies and fleas can infect us with germs when they feed on our blood.

NIGHT-TIME NUISANCE
Cockroaches feed at night, and eat anything from bread to shoe polish. They are very sensitive to vibrations, and scuttle away as soon as they sense danger.

WELCOME VISITORS
Many of the fruits and vegetables we eat have to be pollinated by insects before they will start to develop. Some fruit growers keep honeybees to pollinate their plants.

A DIET OF WOOL
The caterpillars of clothes moths often live in tiny silk bags, and feed on wool. They sometimes chew small holes in woolen clothes and blankets.

POTATO MENACE
The brightly colored Colorado beetle comes from North America. Originally, it fed on wild plants, but it now attacks potato plants in many parts of the world.

ᐧ

DEMOLITION SQUAD
Termites work in darkness, eating wood from the inside. The damage they cause is often hidden until the wood starts to collapse.

FATAL FLEAS
When fleas bite rats and then humans, they can pass on germs that cause the bubonic plague. In the 1300s, outbreaks of this disease killed millions of people.

THE DUNG-BEETLE STORY

Dung beetles are among our most unusual insect helpers. They dispose of animal manure (dung) by using it as food for their larvae. When early settlers imported cattle to Australia, the manure piled up, and the grass began to die. This was because Australian dung beetles were used to the droppings of native animals, but not to those of cattle. The solution to this problem was to bring in dung beetles from Africa, where wild cattle were common. Within a few years, they had cleared the manure away.

DID YOU KNOW?

The most serious disease spread by insects is malaria. It is carried by mosquitoes in their salivary glands. Since the Stone Age, malaria may have caused half of all human deaths. Today, it still kills between 2 and 4 million people every year.

MOUTHS ON THE MOVE
This swarm of hungry locusts in Africa spells disaster for farmers whose crops are in its path. Locusts normally live alone, but swarm when they are on the move.

Looking at Spiders

GIANT FANGS
These fangs stab downwards, pinning prey to the ground as the spider bites. Other spiders have fangs that come together when they bite.

With their hairy bodies and long legs, spiders provoke both fear and fascination. Like an insect, a spider has jointed legs and a hard body case, or carapace. But it differs from an insect in many other ways. Spiders belong to a group of animals called arachnids, which also includes scorpions, mites and ticks. Their bodies are divided into two parts separated by a slender waist, and they have eight legs rather than six. Spiders do not have antennae or wings, but they do have many eyes, and powerful jaws that can deliver a poisonous bite. All spiders are predators. Some eat frogs, lizards and even small birds, but most feed on insects. A spider uses its poisonous fluid, or venom, to paralyze its prey, and then injects it with digestive juices to dissolve the prey's tissue. The spider can then slowly suck it up. About 35,000 species of spider have been identified. They live in many different habitats, including forests, grasslands, caves, fresh water and our homes.

WATCHING FOR PREY
Most spiders have poor eyesight and sense the movement of prey through the hairs that cover their body and legs. This jumping spider however, has unusually good vision.

Leg
Each of a spider's eight legs is attached to the cephalothorax.

HOW SPIDERS MOLT

In order to grow, spiders must periodically molt, or shed their hard outer skin. Just before it starts to molt, a spider hangs upside down and secures itself with a silk thread. Its skin splits around the sides of its cephalothorax and abdomen, and starts to fall away. Meanwhile, the spider pulls its legs out of the old skin, just like someone pulling their fingers out of a glove. When its body is free, it hangs from the thread, and expands to its new size.

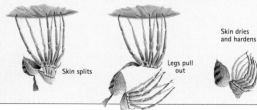

Skin dries and hardens

Skin splits

Legs pull out

BIRD KILLER
The largest spider in the world is the bird-eating spider, or tarantula, from South America. It can be as wide as 11 in (28 cm).

Abdomen
This relatively soft part of the body contains the spider's heart, gut, lungs and the glands that produce silk.

Cephalothorax
This consists of the head and thorax. Its upper surface is protected by a shieldlike carapace.

Eyes
Although most spiders have eight eyes in two rows, their vision is poor.

Pedipalp
Spiders use these leglike body parts to touch and taste. During mating, males transfer sperm through the pedipalps.

Breathing pores
Spiders breathe with small lungs. Many also have air tubes, or tracheae.

Jaw
Each jaw ends in a hollow fang that releases venom. Spiders use their jaws for attack and defense, and sometimes for digging burrows.

A SPIDER'S SHAPE
Although they vary greatly in size, spiders are quite similar in shape. A spider's abdomen is usually rounded, but in a few species it is flattened with spiky edges.

Underside view of a spider

SPIDERS IN WATER
Some spiders live on top of fresh water. They hunt prey on the water surface, in water, and on land. Sometimes these spiders are eaten by fish.

Claws
Spiders use these to cling onto rough surfaces and to walk among the silk threads in their webs.

Spinnerets
Silk emerges from the small nozzles on the spinnerets.

• SPOTLIGHT ON SPIDERS •

Silk and
Web Makers

FOOD PARCEL
This orb-web spider has caught a ladybug.
To make sure victims cannot escape, they are
wrapped in silk, which also prevents stinging
insects from fighting back.

S ilk is a remarkable substance, made by all spiders and
some insects. It starts out as a liquid, but can be turned
into elastic strands that are sometimes stronger than steel.
Spiders make different kinds of silk in special glands in their
abdomens. The glands are connected to nozzles called
spinnerets. As the liquid silk emerges from its spinnerets, a
spider tugs it with its legs, which hardens the silk. For many
spiders, the most important use of silk is in making webs. The
shape of the web and the time spent building it depend on the
species of spider. Once a web is complete, spiders usually lie in
wait, either on the web itself or close enough to touch it with
their legs. If anything makes the web vibrate, the spider
instantly rushes out to investigate. If it
discovers something edible, the spider
often wraps up the victim with sticky
threads before delivering a deadly bite.

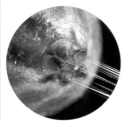

Hunting spider

DIFFERENT FEET
Spiders that hunt their prey
usually have two claws on each
foot, while spiders that trap their
prey in webs have three. The central
claw closes to grip the web.

Web–building spider

COMMUNAL WEBS
In warm parts of the world, some spiders
cooperate to catch prey. This giant web in
Papua New Guinea is several yards long. It
was built by many spiders working together.

OTHER USES OF SILK

S ilk has many uses apart from making webs and wrapping up prey.
Many spiderlings use silk to help them leave the nest and most
spiders use it to produce a dragline, a thin silk thread that trails
behind them as they move. With a dragline the spiders can lower
themselves through the air, but winch themselves back up if they do
not like what they find.
Spiders also use silk for
protecting their eggs
and, as shown here, for
making shelters. This
jumping spider has
used silk to fasten two
leaves together as a
temporary shelter.

PORTABLE TRAP
A net-throwing spider
hangs upside down
holding its web with its
legs. If an insect walks
beneath it, the spider
stretches and lowers the
web to scoop the prey up

SPINNING SILK
Most spiders have three or four
pairs of spinnerets. Here, several
spinnerets work together as a
spider builds its web.

110

TAILOR-MADE TRAPS

Spiders' webs vary from extremely precise structures to untidy tangles of silk threads. Many spiders look after their webs carefully, repairing any damage promptly.

Sheet web
Sheet-web spiders spin a maze of webs to trap their prey.

Orb web
Orb weavers spin a spiral of silk that is covered with sticky droplets.

Triangle web
Triangle spiders hold their webs taut, but release them to entangle prey.

FUNNEL WEB

Funnel-web spiders build a web against rocks or plants and wait at the funnel entrance to grab insects that fall on the web.

HIDDEN HUNTERS
Camouflaged crab spiders keep quite still as they lurk among flowers with their front legs wide open. If a meal, such as a honeybee, lands within range, they strike instantly.

DEATH TRAP
This trap-door spider has opened its door wide, revealing the burrow beneath. Some trap doors are light and flimsy, but others contain earth as well as silk, and close under their own weight.

SLIPPERY CATCH
Raft spiders hunt water animals by sensing the ripples the prey creates. After stabbing a fish with its fangs, this spider hauls its catch ashore.

The Hunters

Not all spiders catch their prey with webs. Many use traps of a different kind, while others set off on patrol and pounce on anything that could make a meal. Spiders that trap their prey rely on disguise for a successful ambush. Crab spiders, for example, camouflage themselves and catch insects that land within reach. Trappers also include many species that build silk tubes, or tunnels with secret doors. If an unsuspecting insect wanders nearby, a trap-door spider flings open the door and lunges at its prey. Spiders that search for food operate either by day or by night. The busiest daytime hunters are the jumping spiders. They have extra-large eyes to help them find their prey. When the sun sets, the jumping spiders hide away, and much larger and more sinister-looking spiders, such as tarantulas, begin to emerge. Instead of hunting by sight, these spiders hunt by touch.

STRANGE BUT TRUE
At dusk, the bolas spider twirls a thread that ends in a drop of liquid silk. Male moths are attracted by a chemical in the silk, and become caught on the sticky blob. The spider then hauls in its prey.

JUMPING ON PREY
Trailing its dragline, this sequence shows a jumping spider leaping through the air. This hunter can jump four times the length of its own body.

HUNTING UNDERWATER

The water spider survives in its unusual habitat by making a silk bubble, as shown below, to store air. It sits inside the air bubble and waits for prey to come along. If a small animal comes within range, the spider dashes out, attacks, and brings the victim back into the air bubble to be eaten. Water spiders also catch animals that have fallen onto the surface of the water, as well as search out prey on the muddy bottom of a pond. They find most of their food by detecting vibrations in the water.

NIGHT STALKERS
This rearing tarantula is more than a match for a mouse. Its diet can also include frogs, lizards, small birds and even young snakes.

Discover more in Predators and Parasites

INVISIBLE SPIDER
This Australian spider rests with its body sideways across a twig. Its dappled colors and knobbly abdomen make it look just like a ridge of bark.

ANT IMPOSTER
Many animals avoid ants because they can bite and sting. However, a close look shows that this tropical "ant" has eight legs. It is a spider in disguise.

PROTECTING EGGS
This spider (in the center) camouflages its egg sacs by disguising them as wrapped up prey. Other animals will be less interested in dead remains than in a spider's living eggs.

• SPOTLIGHT ON SPIDERS •

Spider Defense

Spiders are very effective hunters, but sometimes they can become the hunted. Their enemies are numerous, and include birds, lizards, frogs, toads, centipedes and deadly hunting wasp These wasps paralyze spiders by stinging them, and use the still-livin spider as food for their young. To outwit their enemies, spiders use a range of defenses. Many are camouflaged to blend in with their backgrounds, while some imitate things that are not normally eaten. Others hide away in burrows topped with trap doors, and hold their doors firmly shut if an enemy tries to break in. If this tactic fails and the door is forced open, the owner often retreats into a hidden chamber behind a further door. It remains here until the danger has passed. Despite these defenses, many spiders ar killed. Their best resource in the struggle for survival, however, is that most species lay large number of eggs, so although many die, some always manage to survive.

NASTY SHOWER
A tarantula's hairs have microscopic barbed spines that can make skin itch and burn. When threatened, a tarantula scrapes hairs off its abdomen and showers them on its enemy.

EGG FACTORY
A single garden spider can produc more than 500 eggs. Garden spiders live in the open and ar easy prey, so only a few of the spiderlings survive to become adults.

BITING BACK

Spiders normally use their venom to paralyze their prey, but venom is also a valuable weapon in the fight against predators. Virtually all spiders have a poisonous bite, but to inject their venom into an attacker is not always easy. Of the 35,000 known species of spider, only about 500 can drive their poison into human skin. Once the poison has been injected, however, it can have a rapid, although rarely fatal, effect. The Australian funnel-web spider, shown here, is one of the few spiders that can kill people.

A SECOND DEFENSE
If its burrow is discovered by a hunting wasp, this North American trap-door spider plugs the tunnel with its leathery abdomen. This protects the spider from being stung and makes it very difficult for the wasp to pull the spider out.

Discover more in Insect Defense

115

New Life

Before spiders can reproduce, males and females have to come together to mate. For a male, mating can be a dangerous activity, because he needs to be cautious to avoid being attacked by the female. Once mating has taken place, the male's work is done. Maternal care varies among different species of female spider. However, they all wrap their eggs in a silk bundle called an egg sac, and either hide the sac somewhere safe, or carry it with them as they hunt. Young spiders, or spiderlings, look like miniature versions of their parents. They break out of the egg sac soon after they hatch, and at first cling either to each other, or to their mother's body. A few female spiders find food for their young, but eventually they have to catch food for themselves. From then on each spiderling is on its own.

BREAKING OUT
Most spiderlings molt for the first time while still safe inside the egg sac. After molting, they break through the silk into the world outside.

HITCHING A RIDE
A female wolf spider's egg sac is attached to her spinnerets, and she often warms it in the sunshine (above left). When her spiderlings hatch, they climb onto the top of her abdomen.

LONG LIFE
Guarded by their mother, young tarantulas explore the outside world. Tropical tarantulas are the longest living of all spiders.

TREADING LIGHTLY

Most spiders live alone and do not like to be approached. This creates problems for male spiders, because they could be attacked when they try to court females. The males avoid this fate by using signals. In species that have good eyesight, the male waves its legs or its pedipalps in a special sequence. Web-building spiders often have poor eyesight, so the male

(far left) has to use another signaling technique. This spider tugs on the female's web as it carefully makes its approach.

UNEQUAL PARTNERS
Many male spiders are much smaller than the female. Here a male spider hesitantly advances towards his gigantic, and perhaps hungry, mate.

SECURITY BLANKET
Orb-weaving spiders often cover their egg sac with a blanket of tough silk. This makes it more difficult for predators and parasites to reach the eggs.

FLYING AWAY
To leave the nest, many species of spider use threads of silk as sails to launch themselves into the wind from the tops of plants (far left). When moving around the plants, the spiderlings use draglines as shown below.

STRANGE BUT TRUE
Many female spiders die after they have laid their eggs. For some spiderlings, the mother's body is their first meal. They feed on her remains before setting off to catch food for themselves.

Orders of Insects & Spiders

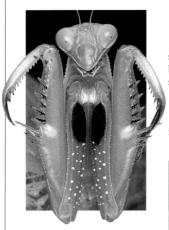

READY TO STRIKE
With its stabbing forelegs raised and ready to strike, this mantis looks like someone at prayer. It belongs to the order Mantodea.

Scientists arrange living things in groups to show how they are related through evolution. The largest groups are called kingdoms, and the smallest are called species. In between, there are classes, orders, suborders, families and genera. Each species consists of living things that breed together, and each one has its own two-part scientific name. So far, scientists have identified and named more than 2 million species of living things. Of these, only about 45,000 are vertebrates (animals with backbones) while more than 1 million are arthropods, which include insects and spiders. The species totals shown on these two pages are recent estimates, but it is certain that many more insects and spiders await discovery.

INSECTS
Class: Insecta

Main insect orders	Meaning of order name	Estimated no. of species	Examples
Coleoptera	hard wings	400,000	beetles, cockchafers, fireflies, ladybugs, weevils
Lepidoptera	scaly wings	150,000	butterflies, moths
Hymenoptera	membrane wings	130,000	ants, bees, wasps
Diptera	two wings	120,000	true flies, hover flies, midges, mosquitoes
Hemiptera	half wings	82,000	aphids, bugs, cicadas, pond-skaters, water boatmen, back swimmers, water scorpions
Orthoptera	straight wings	20,500	crickets, grasshoppers, locusts
Trichoptera	hairy wings	10,000	caddis flies
Collembola	sticky peg	6,000	springtails
Odonata	toothed flies	5,500	damselflies, dragonflies
Neuroptera	net-veined wings	5,000	lacewings
Thysanoptera	fringed wings	5,000	thrips
Blattodea	insect avoiding light	3,700	cockroaches
Pscoptera	milled wings	3,200	booklice, woodlice
Phthiraptera	louse wings	3,000	biting and sucking lice
Phasmatodea	like a ghost	2,500	leaf insects, stick insects
Siphonaptera	tube without wings	2,400	fleas
Isoptera	equal wings	2,300	termites
Ephemeroptera	living for a day	2,100	mayflies
Plecoptera	wickerwork wings	2,000	stoneflies
Dermaptera	leathery wings	1,800	earwigs
Mantodea	like a prophet	1,800	praying mantises
Mecoptera	long wings	400	scorpion flies
Thysanura	bristle tails	370	silverfish

TWO WINGS
Like all other species in the order Diptera, this greenbottle fly has just a single pair of wings. It is a fast and noisy flier.

…TING JAWS
…hese formidable jaws that bite
…ownwards belong to a mygalomorph
…pider, which is a member of the
…uborder Orthognatha.

TRUE SPIDERS
These sideways-biting jaws belong to a true spider, from the suborder Labidognatha. This large group includes the vast majority of the world's spiders.

SPIDERS
Class: Arachnida
Spider order
Araneae

Suborder	Distinctive features	No. of families	Estimated no. of species	Examples and family name
Labidognatha (true spiders)	Their jaws are attached below the head and bite from side to side.	90	32,000	jumping spiders (Salticidae) sheet-web weavers (Linyphiidae) orb weavers (Argiopidae) wolf spiders (Lycosidae) crab spiders (Thomisidae) funnel-web spiders (Agelenidae)
Orthognatha (mygalomorph spiders)	Their jaws bite forwards and down.	15	3,000	tarantulas (Theraphosidae)
Mesothelae (primitive, segmented spiders)	Their abdomens have several segments, like those of insects.	1	24	segmented spiders (Liphistiidae)

HARD WINGS
This scarab beetle belongs to the biggest order, Coleoptera. Its back wings are protected by hard front wings when it clambers across the ground.

STRAIGHT WINGS
Bush crickets belong to the order Orthoptera. Like grasshoppers, they have straight wings, and the front pair is often hard and leathery.

SCALY WINGS
This birdwing butterfly belongs to the order Lepidoptera. Its wings and body are covered with a huge number of tiny, but brightly colored scales.

Reptiles

How does a fringe-toed lizard run on hot sand?

When does a male red-eared turtle flutter its claws?

Which is the world's most venomous snake?

Contents

• I N T R O D U C T I O N •

What Are Reptiles?

SOAKING UP THE SUN
A crocodilian stretches out to absorb heat from the sun so it has energy to hunt later in the day. Warm-blooded animals, such as birds and mammals, generate heat inside their own bodies.

Reptiles have existed for millions of years. Their ancestors were amphibians that lived on land and in water. Unlike their ancestors, however, reptiles have tough skins and their eggs have shells. These adaptations allowed them to break away from water and evolve into a variety of types living in many environments. The four orders of living reptiles are the chelonians (turtles and tortoises), crocodilians (crocodiles, alligators, caimans and gharials), rhynchocephalians (tuataras) and squamates (lizards and snakes). They vary in size and structure, but they all have features in common. They are usually found on land, and they are vertebrates (animals with bony skeletons and central backbones, as shown left). Their skin is covered with scutes or scales to protect them from predators and rough ground. Reptiles are cold-blooded and depend on the sun and warm surfaces to heat their bodies.

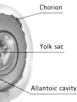

PARTNERS
Reptiles' eggs are fertilized inside the females by males. Amphibians, however, fertilize their eggs outside the body. Water carries the sperm to the eggs.

Chorion

Yolk sac

Allantoic cavity

WONDERFUL EGG
Oxygen, which helps the embryo to grow, enters the egg through the chorion, just beneath the eggshell. The yolk sac nourishes the embryo, and waste is stored in the allantoic cavity.

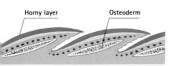

SCALY SKIN

Scales have an outer layer made of hard, horny material similar to that of nails and hooves. Some reptiles also have scales or scutes with bony plates called osteoderms. Scales may also overlap for extra protection (right).

Horny layer   Osteoderm

REPTILES EVERYWHERE

Of the 6,500 species of living reptiles, there are 3,750 species of lizard and 2,390 species of snake. Turtles, tuataras and crocodiles make up the rest of the numbers. Reptiles live in almost every warm environment, from the sea to swamps and rivers, jungles and deserts.

REPTILIAN RECORDS

Sea turtles are the fastest reptiles, and some can swim at 18 miles (29 km) per hour. The black mamba snake, which can slither at 7 miles (11 km) per hour, is the fastest reptile on land. The giant tortoises from the Galápagos Islands are the slowest reptiles. They move their heavy, shelled bodies at 4 miles (6.4 km) a day. At 1,500 lb (680 kg), the leatherback turtle is the heaviest reptile; while the longest is the anaconda at 36 feet (11 m). The smallest and lightest reptiles are the tiny 1½ in (3.5 cm) geckos.

Discover more in Temperature Control

125

A LIVING REPTILE
The Indopacific, or saltwater, crocodile is a giant among today's reptiles, but many extinct reptiles were much larger.

Coelurosauravus, 16 in (40 cm) long, from the late Permian Period, could glide from tree to tree like a flying lizard today.

Although 10-ft (3-m) long *Dimetrodon* from the Permian Period was a reptile, it was also related to the ancestors of mammals.

Hylonomus, 8 in (20 cm) long, from the Carboniferous Period, is known only from fossils found trapped in fossilized tree trunks.

Proganochelys, 3 ft (1 m) long, from the late Triassic Period, had much in common with living tortoises.

• INTRODUCTION •
Early Reptiles

The first amphibians crawled out of the water about 400 million years ago to take advantage of the new habitats available on land. But they still had to lay their jellylike eggs in water. About 300 million years ago, during the Carboniferous Period, some of these animals developed eggs with a waterproof shell that protected the growing young from drying out. The young inside these eggs had a much better chance of surviving on land, and new species began to evolve. The earliest known reptile was *Hylonomus*, and it looked like a small lizard. Later reptiles included pterosaurs, plesiosaurs, dinosaurs, lizards, snakes, crocodiles, turtles and tuataras, which lived during the Age of Reptiles (250 to 65 million years ago). Dinosaurs died out after dominating the land for 150 million years, but the ancestors of today's reptiles survived to evolve into thousands of different species.

AN EXTINCT REPTILE
Scientists study fossil reptiles, such as the dinosaur fossil above, and compare them with living reptiles. Such research can tell scientists much about the bodies of ancient reptiles and the way they lived.

SMALL BEGINNINGS
The outlines shown here are the reptiles from the main illustration. Pterosaurs, dinosaurs, ichthyosaurs and plesiosaurs died out in the Cretaceous Period, but the surviving reptiles went on to evolve into 6,500 species of living reptile.

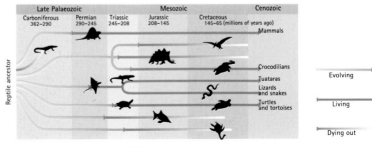

Pteranodon, a pterosaur from the late Cretaceous Period, had a 23-ft (7-m) wingspan. It fed on fish like a modern pelican.

Pachyrachis, 3 ft (1 m) long, from the early Cretaceous Period, may be related to the ancestor of today's snakes.

Stegosaurus, 30 ft (9 m) long, from the late Jurassic Period, was a dinosaur that ate plants, just like an iguana.

Planocephalosaurus, 8 in (20 cm) long, from the late Triassic Period, resembled the New Zealand tuatara.

LIVING IN A NEW WORLD

Amphibians are the ancestors of reptiles. There are some similarities between amphibians and reptiles, but their differences are much more important. Amphibians (their name means "living in two worlds") cannot survive far from a moist environment. They lay their eggs in water, and their young go through a larval stage in water. Reptiles, however, can live in dry places. Their eggs have a shell that prevents the baby reptile from drying out.

Deinosuchus, from the Cretaceous Period, may have grown to 49 ft (15 m) long. It could be the largest crocodile ever to have lived.

Archelon, 12 ft (3.7 m) long, from the late Cretaceous Period, may have fed on jellyfish like a leatherback turtle.

Ichthyosaurus, 7 ft (2 m) long, from the early Jurassic Period, was streamlined and ate fish, like a living dolphin.

Elasmosaurus, a 46-ft (14-m) long plesiosaur, from the late Cretaceous Period, had the longest neck of any marine reptile.

• TURTLES AND TORTOISES •

Chelonians up Close

C helonians, or tortoises and turtles, appeared more than 200 million years ago and have changed very little since then. They are the only reptiles with bony shells as part of their skeletons. Many can pull their heads and legs inside their shells, making it difficult for predators to eat them. Living chelonians are divided into two groups according to the way they draw their heads into their shells. The 200 or so species of straight-necked turtle, freshwater and semi-terrestrial (semi-land) turtle and tortoise have flexible necks that they can pull back (retract) straight into their shells. The 60 or so species of side-necked turtle, which live in Africa, South America and Australia, bend their necks sideways and curl their heads under the front of their upper shell. A chelonian's shell varies in shape, color and hardness. The shape of the shell tells us much about how chelonians move and the different environments in which they live (as shown in the shells below). All chelonians lay eggs, which they usually bury in a hole dug in the sand or earth.

TOP LAYER
The layer of horny plates, or scutes, that covers the carapace and plastron is made of a material called keratin—the same substance as the outer layer of your fingernails.

BONY LAYER
The radiated tortois has striking pattern on its high-domed, heavy shell. The she is fused to the spin and ribs of the tortoise. The upper shell is called the carapace; the lowe shell is called the plastron.

Scute

BREAKING FREE
Chelonians fend for themselves as soon as they hatch. They use a sharp bump (which drops off) on top of the snout to break free of their leathery shells.

Land tortoise
Domed shell, slow moving

Semi-terrestrial turtle
Flattened shell for land and water

Pond turtle
Small, flattened shell

128

DINING ON DAISIES
Sea turtles eat shellfish, fish, jellyfish and seagrasses. Young land tortoises eat worms and insects as well as plants. Adult tortoises, which move too slowly to catch prey, eat flowers, fruit and plants.

THE LONG AND THE SHORT OF IT

A side-necked turtle has a long neck and a flattened shell. It has to turn its head to one side (below left), perhaps because it does not have enough space inside the shell to pull its head back into it. Most straight-necked turtles and tortoises have shorter necks and can easily retract their heads (below right). Straight-necked tortoises with long necks, such as the giant tortoises of the Aldabra and Galápagos islands, have plenty of room inside their large, domed shells to retract their necks.

Retracting neck

OPEN WIDE
Ancient chelonians had small teeth, but modern chelonians do not have teeth. They use their sharp-edged jaws to grasp and cut plant and animal food.

Land tortoise

SUITABLE LIMBS
Chelonians' legs have evolved to suit different environments. Land tortoises have column-shaped legs with claws. Pond turtles need to move on land and in the water, so they have webbing between their claws. Sea turtles have flippers to propel them through the water.

Carapace

Plastron

Sea turtle

Sea turtle
Streamlined shell for swimming

Pond turtle

Land Tortoises

Many land tortoises live in dry environments or deserts. Most have high-domed shells to protect them from predators and perhaps to provide room for larger lungs. As their shells are very strong and heavy, land tortoises are slow moving—the most they could move in an hour would be about 295 ft (90 m)—and use very little energy. In hot areas, they are active only in the morning and late afternoon. They lie in the shade of shrubs and trees or in burrows in the soil during the blistering heat of the day. There are about 40 species of land tortoise, and they can be found in Asia, Africa, Europe, and North and South America. Most species are plant eaters, though some also eat insects and snails. The larger land tortoises can live for 100 years or more, but many species, especially those that live on islands, are endangered.

Pigs and rats eat both eggs and young tortoises.

KEEPING COOL
The desert-dwelling gopher tortoise digs a burrow and retreats into it during the heat of the day and the cold of winter.

LITTLE AND LARGE
Land tortoises range in size from the 4-in (10-cm) long Madagascan spider tortoises to the 8-in (20-cm) long South American tortoises and the wheelbarrow-sized giants of the Aldabra and Galápagos islands.

A NARROW FIT
The African pancake tortoise lives among rocks. Unlike other land tortoises, which usually have domed shells, it has a flattened, slightly soft shell so that it can squeeze into narrow crevices for protection.

LAYING TIME
Land tortoises lay their eggs in nests scraped out of the soil. Like all chelonians, they leave the eggs. The hatchlings must look after themselves.

DID YOU KNOW?
For many years, sailing ships on long voyages across the Pacific Ocean stopped at the Galápagos Islands to collect giant tortoises. The sailors killed the tortoises when they needed fresh meat.

DIFFERENT SHELLS

When populations of tortoises were isolated from each other on the Galápagos Islands many thousands of years ago, each group adapted to different conditions. Tortoises on the large, wetter islands are called domes because they have developed big, domelike shells (below). Tortoises on the smaller, drier islands, where plants grow tall, have long legs and a smaller "saddleback" shell. This is raised in front so the tortoises can stretch their necks up to reach cactus leaves.

SADDLEBACK STRETCH

In dry times, giant saddleback tortoises get water and food from tall cactus plants. But when it does rain, dozens of tortoises collect around puddles and drink as much as they can.

In and Out of Water

Most chelonians live in or near fresh water such as lakes, rivers, swamps and estuaries. There are 200 or so species of freshwater turtle, from pond turtles, softshell turtles, mud and musk turtles to river turtles. Almost all of these have webbed feet with claws, and light, flat shells covered with horny plates. Many of them take in oxygen from the water as well as from the air. Most freshwater turtles lay their eggs in soil or in sandy river banks—the Australian northern snake-necked turtle is the only chelonian to lay its eggs underwater. They ambush their prey of aquatic insects and fish underwater and can stay submerged for long periods (some species hibernate underwater for weeks). Semi-terrestrial (living both in water and on land) turtles are closely related to freshwater turtles. They hunt on land as well as in the water, and eat both plant and animal food. Semi-terrestrial species may hibernate in the mud underwater or in burrows and holes on land.

VACUUM MEALS
The mata-mata is a freshwater turtle from South America. It sucks up prey with its wide mouth.

BIG HEAD
The Asian big-headed turtle spends most of its time in water, where it hunts like a snapping turtle by ambushing prey.

SOFTSHELL TURTLES
Three families of turtles lack horny plates. The largest of these families, the softshell turtles, have flat shells and leathery skin. They are fast swimmers and can hide from predators on the bottom of muddy ponds.

WARMING UP
Like all reptiles, turtles are cold-blooded. These pond turtles soak up warmth (energy) from the sun before they set off to hunt for food in cool water.

MAKE IT SNAPPY
The alligator snapping turtle is camouflaged by a muddy brown shell and skin, and by algae growing on its shell. It waves its wormlike tongue to lure fish into its strong jaws, which could easily bite off your finger.

LOVE DANCE
As male and female turtles usually look the same, they recognize each other through behavior rather than by appearance. Male turtles bite or head-butt females, or "dance" in the water to attract a female's attention. During the spring breeding season, this male red-eared turtle courts a female by fluttering his claws in front of her face.

TUCKING IN
The ornate box turtle lives in the woodlands of North America. It draws its head and legs into its domed shell to protect itself from predators and from drying out.

Sea Turtles

The seven species of sea turtle have flattened, streamlined shells and large front flippers. They can swim at speeds of up to 18 miles (29 km) per hour when they are escaping from predators such as sharks. Usually, they swim much more slowly, using the ocean currents to help them search for food. They eat fish, jellyfish, sponges, seagrasses, crabs—and sometimes floating garbage, which they mistake for food. Some sea turtles spend most of their lives wandering tropical oceans and traveling thousands of miles. They mate for the first time when they are several years old. Each year, the turtles return to the same beach (often great distances away from their feeding grounds) to breed. The females scoop deep holes where they lay up to 100 eggs at a time. Even though sea turtles produce many young, these hatchlings have a perilous life and few survive to become adults. Adult turtles also face many hazards. They often become tangled in fishing nets and drown. Some, such as the green, flatback, hawksbill and leatherback turtles, are killed for food or their shells.

RACE TO THE SEA

Hatching is the most dangerous time for a flatback turtle. Guided by the low, open horizon, newborn flatbacks race to the sea, relying on safety in numbers to help them escape from predators such as birds and crabs. Some reach the sea, but even then they are not safe. Sharks and other fish patrol the shallow waters, ready to eat the hatchlings. Scientists estimate that only one turtle in 100 will live to become an adult.

STRANGE BUT TRUE

Folk tales tell of sea turtles crying when they leave the ocean. In fact, sea turtles, such as this loggerhead, "cry" to get rid of salt. Special glands close to the eyes produce salty "tears" all the time. These tears are washed away when the turtles are in the water, so we can see them only when the turtles are on land.

WITH ALL THEIR MIGHT

Green turtles swim gracefully in the ocean but move clumsily on land as they haul themselves slowly onto the sand to lay their eggs.

OCEAN GIANTS

Most sea turtles return to the beaches where they hatched to mate and nest. Sea turtles such as these olive ridleys mate offshore from the nesting beach.

DANGER IN SIGHT

Hawksbill turtles are endangered because the scutes (the large scales of their carapaces) can be turned into luxury tortoiseshell items such as eyeglass frames.

Crocodilian Characteristics

Crocodilians are some of the world's largest and most dangerous living reptiles. Lying submerged, with only their eyes, ears and nostrils showing, these fierce predators attack with a sudden rush, surprising an antelope drinking at the river's edge or even a bird roosting above the water. The 12 species of crocodile, one dwarf crocodile, one tomistoma, one gharial, two alligators and five caimans can be found in tropical regions around the world. The biggest species, the Indopacific or saltwater crocodile, can grow to 23 ft (7 m), and has been seen swimming in the open ocean, 620 miles (1,000 km) from land. Crocodilians eat everything from insects, frogs and snails to fish, turtles and birds. Some large crocodilians even eat mammals as big as horses and cattle. Crocodilians are cold-blooded, but many species control their temperature by their behavior. An adult Nile crocodile, for example, basks in the sun on a river bank during the day. But at night, as the temperature drops, it retreats to the warmer water.

DID YOU KNOW?

Crocodilians have hundreds of teeth during their lives—but not all at the same time. Crocodilians break or lose their teeth constantly when they hunt. New teeth grow to replace the broken or missing ones.

BRIGHT SHINING EYES
Crocodilians have well-developed eyesight. They can probably see color, and their eyes have a reflective area at the back to help them see at night.

BIG AND SMALL
Crocodilians vary in size. Cuvier's dwarf caiman is 5 ft (1.5 m) when fully grown and is the smallest crocodilian. The tomistoma is a medium-sized crocodilian, but it is only about half the length of the enormous Indopacific or saltwater crocodile.

SNEAK ATTACK
Large crocodilians drift
slowly towards their prey:
large animals drinking at
the side of a river bank.
Crocodilians have buoyant
bodies and can save their
energy for an attack by
floating in the water.

UNDERWATER ADAPTATIONS
A crocodilian can breathe while
it is half submerged because it
has external nostrils that remain
above the water. It also has a
throat flap that stops water
entering the trachea (windpipe)
when the crocodilian
is struggling with
prey underwater.

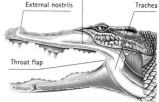

Internal nostrils

External nostrils

Trachea

Throat flap

MESSY EATERS
Crocodilians' teeth are
designed to grip, not cut.
Because they cannot
chew their food, they
swallow prey whole or
tear it into large pieces.

A HEAD AND SIDE VIEW

Crocodilian snouts vary in shape and size,
according to their diets and the way they live.

Crocodiles' snouts
are usually pointed.
When crocodiles
close their mouths,
the fourth tooth in
the lower jaw is
still visible.

American
crocodile

Alligators and
caimans mostly have
broad snouts. Species
with broader snouts
eat larger prey. When
alligators and caimans
close their mouths,
the fourth tooth of
the lower jaw is
not visible.

Black caiman

Gharials have
long, narrow snouts
and many small,
pointed teeth,
which they use
to grasp slippery fish.

Gharial

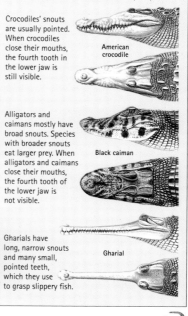

ON LAND
On mud banks, crocodilians slide on their
stomachs. For longer distances, they walk on
their short legs, carrying their bellies off the
ground. Some species, such as the common
caiman, can walk for many miles in search
of new hunting territories.

Mother Care

Crocodilians are some of the most ferocious reptiles in the world, but female crocodilians look after their eggs and young more carefully than most reptiles. Some species make nests by scraping soil and vegetation into mounds; others bury their eggs in holes in the sand or soil. In South America, Schneider's dwarf caimans make nests in shady rainforests. As there is no heat from the sun to warm the eggs, the female builds a nest beside a termite mound by scraping together plant material, which she then uses to cover the eggs. Heat from the rotting vegetation and from the termite mound warms the eggs. All female crocodilians guard their nests, scaring away predators such as large lizards, birds and mammals. The eggs take 60 to 100 days to develop, depending on the species and the temperature of the nest. When baby crocodilians are ready to hatch, they call to their mothers, who scrape away nesting material to release their young. The mother and her young often stay together for several weeks or more until the young can fend for themselves.

LIFEGUARD
A female crocodile guards her nest covered with warm, rotting plant material for up to 100 days. During this time she does not leave the nest and will attack any intruder that comes too close.

BODYGUARD
Newly hatched crocodilians are eaten by many predators, from fish to birds (sometimes even other crocodilians). They stay close to their mother after they hatch, sometimes resting on her back, where no predator would dare to attack.

DID YOU KNOW?

Most female crocodilians continue to guard their own hatchlings for several weeks or months. But any adult crocodilian will answer a call of distress from a young crocodilian—even one that is five years old.

A SAFE PLACE
An alligator's jaws can be lethal, but this hatchling sits safely in its mother's mouth. It is being carried to a quiet pond, where the female alligator will protec it from predators.

MALE OR FEMALE?
A newborn male Nile crocodile crawls from its egg. The sex of a crocodilian is determined by the temperature inside the mother's nest. In the American alligator, for example, temperatures of 82°–86°F (28°–30°C) produce females; temperatures of 90°–93°F (32°–34°C) produce males. Temperatures in-between produce a mixture of males and females.

AGAINST THE ODDS

Female crocodilians care for their eggs and newly hatched young, but only a small number of hatchlings survive to become adults. Eggs can be crushed by a careless or inexperienced female, or dug up by large lizards, birds or mammals, such as mongooses. Hatchlings are eaten by water birds (below), hawks and eagles, fish and turtles—even larger crocodilians.

The Tuatara

The tuatara has changed little in 240 million years. It is often referred to as a "living fossil." Found only on a few small islands off the coast of New Zealand, tuataras are the oldest living relatives of today's snakes and lizards. The gray, olive or reddish tuatara looks a little like an iguana, but it is not a lizard at all. The two species of tuatara are the only living members of a group of small- to medium-sized reptiles called Rhynchocephalia, or "beak-heads." Rhynchocephalians lived in most parts of the world while the dinosaurs were alive. But by 60 million years ago, they were extinct everywhere except New Zealand, which had become isolated from other landmasses. When the Maoris of New Zealand first saw this unusual reptile, they called it "tuatara," which means "lightning back" and refers to the crest of large spikes on the male's back. Tuataras live in burrows. They eat earthworms, snails and insects, and hunt small lizards and hatchling birds. They crush and cut prey with their sharp, triangular teeth. Unlike the teeth of lizards, tuataras' teeth are permanently fused to the jaw.

SLOWLY DISAPPEARING?
Tuataras could once be found throughout the two main islands of New Zealand, but now they are restricted to 30 small islands off the northern coast of the North Island.

SIMILAR BUT NOT THE SAME
Tuataras may look like lizards, but they are very different. Tuataras, for example, have an extra bone in the skull. Lizards have two penises, but tuataras have none. A male and female tuatara mate by touching cloacae.

NIGHT BEAT
Tuataras hunt insects and other prey at night. They spend the day sleeping in their burrows or basking in the sunshine at their burrow entrances.

BIGGER ALL ROUND
A male tuatara (bottom) has larger spines on its neck and back, and is heavier and larger than a female. Males weigh up to 2.2 lb (1 kg), which is double the weight of a female (top). Males can grow to 2 ft (60 cm) in length—6 in (15 cm) longer than a female.

ISOLATED ON AN ISLAND

Eighty million years ago, New Zealand became separated from other landmasses. While rhynchocephalians in other parts of the world died out, tuataras in New Zealand survived. Apart from birds, no large predators reached New Zealand until humans arrived a few thousand years ago. But humans brought with them dogs and Polynesian rats, and these animals began to eat tuatara eggs and hatchlings. Today, tuataras can be found only on islands without rats.

DINNER TIME
Tuataras are not fast runners. They sit still and wait for prey to come close enough so they can lunge at it. This tuatara has spotted a large weta, or New Zealand cricket, and is waiting for a chance to pounce.

DID YOU KNOW?
Tuataras in the south live in a much colder environment and grow more slowly than tuataras in the north. No-one knows exactly how long tuataras live, but it may be for up to 120 years.

Discover more in Early Reptiles

141

BITE–SIZED
This baby Madagascan chameleon will grow to 3½ in (9 cm). But the smallest lizard, the Virgin Islands gecko, is only 1½ in (3.5 cm) when fully grown.

Looking at Lizards

FLYING LEAP
The flying gecko of Southeast Asia has flaps of skin along its sides, and glides from tree to tree to escape predators

There are approximately 3,750 species of lizard in the world. They come in all shapes and sizes, from the tiny gecko to the 10-ft (3-m) long Komodo dragon. Some are short and flat; others are legless and snakelike. Some lizards are brightly colored, while others are dull and blend into the background. Although most lizards are tropical, they are also found in cold climates and from sea level to mountains as high as 16,400 ft (5,000 m). Some Asian and North American skinks hibernate over winter in burrows beneath the snow, emerging in spring to feed on insects attracted to spring flowers. Most lizards are predators, and eat everything from ants and insects to other lizards and animals as large as goats. Lizards also play an important role in controlling insect pests. A house gecko, for example, can eat half its own weight in small insects in a single night. Many large lizards, such as skinks and iguanas, eat mainly plants and fruit. The marine iguanas of the Galápagos Islands eat mostly seaweed.

ON THE LOOKOUT
With long legs and a strong body, monitor lizards are fast runners that usually live in deserts or grasslands. Monitors are found in Africa, Asia and Australia, and include the largest of the lizards, the Komodo dragon.

DID YOU KNOW?
The horned chameleon's eyes are mounted in turrets and can look in different directions at the same time. It can find prey with one eye and watch for predators with the other.

A wall lizard has the most common lizard shape—ideal for hunting and hiding.

The sail-tailed water dragon swims with its high, flattened tail.

A monitor has a long, flexible body for hunting over long distances.

The legless lizard has a streamlined body for moving in narrow places.

The flat body of the dese short-horned lizard helps it hide from predators.

Q: Why would it be difficult to surprise a horned chameleon?

EVERY TAIL TELLS A STORY

Lizards are all shapes and sizes, and so are their tails. Long, short, fat or thin, the tail of a lizard is a useful thing.

Tree-living chameleons have prehensile (gripping) tails that help them hang on to twigs when they are moving about.

Australian shinglebacks live in dry places. Their clublike tails store fat—a source of energy and water.

Skinks' tails are long and streamlined. Most skinks can shed their tails if attacked by a predator.

Leaf-tailed geckos live in rock crevices or trees, and have flattened, camouflaged tails.

A FINE FIGURE
Boyd's forest dragon, from northeastern Australia, is one of the largest dragon lizards in the world. It can puff out its dewlap (a flap of skin on its throat) to communicate with other forest dragons in its rainforest home.

Lizard Facts

Lizards can be found in almost every environment, from rainforests to baking deserts, but they have many features in common. All lizards, for example, have scaly skin. Daytime lizards have rough skins, while night-time lizards, such as geckos, have small, beadlike scales. Most burrowing lizards have smooth scales to help them push through the soil. Lizards have developed special features for their different habitats. Those that live above the ground have external ear openings and large eyes. Lizards that live beneath the ground have tiny eyes, and their external ear openings are covered by scaly skin. Most lizards have fleshy pink tongues, but monitor lizards have slender forked tongues, which they use to "taste" chemicals in the air. Some lizards have flashy blue tongues that they stick out to startle predators. Lizards eat mainly insects and other invertebrates, which they crush with their pointed teeth. Plant-eating lizards have flattened teeth for chopping their food, while lizards that eat snails have flat, rounded teeth for crushing shells.

A GOOD GRIP
A gecko's toe pad has thousands of fine hairlike projections. These cling to invisible rough spots and allow a gecko to walk on walls and upside down on ceilings.

A MOUTHFUL OF FOOD
Most lizards have pointed teeth that are all the same shape. This means that lizards cannot cut up or chew their food. Instead, they crush prey with their teeth and then swallow it whole.

DID YOU KNOW?

A legless lizard and a snake may seem similar, but look at them closely. Most legless lizards have small ear openings behind the eyes, but snakes have no ears at all. Legless lizards also have pointed tongues while snakes have forked tongues.

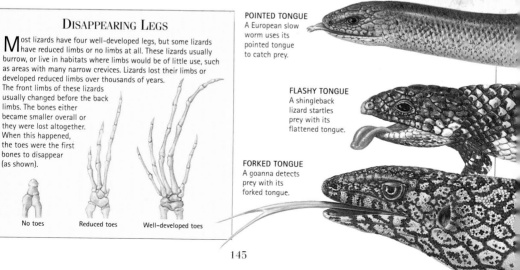

LONG, STICKY TONGUE
Moving slowly towards its prey, this chameleon shoots out an incredibly long tongue, which is coated with sticky mucus.

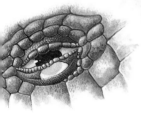

WINDOW WITH A VIEW
Many lizards have a small clear area on their lower eyelids. This allows them to watch for predators while their eyes are closed and protected from dust and from drying out.

DISAPPEARING LEGS

Most lizards have four well-developed legs, but some lizards have reduced limbs or no limbs at all. These lizards usually burrow, or live in habitats where limbs would be of little use, such as areas with many narrow crevices. Lizards lost their limbs or developed reduced limbs over thousands of years. The front limbs of these lizards usually changed before the back limbs. The bones either became smaller overall or they were lost altogether. When this happened, the toes were the first bones to disappear (as shown).

No toes   Reduced toes   Well-developed toes

POINTED TONGUE
A European slow worm uses its pointed tongue to catch prey.

FLASHY TONGUE
A shingleback lizard startles prey with its flattened tongue.

FORKED TONGUE
A goanna detects prey with its forked tongue.

145

The Next Generation

M ost lizards lay eggs. Some geckos and skinks lay only one, while larger lizards may lay as many as forty. A few lizards guard their eggs against predators, but most simply lay their eggs, cover them with soil or leaves, and leave them. Other lizards give birth to fully formed ("live") young. The eggs are protected inside the female bodies, and the developing young are nourished by yolk in the same way as young that grow in eggs outside the body. The female European common lizard lays eggs in warm climates, but in cool mountain climates where the temperature may not be high enough for eggs to develop properly, the female gives birth to live young. Lizards are able to look after themselves as soon as they hatch, but dangers await the next generation. There are many creatures, such as spiders, insects, lizards, snakes, birds and mammals, waiting to eat them. Very few young lizards survive to breed.

HOUSE GUESTS
Some species of goanna (Australian monitors) keep their eggs warm and safe by laying them in termite mounds. The female has to scrape away the hard soil to help her hatchlings escape.

RIGHT TIME
he female collared lizard can store eggs
her body until laying conditions are
ght; for example, there must be enough
oisture in the ground to keep
e eggs from drying out.

BREAK-OUT
A collared lizard cuts its way out of the
egg with an "egg tooth"—a special tooth
on the tip of its upper lip—which drops
off soon after hatching. It fends for
itself as soon as it is born.

SINGLE PARENTS

Some chameleons, dragon lizards, night lizards, whiptail lizards (below), wall lizards and geckos reproduce without males. The eggs of these lizards do not need to be fertilized by males. These all-female lizards increase in number faster than those that have male and female parents.

A SMALL LITTER
Many skinks give birth
to live young rather
than laying eggs. The
Australian shingleback
usually gives birth to
two live young—
a small litter
for a lizard.

A LARGE LITTER
The Australian
blue-tongue skink
gives birth to several
lizards. These young,
however, are smaller than
lizards born in a small litter.

Discover more in Temperature Control

Temperature Control

COOL CHANGE
In hot climates, lizards hide in crevices or burrows during the hottest part of the day. These cool places often trap a little water, and the sheltered lizard can breathe moist air, which also helps to keep it cool.

L izards and other reptiles regulate their body temperature by their behavior. To warm up, they move into the sun or onto a warm surface and expose as much of their body as they can to the heat. To cool down, they expose as little of their body as possible to the heat, or they move into the shade or a crevice. Many desert and tropical lizards can be active at night because the night-time temperatures in these environments are mild. In extremely cold climates, lizards spend the winter in a deep burrow or crevice. Birds and mammals are called warm-blooded because they regulate their body temperature internally and are always warm. Warm-blooded animals must constantly use energy to stay warm. Reptiles, however, are cold-blooded animals. They cool down when they are not warmed by outside heat, and use a lot of energy only when they are warm and active.

Energetic
With its body warmed, a sand lizard has energy for hunting, mating and defending its territory.

SHADES OF THE DAY
In the morning and late afternoon, the skin of rhinoceros iguanas is dark, to absorb the heat of the sun. During the hottest part of the day, their skins are lighter. This helps them to reflect as much heat as possible.

A MIDDAY BURROWER
This common barking gecko is nocturnal and emerges to hunt in the early evening.

Resting
A sand lizard basks in the sun to warm its body and get energy for a day of activity.

Waking
A sand lizard wakes with the sun, and emerges from its shelter.

Did You Know?
Cold-blooded animals, such as reptiles, are able to survive extreme conditions such as drought and cold weather. Their heart rate slows down, they breathe more slowly, and their digestive systems stop working.

NIGHT LIFE

Some lizards, such as geckos, are active at night. They emerge shortly after dark and take advantage of the still-warm ground to hunt insects. Nocturnal lizards need to be able to see in the dark. They have big eyes and their pupils—the transparent "holes" that let light into the eyes—are large, vertical slits. At night, these open wide to let in as much light as possible.

Hiding out
. sand lizard seeks shelter during the warmest
.art of the day to avoid overheating.

Energetic
In the early
afternoon,
a sand lizard
resumes its
activities.

SUN BATHING
Even if clouds hide the sun in
the afternoon, lizards can soak
up heat (energy for afternoon
activities) by pressing
against rocks that have been
warmed earlier in the day.

DAY IN THE
FE OF A LIZARD
.ke most land reptiles
.at are out in daylight,
. sand lizard moves
.round and rests during
.e day. The temperature
.nd the surroundings
.fluence the way
.e sand lizard
.ends its day.

Resting
Late afternoon
is the time
to bask and
digest the
day's meal
of insects.

End of the day
As the sun sinks, a
sand lizard begins to
move into its retreat.

.ady for sleep
.and lizard curls up to stay as
.otected as possible through the night.

149

VENOMOUS MONSTER
The 18 in (45 cm) Gila monster of North America is one of the world's two venomous lizards, though its bite is rarely fatal to humans. The Gila monster stores fat in its thick tail, and uses this supply of energy to survive without food for several months.

"HOT-SPOT" TACTICS
A zebra-tailed lizard mesmerizes its predator with the black-and-white pattern under its tail. Then it races off, leaving the predator staring fixedly at the spot where the waving tail once was.

PRICKLY CREATURE
The thorny devil of central Australia may look fearsome, but it is actually a harmless eater of ants. It is very well adapted to desert life: for example, the pattern of scales on its body channels rainwater to its mouth.

• A LIZARD'S LIFE •
Living in Dry Places

Lizards that live in dry or arid places have to cope with high temperatures and little water. They deal with scorching temperatures in different ways. Many species, for example, are nocturnal. They hunt in the early evening for several hours when the ground is still warm. Daytime species burrow into cool sand or hide in crevices and beneath rocks during the hottest part of the day. Some raise themselves on their toes to keep away from hot sand, or they run to shelter. Finding water is a more serious problem. Most desert lizards, such as the one above, get most of the water they need from food. Their bodies convert the prey they eat into fat, which they store. The fat is then converted into energy, a process that produces water for the body. All lizards produce droppings that are almost dry, which minimizes the precious water they lose from their bodies.

SMOOTH MOVES
Desert-burrowing lizards are known as "sand swimmers" or "sand fish," because they seem to be able to swim through loose sand. Sand swimmers use their wedge-shaped snouts to "dive" beneath the surface of the sand to escape predators.

FOOT SPECIALISTS

Many sand-dwelling lizards have webbed feet or fringed toes to help them grip shifting sand. A desert gecko's foot (right) is webbed to help it dig burrows and to move across sand dunes to look for food or to escape from predators. The toes of the fringe-toed lizard (below) have featherlike scales to grip sand when the lizard needs to chase prey or run from predators.

The fringes on its toes may also help this lizard to cool its feet so that it does not become too hot.

TOO HOT TO HANDLE

This desert fringe-toed lizard lifts one front leg and the opposite back leg, then balances on its other legs for a few moments to cool its feet. Some dragon lizards of dry inland Australia avoid hot surfaces by raising their hind toes.

Discover more in Land Tortoises

PREY UNDERGROUND
Worm lizards can dig quickly to reach insect prey, which they detect from underground vibrations. They also use their sharp teeth and powerful jaws to crush any invertebrates they meet while they are digging their tunnels.

DIGGING FROM SIDE TO SIDE
Keel-snouted worm lizards use their wedge-shaped snouts to scrape soil from the front of the tunnel. They compress the soil into the side of the tunnel with their heads as they move forward.

DIGGING UP AND DOWN
The shovel-snouted worm lizard grows to 4–30 in (10–75 cm) long. It uses its broad, hard head to push soil upwards and compacts it into the top of the tunnel. Body scales arranged like tiles help to keep dirt from building up on its body.

Underground Life

A mphisbaenians (worm lizards) are some of the strangest lizards in the world. All 140 species of amphisbaenian ("am-fizz-BEEN-ee-an") spend most of their lives underground, beneath leaf-litter in the forests of the warmer parts of Africa, Southeast Asia, Europe and the United States. There are four families of worm lizards, and three of these have no legs at all. Mexican worm lizards, however, have two strong front legs. Worm lizards have cylinder-shaped bodies and burrow through tunnels with their hard, strong heads. Most lizards move by using their legs, but worm lizards move like snakes in confined spaces: they inch their way through tunnels in a straight line. All worm lizards have simplified eyes that are covered by clear skin. They crush insects and other invertebrates with their sharp teeth and strong jaws. They have no external ear openings (these would be clogged by dirt), but they can sense prey and predators through vibrations in the soil. Most species lay eggs, but a few worm lizards give birth to live young.

HEADS AND TAILS

The exposed tail of a burrowing worm lizard is protected from predators because it is very hard. The worm has large head scales to strengthen its head for digging.

DIGGING TOOLS

The Mexican worm lizard has strong front legs that are flattened like paddles to help it move above ground. When it begins digging a tunnel, the lizard swings its legs forward and sweeps soil back past its head.

DIFFERENT HEADS

Round-headed

Keel-headed

Shovel-headed

Chisel-headed

Most worm lizards burrow with their heads. The way different groups of worm lizards burrow is reflected in the different shapes of their heads. Round-headed species push forward into the earth and turn the head in any direction to make the burrow. Keel-headed species push the head forward and then to the side. Shovel-headed species push forward and then push the head up. Chisel-headed species rotate the head in one direction and then in the other.

THE TAIL END

This worm lizard looks as if it has two heads, but one end is in fact its tail. Like many other lizards, worm lizards can shed their tails if they are grabbed by a predator.

Invisible eye
The worm lizard's eye is very simple and sometimes not even visible. It can barely see movement, and can only distinguish between light and dark.

Hard snout
A worm lizard has a large reinforced scale as a snout. This helps it to force its way through the soil.

Tucked-in mouth
The worm lizard's mouth is tucked beneath the snout, so dirt cannot get into it when the worm is burrowing.

Discover more in Looking at Lizards

Defense and Escape

Lizards have many enemies. Spiders, scorpions, other lizards, snakes, birds and mammals all prey on them. The Gila monster and the Mexican beaded lizard are the only venomous lizards; other species of lizard have special tactics to defend themselves or to escape from an attacker. Most lizards are well camouflaged and may keep absolutely still until a predator passes by. Chameleons can change their color to blend in with their background, and also stay completely still when a tree snake or other predator approaches. Some lizards surprise or distract a predator to give themselves a chance to escape. The Australian frilled lizard opens its frill suddenly. Other lizards extend their neck or throat crest, hiss, or swallow air to look bigger than an attacker (or too big to swallow). Some even stick out their colored tongues! Many lizards have an unusual method of escape. If grabbed by the tail, they leave it behind. A wriggling tail helps to distract an attacker. Running away, out of a predator's reach, is also a good defense. Some lizards have sharp spines that can injure a predator's mouth, or slippery scales that make them hard to grip.

ON GUARD!
The armadillo girdle-tailed lizard curls itself into a ball when it is threatened and protects its soft belly with a prickly fence

THE TRUTH OF THE TAIL

If a predator grasps them by the tail, many lizards (especially geckos and skinks) are able to shed their tails. The predator sees the writhing, twitching tail on the ground and thinks it is the whole animal. Meanwhile, the lizard can escape—leaving its tail behind. The lizard loses very little blood and a new tail grows over the next few months. The vertebrae in the tail are replaced by a tough elastic tissue and the muscles and scales are often irregular (as shown here).

STRANGE BUT TRUE

The regal horned lizard scares off predators with a strange weapon—its own blood. It uses special muscles to burst tiny blood vessels in and around its eyes. It can squirt a stream of blood up to 3 ft (1 m) to frighten its attacker.

RUNNING ON WATER

The basilisk, an iguana from Central America, escapes predators by going where they cannot follow. It runs on water for several feet, supporting itself with fringes on its toes, before diving in and swimming to safety.

LOOK A LITTLE CLOSER

Tree-dwelling dragon lizards defend themselves by becoming "invisible." Many predators react to small movements, so this dragon keeps very still and tries to look like part of the tree.

Discover more in Defense Tactics

155

Keeping in Touch

Most lizards live alone. They come in contact with other members of their species only for courtship and mating, and to fight over living areas. Lizards communicate in a number of ways such as raising crests, extending or curling dewlaps, waving a front limb or lashing the tail, or changing color. Iguanas and dragon lizards wave one leg in the air, bob their heads or move their bodies up and down to let other lizards know they are ready to mate, or to warn invaders to leave their territories. Male chameleons change color to threaten rivals, while other male lizards change color to let females know they are ready to mate (some female lizards change color after they have laid their eggs to let males know they are not interested in mating). Most geckos are active at night when color and movement are not easy to see, so some species keep in touch by calling to each other. Barking or chirping sounds, for example, warn other geckos to keep away.

RED IN THE FACE
Male chameleons can change their dull camouflage colors to bright colors to warn other males away from their territories. This species changes color from a calm green to a threatening red to intimidate a rival.

MATING SIGNALS
Male and female marine iguanas of the Galápagos Islands are usually a grayish-black color. In the breeding season, the spiny crests and front limbs of the males turn green and the sides of their bodies become rusty red. Females know the males are ready to mate.

TOO BIG A MOUTHFUL

Bearded dragon lizards open their brightly colored mouths to surprise predators. They also expand their throats to make themselves look too big for a predator to eat, or too big for a rival dragon to fight.

DANGER SIGNALS

Male anole lizards have a brightly colored dewlap that they expand in a sudden flash of color to warn other males or to attract females.

CHEMICAL COMMUNICATION

Lizards need to figure out if another lizard is a potential mate or a rival. One way they do this is through pheromones, special chemicals produced by glands in the skin. Pheromones are detected by the nose and by a structure in the roof of the mouth called Jacobson's organ. When the lizard flicks out its tongue (below), it picks up important chemical scents and pheromones from the ground or the air. The tongue then carries these molecules back to the roof of the mouth.

WORSE THAN THEIR BITE
In Southeast Asia, barking house geckos (called "dup-dups" in Malaysia because of the sound they make) keep in touch with their mates or warn other geckos away from their hunting territories with chirping sounds or sharp barks.

Sizing up Snakes

There are almost 2,400 species of snake. From the 8-in (20-cm) long thread snake to the giant anaconda, which can reach 36 ft (11 m) and weigh 440 lb (200 kg), snakes have many different colors, patterns and ways of killing their prey. Snakes eat everything from ants, eggs, snails and slugs to animals as big as caimans and goats. Snakes can swallow large prey because they have elastic connections between some of the bones in their skulls, especially those between the skull and the lower jaws. Some snakes are very venomous: a single drop of venom from the Australian small-scaled snake can kill thousands of mice. Certain kinds of cobra spit venom to blind their predators, while non-venomous pythons wrap themselves around their prey, tightening their grip to overcome it. Some snakes have smooth skin, while the skin of others is very rough. Filesnakes use their sandpaper-like skin to hold their slippery prey of fish.

ENTWINED IN VINES
The vine snake of Central and South America grows to 7 ft (2 m), but its body is no more than ½ in (1.3 cm) round. Its green colors blend in with leaves, and its slender body enables it to move rapidly across branches in search of prey such as small birds in nests.

PATTERN WITH A PURPOSE
Many snakes, especially venomous ones, are brightly colored to warn predators that they are very dangerous. Some harmless species, such as this milk snake, copy the colors of venomous snakes for the same effect.

158

Python

Horned viper

Burrowing snake

Tree snake

HEADS
A python has
a large head to
hold the many teeth
it needs to grip its prey.
A viper has a short head and
two large, venomous fangs.
A burrowing snake pushes through
the soil with a solid, blunt head.
A tree snake has a slender head
to help it slip between twigs.

BIG BOA
The yellow anaconda is one of
the heaviest snakes. It hunts
fish and caimans in streams, but
uses stealth rather than speed
when capturing prey on land. It
will wait beside an animal trail
for days to ambush its prey.

DID YOU KNOW?
The reptile *Pachyrachis*, which lived
about 100 million years ago, had the
body of a snake. Some scientists think
it was closely related to the ancestor
of all modern snakes.

SHAPED FOR SUCCESS

Snakes have different body shapes to suit their
different environments.

A ground-dwelling
snake has an almost
circular body. It has
strong muscles to
grip slippery sand and
soil, or rough rocks.

A tree snake's body
is shaped almost like
a loaf of bread so
that it can grip
small crevices and
notches on
the branches.

A sea snake has
a flattened body.
This gives it a
larger
surface area with
which to push
against the water.

THE LONG VIEW
Snakes have three
general body shapes and
lengths: small and slender
(the blind snake), short and
thick-bodied (the viper)
or large and shaped
like a cylinder (the
reticulated python).

Blind
snake

Viper

Reticulated
python

Discover more in Finding a Meal

Snake Specifications

A s snakes evolved from lizards, they became long and slender, and lost their limbs. Some of their internal organs, such as the liver and the lungs, also became long and thin. Others, such as the kidneys and reproductive organs, were rearranged one behind the other in the body.
In many snakes the left lung even disappeared! Unlike animals with limbs, snakes can escape from predators or hunt prey by squeezing into narrow spaces. Snakes have sharp, pointed teeth and, in some cases, venom to help them kill prey. With their long, supple bodies, snakes can form tight coils to strangle their prey, wrap around their eggs to keep them warm, or curl into a ball to deter predators. Snakes live in many environments and their scales can be rough or smooth. As a snake grows, it sheds its scaly skin and reveals a new skin underneath.

SHEDDING
Snakes shed their skins when they grow too big for them. To loosen its skin, a snake rubs its nose against a hard surface. Then it wriggles free. The old skin (including the snake's clear eyelids) comes off inside-out.

DID YOU KNOW?
Some pythons and blind snakes have tiny leftovers of their hind limbs. These are visible as a pair of "spurs" on the sides of the body, close to the snake's tail. Male pythons use their spurs in combat and courtship.

CLOSE TO THE GROUND
Snakes have completely lost their limbs. They move by using the muscles attached to their ribs.

A USEFUL SCALE

Snake scales give us clues about how and where snakes live. Most snakes that live in wetlands and fresh water have keeled scales. These help to balance side-to-side movement and provide a larger surface area for heating and cooling. Snakes that burrow usually have smooth scales, as these make it easier for them to push through the soil. Many water and sea snakes have "granular" scales with a rough, grainy surface like sandpaper, which helps them to grip their slippery prey.

Keeled scales

Smooth scales

Granular scales

CONTACT LENS
Snakes do not have movable eyelids. Their eyes are covered by a special clear eyelid that protects the eye from damage. Nocturnal species often have vertical pupils, like the eyes of cats.

SMALL EYES
Nocturnal snakes are active at night. They have small eyes and do not rely heavily on sight to hunt. Instead, they use their tongues to detect their prey, or special heat-sensing organs to sense warm-blooded animals.

BIG EYES
Diurnal snakes, which are active in daylight, have large eyes because they rely mainly on sight to find their prey. However, these snakes also use their tongues to detect prey and predators.

TARGETED
A rattlesnake's heat-sensing organs are very accurate: it can even strike in total darkness. Its fangs, which normally lie flat against the roof of its mouth, swing forward to inject fast-acting venom into prey.

EGG MEAL
The African egg-eating snake stretches its jaw to wrap its mouth around the egg.

CRUSHED
The eggshell is crushed by the ridges that project into the snake's throat from its backbone.

SHELL REJECTED
After swallowing the liquid contents of the egg, the snake regurgitates the crushed eggshell.

Finding a Meal

All snakes eat animals. Some will ambush, stalk or pursue their prey. Others eat "easy" prey, such as the eggs of birds and reptiles (including those of other snakes). A few snakes eat snails (which they pull out of their shells), worms and crabs. Many snakes, such as pythons and boa constrictors, kill their prey by constricting, or squeezing it. A python, for example, wraps itself around an animal. Whenever the animal breathes out, the python squeezes a little tighter, until the animal suffocates. More than half of all snakes kill their prey with venom, which is produced by highly evolved mouth glands and injected through hollow or grooved fangs. Rattlesnakes have small pits on the front of their faces; many pythons and some boas have pits in their lip scales. These pits contain heat sensors that can detect temperature differences of one thousandth of a degree. They tell the snake how far away its prey is and even where the heart (the warmest part of the animal) is. This means the snake can strike its prey with deadly accuracy.

DID YOU KNOW?

Most snakes eat only one large prey at each meal. Burrowing snakes and blind snakes (shown), however, are unusual. Like lizards, they eat small prey, such as ant eggs, frequently.

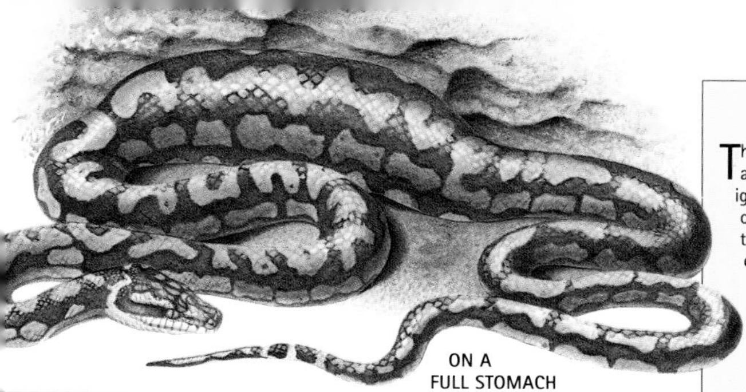

ON A FULL STOMACH
After a large meal, most snakes seek a sunny, sheltered spot to digest their food. The snake positions itself in the sun because heat helps it digest its prey quickly.

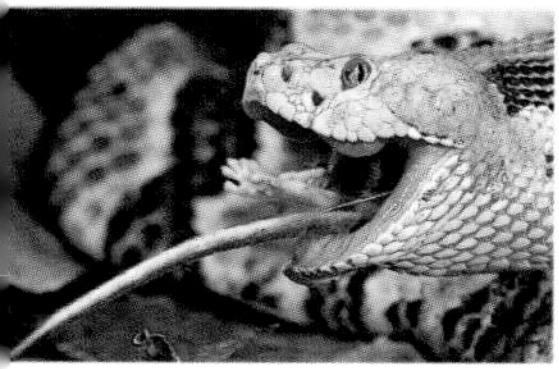

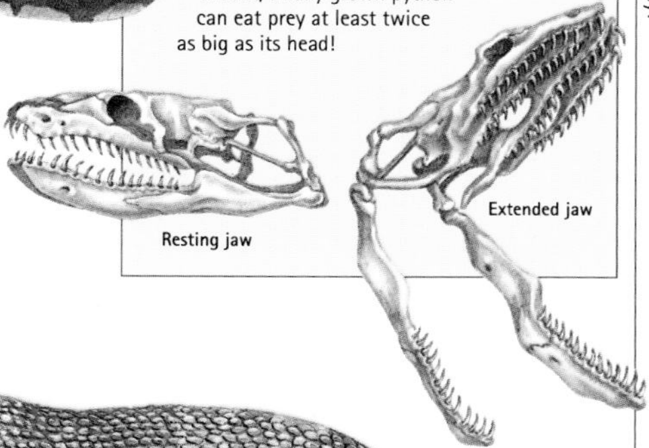

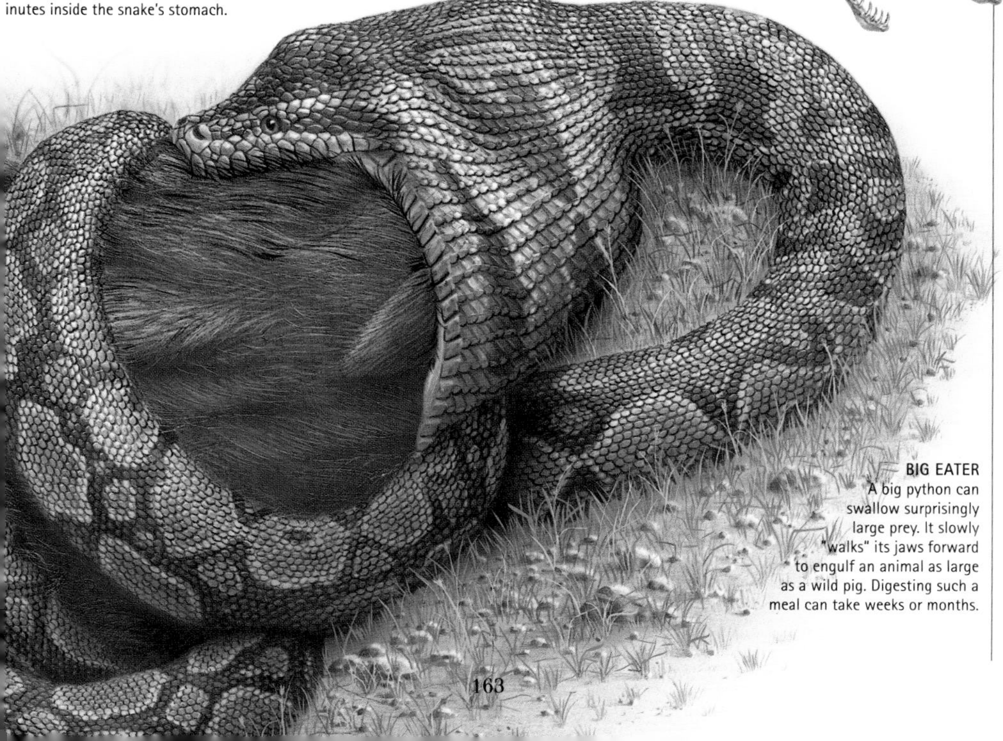

WRIGGLING CATCH
snake swallows prey headfirst so the ıimal's legs do not get stuck in its throat. mouse or rat will suffocate after a few inutes inside the snake's stomach.

COMING UNHINGED

There is an old saying that you should not eat anything bigger than your head. Snakes can ignore this, as they have "elastic" jaws that can open wide to swallow food that is larger than their heads. The bones of their jaws (and some of the bones in their skulls) are attached by elastic connections that allow the bones to move apart and stretch the snake's entire mouth to swallow a large animal. In fact, a fully grown python can eat prey at least twice as big as its head!

Resting jaw
Extended jaw

BIG EATER
A big python can swallow surprisingly large prey. It slowly "walks" its jaws forward to engulf an animal as large as a wild pig. Digesting such a meal can take weeks or months.

Q: How does a snake detect its prey?

Venomous Snakes

S ome snakes can bite and kill their prey with a toxic secretion called venom. The venom is secreted through fangs in the snake's mouth and is so powerful that the prey succumbs within minutes, sometimes even seconds! Venomous snakes have different kinds of fangs. Some are firmly attached to the jaw, while others are hinged; some fangs are grooved while others are hollow; some are in front of the mouth and others are at the rear. Snakes with hollow fangs inject venom into their prey, while snakes with grooved fangs let the venom ooze into the victim. Cobras, kraits, taipans, mambas, coral snakes and sea snakes have fixed, hollow fangs in the front of the mouth, which are firmly attached to the upper jaw. Vipers and rattlesnakes have hollow front fangs that swing forward as the snake strikes its prey. The venom from vipers not only kills, it even helps to break down the tissues of the prey's body, making it easier for the snake to digest its meal. Rear-fanged snakes have grooved, fixed fangs at the back of the mouth. Their bites are rarely dangerous to humans and they must chew their prey for the venom to enter the victim.

POTENT VENO
The Australian small-scale snake, a relative of the taipan, the world's deadliest snake. I venom is so strong that a sing drop could kill 217,000 mic

CAMOUFLAGED KILLER
While the cobra and its relatives are active hunters, vipers and rattlesnakes tend to ambush their prey. They are often camouflaged, and will wait beside an animal's path for days until suitable prey comes along.

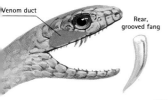

Venom duct

Rear, grooved fang

REAR FANGS
Rear-fanged snakes have fixed fangs, located towards the back of the mouth. Venom travels down grooves along the length of the fangs.

FIXED FRONT FANGS
Cobras and their relatives have hollow, fixed fangs in the front of the mouth.

Venom duct

Hollow, fixed fang

Hollow, swinging fang

Venom duct

SWINGING FRONT FANGS
Vipers and rattlesnakes have large, hollow fangs that swing forward to the front of the mouth.

CHOOSE YOUR POISON

Snake venoms affect their prey in one of two different ways. The neurotoxic venoms of the cobras and their relatives act on the nerves to stop the heart and damage the lungs. The hemotoxic venoms of vipers and rattlesnakes destroy muscles. Snake venom probably evolved to help snakes capture prey, but they also use it to defend themselves. Most venomous snakes are highly resistant to their own venom.

SUDDEN DEATH
A rattlesnake's venom is not as powerful as that of the cobra and many of its relatives, but it injects a large amount through its long fangs. The venom acts quickly, paralyzing or killing prey, such as rodents.

THE FIRST APPEARANCE
A baby green mamba uses its temporary "egg tooth" at the tip of its upper lip to break free of the shell. Snakes' eggs are not hard like birds' eggs. They have the texture of thick, strong paper.

MOTHER CARE
Some pythons coil around their eggs to keep them warm and protect them from predators, but they do not look after the young once the eggs have hatched.

• SNAKES •

Early Life

Each spring in mild climates, or just before the rainy season in the tropics, snakes begin to mate and reproduce. In most egg-laying species the female looks for a safe, warm and slightly moist place—such as a rotting log, or beneath a rock—to lay her eggs. Once she has laid the eggs, she covers them and leaves the eggs to develop and hatch on their own. A few species of snake, however, do stay with their eggs until they have hatched. Female pythons coil themselves around the eggs to keep them warm, and both male and female cobras guard their eggs. But once the young have hatched, pythons and cobras also leave them to look after themselves. Some snakes, such as most vipers and various water snakes, give birth to fully developed young. "Live-bearing" snakes tend to live in cool climates or watery habitats. Scientists believe this type of birth occurs in cool climates because the eggs would be generally warmer in the mother's body than in the soil. Snakes in wet environments give birth to live young because eggs could drown in water or become moldy in soil.

DID YOU KNOW?
Many snakes eat cold-blooded prey, such as lizards, when they are young but eat warm-blooded prey, such as birds and mammals, when they are older. Some zoo keepers found that young snakes will eat warm-blooded prey if it is rubbed and scented with a cold-blooded animal.

BRIEF ENCOUNTERS
Snakes are usually solitary animals and live by themselves. They come together briefly either to mate, or when two males fight to test their strength.

BRIGHT CAMOUFLAGE

Green tree pythons, which live in northern Australia and New Guinea, are bright yellow or brick brown when they hatch. They become the green color of adults in one to three years.

ON THEIR OWN

Although some female snakes protect their eggs and keep them warm, they do not care for the newly hatched young. Once snakes hatch, they face many predators, including other snakes.

LIFE IN A COLD CLIMATE

Snakes that live in cool climates must seek shelter during the winter. They choose a dry place, such as a burrow or a crevice. Their metabolism slows down as the temperature drops, and this allows them to conserve their energy stores. Some cool climates may have such short warm seasons (when snakes are active) that the snakes can only gather enough energy to breed every two years.

Discover more in The Next Generation

167

Snakes on the Move

Whether snakes evolved from their lizard ancestors, they gradually lost their limbs—perhaps to take advantage of narrow spaces where limbs were not much use. Without limbs, however, snakes had to develop new ways of moving. Their longer, more supple bodies provided the solution. Instead of using legs, snakes lever themselves along on the edge of their belly scales, pushing with tiny muscles attached to the ribs. Snakes have developed four different ways to push their bodies along in their different habitats. Snakes move rapidly whether they are on land or in water by a process called lateral undulation. If they are in confined spaces, such as narrow crevices and tunnels, snakes use concertina movement (bunching the body together, then apart). Some heavy-bodied snakes use rectilinear (in a straight line) movement when they are moving slowly. Sidewinding movement is used only by a few snakes that live on loose, slippery surfaces, such as sand dunes.

LOW SPEEDS
Many heavy-bodied snakes, such as pythons and vipers, crawl in a straight line by pushing back with various sections of their belly while bringing other sections forward. This is called rectilinear movement

ROWING IN THE WATER
Sea snakes and other water snakes move just like land snakes. Using lateral undulation, they push against the water with the sides of their curved bodies. Sea snakes have flattened tails to give them additional "push."

TRAVELING AT SPEED
With lateral undulation, a snake can move fast by pushing the side curves of its body against the surface it is traveling on or through. This anchor enables the snake to push forward.

CONCERTINA MOVEMENT
In a narrow space, a snake may anchor the front part of its body by pressing the coils against the sides of the space. It then draws up the rest of the body behind it. The snake anchors this part of the body and pushes the front part to a new anchor point.

DID YOU KNOW?

Snakes usually move at about 2 miles (3 km) per hour, and most species cannot "run" at more than 4 miles (7 km) per hour. The fastest reliable record is for an African black mamba, which moved at 7 miles (11 km) per hour over a distance of 141 ft (43 m).

GET A GRIP
Some tree snakes have a ridge running along the sides of their bellies. This helps them to take advantage of any knob on a branch or twig to push against in lateral undulation.

A WINDING ROAD
The sidewinder, a desert rattlesnake from North America, moves sideways across loose sand with only small sections of its body touching the hot ground at any one time. The snake anchors its head and tail in the sand and lifts its trunk off the ground, moving sideways. The head and tail then move into the same position.

GLIDING TO SAFETY

The flying tree snake can glide from one tree to another, or to the ground. Using lateral undulation, it launches itself into the air where it assumes a more or less straight position. Its belly is curved in, and acts like a parachute. These snakes probably use gliding as a way to escape birds or other predators in trees.

Discover more in Sizing up Snakes

169

Defense Tactics

Most people fear snakes. We see them as deadly, cold-blooded killers, preying on all kinds of animals. But snakes are also preyed on. They are killed and eaten by fish, lizards, other snakes, birds of prey (snakes are a large part of the diet of some eagles, kingfishers and the Australian kookaburra) and mammals. Snakes have evolved a number of ways to defend themselves. Some rely on bright colors to let predators know they are venomous—there are harmless species that even mimic these colors! Others camouflage or bury themselves to hide from danger. Some snakes surprise their enemies by making themselves look bigger, hissing or lashing out with their bodies. Others keep perfectly still, as many predators depend on movement to find their prey. There are also snakes that rely on speed for escape, moving quickly into the cover of a burrow or up into a tree.

DEAD AND STINKING
The hog-nosed snake confuses predators by playing dead and refusing to move if it is touched. If a predator persists, the snake releases a foul smell.

PUMPED UP
If a twig snake is threatened by a predator, it suddenly inflates the loose skin on its chin and throat and makes itself look too big to attack.

Venomous Mayan coral snake

Non-venomous false coral snake

FALSE COLORS
Some harmless snakes avoid predators by imitating venomous species. These two snakes live in the same region of Guatemala in Central America and look almost identical—they even have the same incomplete black bands! The only obvious difference is the red in the false coral snake's tail.

STRANGE BUT TRUE

The king snake is not venomous, but it hunts and eats venomous rattlesnakes! Strangely, rattlesnakes never make any attempt to defend themselves by biting their attackers.

170

DEADLY CAMOUFLAGE
The desert adder hides from predators and ambushes its prey by burying itself in the sand. Only its head and camouflaged eyes can be seen.

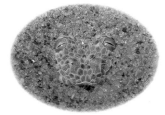

TRICK OF THE EYE
Cobras and some other front-fanged venomous snakes flatten their necks to make themselves look bigger than they really are.

The Rattlesnake's Rattle

The rattlesnake's famous rattle is made up of several interlocking horny segments that have the same structure as the horny scale at the tip of a "normal" snake's tail. When the snake vibrates its tail, the rattle segments move across each other to create a buzzing sound. This warns grazing animals that a rattlesnake is nearby. The natural curve of the segments lifts the rattle off the ground, which places it in the best position for making sounds and keeps it from becoming worn as the snake slides along the ground.

WARNING COLORS
A regal ring-necked snake displays its red-coiled tail to deter a predator. If the predator flips the snake over, it also sees the snake's orange belly. The colors orange and red signal danger to the predator.

Discover more in Snake Specifications

Reptiles in Danger

Many reptiles around the world are endangered. Some small, inconspicuous species of lizard and snake are likely to become extinct during your lifetime, but most people will probably not even notice they have gone. There are many big and spectacular species, such as some crocodilians, large lizards, pythons, tortoises and sea turtles, which are also endangered. They will continue to decline. Reptiles are threatened when their habitats are destroyed for farms, cities and towns; when they are hunted for meat, skins and other body parts; when they are collected as "pets;" and when they are preyed on by introduced animals such as pigs, foxes, cats, mongooses and rats. Species that live on islands or in other small areas are especially vulnerable because they often occur in small numbers. Humans are the main danger to reptiles, but we also have the power to prevent them from becoming extinct. We can stop, or control, all the activities that continue to endanger them.

EXPLOITATION
Crocodilians are endangered because their skins are used for leather. Even baby caimans are killed to make items such as key rings. Countries around the world are making laws to control the trade in crocodilian skins and the killing of hatchlings for souvenirs.

HABITAT INVASION
Habitat destruction is the greatest threat facing reptiles today. We t to conserve individual species in zoos and scientific laboratories, bu if we do not conserve their habitats, the species have no long-term future. A green turtle should be swimming and feeding in the open, unpolluted ocean and nesting on undisturbed beaches. An aquarium will never be a good substitute for its natural environment.

A VALUABLE REPTILE
For many people living in developing countries, a crocodile or python skin can be worth a month's wages. These people kill native reptiles to help raise their standard of living.

BACK FROM THE DEAD
The Australian pygmy blue-tongue skink, which had not been seen alive for 33 years, was rediscovered in 1992. Scientists are studying it closely to see how we can make sure it continues to survive.

PET TORTOISES

Tortoises used to be exploited for their meat and their shells. Today, tortoises are exploited as "pets." In some countries, they are now in danger of being crushed by cars and trail bikes. Tortoise habitats around the world are also being turned into agricultural land and housing subdivisions.

EGGS FOR SALE

Today, turtle eggs are eaten as delicacies in many countries. But young turtles already face many dangers. Harvesting turtle eggs reduces even more the number of hatchlings that will survive to become adults.

A PRECIOUS NECKLACE

People in many cultures use pieces of reptiles in special ceremonies, or they wear them as decoration, such as this crocodile-tooth necklace. These craft items are also sold and sometimes exported to other countries around the world.

A HIGH-PRICED HAT

Some reptiles, such as crocodilians and venomous snakes, can be dangerous to animals and people. But this is not a reason to kill or exploit them.

CHAMELEON EXPORTS

Some poor countries export their live, exotic reptiles to wealthy countries as "pets." Chameleons are among the most sought-after reptiles, but they are also the hardest to look after. Many will die if they are not taken care of by people who know about reptiles.

173

Mammals

Which mammal has a duck's bill, an otter's body and a beaver's tail?

Which is the largest mammal on land?

Are there poisonous mammals?

Contents

FAMILY LIFE
Lions are typical mammals in many ways. Their bodies have fur, they work together to find food, and their young need to be cared for and fed with milk. Mammals look after their young longer than other vertebrates do. Lion cubs continue to nurse for up to six months.

SLEEPING OVER
Because food is scarce in winter, many mammals conserve energy and live off the fat stored in their bodies by sleeping for long periods. This is called hibernation. It lowers their body temperature, heartbeat and breathing.

• THE WORLD OF MAMMALS •

Introducing Mammals

Most of the animals we keep as pets, such as dogs, cats and rabbits, and the animals we use for work, such as horses, are mammals. Humans are mammals too. Mammals belong to a group of animals called vertebrates, all of which have backbones. They are warm-blooded, which means they have a constant body temperature, no matter how cold or hot their surroundings may be. There are nearly 4,000 species of mammal, and most of these have hair or fur on their bodies. Except for the platypus and echidna, all mammals give birth to live young. Unlike other animals, they feed their young with milk. Mammals evolved from reptiles that had several bones in the lower jaw, but mammals have only one bone in the lower jaw.

EARS AND NOSES
The African aardvark has a large nose and big ears. Like many other mammals, it has a well-developed sense of smell and good hearing.

GROWL!
Like many other mammals, wolves work together to find food. This wolf is baring its sharp teeth to let other wolves know that it is angry.

TYPES OF MAMMAL

The three main groups of mammal are monotremes, marsupials and placental mammals. Monotremes (the platypus and echidna) have many features in common with mammals' reptile ancestors. They have a single opening, called a cloaca, for reproduction and body wastes, and they lay eggs. Female marsupials, such as opossums and wallabies, give birth to young that are not fully developed, and are protected in pouches until they can fend for themselves. The young of placental mammals, such as bushbabies, are fed inside the females' bodies by a special organ called a placenta and are more developed than marsupials when born.

Platypus

Rock wallaby

Bushbaby

DID YOU KNOW?

The smaller the mammal, the faster the heartbeat. In one minute, a shrew's heart beats about 200 times, a human's heart beats about 65 times and an elephant's heart beats about 25 times.

BREAK-OUT
The odd-looking star-nosed mole from North America uses its spadelike front feet to dig through the soil. It detects its prey of worms and insects with its sensitive star-shaped nose.

Designs for Living

Mammals are among the most successful animals ever to have lived. Because they are warm-blooded, they can survive in almost any environment. To take advantage of different environments, mammals have evolved different body shapes. They have adapted to life in the jungles, deserts and high mountains; in the polar regions; in the air and in the trees; beneath the ground and in the oceans. They have also adapted as they moved from one environment to another. The ancestors of today's horses, for example, lived in forests and were small enough to move among trees and undergrowth. When they began to live on the open plains, however, they grew larger and stronger so they could migrate in search of fresh food, and faster so they could escape the fast-moving predators of the plains.

HIDDEN FROM SIGHT
The three-banded armadillo searches for food at night. But if it is attacked by a predator, such as a puma, it rolls into a ball and uses its horny skin as armor plating.

Gray-headed fruit bat
(male/female)
Length: 11 in (28 cm)
Wingspan: 2 ft 7 in (80 cm)
Weight: 2 lb (800 g)

Gorilla (male)
Height: (standing on knuckles)
5 ft 3 in (1.62 m)
Weight: 375 lb (170 kg)

Human (female)
Height: 5 ft 2 in (1.59 m)
Weight: 110 lb (50 kg)

Black-handed
spider monkey (female)
Height: up to 2 ft (60 cm)
Weight: 9 lb (4 kg)

ALL SHAPES AND SIZES
Mammals have evolved different body shapes to allow them to live in almost every kind of environment. The sizes given here are the averages for each of these mammals.

Blue whale (female)
Length: 91 ft (28 m)
Weight: 91 tons (90 tonnes)

Australian sea lion (male)
Length: 6 ft 8 in (2.1 m)
Weight: 660 lb (300 kg)

Gemsbok (male)
Height: 4 ft (1.2 m)
Weight: 450 lb (204 kg)

LOOKING ALIKE

Some mammals look similar and live in similar ways even though they are not related to each other and live in different parts of the world. Scientists call this convergent evolution. Many Australian mammals have evolved to resemble unrelated mammals in other parts of the world. The striped possum has a long, narrow finger just like that of the aye-aye from Madagascar. They both hook grubs out of holes in trees with their long fingers. Like the pangolins of Africa and Asia, echidnas have long noses, long sticky tongues and no teeth. Koalas look similar to the sloths of Central and South America. Both live in trees, eat leaves and move slowly.

Aye-aye

Striped possum

Short-beaked echidna

Pangolin

Koala

Sloth

TREE GLIDING

Despite their name, flying squirrels cannot fly. They glide from tree to tree, tightening a flap of skin between their front and back legs, which acts like a parachute.

WINTER COAT

Mammals that live in harsh environments, such as the Arctic, adapt to different seasons by changing color. The Arctic fox has a brown coat in summer, but grows a white coat for camouflage in winter.

Giraffe (male)
Height: 16 ft (4.95 m)
Weight: 2,600 lb (1,180 kg)

African elephant (male)
Height: 11 ft (3.35 m)
Weight: 5 tons (5.1 tonnes)

Black rhinoceros (male)
Height: 5 ft (1.52 m)
Weight: 1¼ tons (1.3 tonnes)

Beaver (male/female)
Length: 3 ft 3 in (1 m)
Weight: 66 lb (30 kg)

Discover more in Finding Food

GOOD DOG

Cynognathus, whose name means "dog jaw," was a mammal-like reptile that lived 240 million years ago. It grew to about 3 ft (1 m) in length, but its head, with massive jaws, was more than 1 ft (30 cm) long.

PICTURING A MAMMAL

Fossilized bones provide clues to the appearance of an extinct mammal. From them, we can reconstruct a model such as this tree-dwelling *Thylacoleo*, a meat-eating relative of today's kangaroo.

• THE WORLD OF MAMMALS •

Mammal Beginnings

The first mammals were small, shrewlike animals that were about 5 in (12 cm) long. Related to today's monotremes, they first appeared during the Triassic Period, about 220 million years ago. They were descended from reptiles called synapsids, which appeared about 300 million years ago. These primitive mammals evolved into different groups during the Jurassic and Cretaceous periods (208–65 million years ago). Most of these early mammals were carnivores (meat eaters), but some, such as the tree-living multituberculates, which ranged from animals the size of mice to some as big as beavers, ate plants. The ancestors of today's marsupials, insectivores and primates first appeared in the Cretaceous Period (145–65 million years ago). When the dinosaurs died out at the end of the Cretaceous Period, these modern mammals spread to every continent and evolved into thousands of new species.

DID YOU KNOW?

Camels and their near relatives now live in South America, Asia and Africa. They evolved in North America but died out there during the Pleistocene Period, about 12,000 years ago

SPIKY ANCESTOR

Sail-backed *Dimetrodon* was a mammal-like reptile. It belonged to a group of animals that had large openings in their skulls behind the eye sockets. Mammals gradually evolved from members of this group.

THE FIRST MAMMAL

Megazostrodon, which lived in Africa about 220 million years ago, is the oldest known mammal. This insect eater was only 5 in (12 cm) long and probably laid eggs like today's monotremes.

FIRST PERSON

The earliest known human was *Australopithecus afarensis,* who lived in northern Africa about 3 million years ago. About 4 ft (1.2 m) tall, *Australopithecus* was first identified from a series of footprints found in hardened volcanic ash. In 1974, the skeleton of a female *Australopithecus,* named "Lucy" by its discoverers, was found in Ethiopia.

CIRCLING THEIR PREY

On the plains of northern Africa 40 million years ago, a female *Arsinoitherium* defends her young against a pack of 4-ft (1.2-m) long predators called *Hyaenodon.* Although *Arsinoitherium* grew to nearly 13 ft (4 m) long, they were actually relatives of today's rabbit-sized hyraxes.

Hyenas are scavengers during the day and
wait to feed on animals killed by lions. At night,
however, they become hunters themselves!

Finding Food

Mammals use many different strategies to find food. Some mammals are hunters, while others are scavengers and dine on leftovers. Some migrate in search of food and others hoard food for winter. Mammals eat almost anything, from plants to other mammals. Vampire bats live on blood, echidnas eat ants and a pack of wolves will eat a moose or other large mammal. The amount of food a mammal eats varies greatly. Very small mammals cannot store much energy and warmth inside their bodies. Because they lose energy quickly, they have to eat a lot of food. A shrew, for example, must eat more than its own body weight every day or it will freeze to death. Strangely enough, the largest mammal—the whale—also eats large amounts of food. This is because it grows quickly (a newborn blue whale gains about 200 lb [90 kg] every day!) and because it has to swim long distances in search of food.

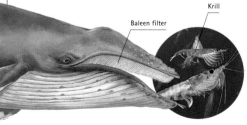

Krill

Baleen filter

FILTERING THROUGH
Baleen whales have long, fringed plates of horny baleen instead of teeth. They filter hundreds of 2-in (5-cm) long shrimp called krill through the baleen and trap them inside their mouths.

184

ON THE MOVE

Many plant-eating mammals migrate to where their food is plentiful. Reindeer in the Arctic travel away from the snow in search of fresh green grass.

DESERT DINING

The gerenuk, or giraffe-gazelle, lives in eastern Africa. It is so well adapted to life in the desert that it never needs to drink. With the help of its long neck, it gets enough moisture from the tender leaves of prickly bushes and trees.

SAVING UP

Squirrels collect nuts and seeds and hide them in hollow trees. They save them to eat during long winters and to have a supply of food ready for the spring.

HUNTING TOGETHER

Many carnivorous mammals cooperate to find food—even humpback whales work together to herd schools of fish. Dolphins, porpoises and seals, lions, hyenas, wolves and other dogs work together to save the energy of individual hunters and to make sure that every member of the group eats enough to survive. Here, a group of African wild dogs corners a wildebeest.

Mammal Society

PART OF A GROUP
Meerkats are very sociable and live together in packs. Living in a group makes it easier to defend the pack and care for the young.

S ome mammals, such as bears, orang-utans and koalas, are solitary animals. They live alone and only come together to mate. But most mammals are social and live in groups. Living in groups has many advantages. Mammals that might be preyed on by birds, reptiles or other mammals can defend each other and their young. Because a predator has many targets to choose from in a group, most members have time to escape. Humans are the only mammals who use words to communicate. Other social animals use smells, facial expressions or body language to "talk" to each other. Dogs, for example, wag their tails when they are happy, and snarl, bare their teeth and growl when they are being aggressive. Most mammals communicate to tell other members of the group how they are feeling, or to warn them of danger.

GETTING TO KNOW YOU

Social mammals spend a lot of time getting to know each other before they mate, because most species bring up the young together.

⬛ORE FOR SHOW

⬛erious fights are rare among social ⬛imals. Male elephant seals push, ⬛ar and slash each other, but they ⬛ldom do real harm.

BRINGING UP THE FAMILY

Gibbons live in South and Southeast Asia. They are social apes and move through the tree tops in family groups, searching for fruits, grubs, insects and leaves. The young take two years to wean, but they stay with the family until they are fully mature and help to take care of their younger siblings.

Platypuses and Echidnas

COVER UP
Strong muscles control a fold of skin that tightens to cover the platypus's eyes and ears when it dives. Instead of sight and sound, it uses its sensitive bill to find its way underwater.

FLOATING RESTAURANT
Platypuses store their prey in cheek pouches, then eat while they float on the surface. Because they do not have teeth, they crush their food between the tongue and horny plates inside the mouth.

The Australian platypus, the short-beaked echidna of Australia and New Guinea, and the New Guinea long-beaked echidna are monotremes. These very primitive mammals have many reptile features, such as a cloaca, which is used to get rid of body wastes and to lay eggs. These mammals ooze milk for their young from special patches of skin. Both platypuses and echidnas have a lower body temperature than other mammals, and echidnas hibernate in winter. Male platypuses and echidnas have a long spur on each hind leg. In platypuses, this is connected to a venom gland and is used in fights between males. Special organs in the rubbery skin of the platypus's bill can detect the muscle activity produced by its prey of shrimp, freshwater crabs and other invertebrates. Echidnas may also be able to detect their prey in this way.

Watertight
The platypus keeps its eyes and ears tightly closed while it is underwater.

Webbed feet
Platypuses use of their powerful fr feet for swimmir

SMOOTH SWIMMER
The platypus is perfectly adapted for an underwater life. It has webbed feet and fur that holds a layer of air next to the skin for warmth. Its bill detects prey in crevices and on the river bed.

WET AND DRY
On land, the platypus pulls back the webs on its front feet so that it can use its claws to walk and to dig burrows.

A Perplexing Mix

When the first specimens of a platypus were sent to England in 1798, many zoologists believed this strange creature was a fake, made of different animals sewn together. They believed it was impossible for one animal to have a duck's bill, an otter's body and a beaver's tail.

TICKY BUSINESS

he short-beaked echidna's tongue is four times as long s its snout and is covered with sticky saliva. It picks up housands of ants, termites and other small insects during a day's feeding.

Digging claws
Short, strong front limbs equipped with thick claws allow the short-beaked echidna to break into the cement-hard nests of termites.

Fur coat
The echidna's coarse fur stops it from losing heat. Sharp spines, which can be raised or lowered by special muscles, protect it from predators.

oisonous spur
ale platypuses use the ur on the hind foot in ghts with other males.

SINKING FEELING
Echidnas burrow straight down into soft soil to escape attack. They bury themselves until only their prickly spines are visible.

HAPPY WANDERER
Long-beaked echidnas are nocturnal and have large feeding territories. They use backward-facing spikes on the tip of the tongue to "spear" their prey of worms.

189

ON THE INSIDE
A newly born kangaroo can spend several months in its mother's pouch, where it is warm and protected, before it is able to survive on its own.

Pouched Mammals

There are about 280 species of marsupial. Seventy-five of these are opossums that live in North, Central and South America, while the remaining species, which vary in size, shape and way of life, live in Australia, New Guinea and on nearby islands. They range from mouse-sized honey possums, which eat pollen and nectar, to 6-ft (1.8-m) tall kangaroos, which eat grasses and plants. Marsupials live in many environments, from deserts to rainforests, in burrows, in trees and on the ground. They glide, run, hop and swim, and eat plants, insects, carrion (the flesh of dead animals) and meat. All marsupials have pouches, although some are very small. Because the young are born at an early stage of their development, they shelter in the pouches and feed on their mother's milk until they are old enough to be independent.

PIGGYBACK
Although the koala's pouch faces downwards, the muscles inside hold the baby safe while its mother climbs trees. Later, the young koala rides on its mother's back as she feeds on leaves.

DID YOU KNOW?
The expression "playing possum" comes from the American opossum's unusual habit of pretending to be dead when it is threatened by a predator. This tactic seems to work, because most predators will not attack and eat an animal that is already dead.

FINDING THE POUCH
A wallaby is no larger than a peanut when it is born. It makes its way from the mother's birth canal to her pouch, where it will stay warm and safe for the next five to eleven months.

A BOXING BOUT
Most of the 59 species of wallaby and kangaroo live in family groups. In the mating season, the competition between male kangaroos is fierce. They have kicking and pushing contests and the winners mate with the females.

TIGER WITH A POUCH

The last known wild thylacine, or Tasmanian tiger, was captured in 1933 and died in 1936. Since then, despite many supposed sightings, there has been no proof that the species still exists. The thylacine was more of a marsupial wolf than a tiger. Its teeth, head and front legs were very similar to those of a dog, but unlike most dogs, it could not run fast, and it lived alone or in pairs.

IN AND OUT OF THE POUCH

A young kangaroo pushes its front feet and head into its mother's pouch.

It twists around so its head is on the bottom of the pouch.

Then it turns so that it can see out of the pouch, and is ready to jump out.

HIDE AND SEEK
Moles use their noses
to find prey. Their stumpy
tails are also covered in
sensitive hairs so they can
detect a predator behind
them in their tunnels.

DID YOU KNOW?
The tenrec of Madagascar is a record
holder. Females can produce up to
32 embryos—more than any other
mammal. However, not all the
embryos survive until birth.

• INSECT EATERS AND BATS •

A Nose for the Job

There are nearly 4,000 species of mammal, and more than half of these eat insects as part of their diet. One group of mammals, the insectivores, eats mostly insects, although some do feed on meat, such as frogs, lizards and mice. The 365 species of insectivore include small mammals such as shrews, hedgehogs and moles. Insectivores are often solitary, nocturnal mammals. They are fast-moving hunters with a relatively small brain, but a well-developed sense of smell, which they rely on far more than their sense of sight. Most insectivores also have long, narrow snouts to sniff out their prey, and up to 44 sharp teeth. Another group of insect-eating mammals, the xenarthrans (pronounced zen-<u>arth</u>-rans), are also called edentates, which means "toothless." The South American anteaters, however, are the only edentates that have no teeth at all.

A PROBING NOSE
The Pyrenean desman is a mole, but it looks like a shrew. It hunts its prey underwater, and probes beneath rocks for insects with its long, flexible snout.

LITTLE DIGGER
A European mole hunts worms and insects underground. It relies on its sensitive nose to smell and feel its prey.

SPIKY DEFENSE
The nocturnal Algerian hedgehog is protected by its spiny coat. It has a short, pointed snout with sensitive bristles, and eats everything from insects to mushrooms.

HANGING AROUND
The South American giant ground sloth, which grew to 20 ft (6 m) long, became extinct in the last 10,000 years. Its five living relatives live in trees and eat leaves. The largest is the three-toed sloth (above), which grows to 2 ft 2 in (67 cm) long.

POISONOUS MAMMALS

Two insectivores use venom to help them catch animals that may be larger than they are. The North American short-tailed shrew and the solenodons of Cuba and Haiti produce poisonous saliva to help them subdue struggling prey. They quickly bite their prey and inject it with a small amount of saliva, which causes paralysis. This poisonous saliva is very painful, but not fatal, to humans. Other mammals also use poison. Male platypuses have a poison spur on each ankle, and scientists believe they use these in fights with other males.

Solenodon

Short-tailed shrew

FURRY VACUUM CLEANERS

There are four species of South American anteater. Three of these are small, shelter in trees and have prehensile (gripping) tails. But the giant anteater, which grows to 6 ft (1.86 m) long, lives only on the ground. Female giant anteaters carry their young on their backs for several months.

VAMPIRE BAT
Found only in
North, Central and
South America, true
blood-drinking vampire bats
have razor-sharp front teeth
that slice open the skin of a bird
or mammal. Their saliva stops blood
clotting while they lap up their meal.

BAT FACES
Some bats have long ears and
flaps of skin around the nose to
detect echoes from prey. Other
bats have tube-shaped nostrils
that help them sniff out food.

Long-eared bat

Tent-building bat

Lesser bare-backed fruit bat

• INSECT EATERS AND BATS •

Hanging Around

About 50 million years ago, a group of insectivores took to the skies, gliding from tree to tree. These gliders evolved into bats—the only mammals that are capable of powered flight. Bats are active mainly at night when there are very few flying predators to threaten or compete with them. They have spread to most parts of the world, except for polar regions and cold mountain areas. Today, there are about 160 species of fruit bat, some of which have wingspans of 5 ft (150 cm), and about 815 species of insect-eating bat, which hunt frogs, fish, birds and small mammals as well as insects. Vampire bats live on the blood of birds and large mammals. Many insect-eating bats eat while they are flying, holding their prey in a special tail pouch. Most bats roost in trees or in caves. Bats that eat fruit and insects use echolocation to navigate and find food. The sounds they make, which are too high for humans to hear, bounce off objects around them.

FLYING FREELY
Free-tailed bats get their name
because their tails extend past
the flap of skin that joins the
hind feet to the tail. There
are about 90 species of
free-tailed bat, and they
are found all over the
world. They roost in caves,
hollow trees or beneath
tree bark.

FRUIT FLYER
Most fruit bats drink the nectar of the fruit and
eat its blossoms, but they do not eat the fruit. Some
land in trees to eat, but many hover above flowers.

ECHOLOCATION

Most small bats find their way around by using echolocation, which is similar to radar. A bat produces sounds, such as high-pitched squeaks, then listens to the type and position of the echo to detect its prey or its surroundings. It can tell what kind of insect or other prey it is "hearing," and how fast and in what direction that prey is moving. Fishing bats "listen" to ripples on the surface of streams, and can tell which ripples are caused by the current, and which are caused by a fish that is below the surface.

Bat
Produces rapid, high-pitched sounds.

Moth
The bat's sounds bounce off the moth, back to the bat.

PRIMATE HANDS AND FEET

One of the distinctive characteristics of primates is their special thumb (and sometimes their big toe) that enables them to grasp small objects.

Indri foot   Indri hand

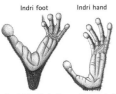

The indri, a kind of lemur, lives most of its life in trees. Its hands and feet are designed to help it climb.

Aye-aye foot   Aye-aye hand

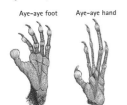

The aye-aye, a kind of lemur, uses its long, thin, second finger to hook insect larvae out of holes in tree branches.

Gorilla foot   Gorilla hand

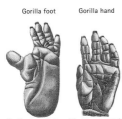

Gorillas have flattened feet to support their heavy bodies. Their hands are designed to grasp leaves, bark and fruit.

NOSING IN
The proboscis monkey of Southeast Asia has a large nose. It lives on the leaves and fruit of mangroves and other trees.

• PRIMATES •

About Primates

Primates are divided into two groups. The lower primates are lemurs, bushbabies, lorises and tarsiers, while the higher primates are monkeys, apes and humans. Most primates live in trees in tropical regions where their food grows all year round. Many monkeys from Africa and Asia live mainly on the ground in drier environments. They eat a wide variety of food, from seeds and nuts to birds' eggs and nestlings, reptiles and small mammals. Lower primates still have much in common with their insect-eating ancestors. Higher primates, however, have large brains and are quite intelligent. They have good eyesight and binocular vision. They have a highly developed sense of touch because they have sensitive pads on the fingers and toes, and nails instead of claws. Their thumbs are opposable—they can reach around to touch the tips of the other fingers, which helps them to hold and eat food.

EARS AND EYES
Tarsiers live in the rainforests of Southeast Asia. They have large ears and eyes, and leap from branch to branch with their long hind legs as they hunt insects, lizards and small birds. Tarsiers also eat fruit and leaves.

196

IN THE TREE TOPS

Cotton-top tamarins, which
are found in Central America,
are typical of monkeys from this
part of the world. They live in family
groups and spend most of their lives high in the
rainforest trees, eating fruit, leaves and insects.

INTRUDERS BEWARE!

Primate society is very complex. Some
primates, such as orang-utans, live
alone. Others, such as baboons, howler
monkeys and chimpanzees live in
extended family groups of up to
40 animals. Male gorillas even have
harems of females. Gibbons are highly
evolved apes from South and Southeast
Asia, and the only primates that mate
for life. In this picture, a pair of gibbons
search for fruit, leaves, insects, grubs
and spiders in their own feeding
territory. They "mark" this area every
morning by hooting and howling, which
warns other gibbons to keep away.

IN FLIGHT
When threatened, sifakas can run for short distances, holding their arms above their heads. But they return to the trees as soon as they can.

ON PATROL
Waving their tails like flags, a family group of ring-tailed lemurs forages for fruits and insects on the forest floor. Like other lemurs, ring-tails are very social animals and have unusual adaptations for grooming. The second toe on each foot has a claw that they use to clean their ears. They comb each other's fur with the front teeth in their lower jaw.

• PRIMATES •

The Lemurs of Madagascar

Lemurs are unusual, primitive primates. They have ghostlike faces and cry eerily at night. Their name comes from the Latin word for "ghost." Lemurs once lived throughout Africa, Europe and North America, but became extinct in these regions because they had to compete with more advanced monkeys. For the last 50 million years, they have survived only on the African island of Madagascar. There are more than 20 species of lemur. They range from the 11-in (29-cm) long mouse lemur, which includes its long tail, to the 3-ft (90-cm) long indri, with a surprisingly short tail! Most live in the wet forests of eastern Madagascar, where they eat fruit, leaves, insects and small animals such as geckos. Many are nocturnal, and most live in groups of up to 24 animals. All lemurs are endangered because their forest habitat is being destroyed.

CLOSE RELATIONS
Indris are one of the families of lemur. They feed on fruit and leaves, and have to hop on the ground because their hind legs are much longer than their front legs.

AYE-AYE

The aye-aye is nocturnal,
solitary and shy. Famous for
its bad smell, it is found only on
Madagascar, although a similar
species once lived in eastern
Africa. The aye-aye eats
insects and hunts for larvae
beneath the bark of trees.
It listens for their movements,
then bites away the bark
and uses its thin second
finger to mash them into a
paste. Aye-ayes also use this
specialized finger to scoop the
soft flesh from fruit.

SAFE RIDE
South American spider monkeys use their prehensile tails as a fifth limb to hang on to slender branches as they travel. A baby spider monkey also uses its tail to keep a firm grip on its mother.

OLD AND NEW

Old World monkeys
Monkeys from Africa and Asia have prominent noses with narrow nostrils that face forward.

New World monkeys
Monkeys from Central and South America have flattened noses with nostrils that face sideways.

• PRIMATES •

Monkeys

About 40 million years ago, new kinds of primates—monkeys and apes—began to take over from the lemurs. Today, there are two groups of monkeys: the Old World monkeys, which live in Africa and Asia; and the New World monkeys, which live only in Central and South America. The 80 or so species of Old World monkey include macaques, langurs, mandrills, baboons, guenons, leaf and colobus monkeys. They have thin, forward-facing nostrils and walk on all fours. Old World monkeys do not have prehensile (gripping) tails and many spend a lot of time on the ground. They eat insects and other animals as well as plants. There are about 65 species of New World monkey, including marmosets, spider monkeys, howlers, capuchins and woolly monkeys. They have widely spaced nostrils that face to the sides, and they spend most of their time in trees. Most New World monkeys are herbivores, or plant eaters. They live in family groups and most have prehensile tails.

MOTHER LOVE
Langurs live in peaceful extended family groups of 15 to 25 animals. Young animals are cared for by their mothers and are protected by other members of the group for up to two years.

MORE SNARL THAN SMILE
Mandrills are the most brightly colored of all monkeys. Males have a red nose, an orange beard, and blue, violet and red buttocks. They bare their large, fanglike canine teeth to express anger or aggression.

Color Codes

Geladas live in families that are dominated by a male and gather in groups of up to 400 animals. They move through large feeding territories in search of grass, roots, seeds and insects. Although geladas look like baboons, they are not related to them. Geladas use color to communicate. The males have a mane of hair and a bright red patch of naked skin on the chest, which they use to attract females and to warn other males away from their mates.

WINTER WOOLLIES
Most monkeys live in tropical climates, but the Japanese macaque (also called the snow monkey) lives in mountains in Honshu (the main island of Japan), which are covered in snow for more than six months every year.

Discover more in About Primates

The Apes

Apes are the most highly evolved primates. There are four species: the orang-utan, the gorilla and two species of chimpanzee. Like humans, apes have flattened fingernails, no tail and an opposable thumb that can move to touch each of the other fingers. Orang-utans, which live in Sumatra and Borneo, are solitary animals. They live in trees and eat fruit, leaves and occasionally small animals and eggs. Chimpanzees and gorillas are found only in Africa. They live mainly on the ground and walk on all fours, supporting their arms on their knuckles. Chimpanzees are very social animals with many different facial expressions and sounds. They eat fruit, leaves, birds' eggs, insects and mammals such as antelopes and monkeys. Although gorillas seem huge and fierce, they are actually peaceful vegetarians. They build nests in trees each night, safe from predators and away from the cold ground.

TEACHING TOOLS
Apes learn how to use tools and then pass on the knowledge to their young. Chimpanzees use sticks as tools to scoop termites out of their nests.

PROTECTING THE FAMILY
Gorillas move through the mountain forests of eastern and central Africa in family groups. Each family is led by a large silverback male. He warns younger males away from his mates and children by standing upright, roaring and slapping his chest.

LOOKING AT ORANG-UTANS

Male orang-utans (below) grow to 5 ft 6 in (1.7 m) tall, almost twice as large as females. They have broad, flat faces and large cheek flaps.

SWINGING FROM TREE TO TREE

There are nine species of plant-eating gibbon, which are closely related to the apes. These tree dwellers live in Asia in family groups. Males and females are the same size.

TALKING TO CHIMPS

Scientists have found recently that chimpanzees have almost the same ability to learn as we do. They cannot make human sounds, but they can be taught to communicate with humans using special symbols. This chimp, for example, can ask a human friend to play by touching the symbol that means "chase," then running away. Chimps can also be taught to understand spoken questions. If asked "Can you make the dog bite the snake?," this chimp will put a rubber snake into a toy dog's mouth.

203

Carnivores

There is one large group of mammals called the Carnivora that has adapted special features for a meat-eating diet. The seven families of carnivore, which are found all over the world, are made up of dogs; bears (including the giant panda); raccoons; weasels, martens, otters, skunks and badgers; civets; hyenas; and cats. These carnivores have two pairs of sharp-edged molars called carnassial teeth and digestive systems that can process food very quickly. But few carnivores eat only meat. Most eat at least some plant material. Bears, for example, eat more plants than meat and their carnassial teeth are rounded so they can grind hard stems and seeds. Although many carnivores are social animals, others are solitary. They drive other members of their species from their hunting territories, except during the mating season.

TREETOP SLUMBERER
The red panda lives in trees where it sleeps most of the day. It eats roots, grasses and eggs as well as fish, insects and mice.

CATLIKE CARNIVORE
The Madagascan fossa looks like a cat, but is actually related to civets. It has a flattened face, and eyes that point forward so it can judge distances when it pounces on its prey.

KILLING BITE
Lionesses hunt together and exhaust their prey before killing it with a fatal bite to the throat. They have powerful jaws and huge canine (stabbing) teeth.

DID YOU KNOW?

Indian and African mongooses eat lizards, insects and venomous snakes! They slowly build up an immunity to snake venom so that, eventually, some can even survive a cobra bite that would kill a human.

Hunting Failures

Despite their reputations as fierce hunters, most large carnivores fail to catch their prey more times than they succeed. Although cheetahs (right) are the fastest land animals in the world, they are designed for speed, not stamina. If they have not caught their prey within 1,476 ft (450 m), they must give up the chase because they cannot run any further. Lions succeed once in every ten of their hunting attempts, and even large groups of wolves capture their prey only once in every five attempts.

Ocelot

Dog

Grizzly bear

Raccoon

Weasel

Civet

Hyena

TABLE MANNERS
Sea otters grow to
4 ft (1.2 m) long, and
hunt fish, sea urchins
and shellfish. They float on
their backs to devour their
catch and later, to sleep.

Discover more in Mammal Society

205

ATTACK AND DEFENSE

Back off
The margay shows it will defend itself by staring with wide eyes.

Ready to attack
The margay gives its enemy a last chance to retreat. It tucks its ears out of the way, opens its mouth wide and shows its sharp teeth.

INVISIBLE HUNTE
A tiger follows its prey silentl<
Suddenly it leaps, grips the anima
with its claws and grabs it by th
neck. To make sure a large anima
is dead, the tiger bite
into its throat so
cannot breathe

DID YOU KNOW?

Leopards, which can kill animals as large as a baby giraffe, have very strong neck and back muscles that enable them to drag their prey high into trees to protect it from lions and scavengers.

• MEAT EATERS •

The Cat Family

There are 36 members of the cat family. They range from the South American oncilla, which is half as big as a domestic cat, to the Siberian tiger, which grows to 12 ft (3.7 m) long, but they have many features in common. All are hunters, most species eat nothing but meat, most are shy and live alone, and many are nocturnal. Cats hunt in similar ways—stalking their prey silently then attacking in a sudden rush, wrestling their prey to the ground and killing it with a bite to the neck or throat. Most cats use their razor-sharp claws to hold prey, and all except cheetahs pull in their claws so they do not become blunt. Cats have tiny muscles in their tongue so they can change its surface. They groom themselves or their young with a smooth tongue and scrape the skin off their prey with a rough tongue. Sixteen species of cat are endangered, and humans are the biggest threat to their survival.

206

FISHING CATS

The fishing cat, which grows to 4 ft (1.3 m) long, lives in Southeast Asia and India. It scoops fish out of streams with its webbed paws. It also eats crabs and birds, and has even been known to kill calves, dogs and sheep.

PRIDE OF THE PLAINS

Most cats live alone. But lions are social and live in a family group called a pride, which includes up to 30 animals. Most of these are females (there can be three generations of lionesses in one pride) and their cubs. There are often two dominant males, and they are usually brothers. Young males lead a solitary life until they are older and stronger. Then they challenge the dominant males for control of the pride.

The Dog Family

Dogs were among the first carnivores, and their way of life, as well as some features of their anatomy, still resembles that of their ancestors of 40 million years ago. They are highly adaptable mammals and are able to take advantage of new habitats and new feeding opportunities. Of the 35 species of wild dog that have now spread to almost every part of the world, 27 species are small, solitary foxes, while the remaining eight species are social dogs that hunt in packs. No matter how they live, all dogs have features in common: keen sight, hearing and smell; strong, sharp canine teeth; and special scissorlike molars (carnassial teeth) that are used for tearing flesh. Dogs are mainly carnivorous, but they also eat insects, fruit, snails and other small prey. Some dogs have evolved to chase prey in open grassland, and one species, the grey fox of North America, even climbs trees in search of food.

PREY AND PREDATOR
Dingoes are wild dogs of Australia. They are found throughout the country, and eat everything from grasshoppers to kangaroos and large monitor lizards.

DESERT FOX
The cat-sized fennec fox of the Sahara in North Africa has adapted to desert life. It has large ears that help it keep cool by spreading and getting rid of its body heat. Its ears also help the fox to detect its prey moving at night.

DID YOU KNOW?
All dogs protect their young, but African wild dogs care particularly for their pups, such as the one shown here, by providing and sharing food with them.

ON THE PROWL

Wolves are intelligent, efficient hunters that cooperate to tire out their prey. They communicate with body language, facial expressions and howls. The howling chorus of a wolf pack can be heard for about 6 miles (10 km) and tells other wolves to keep away.

As Cunning as a Fox

Foxes have a reputation for being clever because they are quick to learn and to adapt to new habitats. These shy, alert animals are very difficult to approach or trap. They hunt at night and rest during the day in dens, hollow trees or even in drains. Foxes have learned how to survive in cities as well as in the countryside. They eat rabbits, fruit, garbage and pet food.

COYOTE FACES

Coyotes use facial expressions to communicate. They use their ears and mouths to show their feelings, and bare their teeth to express fear and aggression.

Friendly

Submissive

Playful

Attacking

Defending

Q: Do all members of the dog family hunt food on the ground?

SUN BEAR
The sun bear of Burma, Sumatra and Borneo is the smallest bear, growing to only 3 ft (1 m). It loves honey, which it licks from beehives with its long tongue.

AN EASY CATCH
Brown bears station themselves at waterfalls on North American rivers and wait for salmon to migrate upstream to lay their eggs. Skilled bears can catch salmon in their mouths.

The Bears

Bears evolved about 40 million years ago in Europe. They spread to Africa, where they are no longer found; Asia; and North and South America. Today there are only eight species of bear. They include the largest of the meat eaters, the polar bear, which can grow to more than 11 ft (nearly 3.5 m) long and weigh 1,600 lb (725 kg), and the slightly heavier North American grizzly. Bears eat anything from plant roots to small and large mammals. Polar bears feed almost entirely on seals and fish, although they can kill reindeer. Bears in colder regions do not hibernate (sleep through winter). When food is scarce, they sleep on and off in dens they dig in hillsides or in snow banks. Females give birth in their dens, where the cubs stay warm until spring. Tropical species, such as the South American spectacled bear, and the Asian sun and sloth bears, are much smaller than their northern relatives.

THE POLAR BEAR'S YEAR

Winter
Females dig dens in snow banks and give birth to their cubs. Males wander along the pack ice at sea and hunt seals.

Spring
The cubs emerge from the den and learn how to hunt. Their mother guards them from predatory males, which will kill and eat the cubs.

Autumn
Bears feed on seals and store fat for winter. Pregnant females move to areas of permanent snow to dig their dens.

Summer
This is the mating season. Polar bears can swim well, and often cross large stretches of open ocean to new hunting grounds.

DID YOU KNOW?

The sloth bear, which lives in India and Sri Lanka, is the largest mammal to feed almost entirely on termites. It forms its large lips into a tube and uses the wide gap between its front teeth to suck termites out of their nests.

GIANT PANDAS

Giant pandas were unknown outside China until the nineteenth century, and are still mysterious animals. Although they sometimes eat birds and small mammals, they live almost entirely on bamboo and spend up to 12 hours a day chewing tough bamboo stalks. As pandas do not digest the bamboo very well, they have to eat up to 44 lb (20 kg) of bamboo a day to survive. Pandas have an extra thumblike structure (part of their wrist bone) on their front paws, which they use to help them grip the bamboo stems.

LIVING IN THE ARCTIC

Polar bears are perfectly adapted to life in the Arctic. They have just enough blood in their feet so their toes do not freeze, and their fur consists of hollow, clear (not white) hairs that trap heat.

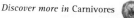

Discover more in Carnivores

211

ELEPHANT'S FOOT
An elephant has five toes on each of its front feet. They are enclosed in a tough, hooflike covering of skin.

ON THEIR TOES
All hoofed mammals walk and run on their toes. Odd-toed hoofed mammals have a middle toe larger than the other toes. Even-toed hoofed mammals walk on their middle two toes.

UNLIKELY RELATIONS
Despite the differences in their appearance and size, hyraxes are the closest living relatives of elephants. Both animals walk on all five toes.

Zebra
Zebras, like horses, run on the central toe of each foot. The other toes are only stumps of bone.

Camel
Camels walk on the third and fourth toes of each foot. The other toes have disappeared.

• GRAZERS AND BROWSERS •

Hoofed Mammals

About 100 million years ago, when plant-eating mammals began to take advantage of open grasslands, they found that the only way they could escape predators was to run. Because it was easier to run on their toes than with a flatter foot, their claws gradually turned into hard hooves, and toes that were not needed for support disappeared or became smaller. Today, there are about 210 species of ungulate, or hoofed mammal, divided into three groups. The primitive ungulates—the elephants, the aardvark, the hyraxes, and the manatees and dugongs (both of which have evolved to live entirely in water)—still have most of their toes. The perissodactyls, or odd-toed ungulates, have three toes (tapirs and rhinos) or one toe (horses and their relatives) on each foot. The artiodactyls, or even-toed ungulates, have two toes (pigs, hippos and camels) or four toes (deer, cattle, sheep, goats, antelopes and giraffes).

DID YOU KNOW?
Camels do not walk on their hooves at all. They actually use their footpads, which give them a good grip on the ground. Their large toes help to prevent them from sinking into the sand.

DIGESTIVE SYSTEM

Some hoofed mammals, such as camels, sheep and deer, have complex stomachs (colored green in top diagram) in which they process food. Many can regurgitate the partially processed food from the rumen to the mouth, where they break it down even more with their specialized grinding teeth. This is called "chewing the cud." This food is swallowed again and passes on to the omasum, where nutrients can be absorbed. The animals process food very thoroughly so they can make maximum use of the nutrients it contains. Horses, rhinos and elephants have a simple stomach where they break down their food. They then process it in a very large caecum. They eat large amounts of food, which is often of a poor quality, to get the nutrients they need.

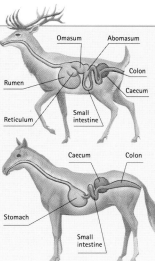

Omasum
Abomasum
Colon
Rumen
Caecum
Small intestine
Reticulum

Caecum
Colon
Stomach
Small intestine

LOUNGING HIPPOS

Hippopotamuses are even-toed ungulates, with four large toes on each foot. Their long, broad toes allow them to walk on the bottom of lakes and swamps as well as on land.

Reindeer
Reindeer have four toes, which can spread to provide support on soft snow.

White rhinoceros
White rhinos have three toes on the front foot. The first and fifth toes have disappeared.

213

Elephants

The first elephants were pig-sized creatures without tusks or trunks that lived in northern Africa about 50 million years ago. Today there are only two species of elephant: the Indian elephant and the African elephant–the largest mammal living on land. Both species live in family groups, which sometimes join to form herds of hundreds of animals. Elephants spend up to 21 hours a day eating as much as 700 lb (320 kg) of leaves, bark, fruit and grass, or traveling in search of food and water. An adult elephant needs to drink 15–20 gallons (70–90 liters) of water a day. Elephants travel through forests on traditional paths called elephants' roads. These intelligent animals have good memories and can live for more than 60 years. Both Indian and African elephants are endangered because humans take over their habitats for farming and poachers kill them for their tusks.

HEAT AND DUST
Elephants stay cool by spending several hours each day in water, or by sucking water into their trunks and spraying it over their bodies. They also coat themselves with mud and dust to protect their skins from sunburn and to keep insects away.

BEAST OF BURDEN
Indian elephants are strong and calm. People have used them to carry logs, cattle, food—even soldiers into battle—for thousands of years.

SPOT THE DIFFERENCES

African elephants grow to 13 ft (4 m) high at the shoulder, have large ears and a sloping forehead, and their hips are as high as their shoulders. They have three toes on each hind foot, and two "fingers" at the end of the trunk.

Indian elephants grow to 10 ft (3.2 m) high at the shoulder, have small ears, a domed forehead and a sloping back. They have four toes on each hind foot, and only one "finger" at the end of the trunk.

FAMILY LIFE

Elephants are very social animals. They communicate by trumpeting and by making sounds that are too low for humans to hear. Family groups are led by an old, experienced female. She passes on what she has learned to younger elephants. When male elephants are between 10 and 15 years old, they join an all-male group. They come near the females only during the mating season.

NOSE WRESTLING
In the mating season, male elephants wrestle each other with their trunks and tusks to decide which elephants will mate with the females.

GROWING ANTLERS

Early spring
Covered in soft skin called velvet, the antlers bud from beneath the fur of the deer's head.

Late summer
Nourished by blood vessels inside the velvet, the antlers grow to their full extent. New points, or tines, are added every year or so.

Autumn
The velvet dries and is rubbed off against rocks and tree trunks. The deer uses its shiny antlers to let other males know it is ready to fight for control of the herd.

Winter
After the mating season, the antlers become brittle at the base, and are easily knocked off against trees.

Deer and Cattle

Deer and cattle live in most parts of the world, from the Arctic tundra to Southeast Asian rainforests. They range in size from the cat-sized pudu to the North American moose, which can reach more than 7 ft (2 m) at the shoulder. All deer and cattle are herbivores and most eat grasses, leaves and fruit, although caribou eat lichen and moss. There are 38 species of deer, and 128 species of cattle, including sheep, goats, buffalo and the pronghorn antelope. Cattle evolved only about 23 million years ago and have very efficient digestive systems. Many species of cattle have been domesticated. Cattle, sheep and goats have horns that grow throughout their lives. Although the water deer of Asia has tusks, most male deer have antlers that are shed each winter and grow again in spring. They range from simple spikes to racks with many branches. Males fight with their antlers, and the strongest wins control of the herd.

A CLOSED CIRCLE
Musk oxen, which live in the Arctic, are related to goats. When threatened by predators such as wolves, the adults form a protective circle around the calves.

RUNNING FROM DANGER
The Indian nilgai is a medium-sized antelope with short horns. Nilgai rely on speed to escape predators such as leopards and tigers.

SMALLEST OF ALL
The pudu of southern Chile (below) is the world's smallest deer. It weighs 13–15 lb (6–7 kg). The mouse "deer" is smaller, but it is related to antelopes and is not a true deer.

LOCKING IN TO WIN
The antlers of all deer are designed so that they rarely become accidentally entangled. Male caribou lock antlers, then push to see which is stronger. The winner mates with the females of the herd, while the loser waits for another chance to prove its strength.

ODD ONE OUT
Scientists have traditionally put the North American pronghorn into a family of its own because it has many peculiar characteristics. Like cattle, it has horns, not antlers; but like deer, it sheds the outer layer of its horns each year. Today, many scientists include the pronghorn in the family that contains cattle, sheep and goats.

DESERT DWELLERS

Gerbils live in the deserts of Africa and Asia. They belong to the mouse family, which is the largest mammal family. These small, nocturnal seed eaters are well adapted to desert life. They get all the water they need from their food and never need to drink.

BEAVERS AT WORK

There are two species of beaver—one in Europe and one in North America. Both species eat bark and leaves and live in water. Beavers protect their large nests, called lodges, by damming streams to form ponds that predators cannot cross.

Rodents

More than a third of all the world's mammals are rodents. From the pygmy jerboa, which could fit into a matchbox, to the capybara, which grows to 4 ft (1.25 m) long and weighs 110 lb (50 kg), rodents live in almost every environment, from the Arctic to the desert. Some species spend almost all their lives in trees, while others live underground. Several species, including beavers, spend much of their time in water. Rodents have many predators. Few species apart from porcupines can defend themselves, and most produce large numbers of young to ensure the survival of their species. Rodents' incisor, or front, teeth grow constantly, ready to gnaw into hard-shell nuts, tree bark or other plant food. Some rodents eat insects and other small animals as well as plants. Others have special diets—bamboo rats, for example, feed almost exclusively on bamboo.

...STE TREAT

...rvest mice eat grain and seeds and ...ild their nests in long grass or fields ...wheat. People in ancient Rome and ...China once cooked and ate harvest ...ce as snacks!

CITIES ON THE PLAIN

Black-tailed prairie dogs, a type of rodent, live on the treeless plains of western North America. They hide from predators and protect each other in "towns." These huge complexes of burrows can cover 75 acres (30 hectares) and house more than 1,000 animals. Each burrow is occupied by a family—a male, three females and about six young. One of the adults stands guard at the mouth of the burrow to warn the others if a predator such as a coyote, fox or hawk approaches.

TYPES OF RODENT

There are many species of rodent, but they look fairly similar. Their behaviour and habits, however, vary greatly.

Capybara

Lemming

Black rat

Crested porcupine

ESCAPE PLAN
A hare's long hind legs give it the speed to avoid predators and the ability to change direction to confuse a hunter such as a hawk, which cannot make sudden twists and turns as quickly.

• BURROWERS AND CHEWERS •

Rabbits and Hares

Rabbits, hares and pikas are called lagomorphs. The 65 or so species of lagomorph live in most environments in Africa, Europe, Asia and the Americas, but they have also been introduced to other parts of the world by humans. They are similar to rodents, but are also different enough for scientists to place them in a separate order. Unlike rodents, lagomorphs have hair on the soles of their feet, but do not have sweat glands. Like rodents, however, lagomorphs' eyes are set at the side of their heads so they can see predators approaching from above and behind, and their gnawing incisor teeth keep growing. Pikas live in deserts and mountain areas in Asia and North America. They have small ears and look a little like large lemmings. Rabbits and hares, however, have long ears, long front legs and very long hind legs, which they use to run and hop. All lagomorphs eat plants, and most emerge from their nests at sunset to feed.

BIG EARS
The black-tailed jack rabbit lives in North American deserts. Its lar ears contain hundreds of tiny blo vessels that radiate heat and help the rabbit keep cool during th day. Such big ears also help it hear predators approaching.

220

PIKAS

Pikas are short-legged relatives of rabbits and hares. They collect large amounts of green plant material in summer and dry it in the sun to make hay. They store the hay in their burrows to provide food through the long winter.

FIGHTING FIT

Arctic hares breed in spring. Males and females chase each other and have boxing matches. This gives each hare a chance to see how healthy and strong its potential mate is.

POPULATION EXPLOSION

Lagomorphs are preyed on by many predators. Like rodents, they give birth to many young so that at least some will survive to breed. European rabbits were introduced into Australia in 1788, but they did not begin to spread until 24 wild rabbits were brought to the country in 1859. Within 10 years there were at least 10 million rabbits, and they have plagued Australia ever since.

THE FAMILY BURROW

European rabbits first evolved in northern Africa. They live in burrows called warrens, which protect them from the weather and predators. Female European rabbits give birth to several young up to six times a year. They keep them warm in grass-lined chambers.

BOTTLENOSE DOLPHIN
This dolphin is a fast swimmer. It has up to 160 small, pointed teeth and feeds on small fish, eels and squid.

MINKE WHALE
The minke whale has 230–360 baleen plates each 8 in (20 cm) long in its upper jaw. It feeds on herring, cod, squid and krill.

SOUTHERN RIGHT WHALE
Named because it was considered "right" for hunting, this whale has 500 baleen plates in its upper jaw. It feeds on krill.

SPERM WHALE
Largest of the toothed whales, sperm whale has up to 50 teeth the lower jaw only. It feeds on squid and octopuses.

• MAMMALS OF THE SEA •

Whales and Dolphins

Today's whales and dolphins, which include the biggest mammal that has ever lived—the blue whale—evolved from ungulates (hoofed mammals) about 65 million years ago. Whales, dolphins and porpoises are now perfectly adapted to life in the sea. They have sleek, streamlined bodies and a flattened tail that propels them through the water. Like all mammals, they feed their young on milk. Whales come to the surface to breathe air through a nostril—called a blowhole—on the top of their heads. There are 63 species of toothed whale, which range from the 59-ft (18-m) long sperm whale to 5-ft (1.6-m) long dolphins and porpoises. They feed on squid, fish and octopuses and, like bats, use echolocation to navigate and to find their prey. Some migrate long distances. Baleen whales have no teeth. They use long, hairlike sieves called baleen to strain their food (mainly small fish and shrimp called krill) out of the water. The 11 species of baleen whale roam the world's oceans and migrate when the seasons change.

SPEEDY SWIMMERS
There are 31 species of dolphin. Their fishlike shape, smooth skin and flattened tails mean they can swim at high speed without using much energy. Some dolphins have been recorded swimming at 25 miles (40 km) per hour for several hours.

KILLER WHALES

Orcas, or killer whales, are the largest and most intelligent dolphins. Like wolves and lions, they hunt their prey together. An orca, for example, sometimes frightens seals by coming right up onto the beach. The startled seals try to escape into the sea, where other orcas are waiting to catch them.

WHALE TALES

The blue whale grows to 96 ft (29.4 m) long and can weigh 98 tons (100 tonnes). Its mouth is 19 ft (6 m) long, and its heart, which is the size of a small car, pumps 9.5 tons (9.7 tonnes) of blood around its huge body.

Sperm whales have the largest brain of any animal. It is about six times heavier than the average adult human brain. Sperm whales are deep divers and can dive more than 5,000 ft (1,500 m) beneath the ocean's surface.

The narwhal, which lives in Arctic waters, grows to 15 ft (4.5 m) in length. The male has one tusk (and rarely, two) up to 8 ft (2.5 m) long, growing forwards from its snout.

Humpback whales "sing" long, complicated songs that can last for more than an hour and can be heard up to 750 miles (1,200 km) away. Scientists believe humpback whales sing to let other humpbacks know where they are and whether they are males or females.

Humpback whale tail

Q: What is the largest toothed whale?

• MAMMALS OF THE SEA •

Seals and Walruses

About 50 million years ago, mammals that resembled today's sea otters were amphibious: they lived both on land and in the water. Gradually, they began to spend more time in the sea. Their front and hind legs shortened and became flippers. They grew larger and developed a thick layer of fat to protect them from cold oceans. By 10 million years ago, they had evolved into pinnipeds: seals, sea lions and walruses. Today there are 14 species of sea lion, or eared seal, which have small but visible ears, and which can turn their hind flippers around to walk on land. There are also 19 species of "true" or earless seal, which cannot turn their hind flippers, and move like caterpillars on land; and one species of walrus. Pinnipeds are carnivores. They eat crabs, fish and squid. The leopard seal of Antarctic waters also hunts penguins, while walruses, which live in the Arctic, use their tusks to find shellfish and crabs. Pinnipeds breed on land in colonies that can number thousands of animals.

HALF THE SIZE
Male elephant seals, the largest of all seals, reach 20 ft
(6.1 m) in length and weigh 3.9 tons (4 tonnes). Female
elephant seals (above) are half the size of the males.

DID YOU KNOW?
A male walrus's tusks can
grow to 2 ft 3 in (68 cm)
long. Walruses use their tusks
to rake shellfish from mud in
shallow waters, to pull themselves
out of the water onto ice floes,
and to battle other males for
control of females.

SEA LION LIFE

Australian sea lions often hunt squid or fish together. Superbly adapted to life at sea, they can swim a month or so after being born. When they dive, their heartbeat slows from about 100 beats a minute to as low as 10 beats a minute.

DECEPTIVE LOOKS

Manatees (right) and dugongs may look similar to seals, but they are not related. In fact, their closest living relatives are elephants. These sea cows have a smooth, fat body shape and their flippers are similar to those of seals. Unlike seals, however, manatees and dugongs give birth in water, not on land.

BEACH CULTURE

Walruses are social animals that gather in colonies of up to 3,000 in the breeding season. A fully mature male walrus, which can reach 12 ft (3.65 m) in length, may have a harem of as many as 50 females.

Endangered Species

A t least 27 species of mammal have become extinct in the last 200 years, and more than 136 species are rare or endangered. Some species, such as snow leopards, tigers and other big cats, have become endangered because their skins are valuable. Others, such as wolves or cougars, have been killed because people think they are dangerous. The Hawaiian monk seal and several species of baleen whale have almost been wiped out for their fur or meat. Most endangered mammals are threatened because their habitats have been destroyed by logging, clearing or draining for farmland.

Golden lion tamarin

Northern hairy-nosed wombat

Black-footed ferret (North America)
The black-footed ferret (found from Canada to Texas) is endangered because agricultural practices, such as the poisoning of the prairie dog, have robbed the black-footed ferret of its main prey.

Hawaiian monk seal (Hawaii)
There are two or three species of monk seal. The Caribbean monk seal may already be extinct, and the Mediterranean

Hawaiian monk seal

monk seal is threatened by pollution. The Hawaiian monk seal is endangered because many thousands were slaughtered on their breeding grounds in the Hawaiian islands. The population of Hawaiian monk seal seems to be recovering, but so little is known about this species that we cannot be sure if it will survive.

Northern hairy-nosed wombat (Australia)
Living in dry, open country rather than forests, the northern hairy-nosed wombat was never as widespread as the common wombat. In fact, it was unknown until 1869. It was once found from southern New South Wales to central Queensland, but it disappeared shortly after European settlement. It is now found in eastern Queensland, which is only one small part of its former range.

Giant panda (East Asia)
Giant pandas have always been uncommon because they do not breed very often. The species has become endangered in the twentieth century because they are hunted for their skins and meat, and their habitat is destroyed for farming. Many pandas starve when the bamboo on which they depend flowers and dies every 50 to 100 years.

Wisent (Europe)
Standing 7 ft (2 m) at the shoulder, the wisent, or European bison, is Europe's largest mammal. The species became extinct in the wild when the last

animals were killed in eastern Europe in the 1920s. Some survived in captivi[ty] however, and animals from captive her[ds] have since been successfully reintrodu[ced] into the wild.

Golden lion tamarin (South America)
Five of the 19 species of tamarin monkey, all of which live in tropical Central and South America, are endangered. As some species became popular as pets, thousands were trappe[d] and shipped to other countries—a voya[ge] that killed most of them. The golden li[on] tamarin, however, is endangered becau[se] its forest habitat is being logged and cleared for farmland.

Northern right whale
The northern right whale, the rarest of the baleen whales, was almost extinct in European waters by 1700. By 1785, a North American right whale hunting company had closed down because there were not enough northern right whales left to hunt. Even today there are probably only a few thousand righ[t] whales in the world.

Orders of Mammals

Monotremata
Monotremes are reptile-like mammals that live in Australia and New Guinea. There are three species of monotreme: the platypus, the short-beaked echidna and the long-beaked echidna.

Marsupialia
Marsupials, or pouched mammals, live in North and South America, Australia and New Guinea. There are about 280 species, from opossums to koalas and kangaroos.

Xenarthra or Edentata
There are 29 species of anteater, sloth and armadillo. They eat leaves or insects and are found in Central and South America.

Pholidota
The seven species of pangolin (scaly anteater) live in Africa and Southeast Asia. They are all protected by hard, scaly skin.

Insectivora
There are 365 species of insectivore, including tiny shrews, moles and rat-sized hedgehogs. Insectivores are on all continents except Australia and Antarctica.

Macroscelidea
The 15 species of insect-eating elephant shrew, which spend almost all their time on the ground, are found only in Africa.

Scandentia
The 16 species of tree shrew, which live only in Asia, are insect eaters that have features in common with primates as well as insectivores. Only one of the species is nocturnal. The rest feed during the day and night.

Dermoptera
The two species of colugo (flying lemur) both live in Southeast Asia. Their name is misleading because they are not lemurs and they glide, not fly, from tree to tree.

Chiroptera
This is the second largest order of mammals. There are 977 species of bat, with wingspans ranging from 4 in (10 cm) to 5 ft (1.5 m).

Fruit bat

Primates
Most of the 201 species of primate are monkeys, tarsiers and tree-dwelling prosimians, such as lemurs. The apes are the largest of the primates.

Carnivora
Meat-eating or carnivorous mammals are found on almost every continent. There are 269 species, including 34 species of seal, sea lion and walrus.

Tubulidentata
This order has only one species: the short-legged, long-nosed aardvark. This pig-sized anteater is found only in Africa, south of the Sahara Desert.

Sirenia
The four species of manatee and dugong are found in the warm, shallow waters of the western Pacific and Indian oceans; in North, Central and South America; and in the rivers of West Africa.

Hyracoidea
There are eight species of rabbit-like hyrax. They live in Africa and the Middle East and share some features with elephants.

Proboscidea
There are only two species of the largest living land mammals—the elephant. One lives in Africa, the other is in Asia.

Perissodactyla
The 16 species of horse, tapir and rhino—the odd-toed ungulates—are native to Africa, Asia and South America.

Artiodactyla
There are 194 species of even-toed ungulate, including pigs, deer, camels, hippos, antelopes, giraffes, sheep, goats and cattle. They are native to every continent except Australia and Antarctica.

Cetacea
The 77 species of whale, dolphin and porpoise are found in all the world's seas. There are also five freshwater species of dolphin.

Lagomorpha
There are 65 species of rabbit and hare. They are native to Africa, Europe, Asia and North and South America. They were introduced into Australia and the Pacific islands.

Rodentia
This is the largest order of mammals, with 1,793 species. They are found all over the world except Antarctica.

Note: We have divided mammals into 20 orders. Some scientists believe there are only 16 orders of mammals, while others say there are as many as 23 orders. This is because taxonomy, which is the study of classifying animals, changes as scientists learn more about mammals and how they are related to each other.

African buffalo

227

Dangerous

How long can a crocodile survive without a meal?

How does a snake swallow a pig or an antelope?

Do vampire bats really exist?

Animals

Contents

Death adder

Why Are Animals Dangerous?

The world is full of dangerous animals with powerful weapons for capturing prey and fighting off predators. A hunting tiger can kill with just one bite to the neck. A rhinoceros can spear a soft belly with its horn. Even a tiny spider can kill with venom-filled fangs. Animals' weapons are complex and varied. Teeth and claws, horns and hooves, fangs and stingers, spurs and spines, poisons and venoms, speed and stealth are all used to eat and avoid being eaten. Dangerous animals, such as snakes, seldom single out people as prey. People usually become victims when they scare or threaten an animal. Mosquitoes, ticks and flies, which cause disease and death, are very dangerous to people. But the most dangerous creatures of all are people.

TAIL STING
A scorpion's stinger injects predators or prey with powerful venom.

Did You Know?
Beware a black spider with red markings. This could be the female black widow, one of the most feared spiders in the world. A bite from this ferocious creature can cause dreadful pain, dizziness and death.

SEEING CLEARLY
Good eyesight helps predators such as lions and eagles to find prey. Other animals, such as sharks and bears, have poor vision. They can mistake people for their natural prey.

232

DEATH TRAPS
Birds of prey use powerful, sharp-edged beaks to kill their victims.

Barracuda

FATAL FUNNEL–WEB
A bite from the toxic fangs of Australia's funnel-web spider can be fatal, especially for children.

BULLDOG ANTS
Bulldog ants use their knife-edged biting jaws and venom-filled stingers to kill prey and scare off predators.

HORNS OF POWER
Plant-eating mammals, such as rhinoceroses and deer, use their horns and antlers to spear, stab and gore predators that threaten to make a meal of them. The males fight furiously with these weapons in battles over females.

A REAL MOUTHFUL
With up to 32 teeth in the upper jaw and 40 in the lower, a crocodile has the edge on most prey. Few animals can escape their fate if they are caught in a crocodile's teeth and jaws.

IPPERS
bear's claws can tear part almost anything its path.

Male narwhals have an overgrown
left incisor tooth. It can reach 10 ft
(3 m) in a narwhal that is 16½ ft
(5 m) long. Scientists believe
that male narwhals use these bizarre
spiral tusks to fence for females.

Bone

Bone that is shed

Tooth/enamel

Keratin

Bongo

White-tailed deer

Walrus

Black rhinoceros

SKIN AND BONE

Tusks, horns and antlers are made of different things.
Walrus and elephant tusks are actually overgrown
teeth. Bongo, cow and gazelle horns are bone, covered
with hard skin called keratin. Rhinoceros horns are
also made of keratin. Like all skin, they will grow back
if worn down or cut off. The bone of deer, elk and
moose antlers is covered with soft skin, called velvet,
which falls off when the antlers reach full size. Horns
are permanent, but antlers are temporary.

• TUSKS, HORNS AND ANTLERS •

Tusks, Horns and Antlers

Tusks, horns and antlers are very different structures,
but they are used for similar purposes by the mammals
that possess them. Males use these weapons in battles
with other males over females, in disputes over territory or
to assert their dominance in a group. Tusks, horns and
antlers are symbols of a male's age, strength and status, and
they can also help to prevent physical combat. A male with
long tusks or elaborate antlers can beat a male with lesser
weapons without exchanging a single blow; the weaker
male knows it would be foolish to fight. In many species,
only males grow tusks, horns and antlers. In others, females
have smaller ones than males. But any male or female
mammal with these weapons is potentially dangerous. If the
animal uses them on a threatening predator, or a person,
they can cause death.

234

CURIOUS CREATURE

The legend of the unicorn, a mystical creature with the body of a horse and a single, long horn on its head, probably came from exaggerated descriptions of rhinoceroses. In the past, people thought that unicorns had magical abilities. They believed that if they drank from a cup made of "unicorn" horn (probably acquired from a narwhal or a rhinoceros), they would be protected against poisoned liquids.

CLASHING ANTLERS

During the mating season, rival male moose have contests to find out which is the stronger. They will confront each other, nose to nose. If one does not retreat, they will bellow out challenges, then lock their antlers in a battle of strength and endurance. Straining every muscle to outpush each other, they will clash head-on. Usually the weaker one will turn away, but sometimes they will fight to the death. The winner mates with a moose cow and stays with her for several days.

Moose antlers

One year

Four years

Eight years

SYMBOLS OF GROWING STATUS

Each year, a moose loses its antlers and grows more. The antlers become bigger and heavier as the moose gets older. Antlers are signs of a male's status and dominance in contests for food and females.

235

Elephants and Hippopotamuses

AFRICAN ELEPHANT
African elephants have very large ears, which they flap when they w to cool down. They often wallow i thick mud, which protects their sk from the sun and insects.

A frican and Asian elephants and the African hippo are three of the largest land animals. Imagine the combined weights of 90 ten-year-old children. This would equal the weight of one hippo. If you added another 100 children, this would be the weight of an African elephant. The huge size of these animals means that they eat enormous amounts of vegetation. Hippos live mostly in the water, but they feed on grass at night, clipping it with their thick lips to leave what looks like a mowed lawn. Elephants feed on grass, leaves and fruit, sometimes using their tusks to fell trees and uproot shrubs. Male elephants and hippos will fight and defend themselves with their tusks. Predators rarely take on adult elephants or hippos, but lions or tigers may threaten the babies of these animals. Female elephants and hippos will slash or stab menacing predators with their tusks.

ASIAN ELEPHANT
An Asian elephant is smaller than an African elephant, and its back, forehead, belly, teeth and trunk are a different shape.

Pulp cavity
The tusk has a pulp cavity
that contains nerve endings.
These make the tusk sensitive
to pressure.

Cavity
An elephant's skull is honeycombed
with numerous air cells and hollow
cavities that make it lighter.

Tusk
This diamond-shaped pattern
is found only in the ivory
tusks of elephants.

Trunk
An elephant's trunk
is strong enough to
uproot trees and
sensitive enough at
the tip to pick up a
small coin.

LEARNING THE ROPES

An elephant is pregnant for about 22 months and
usually gives birth to one baby, called a calf. A calf and
its mother live in a close family group, made up of related
female elephants and their children. The group is led by the
oldest female. During an elephant's long childhood, it is protected
and taught how to survive by the other elephants. Young male
elephants leave the group when they are about 14 years old.

TOOTH AND JAW

Male hippos often fight viciously to protect
food and to control breeding females. Males
open their mouths as wide as they can and
clash their lower jaws together. They lock
their upper incisor teeth and push each
other for as long as an hour and a half—
bellowing all the while.

Discover more in Dangerous People

• TUSKS, HORNS AND ANTLERS •

Rhinoceroses and Wild Cattle

Wild cattle, such as buffalo and bison, are related to domestic cows, and rhinos are related to horses. Unlike their relatives, however, rhinos and wild cattle are big and aggressive, and armed with formidable horns. There are five species of rhino: three live in tropical Asia and two in Africa. The several kinds of wild cattle can be found in Asia, Africa, North America and Europe. Wild cattle eat grass, while rhinos live on a mixed vegetarian diet of grass, leaves and fruit. Rhinos and wild cattle usually defend themselves by attacking. Faced with a predator— they charge. Competing males may also charge each other before sparring with their horns. These large mammals are more than a match for predators— except for well-armed people, who have greatly reduced the number of these animals wherever they are found.

ANCIENT ANIMAL ART
The earliest human art showed animals that our ancestors feared, admired or hunted. Wild cattle are the subjects of many ancient paintings. This cave painting of a rhino and a bison was found in Lascaux, France, in an area of the cave called "Shaft of the Dead Man"

THE SIZE OF IT
Asian gaurs and wood bison are bigger than Sumatran rhinos, After elephants, white rhinos are the largest living mammals.

A HORNED DILEMMA
A rhino's horns are very valuable. Female rhinos protect their young from predators with their horns. (A spotted hyena has no chance against this charging rhino.) But rhinos are also killed by poachers for their horns. Scientists dehorned some female black rhinos to see if this would stop poachers from killing them. But the scientists found that without their horns, the rhinos could not defend their babies.

Gaur

Wood bison

White rhino

Sumatran rhino

DID YOU KNOW?

In Greek legends, the Minotaur was a half-man, half-bull monster, which lived in a maze that belonged to the King of Crete. Every year, the king sent 14 young men and women into the maze to be devoured by the bloodthirsty Minotaur. The Greek hero Theseus killed the ferocious creature.

RAGING BULLS

The Spanish city of Pamplona is famed for its bull fights. Each year, the fiesta of San Fermin is celebrated with a "running of the bulls". Thousands of cheering residents and tourists watch people sprint through the city's narrow streets, chased by charging bulls.

Teeth, Jaws and Beaks

Many dangerous vertebrates use teeth to catch, kill and eat prey. Teeth come in different shapes and sizes for different jobs. The razor-sharp teeth of a barracuda can tear hunks of flesh from fish. A crocodile's sharp, curved teeth both grasp and tear. Fish and crocodiles have just one kind of teeth, but mammals such as lions have several kinds. A lion's long canine teeth stab and hold like knives. Its scissor-like molars grip and rip chunks of flesh; incisors with serrated edges like a steak knife shear the last bits of meat from bones. Birds have no teeth at all. Instead, the beaks of some birds come in different shapes and sizes to spear, grip, bite, crush or tear flesh from prey. The power of teeth or beaks depends on the shape and size of an animal's jaws, and how the muscles attach the lower jaw to the rest of the skull.

DID YOU KNOW?

The crocodile has been feared and worshipped for centuries. The ancient Egyptians believed that the crocodile was Sebek, the god of the Nile. Children often wore necklaces of crocodile teeth to protect them from harm.

CONSPICUOUS CANINES

The sabertooth cat, which is now extinct, had extraordinary teeth. The sabertooth's skull was about the same size as that of a lion, but its impressive canines were more than twice as long as a lion's teeth. However, these long curved teeth with sharp serrated edges were not very strong and broke easily. Lions use their canines to crush neck bones or strangle prey. Sabertooth cats stabbed their prey's soft fleshy areas, such as the abdomen, with their unusual canines, before tearing out the inner organs.

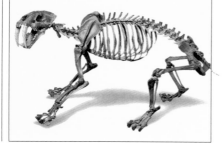

SLIP, SLIDING AWAY
Mergansers are a type of duck. They are sometimes called sawbills because they have unusual long, thin beaks with sharp jagged edges. Mergansers capture and hold onto small slippery fish with their sawlike "teeth." Then they swallow the fish whole, rather than chewing it.

MIXED DIET

...ear has relatively short canines, which it uses
...catch and kill prey. Its flattened upper and
...wer molars, however, show that the
...ar is not a strict meat eater. It
...es its grinding molars to
...ed and break down the
...nts, nuts and berries
...at form a large part
...its diet.

CUTTING TEETH

A crocodile can puncture, grip and crush prey with its many
teeth, but it cannot chew with them. Crocodile teeth do not
have strong roots and they come out easily with wear. Luckily,
for the crocodile anyway, it continually
replaces old teeth with new.

HIGH-SPEED CHASE

Barracudas use rapid charges and daggerlike
teeth to capture all kinds of fish. Sometimes they
herd schools of fish to make them easier to
catch. The largest of the barracudas lives in the
western Atlantic and can grow to be as long as
an adult man.

241

A NUTRITIOUS MEAL
A grizzly bear uses its sharp claws and teeth to eat a tasty meal of salmon from the river.

FLYING FISHER
An osprey is the envy of any fisher: it can catch a fish in nine out of every ten attempts. A hunting osprey flies in a figure eight, high above the water. When it spies a fish, such as a mullet, it plunges feet first to grab the fish out of the water. Spiny growths on the back of its strong toes help the osprey keep its grip on the slippery fish while it carries the prey off to a perch to be eaten.

• TEETH AND CLAWS •

Feet, Claws and Talons

Dangerous animals use their claws, talons and feet to capture prey. Claws and talons are stronger, sharper versions of the nails that protect the tips of your fingers and toes. Some mammals, such as jaguars, use long, sharp claws to grab and hold prey before killing it with their teeth. Polar bears seize seals in their clawed forefeet, while grizzly bears snare salmon with theirs. Sturdy claws are also useful for climbing trees, digging up roots and slashing a predator or rival. Some birds rely on their feet and talons to get food. Osprey plunge from the sky, grabbing a fish with their strong feet and piercing it with their talons. Peregrine falcons swat birds with their powerful feet, then catch the stunned creatures in mid-air.

SWITCHBLADES

Cats depend on claws to catch their prey. A claw works like a switchblade. The blade's usual position is folded into a knifecase, but it springs out with a flick of a wrist. In the same way, a cat's claws usually remain retracted (pulled in), protected in sheaths of skin. They emerge from their sheaths only when the cat needs them.

CLAWS IN
In the retracted, or usual, state the elastic spring ligament is contracted and the controlling muscles are relaxed.

CLAWS OUT
When the muscles contract, the ligament stretches and the claw springs out, ready for action.

DID YOU KNOW?

The powerful owl hunts prey at night. Sometimes it holds any remains of the prey in its talons all day, and finishes it off as a snack before the night's hunt.

Sea eagle

Brown goshawk

Sparrowhawk

FINELY TUNED TALONS

A raptor's talons and toes match its prey. Sea eagles have long, sharply curved talons and sturdy toes, which help them to capture large, slippery fish in one foot. A brown goshawk's talons and toes grab squirrel-sized prey. The sparrowhawk's slender toes and needle-sharp talons are designed to snare small birds.

Discover more in Birds of Prey

243

Great Cats

All cats are good hunters. They have razor-sharp teeth, strong jaws, piercing claws and supple bodies. But only lions, tigers, jaguars, leopards, pumas, snow leopards and cheetahs can be called "great cats." These large, powerful beasts prey on animals such as deer and antelope. Occasionally, great cats, such as tigers, lions and leopards, will prey deliberately on humans. Only cheetahs and snow leopards have never reportedly killed humans, although both could easily do so. It is, however, more usual for a great cat to attack people when it is too sick, old, or maimed to capture its normal prey, or when this prey is scarce. We may fear great cats, but they have much to fear from us. Some people hunt them illegally for their skins, while others turn their wild habitats into farms and logged forests. All seven species of great cats are endangered.

FAST FOOD
A lioness slowly and silently approaches a Thompson's gazelle. With an incredible burst of speed, she closes the gap between herself and the gazelle, grabs the frightened animal in her paws and kills it with a piercing bite to the neck. Other lionesses and lions will soon join her in devouring the carcass.

IN FOR THE KILL
Most great cats kill their prey by biting into the back of the neck with their canine teeth to cut the prey's spinal cord. But to kill very large animals, such as buffalo, lions and other great cats squeeze the prey by the throat until it suffocates. The lion's large paws and sharp claws help drag the animal to the ground.

SPOTTED SPEED
Cheetahs outclass all other land animals for short-distance sprinting. A spring-like spine coils and uncoils to help them speed along at 70 miles (110 km) per hour. The cheetah's long, streaming tail acts as a steering rudder.

DID YOU KNOW?

In the past, many people thought that eating the meat of a lion would give them courage. In paintings and books, the lion often stands for power and strength. The Cowardly Lion in the story *The Wizard of Oz* believes he has no courage. He asks the Wizard of the Emerald City to make him brave.

GUARANTEEING THE FUTURE

Big-game hunters killed thousands of tigers for "sport" until laws passed in the 1970s banned tiger hunting for profit or sport. But the 5,000 or so tigers left in the wild are still hunted and poached illegally. Unless this stops, tigers may become extinct in the next 20 years.

A RARE SIGHT
Pumas are large and strong, but very shy. They live and hunt alone, and capture all kinds of prey— from deer and elk to ground squirrels, mice and even grasshoppers, if big game is scarce. Pumas avoid people and very rarely attack them.

Discover more in Size, Strength and Speed

Wolves and Wild Dogs

Wolves travel widely to find prey such as deer and moose. When they sight a victim, they slowly sneak up on it, until, sensing danger, the prey flees. The wolves then rush to attack. Using 42 deadly teeth in their powerful jaws, some wolves bite the prey's rump to slow it down. One wolf, usually the pack leader, darts forward to seize its nose. Others nip and rip its flanks, neck and throat. Within minutes, the prey has been bitten to death and the wolves are tearing into their dinner. Although the wolves cooperate to make the kill, it is every wolf for itself when it comes to eating it. Many of the 35 species of wolves and their wild dog relatives live in groups and hunt large prey together. These groups may number 20 wild dogs, able to take down a zebra, or be as small as a pair of foxes, which often hunt for small prey, such as rabbits and rodents.

THE HUNTER AND THE HUNTED
A maned wolf roams the grassy pampas of Brazil. These long-legged animals can cover long distances, hunting rodents, rabbits and birds. Some people believe that parts of the maned wolf's body, such as the eye, are lucky. As a result, many have been killed, and they are now an endangered species.

TALKING TAILS

If a dog is afraid, it will walk with its tail between its legs. In the same way, a wolf uses its tail to tell other wolves about its moods and intentions.

NO PROBLEM
This is the tail of a relaxed wolf or dog. Wolves that are eating or just looking around casually will hold their tails loosely, and their fur will be slightly fluffed.

NO THREAT
A wolf holding its tail close to its body, with the tip curved back and the fur flattened, is saying, "I'm no threat." It may be approaching a dominant wolf, perhaps to beg for food.

FEARFUL
When a wolf is afraid, its tail touches its belly. A wolf holds its tail like this when it loses a serious fight with a dominant wolf.

BACK OFF
With its tail held high and the fur fluffed out to make it look bigger, this wolf is saying, "I can beat you, so you had better back off."

ATTACK
If you see a wolf or an unfriendly dog holding its tail straight out behind it, think about how to escape— quickly! This animal plans to attack.

HOWL AWAY
At close range, wolves communicate with whimpers, growls, barks and squeaks. But howling can capture the attention of wolves far and wide. When all pack members join in an echoing chorus, they can be heard as far as 6 miles (10 km) away. Group howling sends a message to neighboring packs: stay away, or come prepared to fight. Wolves also howl to locate pack members that have lost one another during a long chase after prey. Once reunited, they howl in celebration.

Bears

What do you picture when you think of a bear? A giant panda, a fierce grizzly bear or maybe the honey-loving, storybook character, Winnie the Pooh? It probably depends on where you live. One or more of the eight species of bear lives among people in the ice of the Arctic; the temperate forests in Europe, Asia and North America; and tropical forests in Asia and South America. Bears are enormous creatures with heavy bodies, long, sharp claws and huge heads with long canine teeth. Polar bears use these weapons to kill seals, but other bears use them to dig up roots, strip bark, split bamboo and rip open beehives. These bears eat plants, insects, honey and meat, if they can catch it easily. Giant pandas live on bamboo, spectacled bears prefer fruits and nuts, and sloth bears eat termites. Bears use their teeth and claws to fight each other, to defend their young and sometimes to attack people who get in the way.

DOWN AND OUT
Using its keen sense of smell, a grizzly bear finds a marmot's underground home. It rips off the roof of the marmot's burrow with its claws and scoops out the exposed animal.

A BIRD'S EYE VIEW

A cinnamon-colored black bear snoozes in a treetop. When there are people around, black bears often sleep in places where it would be difficult for someone to creep up on them.

A TALE OF TWO FISHERS

Fishermen and grizzly bears are both attracted by abundant salmon. The catch can be shared peacefully if people follow the rules: do not get close and do not act in any surprising manner. Grizzly attacks usually occur when people startle a mother protecting her cubs, or when they "invite" the bears to dinner by keeping food in their camping tents.

DID YOU KNOW?

The teddy bear is named after Theodore "Ted" Roosevelt, the 26th President of the United States. He refused to shoot a black bear while on a hunting trip.

UP AND AWAY

American black bears are excellent tree climbers. They climb quickly, using their short, sturdy claws to keep a firm grip on the tree. When in danger, bear cubs scramble into the tree tops while their mother fights or flees alone. Later, she returns to fetch them. American black bears also climb into trees to reach food, such as honey from beehives.

WHITE KNIGHTS

Huge male polar bears fight viciously with their large, sharp claws and canine teeth when they compete for females during the breeding season. The loser of the battle is often killed.

• TEETH AND CLAWS •

Birds of Prey

If you see a bird with a hooked beak, big staring eyes and strong feet with sharp talons, you are looking at a bird of prey. These raptors live throughout the world, except in Antarctica. Size, diet and hunting style vary greatly among the 463 species. Robin-sized falconets catch flying insects. Crow-sized sparrowhawks snatch smaller birds off the branches of trees. Secretary birds the size of turkeys hunt for small mammals and snakes on the ground. Condors with wingspans as wide as the smallest airplane eat the meat of dead animals. South America's harpy eagle is one of the largest raptors. It can seize and carry off a monkey the size of a big house cat. Most raptors, such as falcons, hunt during the day, although owls hunt at night. Many birds of prey are strong and spectacular flyers. Golden eagles cover huge distances looking for food and swoop from great heights to attack unsuspecting prey on the ground.

IN HOT PURSUIT
Reaching flight speeds of 80 miles (128 km) per hour, this peregrine falcon will quickly overtake its pigeon prey. If it dives from high to capture a bird below, it can reach speeds of up to 178 miles (288 km) per hour!

NOWHERE TO RUN, NOWHERE TO HIDE

Huge harpy eagles hunt among the trees of the Amazon rainforest. Moving from tree to tree, they listen for the chatter of monkeys, and home in on their prey. A surprised howler monkey is no match for a harpy, which will snatch it up with feet as large as a man's hand.

READING THE MENU

Once or twice a day, most raptors regurgitate parts of their prey that they cannot digest. Scientists search avidly for these pellets, which reveal what a raptor has been eating. Fur in a pellet means mammals were on the raptor's menu, while feathers indicate birds, and scales say snakes. Often, scientists can pinpoint exactly which species of mammal, bird or snake the raptor ate, and how many were included on the menu!

Bones   Claws

Bird pellet

251

Crocodiles and Alligators

Resembling a log lying in the murky, shallow water, a crocodile will wait for an antelope to come for a drink. Only its eyes, ears and nose are out of the water, so it can see, hear and smell a thirsty animal nearing the shore. In a sudden lunge, the crocodile will vault out of the water and seize an antelope's muzzle in its clamping and gripping teeth. The crocodile will then flip or drag the antelope underwater and drown it. Stealth, speed and a snout full of sharp teeth are the weapons of the 22 species of crocodiles, alligators, caimans and gharial that live in tropical and subtropical lakes, rivers and sea coasts. These reptiles range from the length of a bike to as long as a limousine, but all are fierce meat eaters. They prey on any creature they can catch, from small fish to mammals as big as buffalo—and people of all sizes.

TELLING TEETH
Is it an alligator or a crocodile? You can tell the difference by looking at its teeth, but from a distance! Luckily, you do not have to peer too closely to see that an alligator's lower teeth cannot be seen when its mouth is closed. Its lower teeth fit into pits in the upper jaw. In a closed-mouthed crocodile, however, one lower tooth on each side slips into a notch on the outside of the upper jaw.

Alligator
Lower teeth hidden

Crocodile
Lower teeth showing

Alligator

DID YOU KNOW?
Female crocodiles and alligators bury their leathery eggs on land, then guard the nest constantly for 70 to 90 days. When they hear their babies crying, they uncover the eggs and crack the shells gently to help free them.

A WILDEBEEST WORTH PURSUING
A huge Nile crocodile chases a wildebeest. It will provide the crocodile with more meat than it can eat in one meal.

WHAT'S IN A SNOUT?

The snout's width tells about a species' diet. Long, slender snouts are fragile but snap quickly to catch fish. They are useful for poking into burrows to find crabs. Shorter, wider snouts can catch fish and larger mammals.

Gharial

African slender-snouted crocodile

Caiman

Dwarf crocodile

Crocodile

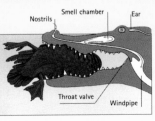

THE LIVING SUBMARINE

If a crocodile is up to its eyes in water and has a mouth full of food, how does it breathe? By using its nostrils, which are on the tip of its snout. When the crocodile inhales, air flows through the nasal passage, and the smell chamber, to the windpipe. A throat valve, formed when a flap of skin at the back of the mouth meets one on the tongue, keeps water from entering the windpipe.

Nostrils
Smell chamber
Ear
Throat valve
Windpipe

ENERGY SAVERS

Crocodiles and alligators are lazy predators. They lie still, mostly submerged in shallow water, and wait for food to come to them. This energy-saving behavior and efficient digestion helps these animals to survive for months without a meal.

Discover more in Size, Strength and Speed

GREAT WHITE KILLER

The great white shark is the famous killer shark of the film *Jaws* and horror stories. Although its evil reputation is exaggerated, the great white shark may be the most dangerous predator of all to humans. Great whites prey mostly on seals and porpoises, but they do encounter people swimming in their hunting grounds. With their poor vision, they may see little difference between the size and sleek lines of a seal and a snorkeler.

• TEETH AND CLAWS •

Sharks

I magine splashing in the surf and suddenly seeing a grey fin slicing through the water towards you. One word comes to mind. Shark! With strong, slender bodies, sharks swim fast and lunge at prey even faster. They attack with a strong mouthful of sharp teeth, which they use to tear off chunks of their victim's flesh. The 350 species of sharks live in oceans throughout the world, from cold polar waters to tropical seas. But you are more likely to drown than see a shark, much less be attacked by one. Many sharks are small and eat fish, shellfish and clams. The biggest types, whale and basking sharks, eat tiny plants and animals called plankton. The most dangerous sharks, such as great whites and tiger sharks, hunt in shallow coastal waters. They may sometimes confuse human swimmers and divers with seals and porpoises, their natural prey.

Tiger shark
20 ft (6 m)

Blue shark
13 ft (4 m)

Bronze whaler shark
6½ ft (2 m)

Diver
6 ft (1.8 m)

THE SIZE ADVANTAGE

Most dangerous sharks are bigger than people. This means that sharks see people as prey they can attack without much risk to themselves. Big sharks are much faster than people in the water— and far better armed.

Sense organs

Pores

Electric sensory perception
Small pores on a shark's snout link to sense organs. They detect weak electrical impulses produced by prey and by the Earth's magnetic field. Sharks use this sense to find prey. It may also act as a compass to help guide sharks when they migrate.

USING SHARKS

To the Chinese gourmet, few dishes are as appealing, or as expensive, as shark-fin soup. In many other countries, shark meat appears regularly on restaurant menus and kitchen tables. People use sharks for leather, fertilizer, oils of various kinds and Vitamin A. Their eyes provide corneas for human eye transplants and shark cartilage is used for treating burns.

OPEN WIDE
Whale sharks, which grow up to 46 ft (14 m), are the world's largest fish. They eat plankton and small fish and use a grill in their mouths to trap and filter food.

Q : Are whale sharks or basking sharks likely to attack people?

Venoms

Many animals produce venoms or poisons to deter predators and capture prey. A spitting cobra can spray a stream of venom into the eyes of an enemy 10 ft (3 m) away. Blind and in terrible pain, the enemy, or an unsuspecting walker, drops to the ground and the snake slithers away. Animal venoms and poisons are complex combinations of chemicals that, drop for drop, are among the most toxic substances known. A dart-poison frog the size of a walnut contains enough poison to kill 100 people. The venom from a box jellyfish can kill someone in less time than it takes to read this page. A tiny fraction of a drop of Indian cobra venom can be fatal to a human. Venomous animals have special structures, such as fangs, spines or stingers, to inject poisons directly into the bodies of their predators or prey. But poisonous animals, such as dart-poison frogs, will kill you only if touched or eaten.

VENOM VARIETIES

AUSTRALIAN PARALYSIS TICK
The females feed on the blood of people and dogs. The saliva of a single feeding female may paralyze and even kill its host unless the tick is removed.

BLACK-HEADED SEA SNAKE
The most poisonous of all snakes, its venom is 100 times more toxic than that of the deadly taipan. It may cause paralysis and death within hours.

BLUE-RINGED OCTOPUS
This creature spits venomous saliva into its bite wound. Death may follow in minutes when the breathing muscles become paralyzed.

STONEFISH
The venomous spines of this fish produce violent pain, which spreads from the foot to the abdomen. Swelling, numbness, blisters, delirium and even death may follow.

NORTHERN AFRICAN SCORPION
This is the most deadly of all scorpions. Its venom attacks the nervous system, and adults may die within minutes of a sting.

FUNNEL-WEB SPIDER
Until antivenin was available, children were especially likely to die from this spider's bite. Males of this species are far more venomous than females.

BOX JELLYFISH
The venom from this jellyfish may lead to death from paralysis within 30 seconds to 15 minutes. Even a mild sting is very painful and leaves long-lasting scars.

POISONOUS PLATYPUS
A male platypus can paralyze a person's leg or kill a dog by wrapping his legs around the victim and jabbing it with venom-filled ankle spurs. These hollow spurs connect to venom glands, which produce more venom during the breeding season than at other times. Males wound and sometimes kill each other with their venomous spurs.

STRANGE BUT TRUE

Some shrews, such as this Eurasian water shrew, are the only mammals with venomous saliva. Shrews are not dangerous to people, but the salivary glands of one American short-tailed shrew have enough venom to kill 200 mice.

LIFE-SAVING LIQUID
Antivenins reverse or relieve the symptoms of some venomous bites and stings. They are available for most dangerous snakes, as well as some scorpions, ants, spiders and bees.

SPITTING COBRA

In most snakes, venom pours out of the open tip of their hollow fangs. like water through a hose nozzle. But in the three species of spitting cobra, the venom sprays in a jet out of the opening, like water spraying from a puncture in a hose. These cobras only spit in defense; while hunting, they bite in typical snake fashion.

Fangs

Spiders and venomous snakes have fangs that deliver venom into prey or predators. The fangs of snakes are very long, slender teeth with grooves or hollow centers through which the venom flows. Pit vipers, rattlesnakes, cobras, coral snakes and others have fangs at the front of their mouths. These fangs are like hypodermic needles and inject venom into the prey's bloodstream. The deadly African boomslang and other snakes have fangs at the rear of their mouths. These snakes catch prey in their mouths and push it to the back of their jaws. As they chew it with their fangs, venom flows into the bitten areas. When the venom takes effect and the prey stops struggling, the snake swallows it. The sharp, thin fangs of spiders, which pierce, hold and tear prey, are the end parts of their paired jaws, or chelicerae. When muscles in the spiders' venom glands contract, venom is injected through the chelicerae. The fangs of a funnel-web spider are particularly intimidating. Like a pair of pickaxes, they are poised, ready to strike any unsuspecting insect.

REAR FANGS
Brown tree snakes have grooved venom fangs at the back of their mouths. They catch and partially swallow prey before using their fangs.

DID YOU KNOW?
Venom can be more dangerous to some prey than to others. The eastern diamondback rattlesnake commonly eats rabbits, and its venom kills them very quickly. But this snake must inject more venom to kill an animal that is not usually on its menu.

STABBING FANGS
The fangs of rattlesnakes, such as this red diamondback, point forward to stab venom into their prey. While the fast-acting venom takes effect, the snake tracks down and eats its dead or dying meal.

BITE AND SQUEEZE
The eastern brown snake of Australia kills prey by injecting venom with its long fangs, or constricting with its coils. It will also strike to defend itself and can inject enough venom to kill a human.

FATAL FANGS

The needle-sharp fangs of a red-back spider puncture and hold its prey while the paralyzing venom begins to work.

Venom gland

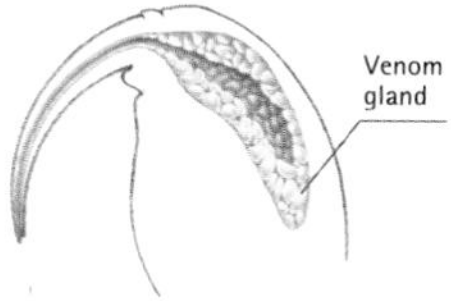

VENOM SACS

The funnel-web's venom is stored in a pair of glands, or sacs, at the base of the fangs. When the spider bites, venom flows from the glands through ducts that end in small holes at the tips of the fangs.

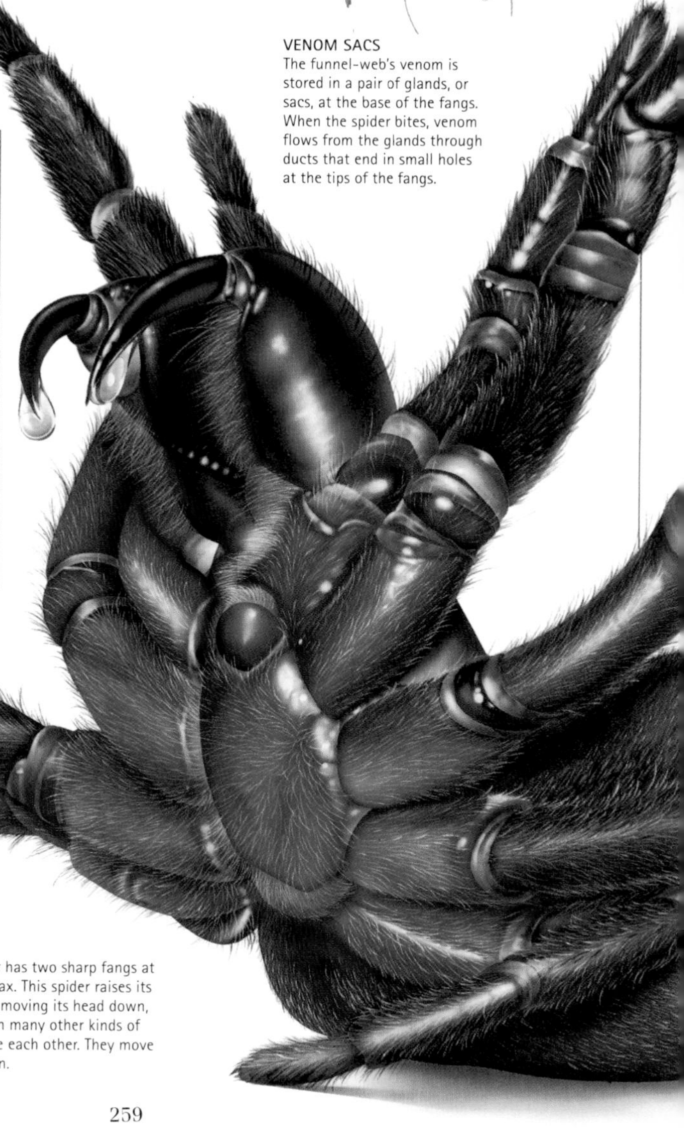

FOLD-AWAY FANGS

Vipers and pit vipers, categories which include adders and rattlesnakes, have the most efficient fangs of all the venomous snakes. When not in use, these very large fangs fold neatly away in the roof of the snake's mouth and are covered by a flap of skin. But when the snake opens its mouth, the flap is pulled back and the fang springs forward and strikes. Pressure on the storage area forces venom down a duct to the fang and into the snake's victim.

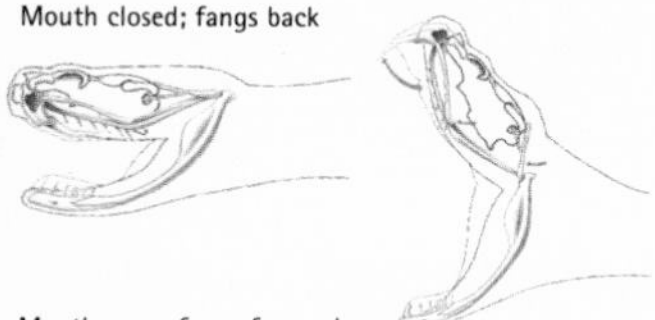

Mouth closed; fangs back

Mouth open; fangs forward

FUNNEL-WEB FANGS

Australia's deadly funnel-web spider has two sharp fangs at the front of its head, or cephalothorax. This spider raises its head to attack and stabs its prey by moving its head down, with the fangs pointed downward. In many other kinds of spiders, the fangs are rotated to face each other. They move from side to side in a pinching action.

DEATH STING
A honeybee can sting only once. To free itself from its victim's skin, it must leave behind its barbed stinger and venom gland. The venom flows until the stinger is removed because small muscles continue to pump venom through the gland. But without this part of its body, the honeybee will eventually die.

Antennae
Wasps taste, smell and feel with their antennae.

Wasp's eyes
These are made up of many lenses.

BEWARE!
The vivid yellow and black coloring of the European wasp warns other animals that it is dangerous. These wasps attack in large swarms when defending their nests, and can sting their victims repeatedly.

• VENOMOUS ANIMALS •

Stingers

Most people know that bees and wasps sting, but some ants can also give a nasty sting or bite. These fierce insects pierce your skin and inject venom into your blood. There are nearly 9,000 kinds of ants, and many are predators that live in colonies and hunt in groups. A swarm of as many as 700,000 South American army ants may sweep noisily through the forest floor, taking any animal in its path that cannot escape the onslaught of bites and stings. There are many thousands of kinds of wasps, but hunting wasps are the familiar ones that might sting you. They use their stings to capture and stun insects, or to defend themselves. Large hunting wasps that live in groups are called hornets. If you ever stir up a hornet's nest— run! Bees eat nectar and pollen from flowers and sting only in self-defense. Some wasps and bees live in groups, but most live alone.

Venom gland
Venom is produced by the venom gland.

Venom sac
Venom is stored in the sac until the wasp stings. It then flows down the hollow stinger and into the victim.

Stinger
Only females have stingers. They have evolved from a tube that other insects use to deposit eggs.

BUMBLEBEE STING
A bee's barbed stinger hooks into the skin of its victim and is torn from the bee's body when the bee tries to withdraw it.

HORNET STING
A hornet can sting more than once because its stinger slips easily in and out of prey like a hypodermic needle.

ANT STING
An ant sting is similar to that of a hornet sting. Like hornets, ants can paralyze their prey by stinging it many times.

On the wings
These delicately paired wings enable wasps to reach speeds of 12 miles (20 km) per hour.

DID YOU KNOW?

The honeybees that forage on flowers and build intricate honeycombs are all females. There may be as many as 80,000 females in a hive, which is ruled by the queen bee. Only the queen bee lays eggs.

BULLDOG ANTS

Australia's bulldog ants are among the most dangerous ants in the world. They have huge biting mandibles, or jaws, with serrated edges. Like bulldogs, after which they are named, they cling to their victims with their jaws. Then, they curl their bodies forward and inject a powerful venom with their long stingers. A bulldog ant guarding a nest recruits others to attack a predator by sending out chemical signals, called pheromones, which are produced in the Dufor's gland. As few as 30 stings from these aggressive ants can kill a human.

Venom duct

Dufor's gland

Stinger

261

HANDY LEGS

Like their relatives the spiders, scorpions have eight legs. Two of them have evolved into large pedipalps, which end in grasping pincers. Male and female sometimes join pincers and perform a dance during mating.

Scorpions

There are nearly 9,000 kinds of scorpions, none of them longer than your hand. A few, such as the Trinidad scorpion and the African gold scorpion, have stings that can be deadly, especially to small children. A scorpion usually lashes out with its stinging tail when a bare-footed person steps on it. But slipping into your shoes may be equally dangerous. Scorpions often seek warm, dark places— such as shoes— to sleep! Most scorpions, however, are harmless. They sting to defend themselves and to kill prey such as spiders, insects and small vertebrates. Their lobster-like pinching legs help them capture and crush prey.

Muscle for moving stinger

Muscle over
poison gland

Stinger

BACKLASH
A scorpion's stinger is a hollow
tube connected to a poison
gland. Muscles force the stinger
into the body of the scorpion's
prey and squeeze poison from
the gland down the tube.

Pedipalp

MANY PAIRS OF LEGS

Centipedes have between 30 and 350 legs. They are
not related to scorpions, but they do catch prey in
a similar way. With their fanged venomous claws,
conveniently close to the jaws, centipedes capture and
paralyze earthworms, cockroaches and even mice. Like
a scorpion's pedipalps, these claws are the first pair of
a centipede's many pairs of legs. In scorpions, however,
the venomous sting comes from the tail, not from the
pedipalps. Some centipedes can give people a painful
sting in self-defense.

DID YOU KNOW?

A slim scorpion with small, slender
pedipalps grasps prey in its pincers, then
stings it to ensure the prey does not escape.
A stocky scorpion with large pedipalps uses
its strong pincers to subdue its victim and
stings only if the prey struggles too much.

Discover more in Venoms

Fish

It may seem surprising, but fish can kill people. Some fish can cause very painful injuries or even death by injecting venom into a victim's flesh with their sharp spines. Some fish have as many as 18 spines on their backs, while others have spines at the ends of their tails. Venomous fish live in oceans around the world. A few, such as catfish, live in rivers. In most fish, venomous spines are a defense against predators. In shallow coastal waters, people can come into contact with venomous fish, such as weevers and stonefish, which lie hidden on the ocean floor. A wader who steps on one is stabbed by the spines. Other venomous fish, such as lionfish and zebrafish, are beautiful and easy to see. People are stung when they touch them.

DANGER BELOW
The lionfish swims slowly and gracefully among the crevices of a coral reef. Its long, lacy and brilliantly colored fins conceal 18 needle-sharp spines full of deadly venom. The spines of a stonefish, lying motionless in the sand, are also venomous. An unsuspecting wader could easily stand on this well-camouflaged fish, which is covered with algae that live on its skin.

SURGEONS' KNIVES

Surgeonfish have thin, flat bodies. With incisorlike teeth, they nibble on small animals and plants living and growing on rocks or coral. These brightly colored, or dull, fish range in size from 8–40 inches (20 to 100 cm). On each side of their tails, surgeonfish carry sharp, venomous spines that flick out like knives when the fish are excited. Surgeonfish swimming in large schools may slash the legs of a wader with these spines, causing deep, painful gashes that are slow to heal.

FLICK OF THE TAIL

Many stingrays live in warm, coastal waters, where they spend much time resting camouflaged on the sandy ocean floor. When someone steps on a stingray's back, it lashes out with its whiplike tail, which has one or more barbed, venom-filled spines. In the largest stingrays, the spines reach up to 1 ft (30 cm) long, but even the smaller stingray spines can inflict terrible, sometimes deadly, wounds.

Discover more in Venoms

Pretty but Poisonous

The world's seas are full of beautiful but deadly creatures that use their weapons to kill prey and defend themselves from predators and competitors. Jewel-like cone shells hide tiny harpoons that shoot out to inject poison into fish and sea worms. Fragile, clear box jellyfish attack and kill fish with up to 20 deadly stingers. Colorful sea anemones wave their pretty, poisonous tentacles. Some sea slugs eat sea anemones, then use the stinging cells of their prey to defend themselves. Other fatally attractive marine invertebrates include sponges, corals, sea cucumbers, starfish and bristle worms. None of the deadly invertebrates preys on people, but many live in the shallow coastal water where people swim. Anyone who crosses their paths may be stung or bitten, sometimes with fatal results.

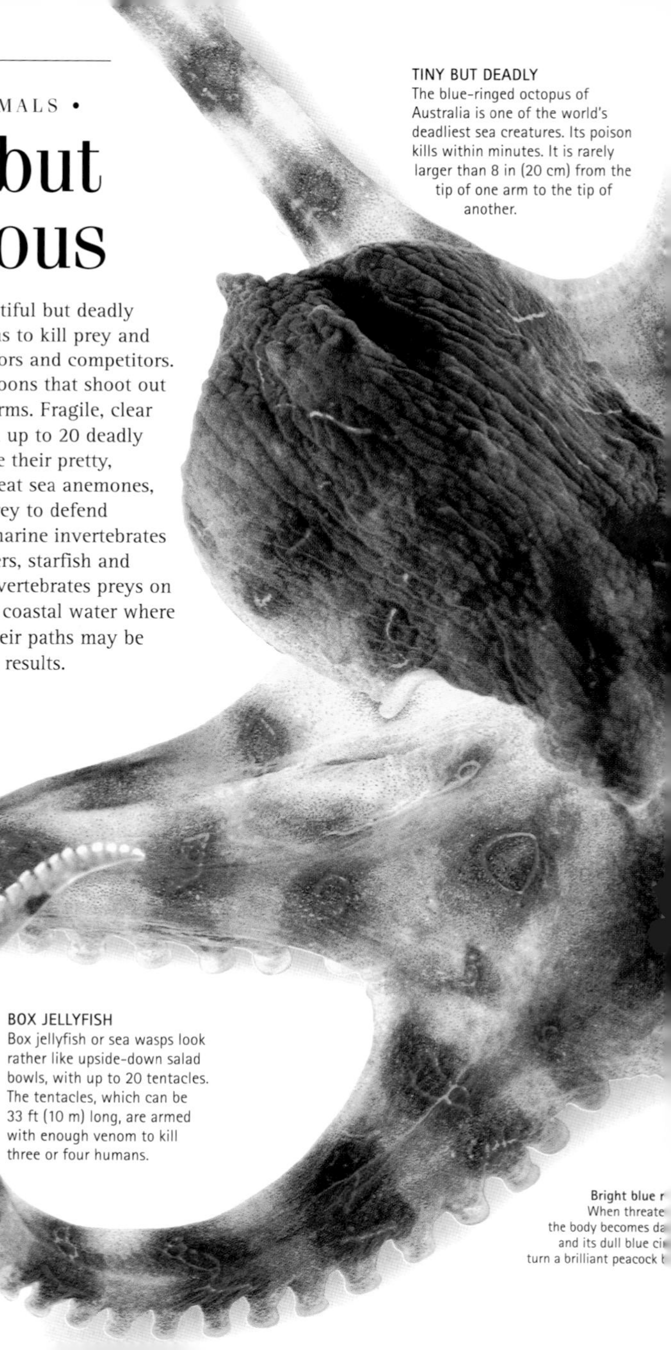

TINY BUT DEADLY
The blue-ringed octopus of Australia is one of the world's deadliest sea creatures. Its poison kills within minutes. It is rarely larger than 8 in (20 cm) from the tip of one arm to the tip of another.

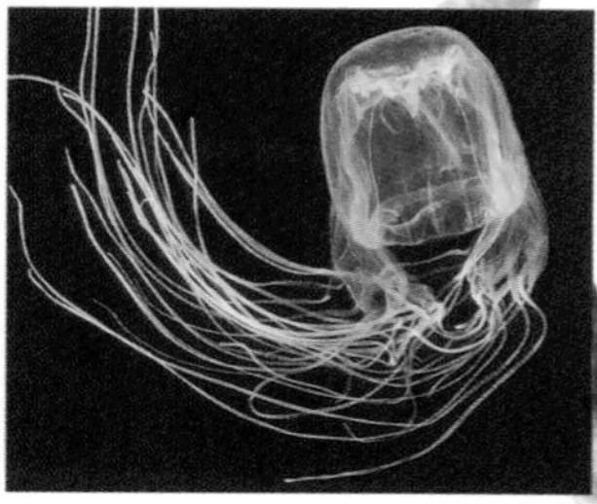

BOX JELLYFISH
Box jellyfish or sea wasps look rather like upside-down salad bowls, with up to 20 tentacles. The tentacles, which can be 33 ft (10 m) long, are armed with enough venom to kill three or four humans.

Bright blue r
When threate
the body becomes da
and its dull blue ci
turn a brilliant peacock t

MAN O' WAR
A Portuguese man o' war is a colony of animals living together. The gas-filled float, or bladder, is one animal, and the stinging tentacles clinging to it are other animals. Their sting may cause sharp pain, headaches and chills.

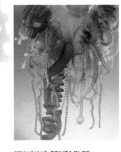

STINGING TENTACLES
Each tentacle of the Portuguese man o' war has black "spring-loaded" stinging cells, which deliver the venom.

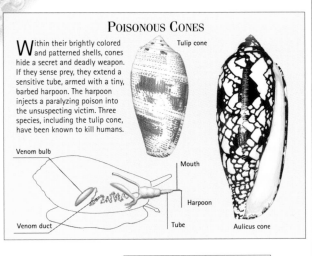

POISONOUS CONES

Within their brightly colored and patterned shells, cones hide a secret and deadly weapon. If they sense prey, they extend a sensitive tube, armed with a tiny, barbed harpoon. The harpoon injects a paralyzing poison into the unsuspecting victim. Three species, including the tulip cone, have been known to kill humans.

Tulip cone

Venom bulb

Mouth

Harpoon

Venom duct

Tube

Aulicus cone

DID YOU KNOW?
The venomous sting of a matamala, a sea anemone from the South Pacific, affects people only mildly. Eating this creature, however, can be deadly.

Tentacles
Octopuses can move their tentacles at lightning speed to catch prey.

267

Hooves and Spurs

Every karate expert knows that a foot powered by a strong leg can deliver a stunning blow. It is not surprising that some animals have evolved kicking legs and feet as weapons. An ostrich, for example, usually runs away from danger. But a cornered ostrich is capable of killing with a kick. Other animals increase the effect of their kicks with additional structures. The toes of horses, deer and similar animals are encased in thick, sharp-edged hooves. Male jungle fowl have razor-sharp spurs, and the toes of cassowaries are like daggers. Animals use kicking mainly to defend themselves against predators. In some species, males kick in battles over females. Horses sometimes kick people who ignore the rule about never standing behind one.

FLYING HOOVES
To defend themselves and other members of their group, zebras kick predators such as African hunting dogs with one or both of their powerful back legs. When hoof meets head, the predator may be stunned, or killed. The hoof's sharp edge may also leave predators with bloody gashes.

HOOVED COMBAT
Even reindeer with antlers use sharp front hooves in fights over food. Rising on their hind legs, reindeer flail at each other with their front legs. In combat, the reindeer smacks a front foot into its opponent's body or slashes it with a sharp hoof.

THE ODD AND THE EVEN

Like ballet dancers in padded toe shoes, ungulates, or hooved mammals, balance on the tips of their toes, which are encased in hard-edged hooves. Some hooved mammals balance on one or three toes, while others use two or four toes. Odd and even ungulates can run quickly and gracefully on tiptoes.

Even toes
Deer are even-toed. Two long middle toes, equivalent to your third and fourth toes, bear their weight. The other two toes are small, and the first toe (the big toe in humans) is absent.

Odd toes
Horses are odd-toed. One large toe, equivalent to your third toe, supports the horse's weight. Heavier ungulates, such as rhinoceroses and hippopotamuses, have three short, wide toes that touch the ground to spread out their weight.

SHARP KICKER
Cassowaries are tall, flightless birds native to Australia and New Guinea. Their powerful kicking legs have stiletto-like toes that can easily rip open a person's stomach or cut off an arm.

A BOXING BOUT
Male kangaroos box by locking their front legs together, then kicking with their muscular back legs. To win the bout, one male must push the other's back to the ground.

POISON FEATHERS
In 1991, scientists discovered that the skin and feathers of New Guinea's pitohui contain a poison similar to that of dart-poison frogs. Pitohuis are the first birds found to be poisonous.

• NATURAL WEAPONS •

Skin, Quills and Feathers

Beware of animals bearing bright colors! Very often, animals with vivid coloring have dangerous chemical defenses. Predators can easily see these creatures, but learn quickly to avoid them, or die. Many caterpillars and butterflies store toxins in their bodies; some cause a rash in people who touch them. The skin of some brightly colored frogs and other amphibians secretes poisons that range from mild to murderous. Some fish also have poisonous skin or flesh. Although scientists do not really know if this discourages natural fish predators, it certainly influences whether these fish appear on human menus! At least one species of bird has poisonous feathers, which, like hair, are a special form of skin. A few species of mammal have evolved different hairs called quills. Quills are not poisonous, but few predators are willing to risk a mouthful of needles.

SNEAKY SALAMANDER
The bright colors of the red salamander mimic those of the North American newt, whose poisonous skin and nasty taste repel birds and snakes. The red salamander is not poisonous, but many predators avoid it just in case.

BALL OF QUILLS

On hard ground, a threatened echidna curls into a tight ball of spiky quills, leaving no soft parts exposed to a predator's teeth. When the soil is soft, the echidna burrows into the ground until only its quills poke above the surface.

TOXIC TOAD

When they are frightened, cane toads, and many other toads, produce a frothy, white foam behind the eyes, which is a poison. The chemicals that make up the poison are strong enough to kill small animals.

A DEADLY MEAL

The skin, blood and internal organs of puffer fish contain a deadly poison. But in Japan, the flesh of the puffer fish, called fugu, is served as a gourmet meal. Fugu chefs are trained to keep the poison away from the flesh, but every year a few people die after a last supper of fugu.

FATAL FROGS

The Choco Indians of South America rub the darts for their blow guns across the backs of the bright yellow dart-poison frogs. Hunters then shoot prey, such as monkeys and tapirs, which die quickly before they can escape into the forest.

LARGE AND LETHAL
The Komodo dragon of Indonesia is the biggest lizard in the world. With its strong legs, fang-like teeth, lashing tail and surprising agility, it can kill water buffalo that are three times its weight.

• NATURAL WEAPONS •

Size, Strength and Speed

A house cat and a tiger capture and kill prey with similar weapons: sharp claws and long canine teeth. One sits in your lap, but the other is a dangerous animal. Size, strength and speed make all the difference with many animals that are dangerous to people. Anaconda boas, for example, can coil part of their long body around a victim and squeeze the life out of it. An elephant can simply crush a person. Right whales have rammed whaling ships or risen underneath and flipped them over. Most large dangerous animals, even lumbering hippopotamuses and bears, can run faster than humans over short distances. You could easily outrun a crocodile or a cobra, but they often strike so quickly that you would not have time to flee. In the animal world, danger really depends on your point of view: a cat purring happily in your lap is very dangerous to a mouse.

BLAST OFF!
A crocodile can leap straight up from the water to snatch a bird out of the air or grab a mammal on the riverbank.

272

DRAGON CLAWS
Komodo dragons use their strong toes armed with sharp claws to bring down large prey such as deer and wild pigs.

STRANGE BUT TRUE
The fire-breathing dragon is a symbol of the Chinese people, but no one really knows the origin of the dragon myth. The Komodo dragon is certainly a fierce creature, and some people believe that the myth of a monstrous dragon was based on a reptile such as a snake, alligator or lizard.

SURPRISE
A group of orcas, or killer whales, swims deliberately close to, and sometimes onto, the shore near unsuspecting seals.

ATTACK!
The seals panic and try to flee into the surf. Here, the orcas may "play" with the seals until they are too weak to escape.

▼ PAST THE POST
tahs are the fastest land mals and can reach speeds ▮ miles (110 km) per hour in nds. Wolves take off more y and at top speed can run out 37 miles (60 km) per . But a wolf can overtake a tah, because cheetahs wear uickly. Wolves are long-distance rs, and can keep going for longer at their slower pace.

Strength in Numbers

Many animals find strength in numbers. Numbers can make harmless animals dangerous—and dangerous animals even more so. Some animals are dangerous to people only because they work in groups. One locust might munch on a blade of wheat, but a swarm of millions of locusts can eat all the food crops of an entire region. The sting of a single killer bee is no worse than any other bee's sting. But killer bees defend themselves by attacking in huge numbers all at once, often killing humans. Social insects, such as bees and ants, send complex messages to each other using chemicals called pheromones. This allows them to coordinate their fierce attacks on predators, and their search-and-devour missions for prey.

ATTACK OF THE KILLER BEES

In the 1950s, Brazilian beekeepers mated aggressive African bees wi[...] Western bees to improve honey production. But swarms of the mi[...] bees escaped and killed people. T[...] bees have since spread slowly nor[...]

DANCES WITH BEES

A honeybee flies in a figure eight[...] waggling her abdomen from side [...] side. This is called a "waggle dan[...] It tells other workers that she ha[...] found food, where it is, and even[...] how good it is!

DEADLY DRIVERS

A raiding swarm of African driver ants kills everything in its path. Confined or injured animals cannot escape 20 million biting mouths. But the swarm travels slowly and humans have time to flee the ant onslaught.

NATURAL INSECTICIDES

The green weaver ants of Asia attack in great numbers, biting their victims ferociously with sharp, powerful jaws. They live in leaf nests and form huge colonies of up to half a million members. Weavers are excellent insect hunters. They forage in groups and work together to kill and carry back to the colony insects that are much bigger than themselves. For nearly 2,000 years, Chinese farmers have used green weaver ants to kill the insects that eat their crops.

A PLAGUE OF LOCUSTS

When the weather is warm, locusts form huge swarms and travel widely in search of green plant food. One of the biggest swarms ever seen in East Africa had 40,000 million locusts. They ate enough grain to feed one million people for a year.

275

Disease Carriers

R ats, blood-sucking mosquitoes, flies and ticks are the mass murderers of the animal world. Each year, dangerous animals such as big cats, crocodiles and cobras kill a few thousand people. But millions of people are killed or made sick by animals without sharp teeth, great size or venomous fangs. These animals carry a variety of microscopic creatures, such as bacteria and parasites, which cause disease and death. Some mosquitoes have a parasite called *Plasmodium*. When people are bitten by a mosquito with this parasite, they can develop malaria, a severe and often fatal disease. Scientists estimate that about half the people in the world, mostly in the tropics, either have malaria or are in danger of getting it. For more than a century, they have been struggling to eliminate the mosquitoes with various pesticides and to kill the parasite with different drugs. But again and again, these animals develop resistance to new types of chemical weapons.

A FEVERISH BITE
Some kinds of mosquitoes pass on the malaria parasite when they bite. Others, such as the one above, transmit the viruses that cause yellow fever and dengue fever.

Before

FULL TO BURSTING
After two days of sucking blood, a female tick blows up to 200 times its weight.

After

THE TICK OF LYME
Ticks live on blood from vertebrates, and many carry deadly diseases from one meal to the next. Deer ticks carry bacteria that causes Lyme disease, which can kill people.

BLACK DEATH

The deadly bubonic plague swept through Europe in the Middle Ages. Between 1346 and 1350, one-third of the population died from this disease, which was spread by fleas living on the black rats of Asia. Today, rats still spread diseases such as typhus.

THE MITES AMONG US

Did you know that eight-legged creatures, too small to see without a microscope, are feeding on your skin at this very moment? Dust mites are everywhere: in the curtains and carpet, in the furniture, in the wallpaper, and even on your mattress. They feed on the millions of dead skin and hair cells we shed continuously. Dust mites get rid of dust, but some people are allergic to them and can suffer from asthma.

THE LIFE OF A MOSQUITO

Mosquitoes lay their eggs in water. The eggs become larvae, which attach to the water's surface with a breathing siphon and feed on tiny plants and animals. Larvae turn into pupae, and then become adult mosquitoes.

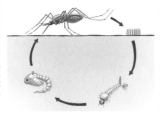

DEADLIER THAN THE MALE

Only female mosquitoes are able to suck blood. They need to have blood after mating so they can lay their eggs.

A REAL VAMPIRE

There are many chilling stories of vampires that suck human blood. It is true that the common vampire bat feeds on the blood of mammals. But does this include people? Very rarely.

Dangerous People

People are the most dangerous animals of all. They kill each other, and they threaten animals and environments everywhere. For thousands of years, people armed with weapons, from simple bone blades to modern submachine guns, have been killing other animals. The first North Americans wiped out mammoths and giant ground sloths. The Maoris in New Zealand destroyed moas and giant eagles completely. European explorers exterminated Steller's sea cows, elephant birds and other animals on islands around the world. Between 1970 and 1993, poachers in Africa slaughtered more than 60,000 black rhinoceroses. With fewer than 2,500 rhinoceroses left, this animal is now on the verge of extinction. Whenever people move into new habitats, other animals are moved out, by one means or another. This process continues as the growing human population, armed with modern weapons, invades the world's last wildernesses.

IVORY IN FLAMES
In 1989, Kenyan wildlife officials confiscated and burned the tusks of about 1,000 elephants to show their support for banning the ivory trade. Ivory prices, and the poaching of elephants, have now declined as a result of the ban.

SMART WEAPONS
People use their natural weapon, intelligence, to make tools that kill at a distance. Even simple bows and arrows allow people to kill the most dangerous prey with little risk to themselves.

THE SKIN TRADE
The beautiful fur of the spotted cat has tempted many hunters, and the numbers of some species have declined dramatically. In the 1970s, most countries agreed to stop the trade in skins of endangered cats.

EXTINCTION IN SIGHT
Rhinoceroses have been hunted for their horns for centuries. Horns are still prized ingredients in some medicines and are valued as status symbols when carved into dagger handles. Modern weapons and vehicles make it much easier to hunt these huge animals. Because of this, all five rhinoceros species may soon be extinct.

CARING FOR KOALAS
Koalas are not usually afraid of people. In the past they were an easy target for hunters who wanted their fur, and two million skins were exported from Australia in 1924. Soon after this, it became illegal to hunt these marsupials.

DID YOU KNOW?
In 1963, only about 400 breeding pairs of bald eagles were left in the United States. A 30-year effort to save them included protecting their habitat, banning the insecticide DDT and hunting. This was so successful that the number of breeding pairs grew to more than four thousand. The bald eagle is no longer an endangered species.

FROM THE OTHER SIDE
This protestor is part of a movement to save rainforests. Each year, people log or burn huge areas of rainforest, and more than 15,000 species of plants and animals become extinct. Unless this stops, all rainforests will be destroyed in the next 30 years.

FATAL FASHION
Crocodiles, alligators, snakes and lizards are killed regularly to make leather boots, belts and purses for the fashion industry. Many species of these reptiles are now endangered as a result.

Discover more in Great Cats

279

—Where in the World?—

Dangerous animals are everywhere. Sharks and venomous jellyfish and reef fish haunt coasts around the world. Poisonous snakes and spiders live in every continent except Antarctica. Most continents have at least one predator— perhaps a crocodile, a bear or a great cat— that is larger than humans.

We are more likely to be struck by lightning than attacked by one of these dangerous animals. But there are many other dangerous animals we should worry about. Disease-carrying mosquitoes, houseflies and rats have invaded nearly every corner of the globe.

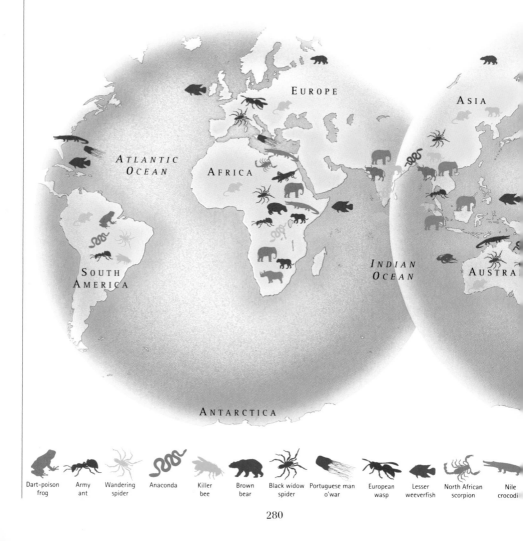

EUROPE
ASIA
ATLANTIC OCEAN
AFRICA
SOUTH AMERICA
INDIAN OCEAN
AUSTRA
ANTARCTICA

| Dart-poison frog | Army ant | Wandering spider | Anaconda | Killer bee | Brown bear | Black widow spider | Portuguese man o'war | European wasp | Lesser weeverfish | North African scorpion | Nile crocodi |

| Tiger | Asian elephant | Gaur | Black rat | Estuarine crocodile | King cobra | Grizzly bear | Western diamond rattlesnake | American alligator | Barracuda | Scorpion |

NORTH
AMERICA

PACIFIC
OCEAN

ANIMALS IN DANGER

People endanger animals. They destroy animals' habitats to build houses and towns, to grow timber, to graze other animals or to use as farmland. People also hunt different animals for their skins, fur or horns. If many animals of one species are killed, there are sometimes not enough left to breed. Two hundred years ago, one animal species died out each year. Today, several species become extinct every day.

POLAR BEAR
People in the Arctic have hunted polar bears for many centuries. In 1973, rules were set down to help control the number of bears being killed.

GORILLA
Gorillas were once hunted for their hands and feet, which were made into tourist souvenirs. It is now illegal to hunt gorillas, but some species remain dangerously close to extinction.

HARPY EAGLE
Harpy eagles live in the lush Amazon rainforest. But this powerful bird of prey is threatened as more and more of the rainforest is cleared.

CHEETAH
Cheetahs are the fastest animals on land, but they cannot escape the danger that faces their species. Much of their habitat has been turned into farms and many are shot when they attack farm animals.

| ppo | Desert locust | White rhino | Spitting cobra | African elephant | Lion | Bulldog ant | Black-headed sea snake | Box jellyfish | Funnel-web spider | Stonefish | Blue-ringed octopus |

The Human Body

What is the largest and heaviest organ in the body?

Where would you find the hammer, the anvil, and the stirrup?

What links the brain to all parts of the body?

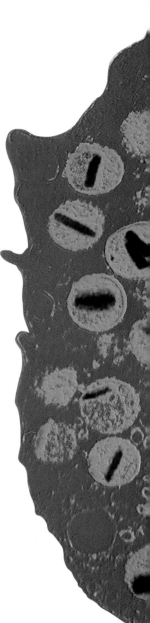

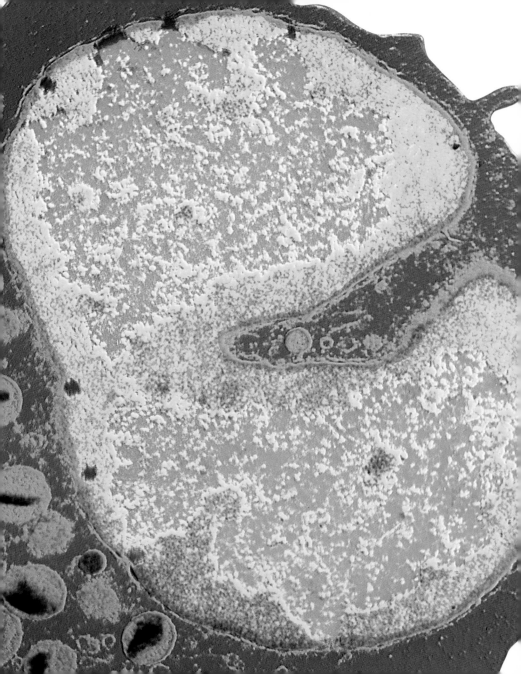

Contents

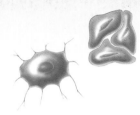

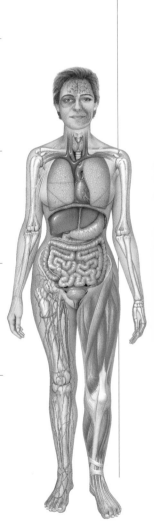

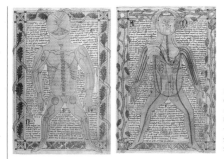

ART AND SCIENCE
Leonardo da Vinci (1452–1519),
an Italian artist and scientist,
cut open and studied more
than 30 bodies. His drawings
of the human body inspired
many people.

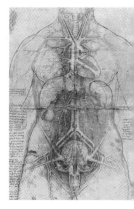

ROME'S MASTER PHYSICIAN
Claudius Galen (129–199) wrote
more than 500 books on the human
body. The Romans believed it was
wrong to cut open human corpses,
so Galen dissected animals and
studied the wounds of gladiators.

• EVERY BODY TELLS A STORY •

In the Beginning

Our knowledge about the human body began long ago. Fossil remains of prehistoric people from 50,000 years ago show that they tried to heal broken bones by setting them in their natural positions. Ancient Egyptians carefully preserved the bodies of pharaohs with a technique called mummification. Ancient Chinese inserted needles into the body to balance life energy called chi. This procedure, called acupuncture, is still used in Chinese medicine. Ancient Greeks, such as Hippocrates, used their knowledge of the body to treat disease and illness. Ancient Romans studied the bodies of slaves and gladiators who had been injured in battles. The teachings of Rome's great physician Claudius Galen were followed for 1,200 years. When the Renaissance began in Europe in the 1300s, artists and scientists began to cast off old beliefs. By the 1500s, people understood much more about what really happened inside the human body.

OPEN TO VIEW
During the Renaissance, students in European
universities and medical schools began to study body
structure, or anatomy. In Padua, Italy, Andreas
Vesalius founded the modern science of anatomy.

BODY ENERGY
The Chinese believe that a life energy
flows along body channels, or meridians.
If the flow is disturbed, a person becomes
ill. The Chinese use acupuncture points
to rebalance the energy flow and make
the person well again.

286

BODY WORSHIP
The Venus of Willendorf is a statue from the Stone Age. The statue is an example of how people have been fascinated with the shape of the human body for centuries.

THE REAL PICTURE

Andreas Vesalius was born in Brussels in 1514. When he was 24, he became a professor of anatomy at the University of Padua, Italy. He studied many human corpses, and sometimes hid them in his room for weeks. In 1543, he published a book called *De Humani Corporis Fabrica* (On the Structure of the Human Body). It contained detailed drawings of bodies, such as the one on the right, and caused huge arguments because it went against the teachings of Galen, Aristotle and others. Vesalius drew exactly what he saw and suggested how body parts worked together. His work was the beginning of modern scientific anatomy.

LOOKING AT CELLS
Early microscopes could magnify cells only up to 100 times. This soon improved to 2,000 times, which revealed many kinds of tiny cells inside the body.

GETTING SMALLER
Electron microscopes use electron beams instead of light beams. They make things look a million times bigger, so they can show the tiniest parts of a single cell.

USING SOUND
Ultrasound scans, developed in the 1950s, beam very high-pitched sound waves into the body and detect the echoes. The echoes are converted into a picture. Ultrasounds are used to check a baby's progress in the womb.

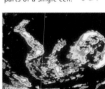

A HEAD IN 3-D
In the 1960s, the CT (Computerized Tomography) scan was the first to show three-dimensional images of body parts. It uses a very weak X-ray beam.

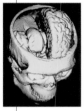

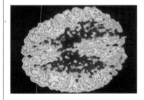

VIEWING THE BRAIN
The PET (Positron Emission Tomography) scan reveals how much energy a body part is using. It shows which areas of the brain are busiest when a person is doing a particular activity.

• EVERY BODY TELLS A STORY •

The Story So Far

In the fourteenth century, scientists began to question traditional knowledge and teachings. They began to study the body in two main ways. The first, called anatomy, looks at how the body is made—its shape and structure. The second, called physiology, tests how the body works—what the parts do and how they function together. New inventions and discoveries revealed more about the body's anatomy and physiology. The microscope, invented about 1608, showed that the body was made up of billions of cells. X-rays, discovered in 1895, allowed doctors to see inside the body without cutting it open. Scanners were invented in the twentieth century with the help of computer technology. These allow images of the inside of the human body to be processed and viewed on a computer or television screen.

SLICES OF THE BODY

Magnetic Resonance Imaging (MRI) was invented in the 1970s. The MRI scanner shows details of soft tissues, such as muscles, nerves and blood vessels, by capturing images in sections, or "slices," of the body. A computer then builds up a picture of the body.

AMAZING IMAGES

In 1895, German scientist Wilhelm Röntgen discovered X-rays. As he experimented with high-voltage electrical equipment, he noticed that it gave off mysterious rays that passed through skin but not through bone. He could see the body's skeleton clearly. Within weeks, doctors were using X-rays to check injured people for broken bones.

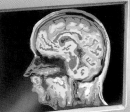

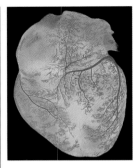

BRANCHES OF BLOOD
The thick, muscular walls of the heart work nonstop. To do this, they need their own blood supply for nourishment and energy. This comes from arteries that branch over the outside of the heart.

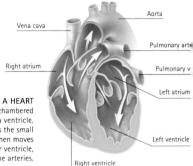

Aorta
Vena cava
Pulmonary art
Right atrium
Pulmonary v
Left atrium
Left ventricle
Right ventricle

INSIDE A HEART
Each side of the heart is a two-chambered pump made up of an atrium and a ventricle. Blood flowing from veins enters the small upper chamber, or atrium. It then moves into the large lower chamber, or ventricle, which squeezes it into the arteries.

• THE VITAL SYSTEMS •

From the Heart

Your heart is about the same size as your fist. This bag of muscle filled with blood squeezes tirelessly once every second of your life to pump blood around your body. The heart is made up of two pumps, which lie side by side. The right pump sends blood through the lungs to pick up the vital oxygen needed by all the cells in the body. The left pump sends blood around the body to deliver the oxygen. The blood then returns to the right pump and so on, round and round the double loop of the circulatory system. The heart pushes blood into tubes called arteries, which carry the blood around the body. When the heart relaxes, it fills with blood that comes back from the body along floppy tubes called veins. A heartbeat occurs every time the heart squeezes and relaxes.

OLD HEARTS
Ancient Egyptians believed that the heart was the home of all thoughts, feelings and memories. They placed heart amulets (above) with the dead to help them on their journey to the afterlife.

A HELPING HEART
Some people with heart disease need a new heart. Surgeons are able to remove a healthy heart from someone who has just died and put it into the body of someone who needs it. People of all ages, such as this group (left), have undergone successful heart transplants.

DID YOU KNOW?
When an embryo is four weeks old, its heart starts beating. By the time it is eight weeks old, the heart is fully developed.

AT THE HEART OF THE BODY

The heart is in the middle of the chest, slightly to
the left side, between the lungs. It is linked into
the circulatory system by arteries and veins.
About every second, it pumps blood out into
the large, strong-walled arteries. These branch
around the body carrying blood. The blood
flows back along floppy, thin-walled
veins, which join together and
return it to the heart.

HELPING THE HEART

The heart has valves that make
sure the blood flows the correct
way. A valve's flexible flaps fold out
of the way as blood moves by. If
blood tries to flow backwards, the
flaps balloon out and their edges
slap together, making a seal. This
action creates the heartbeat sound.
Sometimes a valve may become stiff
or weak and will not close properly,
causing illness. Faulty valves can be
replaced with artificial ones made
from metal and plastic (below).

Parts of a
ball-and-cage valve

Moving Things Around

Blood flows from the heart along arteries. These have thick, tough, stretchy walls that withstand the surge of blood pressure with each heartbeat. Arteries divide many times as they spread around the body, and form millions of micro-blood vessels called capillaries. The walls of the capillaries are so thin that vital substances in blood—oxygen, nutrients, high-energy sugars and hormones (chemical messengers)—can seep through to surrounding cells. Carbon dioxide and other wastes from the cells can pass into blood, which takes them away to be removed from the body by the lungs, kidneys and liver. The capillaries join to make larger, thin-walled veins, which return the blood to the heart. Blood carries white cells that fight germs and disease. It also clots to seal leaks and wounds, and it spreads warmth evenly around the body.

A SYSTEM OF BLOOD
Blood flows around the body through veins and arteries. It delivers nutrients, collects wastes and fights germs.

White cell

White cell

INSIDE A CAPILLARY
Blood is made up of plasma, cells and platelets. Plasma is a watery liquid that contains body sugars, salts and many other dissolved substances. There are billions of doughnut-shaped red cells that carry oxygen. Frilly-looking white cells kill germs and clean the blood. Tiny particles called platelets clot blood in wounds.

Red cell

EXCHANGING BLOOD

People have understood for centuries that blood is vital for life. But they did not understand that people have different types of blood. Transfusions were even tried between humans and animals!

A SAVING DONATION

Donors are always needed to give, or donate, fresh supplies of blood. The blood is transfused into patients who have been injured, or who suffer from blood diseases.

DID YOU KNOW?

A tiny drop of blood the size of a pinhead contains up to 5 million red blood cells, 15,000 white blood cells and 250,000 platelets.

CUT TO CLOT

At a wound, platelets and sticky fibers trap red cells, white cells and germs. A clot is formed that seals the leak.

CLOT TO SCAB

Cells at the wound's edges multiply to make new skin as healing begins. The clot hardens into a protective scab.

SCAB TO SKIN

Capillaries under the skin reseal, and the new cells grow together. Eventually, the scab falls off and the wound is healed.

BLOOD TYPES

Type A

Type B

Type AB

Type O

Each person has a certain type of blood. The main types—A, B, AB or O—depend on proteins called antigens that are in the red cells. Type A blood has antigen A present in the cells and anti-B antibodies in the plasma. Type B blood has antigen B, while type AB has both. A person with type O blood has no antigens in the red cells and both anti-A and anti-B antibodies in the plasma. If a patient receives the wrong blood type, the red cells can fall apart and the blood can clot. Patients must receive blood that matches their own.

A Deep Breath

You breathe in one pint (half a liter) of air every few seconds when you are resting. The air enters through the nose and mouth, goes down the throat and into the windpipe, called the trachea, before entering the two spongy lungs. The lungs absorb oxygen, which makes up one-fifth of normal air. Oxygen is vital because it is an essential part of the energy-giving chemical reactions inside each cell. The lungs pass the oxygen into the blood, which carries it to all body cells. The body's main waste substance, called carbon dioxide, passes in the opposite direction, from the blood to the air in the lungs. You then breathe this up the windpipe and out—before breathing in new air. The body cannot store much oxygen, so you need to keep breathing to stay alive.

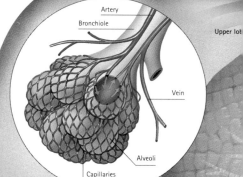

Artery
Bronchiole
Upper lobe
Vein
Alveoli
Capillaries

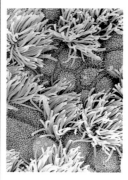

THE DUST REMOVERS
Sticky mucus lines the airways of the nose, throat, windpipe and lungs. It traps dust, dirt and other airborne particles. In the lining of the lungs and windpipe, microscopic hairs called cilia (left) wave to and fro. They push the dirty mucus up to the throat, where it is swallowed.

INSIDE THE LUNGS
In each lung there is a large air tube, called a bronchus, which branches off the trachea. These tubes divide many more times, forming millions of airways called bronchioles. Each bronchiole ends in a cluster of microscopic air chambers, called alveoli, which are surrounded by blood capillaries. Oxygen seeps from the alveoli to the blood in the capillaries.

Lower lobe

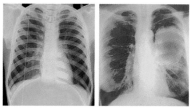

IN THE CLEAR
On an X-ray photograph, healthy lungs (left) show up as faint shapes. Shadowy areas (right) show lungs that have been damaged, for example, by smoking.

Middle lobe

Trachea

INVISIBLE INVADERS

Air may look clean, but it contains all kinds of floating particles, such as dust, pollen grains, bits of animal fur and feathers. Some people are very sensitive to these substances. They sneeze, cough, get runny noses and perhaps attacks of wheezy breathlessness called asthma. Even the powdery droppings of a microscopic creature called the dust mite (right) can float through the air and cause asthma.

Upper lobe

Pulmonary artery

Pulmonary vein

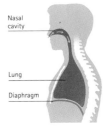

Nasal cavity

Lung

Diaphragm

BREATHING IN
The curved diaphragm under the lungs is the main breathing muscle. It contracts and flattens to stretch the lungs and suck in air.

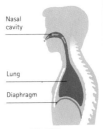

Nasal cavity

Lung

Diaphragm

BREATHING OUT
The diaphragm relaxes as we breathe out. The stretched, elastic lungs spring back to their natural smaller size, and blow out air. Rib muscles also help you to breathe.

Bronchus

Diaphragm

Heart

Lower lobe

Discover more in Moving Things Around

Salivary glands make watery spit, or saliva. When you eat, the saliva flows into the food and makes it soft and squishy. Saliva also contains enzymes that start to digest food.

Salivary gland

Salivary glands

• THE VITAL SYSTEMS •

Open Wide

The food that you eat takes a 24-hour journey through your body. It travels through the digestive tract, a tubelike passage that is about $29^1/_2$ ft (9 m) long and runs from the mouth to the anus. Food is essential for two main reasons. First, the body needs energy to make it go. Food provides the energy needed to power the millions of chemical reactions that take place in the body. Second, food contains the nutrients needed to make new body tissue and to maintain and replace worn-out cells and tissues. Digestion is the process of breaking down the food, by physical and chemical means, into pieces that are small enough to be absorbed by the body. The mouth is designed to bite off bits of food, mix them with watery saliva, chew them into a soft pulp, and swallow them down the esophagus into the stomach.

CUTTERS, CHOPPERS AND CHEWERS

Teeth have different shapes and names. The incisors at the front are wide and sharp to cut and bite. The canines are longer and more pointed to tear and rip. The premolars and molars are broader and flatter to chew and crush. There are 32 teeth in a full adult set. On each side of the upper and lower jaw there are two incisors, one canine, two premolars and three molars. The third molars are called wisdom teeth, but many adults do not have all, or any, of these. Children have only 20 teeth in their first full set.

| Incisor | Canine | Premolar | Molar |

A MOUTHFUL OF FOOD
Each part of the mouth has its own job, but the parts work together as a whole to begin the process of digestion. The lips open to let in food, then seal together to prevent it from falling out. The teeth chop and chew the food while the tongue moves it around. The cheeks bulge as food is squeezed and squashed between the teeth before the tongue presses it into the throat for swallowing.

DOWN IN THE MOUTH
The tonsils are at the very back of the mouth—one on either side. Tonsils are ridges of lymph tissue (left) that help to fight germs and disease. During an infection called tonsillitis, they may swell up with extra fluids, white blood cells and dead germs. If you have tonsillitis, it can be difficult to swallow.

READY
The tongue separates a small portion of the food in the mouth. It presses this against the mouth's roof, or hard palate, to shape it into a soft lump.

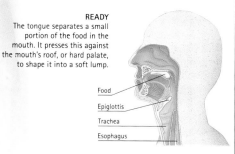

Food
Epiglottis
Trachea
Esophagus

STEADY
The tongue pushes the lump into the upper throat. A flap, called the epiglottis, closes over the top of the trachea to prevent food from going down it.

Food
Epiglottis
Trachea
Esophagus

SWALLOW
Muscles in the walls of the lower throat and esophagus contract in waves. They grasp the lump of food and force it down the esophagus to the stomach.

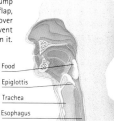

Epiglottis
Esophagus
Food
Trachea

DID YOU KNOW?
Fresh saliva from healthy salivary glands contains no bacteria or other germs. After chewing, it may contain a million bacteria in one droplet. They come from food and the lining in the mouth.

Discover more in Taste Sensations

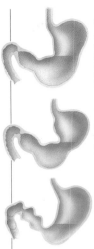

JUST SWALLOWED
The stomach's muscular walls squeeze and squirm to mash food (coloured blue). Its lining produces powerful digestive juices that break down food.

AFTER ONE HOUR
Food is turned into a lumpy soup called chyme. Starchy and sugary foods digest fastest, while fatty foods are the slowest.

AFTER FOUR HOURS
The stomach's job is done. The remains exit through the sphincter, which opens regularly to allow squirts of chyme into the small intestine.

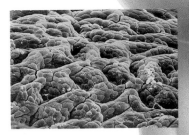

SELF-PROTECTION
The stomach's lining (above) contains tiny glands that make gastric acids, enzymes, and mucus. The lining is coated with thick mucus so that it does not digest itself.

Gall bladder

Duodenum

Liver

Large intestine

Appendix

• THE VITAL SYSTEMS •

The Production Line

The first stop for food swallowed down the esophagus is the stomach. The stomach is the widest part of the digestive tract. It is a muscle-walled bag that can expand to hold about 1/2 gallon (2 liters) of food and drink. The stomach breaks up the food with powerful squeezing actions and strong digestive chemicals. The soupy, partly digested food oozes into the next section, called the small intestine. More enzymes are mixed in for further chemical breakdown. The digested nutrients are absorbed into blood flowing through the lining of the small intestine. The large intestine is shorter, but much wider, than the small intestine. Water, body salts and minerals from the undigested food are absorbed here. The brownish, semi-solid remains are called feces and are stored in the rectum. The final stage is when the remains are passed through the anus.

Esophagus

Stomach

Pancreas

FOOD PROCESSORS

The digestive system includes the digestive tract, pancreas, gall bladder and liver. The pancreas and gall bladder empty juices and bile into the small intestine to digest food there. The liver receives digested nutrients in the blood and stores and processes them.

HEALTHY FOODS

To stay healthy, a body needs a wide variety of foods containing important dietary components. These include proteins for growth, maintenance and repair, and starches and sugars for energy. Some fats (especially plant-based ones) make nerves and tissues healthy, but too much fat can harm the heart and blood vessels. Fresh vegetables and fruits provide essential minerals and vitamins, and also fiber, or roughage. This keeps the digestive tract itself healthy and working well.

Small intestine

DID YOU KNOW?

The small intestine is four times longer than the large intestine. The small intestine is an incredible 20 ft (6 m) long while the large intestine is only 5 ft (1.5 m) long.

FRILLY VILLI

The small intestine's velvety lining consists of thousands of finger-shaped villi (left), each about $1/25$ in (1 mm) long. They form a huge surface, more than 20 times the body's skin area, to absorb digested nutrients.

Rectum

The Work Continues

Liver

The digestive system is made up of the digestive tract, the pancreas, the gall bladder and the liver. The wedge-shaped pancreas gland, just behind the stomach, makes strong digestive juices to help food digest in the small intestine. The gall bladder is under the liver. It stores bile, a yellowish fluid made by the liver, which also helps digestion in the small intestine. The liver, next to the stomach, is the largest organ inside the body. It has more than 600 different jobs, mostly processing nutrients and other substances that are brought by the blood from the small intestine. After body cells have used their nutrients, they make waste products such as urea. The blood collects the waste products, and the excretory system—the kidneys, ureters, bladder and urethra—gets rid of them as a yellowish fluid called urine.

Cortex

Medulla

Renal artery

Renal vein

Renal pelvis

BLOOD'S FILTER
Each kidney's cortex and medulla layers filter blood brought by the renal artery. The filtered blood returns to the heart by the renal vein. Wastes and excess water collect in the renal pelvis as urine.

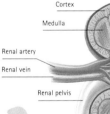

THE EXCRETORY SYSTEM
The two kidneys are in the upper abdomen, just below the liver and stomach. Urine flows to the bladder in the lower abdomen, then out along the urethra.

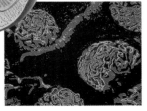

TINY FILTERS
Each kidney contains about 1 million microscopic blood-filtering units called nephrons (above). Every day, the kidneys filter about 42 gallons (190 liters) of blood.

Gall bladd[er]

JUICES FOR DIGESTION
As you eat a meal, the digestive system prepares for action. Bile flow[s] into the small intestine from the ga[ll] bladder along the bile duct. It diges[ts] mainly fatty foods. Digestive juices flow from the pancreas, along the pancreatic duct, into the small intestine. They digest mainly protei[n]

Inferior vena cava

Esophagus

Right hepatic vein

Left hepatic vein

Portal vein

Stomach

Pancreatic duct

Bile duct

Pancreas

Small intestine

LIFE-SAVING TREATMENTS

Kidneys sometimes become diseased and cannot filter blood. This means that harmful wastes can build up in the body. Sometimes the blood can be filtered through a machine, a renal dialyzer, for several hours every few days. Another treatment is to transplant kidneys from a person who has just died, or one from a relative. The kidneys are kept cool and bathed in special fluids (right) before the transplant.

Discover more in The Production Line

The Bare Bones

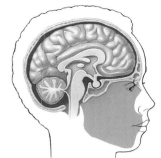

BRAIN PROTECTION
Bones support and protect. The rounded dome of the skull shields the delicate brain from injury. The upper skull, or cranium, is made up of eight curved bones linked firmly at wiggly lines called suture joints.

Most parts of the body, such as blood vessels, nerves and intestines, are soft and floppy. The whole body can stand up straight and move about because it is held together by a skeleton. This is the inner framework of 206 bones, which are stiff and strong. The skeleton has two main parts. The axial skeleton is the central column, and is made up of the skull, vertebrae (backbones), ribs and sternum. The appendicular skeleton is made up of the bones of the arms and legs. About half of all the body's bones are in the wrists, hands, ankles and feet. Each bone in your body works as a movable beam or lever and is specially shaped to support, protect and withstand stresses and strains. Most bones are linked at flexible joints and pulled by muscles, which allow you to walk, run, jump, and perform more delicate movements.

HEAD BONES
The brain is so securely encased in bone that doctors must use scanners to find out if anything is wrong.

Scapula

Humerus

Ulna

Phalanx

Suture joints

Radius

Skull

Metacarpus

Clavic

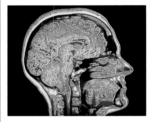

Fibula

Tibia

Femur

Patella

Vertebra

Rib

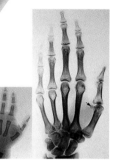

GROWING BONES

Bones grow first as soft, flexible cartilage. This gradually hardens into true bone. It takes many years for some bones to grow, especially those in the wrist and hand. Look at the hand X-rays of a child (left) and adult (right). True bone is the whitest.

Pelvis

Sternum

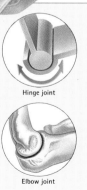

Hinge joint

Elbow joint

AT THE JOINT

Joints, like bones, are designed for their jobs. Joints that allow least movement are the most strong and stable. Suture joints have firmly cemented bones that cannot move. Hinge joints (left) in the knees, elbows and knuckles let the bones move to-and-fro, but not from side to side. Ball-and-socket joints (right) in the hips and shoulders let the bones twist, move to-and-fro, and from side to side. Bones are covered with slippery, shiny cartilage where they meet at the joint. This prevents them from wearing out and keeps the movements of the bones smooth.

Ball-and-socket joint

Hip joint

NES, BONES, BONES

nes are many sizes and shapes.
general, long bones in the limbs are
e supporting beams and movable
ers. Wide, flat bones in the shoulders
d hips anchor many muscles. Each bone
s a scientific name, and many have
mmon names, too. The patella, for
mple, is usually called the kneecap.

303

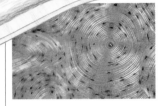

Periosteum

Spongy bone

Compact bone

Bone marrow

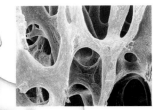

COMPACT BONE
A bone is like a tube. The outside is made of compact bone (left) and is hard and dense, while the inside is jelly-like tissue called bone marrow. A living skin, called periosteum, covers the bone.

• THE ULTIMATE STRUCTURE •

What's in a Bone?

Bone is living tissue that grows and changes throughout your life. Although bones you may see outside the body are dry and brittle, inside the body, they are one-fifth water and are tough, but flexible. Bone tissue is a mixture of three main substances. One is a meshwork of fibers called collagen, which lets bone bend without snapping. The second is masses of crystals, made up of minerals such as calcium, carbonates and phosphate. These make bone tough and hard. The third is millions of cells called osteoblasts, which build and maintain the collagen and mineral crystals around them. Like other body parts, bones have blood vessels to bring them nutrients and nerves to detect pressure and pain. Bones also respond to change. If you decide to take up weightlifting, for example, your bones will grow new tissue to cope with the new stresses.

A BONE DOME
The human body is a marvellous construction, and designers, architects and engineers have learnt much from it. Just like the human skull, some buildings are dome-shaped. This shape is light, but very strong.

SELF-REPAIR
Bones show up clearly as pale shapes on X-rays, or radiographs. These reveal any break or fracture in the bone. A splint, plaster cast or other support holds the broken bone steady in the correct position so that it can heal itself.

BROKEN BONE
Bones have blood vessels and nerves, so they bleed when broken. The blood clots to seal the leaks.

MENDING BONE
Cells at the edge of the break make new hard tissue, which grows into the clot. At first, this is cartilage.

MENDED BONE
The cartilage hardens into true bone. Other cells break up the lumps and "remodel" the bone to its original shape.

RED MARROW, YELLOW MARROW

There are two main kinds of jelly-like marrow in bones. In a baby, most bones contain red marrow, a very busy substance. Each day, red marrow produces millions of new red blood cells, platelets, and some white blood cells, to replace those that die. In adults, red marrow is found in the ends of the long bones, the sternum, ribs, vertebrae and parts of the skull. The other bones contain yellow marrow, which is mainly a store of fats and minerals. Bone-marrow disease may affect the body's disease-fighting immune system, which is based on white blood cells.

Healthy bone marrow

Sick bone marrow

Muscle Power

Trapez

Deltoid

PULLING TOGETHER

Many muscles work in pairs. For example, the biceps pulls the forearm bone to bend the elbow. Its opposing partner, the triceps, pulls the other way to straighten the elbow. Muscles must shorten, or contract, to create movement.

Biceps contract

Triceps relax

Biceps relax

Triceps contract

Every movement you make uses muscles. They allow you to blink, jump, eat, run and sing. Your body has three different kinds of muscles. Cardiac muscle in the heart squeezes life-giving blood around the body. Smooth muscle in the walls of the digestive tract massages food along. The walls of other internal tubes and bags, such as the arteries and lungs, also contain smooth muscle. The most common kind of muscle is skeletal, or striped, muscle. You have about 640 skeletal muscles and these make up two-fifths of your body weight. Some are long, thin and straplike; others bulge in the middle, or are flat and sheet-shaped. Skeletal muscles are joined to bones or to each other. When they contract, they pull on the bones and other tissues, and let you hoist up a huge weight or tie a shoelace.

Hamstring

Gastrocnemius

Triceps

Gluteus maximus

Rectus abdominis

Achilles tendon

DID YOU KNOW?
The biggest muscle in the body is the gluteus maximus, which is in the buttock and upper thigh.
The smallest muscle is the stapedius. This is attached to the tiny stirrup bone, deep in the ear.

LAYERS OF MUSCLES
Dozens of skeletal muscles lie just under the skin. Their narrowed ends form ropelike tendons that anchor them firmly to bones. The muscles crisscross and intertwine to form layers all over the body.

MUSCLE POWER

Skeletal muscle has bundles of muscle fibers. They are giant cells, slightly thinner than hairs, up to 12 in (30 cm) long. These muscles are also called striped muscles because they have a regular banded pattern. Smooth muscle has spindle-shaped cells without banded patterns. Cardiac muscle cells branch and rejoin.

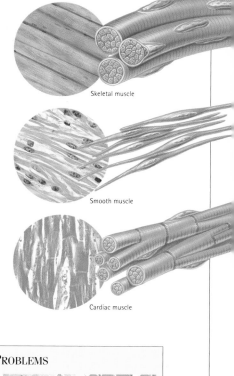

Skeletal muscle

Smooth muscle

Cardiac muscle

FITTER MUSCLES

Exercise makes all your muscles—even the heart and breathing muscles—bigger and more powerful. This makes you feel fit and healthy.

Pectoralis major

ceps

Digital flexor muscle

MUSCLE PROBLEMS

Muscles that are not used and exercised regularly become weak and floppy. They can shrink and waste away. If your breathing, heart and blood-vessel muscles are weak, you can suffer from health problems. Some diseases affect mainly muscles. Muscular dystrophy is the general name for a group of muscle-wasting diseases. The muscle fibers in people with this disease shrink and die and are replaced by fatty and scar tissues.

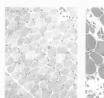

Healthy muscle   Muscular dystrophy

Discover more in On the Move

Skin Deep

Skin is the body's largest and heaviest organ. It covers almost 21 1/2 sq ft (2 sq m) on an adult, and weighs up to 9 lb (4 kg). It varies in thickness from 1/50 in (0.5 mm) on the eyelids to 1/5 in (5 mm) on the soles of the feet. Skin keeps in body fluids, salts and soft tissues. It keeps out dirt, germs, water and most harmful rays from the sun. It protects the delicate inner parts of the body against wear and tear, knocks and physical damage, and extremes of temperature. Skin also helps the body to maintain a constant temperature of 98.6°F (37°C). It turns flushed and sweaty to lose extra warmth, or goes pale to save heat.

It also provides the body's sense of touch, so that we can detect danger and stay out of harm's way.

ONLY ONE YOU
The ridged patterns of fingertip skin are fingerprints. They help to grip small objects and to identify you. No two fingerprints are the same. The skin replaces itself each month, but fingerprints remain through life.

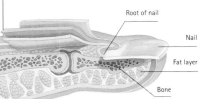

Root of nail

Nail

Fat layer

Bone

AT YOUR FINGERTIPS
A fingernail grows from a fold in the skin at the nail's root. It stays attached along the nail bed. Like a hair, a nail is dead. The nail bed and surrounding skin feel touch and pressure.

LOSING HAIR
Hairs, nails and the tough, dead cells at the skin's surface are all made from a body protein called keratin. An average scalp hair (above) lives for three years before it falls out and is replaced by a new one.

HAIR TYPES
The kind of hair you have depends mainly on its shape. Viewed under a microscope, a cross section of curly hair looks square, wavy hair looks oval and straight hair is circular. Like skin, hair color is determined by melanin.

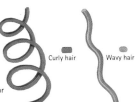

Curly hair   Wavy hair

Straight hair

SEEING INTO SKIN
This close-up of skin shows its two main layers. The epidermis is made of hard, tough cells. A top layer of dead cells rubs off and is replaced by cells multiplying below. The dermis contains many tiny parts such as blood vessels and nerves.

308

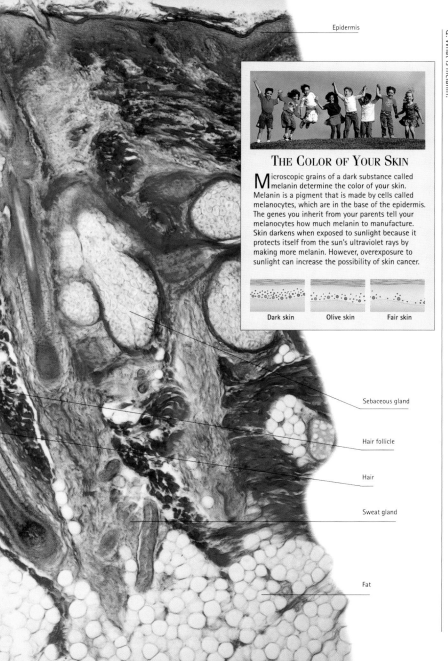

Epidermis

THE COLOR OF YOUR SKIN

Microscopic grains of a dark substance called melanin determine the color of your skin. Melanin is a pigment that is made by cells called melanocytes, which are in the base of the epidermis. The genes you inherit from your parents tell your melanocytes how much melanin to manufacture. Skin darkens when exposed to sunlight because it protects itself from the sun's ultraviolet rays by making more melanin. However, overexposure to sunlight can increase the possibility of skin cancer.

Dark skin

Olive skin

Fair skin

Sebaceous gland

Hair follicle

Hair

Sweat gland

Fat

Looking Around

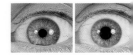

BRIGHT AND DIM
The iris adjusts the pupil. The pupil shrinks in bright conditions to keep too much light from damaging the retina (left), and widens in dim conditions to let in as much light as possible (right).

Five main senses tell the body about the outside world: sight, hearing, smell, taste and touch. Sight is the most important. Two-thirds of all the information processed in the human brain comes in through the eyes. Light enters through the clear, domed cornea at the front. It then passes through an adjustable hole, called the pupil, which is situated in a ring of muscle, called the iris. A lens focuses the light rays so that they cast a clear, sharp image on the retina, which lines the back of the eyeball. In the retina, about 130 million light-sensitive cells generate nerve signals when light rays shine on them. Signals are then sent along the optic nerve to the brain. The images formed on the retina are upside down (like those inside a camera), but the brain interprets them the right way up.

RETINA REVEALED
A doctor or optician sees into the eye with an ophthalmoscope. This shows the retina and blood vessels branching over the eye (left) and gives the doctor valuable information about the eye's health.

Optic nerve

Eye muscle

Retina

CELLS THAT SEE
The retina has two kinds of light-sensitive cells, called rods (yellow) and cones (blue). Rods work in dim conditions and cannot see colors. Cones can detect colors and fine details, but only function in bright light.

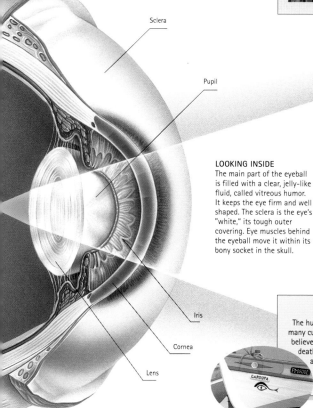

Tear duct

Tear gland

CRYING EYES

Every time you blink, tear fluid is smeared over the eye's surface to wash away dust and germs. The fluid comes from the tear gland, under the upper eyelid. It drains through tear ducts into the nose. This is why crying makes you sniff.

EYE PROBLEMS

Sometimes the eyeball is not the correct shape. If the eyeball is too long, the lens is unable to focus on distant objects and this causes near-sightedness (myopia). If the eyeball is too short, it causes far-sightedness (hyperopia). Glasses or contact lenses are used to correct these problems. If the light-sensitive rods and cones in your retina do not work properly, you can

have problems seeing colors. This can cause confusion between reds and greens. Tests using dots of different colors (left) can reveal color blindness.

Sclera

Pupil

LOOKING INSIDE

The main part of the eyeball is filled with a clear, jelly-like fluid, called vitreous humor. It keeps the eye firm and well shaped. The sclera is the eye's "white," its tough outer covering. Eye muscles behind the eyeball move it within its bony socket in the skull.

Iris

Cornea

Lens

DID YOU KNOW?

The human eye has been a powerful symbol for many cultures through the centuries. Many people believed that dreadful things, such as disease or death, could happen if someone was looked at with the evil eye. Today, some cultures still paint eyes on their fishing boats to ward off the bad luck of evil eyes.

Discover more in The Control Center

311

Listening In

Eyes see light, but they cannot see sound. Sound travels as invisible waves of high and low air pressure and is detected by your ears. The outer ear funnels these waves into the ear canal. They bounce off the eardrum, a small flap of taut skin, and make it vibrate. The eardrum is joined to a tiny bone called the hammer. The vibrations pass by the hammer, and two other miniature bones, the anvil and stirrup. After passing through a flexible membrane called the oval window, the vibrations move into a snail-shaped, fluid-filled area called the cochlea. Ripples are created in the cochlea's fluid. The ripples move microscopic hairs that stick out from rows of hair cells in the fluid. The hairs' movements generate nerve signals that pass along the auditory nerve to the brain.

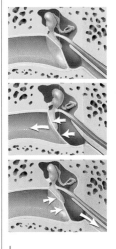

EQUAL PRESSURE
The middle-ear chamber is a tiny air pocket behind the eardrum. The Eustachian tube links it to the throat, and so to outside air.

PRESSURE UP
The outside air pressure is less when you are up high. Because the middle-ear pressure stays the same, the eardrum bulges and your hearing fades.

PRESSURE DOWN
If you swallow hard, the Eustachian tube opens. Air rushes out of the middle ear to relieve the pressure. Your eardrum "pops" back to normal.

EYES AND EARS
The ear canal of the outer ear is 1 1/5 in (3 cm) long. This means the delicate hearing parts of the middle and inner ear are set deep in the head, almost behind the eye. They are well protected inside the thick skull bone.

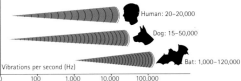

Human: 20–20,000
Dog: 15–50,000
Bat: 1,000–120,000

Vibrations per second (Hz)

0   100   1,000   10,000   100,000

HEARING SILENCE
The pitch or frequency of sound, from low to high, is measured in vibrations per second, or hertz (Hz). Human ears hear about 20 to 20,000 Hz, but animals can hear even higher pitched, or ultrasonic, sounds.

INSIDE THE EAR
The outer ear is large and obvious and guides sound waves into the ear canal. Three tiny ear bones vibrate in the air-filled middle-ear chamber, which is set into the skull bone. The snail-shaped cochlea converts vibrations to nerve signals.

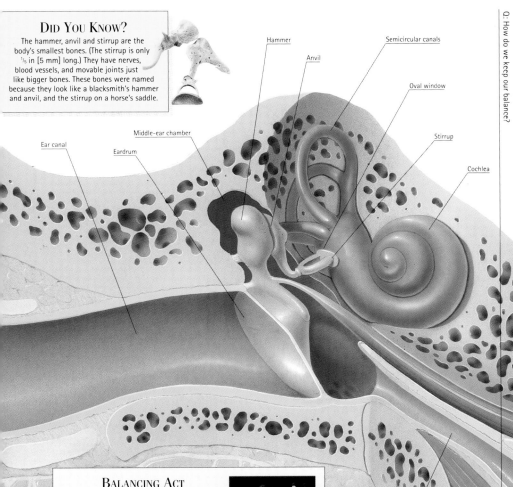

DID YOU KNOW?

The hammer, anvil and stirrup are the body's smallest bones. (The stirrup is only ¹/₅ in [5 mm] long.) They have nerves, blood vessels, and movable joints just like bigger bones. These bones were named because they look like a blacksmith's hammer and anvil, and the stirrup on a horse's saddle.

Hammer

Anvil

Semicircular canals

Oval window

Stirrup

Cochlea

Middle-ear chamber

Ear canal

Eardrum

Eustachian tube

BALANCING ACT

It is difficult to balance. This is because balancing involves various senses, the brain, and muscle actions. The three, fluid-filled semicircular canals inside the ear can detect movement by sensing changes in the flow of the fluid. The eyes and skin, and microscopic sensors in the muscles and joints, also send information to the brain. After split-second analysis, the brain sends nerve signals to the body's muscles to adjust its posture and stay well balanced—even upside down on a narrow beam!

Discover more in Communication

313

ON THE TIP OF THE TONGUE
The tongue has small lumps and bumps, called papillae, which help to grip food. The much smaller taste buds are set into the surface around their edges.

Pharynx

A GOOD SNIFF
When you breathe normally, air flows into the nasal cavity. To smell or sniff, air swirls around the ridged bones in the nose up to the olfactory areas in the nasal cavity's roof.

HAIRS THAT SMELL
Each olfactory area has 10 million cells that detect chemicals. Each cell has a tuft of up to 20 long hairs, called cilia. Different smells settle on these hairs and trigger nerve signals. An average person can identify 10,000 different smells.

• FROM THE OUTSIDE WORLD •

Taste Sensations

Taste and smell work in similar ways. They are both chemosenses, which means they respond to certain chemical substances. Taste detects flavors in food and drink. As you chew, watery saliva dissolves the flavors from foods. These flavors are picked up by more than 8,000 taste buds in the tongue's upper surface. Each taste bud has up to 50 chemical-sensing cells clustered together like segments of an orange. Smell detects odors floating in the air. The different odors around you land on two thumbnail-sized patches inside the top of the nose, called the olfactory areas. Taste and smell can help to warn you if food or drink is bad. They also detect delicious aromas and flavors. Smell alone can also warn you of danger, such as smoke from a fire.

AAAAA...
You sneeze when dust, animal fur or plant pollen irritates the sensitive lining of the nose.

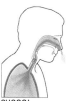

AAAAA...
The throat and windpipe close. Muscles in the chest and abdomen press the lungs and squash the air inside.

CHOOO!
When the windpipe and throat open again, high-pressure air blasts through the nose to blow away the irritants.

TASTES ON THE BRAIN
When the tongue's taste buds detect certain flavors, they send nerve signals along sensory nerves to the taste centers in the brain. These sort the signals and identify the taste. Smell signals run from the olfactory areas in the top of the nose to the olfactory bulb. This sorts out some of the smells and passes the signals on to the olfactory centers in the brain.

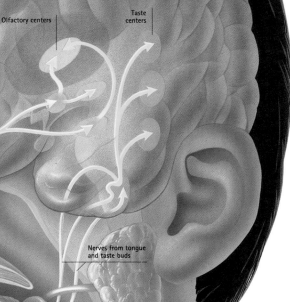

Olfactory centers

Taste centers

Olfactory bulb

Olfactory nerves

Nerves from tongue and taste buds

Salivary gland

Salivary gland

Salivary gland

FOUR FLAVORS

Hundreds of different tastes, from chocolate to lemon, are combinations of four basic flavors: bitter, sweet, sour and salty. Different parts of the tongue sense different flavors. Touch sensors inside the mouth detect pressure, hardness, texture, heat and cold. Although smell and taste are separate senses, the brain adds together their information. "Taste" is really a complicated combination of taste, touch, temperature and smell.

Bitter

Sweet

Sour

Salty

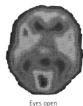

Listening to music   Understanding language   Eyes closed   Eyes open

SEEING THINKING
PET (Positron Emission Tomography) scans show which parts of the brain are busiest as the owner carries out different thoughts and actions. They help to "map" the jobs of various brain parts.

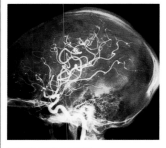

BRAIN'S BLOOD SUPPLY
An angiogram X-ray (above) shows arteries bringing blood to the brain. These angiograms can help to identify problems, such as strokes and brain tumors. If the blood supply to the brain stops for more than just a few minutes, parts of the brain begin to die.

• TOTAL CONTROL •

The Control Center

The brain is the control center of the body. All the nerve signals from the eyes, ears and other sense organs travel to the brain to be sorted and analyzed. These signals tell the brain about conditions outside the body. The brain decides what to do, and sends nerve signals to the muscles that control body movements. There are also sensors inside the body that send nerve signals to the brain, telling it about body conditions such as temperature, blood pressure, and amounts of oxygen, carbon dioxide, nutrients and fluids. The brain automatically controls breathing, heartbeat, digestion and many other inner processes. When nutrients or fluids run low, your brain makes you feel hungry or thirsty. The brain is the place where you think, remember, work out problems, have feelings, imagine and daydream.

DID YOU KNOW?
The brain is one-fiftieth of the weight of the whole body, but it consumes one-fifth of all the energy used by the body. This means the brain is ten times more energy-hungry than any other body part. Whether you are thinking or fast asleep, your brain is using energy constantly.

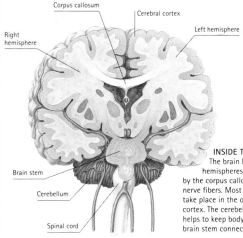

Corpus callosum

Cerebral cortex

Right hemisphere

Left hemisphere

Brain stem

Cerebellum

Spinal cord

INSIDE THE BRAIN
The brain has two parts called cerebral hemispheres. The two hemispheres are linked by the corpus callosum, a bridge of 100 million nerve fibers. Most conscious thoughts and feelings take place in the outer gray layer, called the cerebral cortex. The cerebellum, at the rear of the brain, helps to keep body movements coordinated. The brain stem connects the brain to the spinal cord.

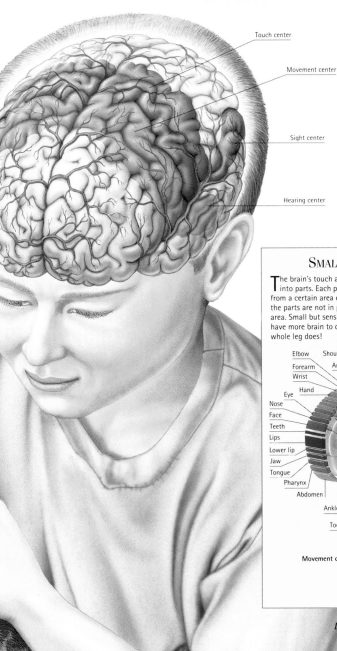

Touch center

Movement center

Sight center

Hearing center

BRAIN CENTERS
The cerebral cortex looks the same all over, but different parts, or centers, do different jobs. The sight center receives and analyzes nerve signals from the eyes. This is where you really "see." Other senses, such as hearing and touch, have their own centers. The movement center sends out signals to the body's muscles.

SMALL BUT COMPLEX
The brain's touch and movement centers are divided into parts. Each part deals with nerve signals coming from a certain area of the body, such as the lips. But the parts are not in proportion to the size of the body area. Small but sensitive areas, such as the lips, can have more brain to deal with their signals than a whole leg does!

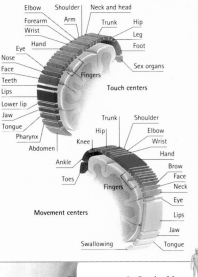

Elbow Shoulder Neck and head
Forearm Arm Trunk Hip
Wrist Leg
Hand Foot
Eye
Nose Sex organs
Face Fingers
Teeth Touch centers
Lips
Lower lip
Jaw
Tongue Trunk Shoulder
Pharynx Hip Elbow
Abdomen Knee Wrist
Ankle Hand
Toes Brow
Fingers Face
Neck
Movement centers Eye
Lips
Jaw
Swallowing Tongue

Discover more in On the Move

HOT FOOT

Long ago, people believed that nerves were tubes of fluid flowing to and from the brain. They thought this fluid carried messages around the body. If you burned your foot, for example, the fluid told your brain to pull your leg away.

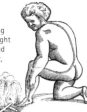

DID YOU KNOW?

If you sit in an awkward position, the nerves are sometimes squashed and blood vessels cannot supply vital nutrients and oxygen. A part of your body may "go to sleep," or feel numb. When you change your position, the pressure is relieved, blood flows, and the nerves begin to work again.

What a Nerve!

The brain is not isolated in its curved casket of skull bones. It is linked to all parts of the body by nerves. Nerves are long, pale and thin, like pieces of shiny string. The main nerve is the spinal cord, a bundle of millions of nerve cells with long, wirelike fibers. The spinal cord is about 18 in (45 cm) long, and is as thick as an index finger. Branches of nerves connect it to the skin, muscles and other body parts, and the upper end merges with the brain. The lower end tapers into a stringy cord inside the vertebrae (backbones) of the lower back. The billions of nerve cells in the brain, spinal cord and nerves are linked into a vast web, or network, which carries tiny electrical nerve signals.

NEURAL NETWORK

Each nerve cell has spidery dendrites that gather signals from other nerve cells at synapses. The signals travel along the cell's main wirelike section, called the axon, before passing on to other nerve cells.

Nerve cell body

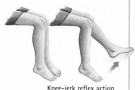

Synaptic cleft

Axon

Synapse

Dendrite

JUMPING THE GAP

Nerve cells link together at trillions of junctions called synapses, but they do not touch. They are separated by a tiny gap called the synaptic cleft. Nerve signals cross this gap as chemicals, called neurotransmitters, before continuing in an electrical form.

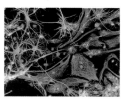

QUICKER THAN THINKING

Sometimes your body reacts quickly, before you even think about it, to avoid harm or danger. If a ball comes near your head, you close your eyes, turn your head and throw up your hands. These quick, automatic reactions are called reflexes. Sometimes the brain is not involved in reflexes. If your fingers accidentally get too hot, the skin sends nerve signals to the spinal cord, which sends other signals straight back to your arm muscles, and you pull your hand away. This is called the withdrawal reflex.

Knee-jerk reflex action

Withdrawal reflex

THE FLEXIBLE TUNNEL

A tunnel formed by holes in the vertebrae protects the spinal cord from knocks and kinks. Like the brain, the spinal cord is wrapped in three cushioning layers, or membranes, called the meninges. Thirty-one pairs of nerves branch out from the spinal cord to other areas of the body.

Vertebra

Spinal cord

Nerve

Intervertebral disk

MOTHER'S MILK
The pituitary "master gland" produces six main hormones. One is called oxytocin. This releases milk from a mother's breast.

FATHER'S BEARD
The male hormone testosterone comes from a man's testicles. It produces certain body features such as a deep voice and facial hair.

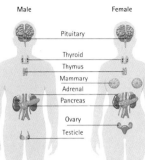

Male   Female

Pituitary
Thyroid
Thymus
Mammary
Adrenal
Pancreas
Ovary
Testicle

HORMONE-MAKING GLANDS
These are the main endocrine, or hormone-making, glands. The kidneys, stomach, intestines, heart and other organs make their own hormones.

CALCIUM CONTROL
The thyroid gland in the neck has four pea-sized parathyroid glands, which make parathormone. This hormone controls the levels of the mineral calcium (above) in bones and blood.

FLIGHT, FIGHT OR FRIGHT!
A roller-coaster ride makes your heart race, blood pressure rise, breath shorten, muscles tense and pupils widen. The hormone adrenalin, made by the adrenal glands above the kidneys, causes these effects. They are known as the "fight or flight" reaction because the body decides whether to face danger or flee from it.

• TOTAL CONTROL •

The Activators

The body is controlled by different systems. The brain and nerves send electrical signals through the body very quickly. The endocrine system works more slowly using chemicals called hormones. This system helps to regulate the amounts of nutrients, fluids and minerals. It activates and controls long-term growth, from baby to adult. The endocrine glands make more than 50 different hormones. Each hormone circulates in the blood and affects the workings of certain areas, such as organs and tissues. The thyroid gland produces thyroxine, which controls how quickly cells use energy. The thymus gland makes hormones that help white blood cells defend the body against disease. The adrenal glands make hormones that regulate sodium and other minerals, and help the body cope with stress and disease. The pea-sized pituitary gland just beneath the brain controls and coordinates the whole endocrine system and links it to the brain and nerves.

MISSING HORMONES

The two main jobs of the pancreas are to make digestive juices and hormones. In some people, the pancreas cannot make the hormone insulin, which controls the amount of energy-giving glucose in the blood. The resulting condition, called diabetes mellitus, can lead to serious illness. Injections of artificially produced insulin replace the missing natural insulin.

ON THE BOIL

A boil is a small-scale or localized area of inflammation, usually due to infection with germs. The germs, white cells and fluids gather in a hair follicle and make it swollen and tender—and fit to burst!

THE BATTLE RAGES

If germs get into the blood and multiply, they cause infection throughout the body. A high temperature is one sign of the body's reaction to invasion.

GERM INJECTION

A mosquito's needle-like mouthparts slide through human skin to suck blood, and inject any germs picked up from previous victims.

KILLERS ON THE LOOSE

White blood cells called T-cells control many features of immune defense. Other cells called killer T-cells (left) destroy invading germs on contact.

• WORKING TOGETHER •

Under Attack

The body is always under attack. Microscopic germs such as bacteria and viruses float through the air, enter skin cuts, and settle on food and drink. The body has many defenses. Tough skin keeps out many would-be invaders. They are trapped and killed by slimy mucus and natural chemicals in the linings of the nose, mouth, throat, lungs and gut. But if germs get in, the body also has internal defenses. The immune system, based on white blood cells called lymphocytes, makes substances known as antibodies. These stick to and destroy any germs that invade the body. The body also reacts to infection by a process known as inflammation. The infected part swells and becomes red, hot and sore, as white blood cells of many kinds rush to tackle the problem.

ATEN ALIVE

...arge white blood cells, called macrophages, crawl
...hrough blood and tissues to gather at the battle site
...their millions. They search for germs, bits of body
...ells and other debris, which they surround and
...ngulf. One macrophage (below) can "eat" more
...han 100 invading bacteria.

STRANGE BUT TRUE

There are complex links between the
brain and the immune system.
Some people believe that they will
become very sick if a medicine
man (above) places a
curse on them.

ALL-ROUND PROTECTION

A pale fluid called lymph flows
around the body through its own
system of lymph vessels and nodes
(glands). This system delivers
nutrients, collects wastes and
removes germs.

WHEN DEFENSES ARE DOWN

Human Immunodeficiency Virus (HIV)
attacks parts of the immune system that
are meant to protect the body against germs.
It destroys particular white blood cells called
helper T-cells. As the body loses its defenses,
after months or years, HIV can lead to the
general condition known as Acquired Immune
Deficiency Syndrome (AIDS). The body is then
open to other diseases, such as infections like
pneumonia and types of cancers.

HIV-infected cell

LETTERS AND WORDS
There are more than 2,000 different written languages. Most of these have an alphabet of basic units called letters, which are combined into groups known as words. Here are just some of the ways the words "the human body" can be written.

.: .•:.•• .: .:.•
Braille

ΤΟ ΑΝΘΡΩΠΙΝΟΝ ΣΩΜΑ
Greek

ΤΕΛΟ ЧЕЛΟΒΕΚΑ
Russian

人體
Chinese

• WORKING TOGETHER •

Communication

Humans communicate with each other every day using sounds and body movements. Most commonly, we share information about the world around us through spoken languages. These are special sounds we make to represent objects, actions, numbers, colors and other features. We use our brains to remember words, put them in the correct order, and make the larynx, or voice box, produce the correct sounds. If a person is unable to speak, he or she can communicate in other ways, often by using sign language. We also have written and pictorial languages, which are signs, symbols and squiggles that represent spoken words. The whole body works together to help us convey our innermost thoughts and feelings through language.

SHAPING SOUNDS
The jaws, tongue, cheeks and lips help to shape sounds, such as words, from the larynx. But not all the sounds from the larynx are words. They can be laughter, sad sobs or screams of pain.

 Aaah
 Eeee
 Oooh
 Mmmm

SOUNDS OF SPEECH
The sounds we make come from the larynx at the top of the trachea. It has two vocal cords at its sides. Air passes silently through the wide gap when we breathe normally. When we speak, the muscles pull the cords close together. Air then flows up the trachea making the vocal cords vibrate to produce sounds.

BODY LANGUAGE

We can communicate without words. All over the world, a smile means someone is happy, while a down-turned mouth and tearful eyes say he or she is sad. Body language involves facial expressions, gestures of the hands and limbs, and general posture and movement—from a slightly raised eyebrow to a low bow. It can convey information on its own, or extend and emphasise the meaning of spoken words.

Larynx

Vocal cords

Trachea

On the Move

GETTING AROUND
Some people cannot move around easily because they have an injury, a disease or a disability. Wheelchairs and other devices help them to move more freely and to take part in sports.

IN THE SWIM
A dolphin swishes its broad tail with powerful back muscles to surge through the water at high speed. Humans can also swim underwater, but they need the help of diving equipment to stay underwater for long periods.

Your body is constantly on the move. Even when you are resting or sleeping, oxygen, nutrients and other chemicals spread throughout the body, and cells grow, multiply and migrate. The heart pumps blood, lungs breathe and food squeezes through your stomach. When you are awake, your body is also in continuous motion—from glancing quickly to jumping in the air. The body's inner parts work together for movement. The brain sends signals along nerves to muscles, telling them to contract. The muscles need the oxygen and energy-rich sugars that are brought by blood, which is pumped by the heart. The lungs absorb oxygen, while the intestines digest nutrients from food. All of this happens in animals, too. Many animals are built for specialized movements—whales can swim, bats can fly and monkeys can climb. But the human body is probably the best all-rounder. People can do many things and they use their brains to invent special equipment to allow them to do even more.

ON THE RUN
A cheetah can run faster than any other animal. With four long, slim legs and a flexible body, it is built for speed. Humans can run short and long distances, but they are never as fast as the cheetah.

THE SKY

...ds can fly because they have extra-light ...dies and powerful chest and shoulder ...scles. Humans need to use equipment, ...ch as a hang-glider, to fly.

UP THE SLOPE

Sloths hang around in trees all day, and all night, too. Their hooklike claws are made for climbing. Humans can climb, but they often need to use picks, ropes and other equipment.

SLEEPING ON THE JOB

Scientists study people to find out what happens when we sleep. They have discovered that the body slows down, and the skeletal muscles are relaxed and still. But the body is still moving and working. The heart

pumps blood, lungs breathe air, intestines digest food, kidneys make urine, and millions of electrical signals fly around the brain. Sleep is vital and a person without it will die sooner than a person without food. By the time you are 60, you will have spent 20 years sleeping.

Discover more in Growing Up

327

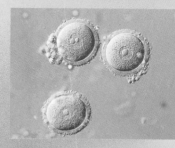

A MASSIVE CELL
The ripe egg is one of the largest cells in the human body. It is full of nutrients for the early stages of a baby's development. Like the sperm, the egg has only a half-set of DNA.

FEMALE PARTS
Each month one ovum, or egg, ripens and passes along the Fallopian tube to the uterus, or womb. The womb lining becomes thick and rich in blood vessels to nourish the fertilized egg as it develops. If the egg is not fertilized, the womb lining is not needed. It breaks down and comes away through the vagina as fluids and blood. This is called menstruation.

Fallopian tube

Uterus

Ovum

Ovary

Bladder

Position of female reproductive system

Urethra

Vagina

How Life Begins

The body has systems for digestion, movement and other activities. It also has a system for reproduction. The reproductive system is different in men and women. The parts of the female system are inside the lower abdomen. Glands called ovaries contain egg cells, or ova. The main parts of the male system are just below the lower abdomen. Glands called testicles contain sperm cells, or spermatozoa. Together, one egg and one sperm contain all the information and instructions necessary to create life. The instructions are in the form of genes which are made from the chemical deoxyribonucleic acid (DNA). When a sperm fertilizes an egg, a baby begins to develop in the woman's womb.

> **DID YOU KNOW?**
> An enormous set of instructions—between 100,000 and 200,000 genes—is needed to create a human body.

ANCIENT ART
People have always known that babies grew in a mother's uterus, or womb. The ancient Egyptians used hieroglyphs, or picture-symbols, such as these to represent the uterus.

COILS AND SUPERCOILS

Every cell contains DNA molecules. These hold all the genetic information, such as height and hair color, that makes you different from every other living thing. A DNA molecule is made up of four chemicals that fit together to form what look like the rungs of a twisting ladder. As a DNA molecule becomes tightly coiled, it forms part of a threadlike object called a chromosome. A sperm and an egg usually have 23 chromosomes each, a half-set of DNA. When they join, every cell in the new human body has 46 chromosomes, a full DNA set.

SEEING THE INVISIBLE
People could not see sperm or egg cells until the microscope was invented. Dutchman Anton van Leeuwenhoek made his own microscopes, such as the one below, and drew the first published pictures of sperm (left) in 1677.

MALE PARTS
The testicles, or testes, contain cells that continually divide to form millions of sperm cells every day. The sperm are stored in a coiled tube called the epididymis. During sexual intercourse, sperm are forced along the vas deferens and then along the urethra by powerful muscular contractions. About 400 million sperm come out of the urethra in a milky fluid called semen.

Position of male reproductive system

Bladder

Penis

Prostate gland

Vas deferens

Foreskin

Epididymis

Urethra

Testicle

Scrotum

TINY SWIMMERS
Sperm cells are like microscopic tadpoles that swim by lashing their tails. The half-set of DNA that they carry is inside the front end, or head, of the sperm.

329

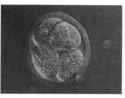

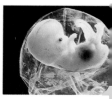

THE SPERM MEETS THE EGG
Hundreds of sperm cells gather around the egg cell as it moves slowly along the Fallopian tube to the uterus. But only one sperm will merge with, or fertilize, the egg.

THE CELLS DIVIDE
The fertilized egg divides into two cells. These split into four cells, then eight, and so on. After a few days, there is a ball of dozens of cells.

AN EMBRYO FORMS
Four weeks after fertilization, cells are multiplying in their millions and forming tissues and organs, such as the brain, the liver and the heart, which has already started to beat.

THE BODY SHAPES ITSELF
Six weeks after fertilization, the grape-sized embryo begins to develop arms and legs. The head is bigger than the body and has eyes and ears.

• FROM THE BEGINNING •

Early Life

When the egg and sperm join at fertilization, they form a single cell that is smaller than the head of a pin. The cell divides into a ball of cells that burrows into the blood-rich womb lining, absorbs the nutrients there and starts to grow. This time is called gestation, or pregnancy. From about the fifth month, the mother can feel the foetus kicking and moving about in the bulging uterus. The foetus floats in a pool of fluid, protected and cushioned from knocks and noises. It cannot breathe air or eat food. It obtains oxygen and nutrients from its mother's blood through an organ the size of a dinner plate, called the placenta, which is in the wall of the uterus. The foetus is linked to the placenta by a curly lifeline called the umbilical cord, through which blood flows. Nine months after fertilization the foetus has developed into a baby who is an average of 19^{1}/$_{2}$ in (50 cm) long and 7^{1}/$_{2}$ lb (3.4 kg) in weight.

READY FOR BIRTH
The powerful muscles in the walls of the uterus contract during labor. They begin to push the fully developed baby into the birth canal.

DELIVERY
The baby's head, its widest part, passes through the cervix, or opening of the womb. It emerges from the birth canal.

LEAVING THE WOMB
The muscles of the uterus continue to contract. The baby slips from warmth and darkness into the outside world.

THE FETUS FORMS

Eight weeks after the sperm joined the egg, the embryo is as big as a thumb and looks human. All major parts and organs have formed, and it is now called a fetus.

SIX MONTHS TO GO

The fetus is about 2¹/₃ in (6 cm) long. It hiccups and moves its arms and legs as it floats in the watery amniotic fluid inside the womb. In the final months, the fetus grows eyelashes and nails and becomes much larger.

DIFFERENT GENES

Each human body has a unique set of genes. Identical twins, however, develop from a fertilized egg that has split into two. Each half then develops into a complete human being. The twins look the same because they have identical genes. Fraternal twins develop together but each comes from a separate egg and sperm. Because their genes are different, they do not look the same.

331

TALL AND SMALL
People who have an excess of the growth hormone grow too much, while those with too little do not grow enough. Doctors can now treat these conditions to help people grow to a normal size.

Growing Up

The body grows by increasing its cell numbers. Growth is fastest in the mother's womb, and continues very rapidly during the first two years. Then, it begins to slow. Growth is controlled mainly by a growth hormone that is made by the pea-sized pituitary gland below the brain. Sex hormones control physical changes when girls are between 10 and 14 years old and boys are between 12 and 14 years old. A girl develops breasts, rounded hips and other female features. A boy develops a deep voice, facial hair and other male features. The body's final height is due largely to the genes inherited from the parents. However, the human body also needs nutrients, energy and raw materials from healthy food to grow properly. As the body develops, so does the mind. We learn how to communicate and perform hundreds of other day-to-day tasks.

David, age 2 years

ON YOUR FEET
Children grow fastest in their first two years of life. By the age of two, most children can walk and run.

FOR THE FIRST TIME
By the time babies are eight months old, they have learned to move their arms and legs and to sit up. They have also grown teeth.

HAND OVER HAND
By the age of seven, children can perform delicate tasks with their hands. They have begun to develop independent thought.

David, age 6 months

David, age 7 years

Growing Older

The average human body peaks in size and physical fitness at about 20 years of age. The body begins to age after this, but for many years the aging process can hardly be noticed. Gradually the aging signs become more obvious. Hair turns gray, skin becomes wrinkled, reactions become slower, muscle strength decreases, height reduces, senses lose their sharpness, and even memory and concentration become less efficient. However, these signs happen at very different ages and rates in each individual.

Sam, age 4

Sam, age 6

Sam, age 8

SELF-PORTRAITS

Some skills combine your physical and mental abilities. To draw, you have to be able to use a pen or a brush. This involves your brain, nerves and hand muscles and feedback from your eyes. But you also show your understanding and experience of the world in your drawings.

David, age 10 years

MENTAL NOTES

about the age of ten, a child's growth once again increases. The child's mental velopment is very important at this age.

David, age 18 years

GROWN UP

At 18–20 years of age, the average person is physically fully grown and is considered adult.

THE CHANGING YEARS

At 12–14, everyday activities are usually mastered. The body goes through puberty and grows very quickly.

David, age 13 years

Spare Parts

Most parts of the body can be replaced by an artificial part called a prosthesis. This is a substitute for a natural body part that did not develop properly or was damaged by an injury or disease. Some prostheses, such as myoelectric hands, do the missing parts' job. Others, such as false eyes, may improve the body's overall appearance. Prostheses can also provide framework and support for the remaining natural parts. A metal plate, for example, can repair a broken bone. Artificial parts that are put into the body, such as metal joints or heart valves, are called implants. Natural body parts that are transferred between bodies, or different parts of the body, are called transplants. Skin is transplanted from one part of the body to another, but organs such as hearts and kidneys are often transplanted from someone who has just died.

A METAL PUMP
Disease may cause the heart to pump at an irregular rate, or to stop pumping altogether. Today, specialists are developing pumps like this to help the heart pump.

FROM THE HIP
This artificial hip joint copies the original ball-and-socket design, with a steel ball on a spike in the thigh bone, and a plastic socket cemented to the hip bone. It can replace a hip joint that has become stiff and painful through a disease such as arthritis.

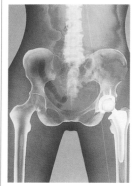

A CLEAR VIEW
Some people wear contact lenses instead of glasses. These help the eyes' own lenses and are less noticeable than glasses.

PLASTIC EYES
Some people have diseases of the eyes. Sometimes their eyeball or eyeballs may be removed to prevent a disease from spreading. Modern plastic eyes look very real, but the wearer cannot see with them.

LOUD AND CLEAR
Electronic engineers have developed a cochlear implant (left) for the part of the inner ear that changes sound vibrations into tiny electrical nerve signals. This implant allows some deaf people to hear again.

ELECTRIC HANDS
The myoelectric hand has an electric motor that moves its fingers and can grip even small, soft objects. Its metal wires and sensors detect signals in nearby nerves and muscles, so the wearer can control it precisely.

A NEW ARTERY
Special tubing (above) can replace diseased or damaged arteries. The inner surface of the tube is coated to prevent blood from sticking to it or clotting in it.

Glass eye

Rigid wooden leg

BODY BUILDING

For centuries, people have used the technology and materials available to them to build spare parts for the body and alter its appearance. False teeth have been made from many different materials, including wood, ivory and even gold! Eyes of glass were created to replace eyes that were lost through injury or disease. Rigid artificial arms and legs were made from wood. As engineering techniques improved, flexible limbs with hinges, levers and even wheels inside were built. Wigs have often been worn to cover baldness, but they have also been used as fashion accessories!

Flexible wooden arm

17th-century wig

A HELPING MACHINE
Sometimes machines help the human body to function properly. When a person's kidneys are diseased, the renal (kidney) dialysis machine filters and cleans their blood. Tubes carry the patient's blood to the machine and back again. Most patients need dialysis for several hours, several times a week.

HI-TECH LEG
The modern artificial leg has a hinged knee joint and a realistic-looking foot. It is a great advance on the wooden peg leg worn by some pirates hundreds of years ago.

SECOND SKIN
Surgeons are able to reuse skin from many areas of the body to help heal or replace skin that has been damaged or diseased in other areas. Specialists have also developed artificial skin, which allows the real skin underneath to heal naturally.

A FALSE BITE
Dental engineers use the hardest types of modern plastics and composites for modern false teeth, or dentures.

Planet Earth

Dinosaurs

Why were dinosaurs the most successful creatures ever to live on Earth?

Which dinosaur whiplashed predators with a heavy club on its tail?

Why did large plant-eating dinosaurs have stones in their stomachs?

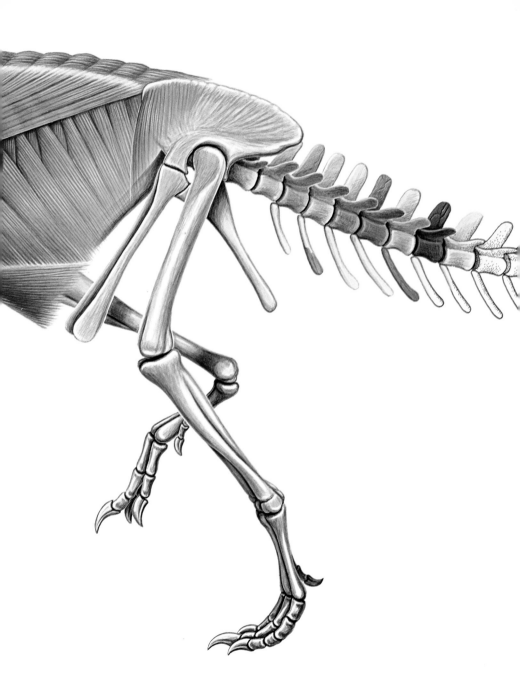

Contents

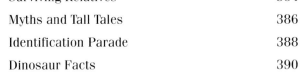

Before the Dinosaurs

Soft-bodied organisms
Fossils of algae, bacteria and jellyfish are rare. Their soft bodies usually rotted quickly, before mud could harden on them.

Blue-green algae and bacteria

Jellyfish

Animals with shells
Between 570 and 250 million years ago, there were more than 10,000 kinds of trilobites. They ranged from 1 in (3 cm) to 1½ ft (50 cm) in length.

Ammonite

Trilobites

Ptero

Drepanaspis

L ife on Earth began 4,600 million years ago. Its long history is divided into different periods, during which an amazing variety of life forms developed or died out. In the beginning, single-celled algae and bacteria formed, or evolved, in the warm seas that covered most of the planet.

In the Paleozoic Era, more complex plants and animals appeared in the sea: worms, jellyfish and hard-shelled mollusks swarmed in shallow waters and were eaten by bony fish. When plants and animals first appeared on land, they were eaten by amphibians that had evolved from fish with lungs and strong fins. Some amphibians then evolved into reptiles that did not lay their eggs in water. Early reptiles developed into turtles and tortoises, lizards, crocodiles, birds and the first dinosaurs. They dominated the world for millions of years.

The first jawless fish
Armor-plated fish such as *Pteraspis* and *Drepanaspis* did not have jaws. They sucked up food from the mud or fed on plankton.

A bony fish
Dunkleosteus, a giant of late Devonian seas, grew to 11 feet (3.4 m). It grasped its prey in sharp, bony dental plates because it did not have teeth.

Scorpior

An amphibian
Ichthyostega could not expand or contract its solid rib cage. This 3-ft (1-m) long amphibian had to use its mouth to push air into its lungs.

An early reptile
Hylonomus, a 8-in (20-cm) long reptile, is known only from fossils found in the remains of hollow tree trunks, where it may have become trapped while hunting insects.

A mammal-like reptile
Dimetrodon, which was 10 ft (3 m) long, may have angled its "sail" to catch sunlight so that it could warm up quickly in the morning.

Thecodontian archosaurs
Ornithosuchus looked like *Tyrannosaurus*, but it was not a dinosaur. It had five toes on each hind foot while *Tyrannosaurus* had only three.

THE DINOSAUR RACE

D inosaurs, which appeared in the Triassic Period, were descended from crocodile-like reptiles, whose legs sprawled at right angles from their bodies. *Euparkeria*, from the early Triassic Period, had straighter legs and carried its body off the ground. The legs of *Lagosuchus*, from the middle Triassic Period, were tucked beneath its body, and it walked on its hind legs. By the late Triassic Period, the predator *Ornithosuchus* looked a little like a dinosaur, but the earliest known dinosaur was *Eoraptor*. It appeared 228 million years ago.

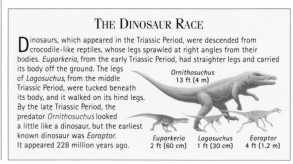

Ornithosuchus
13 ft (4 m)

Euparkeria
2 ft (60 cm)

Lagosuchus
1 ft (30 cm)

Eoraptor
4 ft (1.2 m)

millions of years ago	4,600	2,500	570	510	439	408	362	290	245
	Precambrian Era		Paleozoic Era						
Origin of the Earth	Archaean	Proterozoic	Cambrian	Ordovician	Silurian	Devonian	Carboniferous	Permian	
	First algae and single-celled bacteria appeared in the seas.	First animals with soft bodies and many cells. They looked like worms and jellyfish.	First sponges, segmented worms and hard-shelled animals.	First animals with backbones; jawless fish, then sharks and bony fish.	First land plants. Sea scorpions up to 7 ft (2 m) dominated the seas.	The Age of Fishes and the first land animals with backbones.	The Age of Amphibians. Primitive reptiles hunted insects and small amphibians.	Many species of reptiles that ate plants and meat. Trilobites disappear.	

Dunkleosteus

Ichthyostega

Dimetrodon

Dragonfly

Hylonomus

Ornithosuchus

What is a Dinosaur?

Dinosaurs were very special reptiles. Some were the size of chickens; others may have been as long as jumbo jets. These creatures were the most successful animals that have ever lived on Earth. They dominated the world for nearly 150 million years and were found on every continent during the Mesozoic Era, which is divided into the Triassic, Jurassic and Cretaceous periods. Like reptiles today, dinosaurs had scaly skin and their eggs had shells. The earliest dinosaurs ate meat, while later plant-eating dinosaurs enjoyed the lush plant life around them. Dinosaurs are called "lizard-hipped" or "bird-hipped," depending on how their hip bones were arranged. They stood on either four legs or two and walked with straight legs tucked beneath their bodies. Dinosaurs are the only reptiles that have ever been able to do this.

JURASSIC HUNTERS
In a scene from the Jurassic Period in North America, 69-ft (21-m) long *Apatosaurus* munches on a cycad as a 7-ft (2-m) long *Ornitholestes* pounces on a salamander disturbed by the grazing giant.

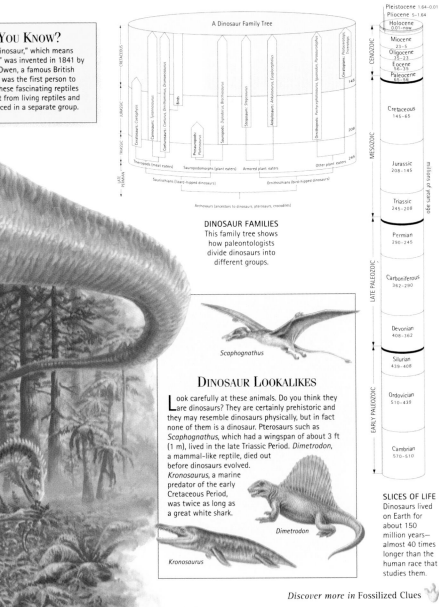

DID YOU KNOW?

The term "dinosaur," which means "terrible lizard," was invented in 1841 by Sir Richard Owen, a famous British scientist. He was the first person to realize that these fascinating reptiles were different from living reptiles and should be placed in a separate group.

A Dinosaur Family Tree

Ceratopsians: Protoceratops, Triceratops

Ornithopods: Parksosaurus/Heterodontosaurus, Iguanodon, Parasaurolophus

Ankylosaurs: Ankylosaurus, Euoplocephalus

Stegosaurs: Stegosaurus

Sauropods: Diplodocus, Brachiosaurus

Prosauropods: Plateosaurus

Coelurosaurs: Coelurus, Ornithomimus, Dromaeosaurus

Carnosaurs: Tyrannosaurus

Ceratosaurs: Coelophysis

Birds

Theropods (meat eaters)   Sauropodomorphs (plant eaters)   Armored plant eaters   Other plant eaters

Saurischians (lizard-hipped dinosaurs)   Ornithischians (bird-hipped dinosaurs)

Archosaurs (ancestors to dinosaurs, pterosaurs, crocodiles)

DINOSAUR FAMILIES

This family tree shows how paleontologists divide dinosaurs into different groups.

Scaphognathus

DINOSAUR LOOKALIKES

Look carefully at these animals. Do you think they are dinosaurs? They are certainly prehistoric and they may resemble dinosaurs physically, but in fact none of them is a dinosaur. Pterosaurs such as *Scaphognathus*, which had a wingspan of about 3 ft (1 m), lived in the late Triassic Period. *Dimetrodon*, a mammal-like reptile, died out before dinosaurs evolved. *Kronosaurus*, a marine predator of the early Cretaceous Period, was twice as long as a great white shark.

Dimetrodon

Kronosaurus

SLICES OF LIFE

Dinosaurs lived on Earth for about 150 million years— almost 40 times longer than the human race that studies them.

Discover more in Fossilized Clues

345

Geologic time scale (right margin):

Era	Period/Epoch	millions of years ago
CENOZOIC	Pleistocene	1.64–0.01
	Pliocene	5–1.64
	Holocene	0.01–now
	Miocene	23–5
	Oligocene	35–23
	Eocene	56–35
	Paleocene	65–56
MESOZOIC	Cretaceous	145–65
	Jurassic	208–145
	Triassic	245–208
LATE PALEOZOIC	Permian	290–245
	Carboniferous	362–290
	Devonian	408–362
EARLY PALEOZOIC	Silurian	439–408
	Ordovician	510–439
	Cambrian	570–510

SPRAWLING
The ancestors of the dinosaurs sprawled on four legs, like a lizard. They had to use large amounts of energy to twist the whole body and lift each leg in turn.

HALFWAY UP
Some reptiles, such as today's crocodiles, have upright hind legs. As their bodies are off the ground, they can run on their hind legs for short distances.

ON TWO LEGS
A dinosaur's weight was supported easily by its straight legs, tucked under its body. As the body weight was balanced over the hips by the weight of the tail, some dinosaurs were bipedal (two-legged) and used their hands for grasping.

TWO-LEGGED PLANT EATER
This 43-ft (13-m) long *Edmontosaurus* has a typical ornithischian pelvis. The pubis points backwards and allows more space for the large intestines that plant eaters needed to digest their food. Conversely, in sauropods (plant-eating saurischians) the intestines are slung forward. This means the forward-pointing pubis does not get in the way of these four-legged (quadrupedal) dinosaurs.

Dinosaur Hips

Dinosaurs walked upright with their legs beneath their bodies. No other reptiles have been able to do this. Dinosaurs had a right-angled joint at the top of the leg bone that fit into a hole in the hip bones. This allowed the limbs to be positioned under the body, so the weight of the dinosaur was supported, and all the joints worked as simple forward and backward hinges. These evolutionary advances were the key to the great success of the dinosaurs. They did not have to throw the whole body from side to side to move their legs, so they could breathe easily while running quickly. They were able to grow bigger, walk further and move faster than any other reptiles. The two main groups of dinosaurs had different kinds of hips. The meat eaters and plant-eating sauropods (called saurischians, or lizard-hipped dinosaurs) had a forward-pointing pubis. In the plant-eating ornithischians, or bird-hipped dinosaurs, part of the pubis pointed backward, to allow more space for the gut.

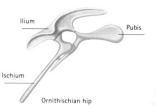

Ilium
Pubis
Ischium
Ornithischian hip

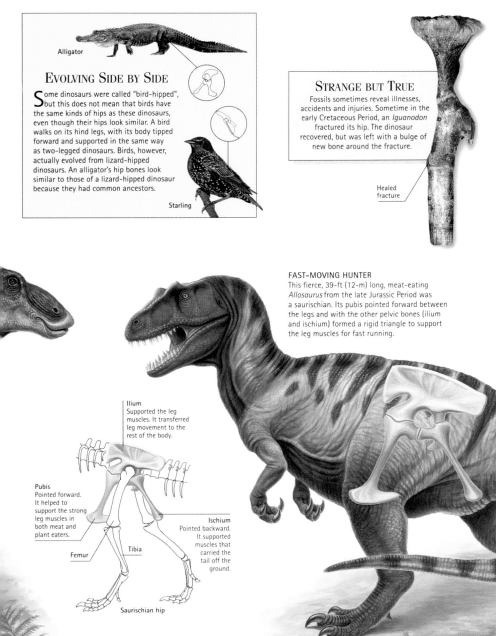

EVOLVING SIDE BY SIDE

Some dinosaurs were called "bird-hipped", but this does not mean that birds have the same kinds of hips as these dinosaurs, even though their hips look similar. A bird walks on its hind legs, with its body tipped forward and supported in the same way as two-legged dinosaurs. Birds, however, actually evolved from lizard-hipped dinosaurs. An alligator's hip bones look similar to those of a lizard-hipped dinosaur because they had common ancestors.

Alligator

Starling

STRANGE BUT TRUE

Fossils sometimes reveal illnesses, accidents and injuries. Sometime in the early Cretaceous Period, an *Iguanodon* fractured its hip. The dinosaur recovered, but was left with a bulge of new bone around the fracture.

Healed fracture

FAST-MOVING HUNTER
This fierce, 39-ft (12-m) long, meat-eating *Allosaurus* from the late Jurassic Period was a saurischian. Its pubis pointed forward between the legs and with the other pelvic bones (ilium and ischium) formed a rigid triangle to support the leg muscles for fast running.

Ilium
Supported the leg muscles. It transferred leg movement to the rest of the body.

Pubis
Pointed forward. It helped to support the strong leg muscles in both meat and plant eaters.

Ischium
Pointed backward. It supported muscles that carried the tail off the ground.

Femur

Tibia

Saurischian hip

In the Sea and in the Air

Longest-winged pterosaur
Pteranodon had a long, toothless beak. It probably scooped up fish in its narrow jaws, just like a pelican.

Fish eater
Dimorphodon, a pterosaur, had a long tail and forward-facing teeth to grasp its prey.

Pint-sized flier
Archaeopteryx, the earliest bird of all, evolved from the dinosaurs. It probably ate insects and small reptiles.

TARGET IN SIGHT

Above the seas in the late Jurassic Period, one of the most common pterosaurs, *Rhamphorhynchus*, spies *Muraenosaurus*, a 20-ft (6-m) long plesiosaur, attacking a school of *Leptolepis* fish. *Rhamphorhynchus* had a leaf-shaped membrane on the end of its tail to help it steer in flight.

D uring the Mesozoic Era, dinosaurs ruled the land, marine reptiles dominated the sea and flying reptiles, called pterosaurs, glided through the skies. Marine reptiles and pterosaurs were only distant cousins of the dinosaurs, even though some marine reptiles looked almost like long-necked sauropods with fins. Pterosaurs were the first animals with backbones to take to the air—on wings made of skin. Many of them hunted fish, but others such as *Quetzalcoatlus*, the largest flying animal of all time, had no teeth and used their jaws to eat decaying animals. Plesiosaurs, pliosaurs, marine turtles, crocodiles and other sea reptiles lived in the waters of the Mesozoic world. The plesiosaurs had long necks and a small sea creatures, while the big-headed, short-necked pliosaurs tackled larger prey with their strong teeth and jaws.

WORLDS APART

There were differences among the flying animals of the Mesozoic Era—differences that can still be seen in flying creatures today. The wings of a pterosaur were skin membranes, supported by a long fourth finger. The wings of a living bat are also made of skin membrane. However, a bat's wings are supported by all its fingers. Modern birds evolved from *Archaeopteryx*. Its wings were made of feathers that were arranged in a similar way to those of a living bird, such as a pigeon.

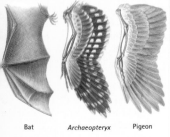

Bat   *Archaeopteryx*   Pigeon

FISHY LIZARD
Ichthyosaurus (meaning "fish-lizard") was about 7 ft (2 m) long, with a streamlined body shaped like a dolphin. Paleontologists think it could reach a speed of 25 miles (40 km) per hour for short bursts.

IN THE SEA

The pliosaur *Peloneustes*, 10 ft (3 m) long, had a short neck but a long jaw full of rounded teeth.

The turtle *Archelon* was almost 13 ft (4 m) long—as big as an automobile.

Triassic *Nothosaurus*, 10 ft (3 m) long, was at home in the water and on the land.

The lizard *Platecarpus* was 13 ft (4 m) long, with a tail as long as its body.

Cretaceous *Deinosuchus* was a giant crocodile, 49 ft (15 m) long.

STRANGE BUT TRUE

Eric, a 5-ft (1.5-m) long Jurassic pliosaur from Queensland, Australia, is one of the most spectacular fossils in the world. As Eric's bones decayed, they were gradually replaced by minerals that formed a precious stone called opal.

Discover more in Surviving Relatives

A VIEW OF THE WORLD
In the Triassic Period, the continents
fitted together into one huge
continent called Pangaea. Fossils
show that most dinosaurs lived near
the center of Pangaea, the area now
divided among North America,
Africa and northern Europe.

Ginkgo tr

FOSSIL SITES OF TRIASSIC DINOSAURS

Coelophysis

• THE ARRIVAL OF THE DINOSAURS •

The Triassic World

The Triassic Period was the "Dawn of the Dinosaurs." The Earth was a huge supercontinent called Pangaea (from the Greek meaning "all Earth"), which had three main environments and was dominated by mammal-like reptiles. Near the coasts, forests of giant horsetail ferns, tree ferns and ginkgo trees were alive with insects, amphibians, small reptiles (such as the first turtles, lizards and crocodiles), and early mammals. The dry, cool areas near the equator had forests of tall conifers (pine and fir trees) and palmlike cycads. The center of Pangaea was covered by hot, sandy deserts. Many different plants and animals developed in these varied climates. There was plenty of food for many life forms, especially one group of animals that first appeared 228 million years ago—the dinosaurs. These extraordinary creatures began to rule the Triassic world.

THE CHASE
In the warm, moist forest
close to the coast of
Pangaea, two *Coelophysis*
chase a *Planocephalosaurus*
up a tree.

AN EARLY DINOSAUR
Eoraptor, the earliest known
dinosaur (a fossilized head
is shown supported by a
human hand), lived 228
million years ago in what
is now South America.
This fast, lizard-hipped
animal did not have a
flexible jaw, so it could
not trap struggling prey.
It probably scavenged food
from animals killed by
larger reptiles.

STRANGE BUT TRUE
Coelophysis was an agile predator that used
its strong, clawed hands to grab small prey.
One fossil was found with the remains of a
baby *Coelophysis* in its stomach. Did this
Triassic hunter eat a member of its
own species?

TRIASSIC DINOSAURS

Zanclodon was a 20-ft (6-m) long, meat-eating carnosaur.

Horsetails

Herrerasaurus was a 10-ft (3-m) long, meat-eating coelurosaur.

Cycads

Procompsognathus was a 4-ft (1.2-m) long, meat-eating coelurosaur.

Saltopus was a 2-ft (60-cm) long, meat-eating carnosaur.

Plateosaurus was an 26-ft (8-m) long, plant-eating prosauropod.

DINOSAUR DIETS

Before flowering plants appeared in the Cretaceous Period, plant-eating dinosaurs grazed on ferns and tree leaves. Many plants had tough, waxy coatings or spines to protect themselves.

Meat-eating dinosaurs such as *Eoraptor* and *Coelophysis* hunted insects such as cockroaches and dragonflies, frogs, mammal-like reptiles and even early mammals —our distant ancestors.

Dragonfly

Tree fern   *Wielandiella*   *Haramiya*

Discover more in Meat-eating Dinosaurs

351

As the two supercontinents moved apart, the centers of dinosaur evolution spread. Most of the plant-eating sauropods, for example, remained in Gondwana, but some theropods, such as *Allosaurus*, spread throughout Laurasia.

Laurasia

Gondwana

Tree fer

FOSSIL SITES OF JURASSIC DINOSAURS

STRANGE BUT TRUE

The forests that covered the Jurassic world survive today—as seams of coal. Dead trees (even whole forests destroyed by storms or floods) were covered by mud and soil. They slowly hardened into material that looks like rock, but burns like wood!

REARING ITS HEAD
A *Diplodocus* rears to defend itself against a predator. Its clawed front feet and lashing tail are ready for battle.

• THE ARRIVAL OF THE DINOSAURS •

The Jurassic World

Toward the end of the Triassic Period, the supercontinent of Pangaea started to divide into two smaller, but still very large, continents—Laurasia and Gondwana. New kinds of dinosaurs began to evolve on these new continents as they moved further apart. The slightly cooler temperatures and higher rainfall of the Jurassic world created a warm, wet climate that was ideal for reptiles. The lizard-hipped dinosaurs continued to break into the two groups that first split in the Triassic Period: the meat-eating theropods, which walked on two legs; and the plant-eating sauropods, which moved on all fours. The bird-hipped dinosaurs remained plant eaters. Giant, long-necked, plant-eating sauropods; plated, bird-hipped dinosaurs such as *Stegosaurus*; and bird-hipped plant eaters such as *Camptosaurus* were some of the mighty dinosaurs roaming the Jurassic world.

Camptosaurus, 20 ft (6 m) long, from Europe and North America

Allosaurus, 39 ft (12 m) long, from North America

Stegosaurus, 30 ft (9 m) long, from North America

Coelurus, 7 ft (2 m) long, from North America

Cycads

A SIZABLE APPETITE

Brachiosaurus was 39 ft (12 m) high and 75 ft (23 m) from nose to tail. It weighed an incredible 78 tons (80 tonnes)—as much as 12 African elephants—and ate the equivalent of 35 bales of hay a day. Its front legs were longer than its hind legs, and its whole body sloped downward from the shoulders (like a giraffe today), so its long neck could reach the tasty young leaves at the tops of the tallest trees.

FOOD FOR DINOSAURS
Jurassic dinosaurs ate many animals, including freshwater turtles such as *Pleisochelys* and perhaps even the earliest bird, *Archaeopteryx*.

Ground cover ferns

Discover more in Long-necked Dinosaurs

353

Conifer forest

MOVING CONTINENTS

Laurasia and Gondwana continued to move apart during the Cretaceous Period. By the end of this period, the outlines of the continents were roughly the same as they are today. There were land bridges between the continents, but dinosaurs tended to evolve separately on each of the land masses.

• THE ARRIVAL OF THE DINOSAURS •

The Cretaceous World

The Cretaceous Period lasted for 80 million years. More dinosaur species evolved in this time than in all the other dinosaur periods put together. But at the end of this period, about 65 million years ago, the dinosaurs disappeared. The early Cretaceous Period was warm. Winters were mild and dry, and most of the rain fell in summer. Later, summers became hotter and winters were colder in the temperate and polar regions. The giant plant eaters disappeared and were replaced by smaller species such as *Triceratops* and the duckbilled dinosaurs. Flowering plants evolved during this period (giant plant eaters during the Jurassic Period ate and trampled down so much of the vegetation that it gave new plants the chance to grow) and were eaten by hundreds of new species of plant-eating animals. There was a huge amount of food to support an enormous number of animals. The animals that ate the flowering plants were also eaten by predators, from snakes (which first appeared in this period) to great predatory dinosaurs such as *Tyrannosaurus*.

Magnolias

PREDATORS AND PREY

In this scene from the late Cretaceous Period in Mongolia, a *Velociraptor* (above right) battles with a *Protoceratops*, squashing dinosaur eggs in the process. An inquisitive *Prenocephale* looks on at the fierce encounter.

354

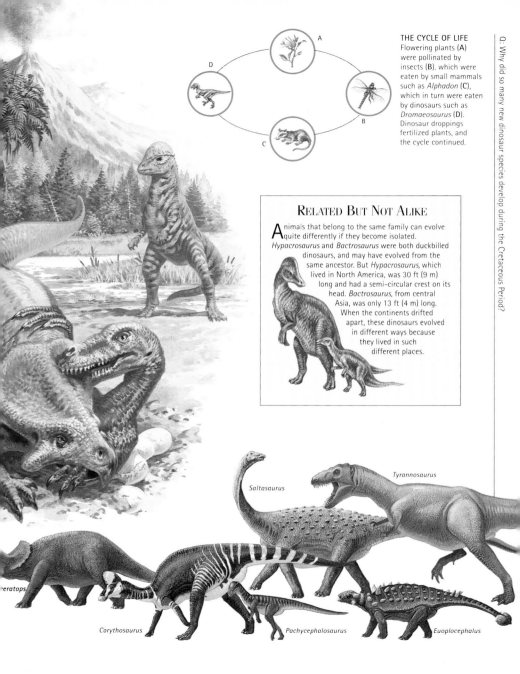

THE CYCLE OF LIFE

Flowering plants (**A**) were pollinated by insects (**B**), which were eaten by small mammals such as *Alphadon* (**C**), which in turn were eaten by dinosaurs such as *Dromaeosaurus* (**D**). Dinosaur droppings fertilized plants, and the cycle continued.

RELATED BUT NOT ALIKE

Animals that belong to the same family can evolve quite differently if they become isolated. *Hypacrosaurus* and *Bactrosaurus* were both duckbilled dinosaurs, and may have evolved from the same ancestor. But *Hypacrosaurus*, which lived in North America, was 30 ft (9 m) long and had a semi-circular crest on its head. *Bactrosaurus*, from central Asia, was only 13 ft (4 m) long. When the continents drifted apart, these dinosaurs evolved in different ways because they lived in such different places.

Saltasaurus

Tyrannosaurus

eratops

Corythosaurus

Pachycephalosaurus

Euoplocephalus

Meat-eating Dinosaurs

Many carnivorous dinosaurs were powerful, fast hunters that ate prey larger than themselves. But there were also smaller meat eaters (*Compsognathus* was no taller than a chicken) that ate eggs, insects, small reptiles and mammals. Carnosaurs, ceratosaurs and coelurosaurs, the three main groups of meat-eating dinosaurs, all had short, muscular bodies, slender arms, and low, powerful tails that balanced strong back legs with birdlike feet. With large eyes and daggerlike teeth, they were formidable predators: the coelurosaur *Deinonychus* had long, slashing claws on its front legs that could rip open a victim's belly; *Megalosaurus*, a carnosaur, had powerful hinged jaws that were armed with curved, saw-edged fangs. Meat-eating dinosaurs had much larger brains than plant-eating dinosaurs. Hunting prey that was large and sometimes armored required good vision and an ability to plan an attack.

THE PREDATOR KING
Tyrannosaurus ("the tyrant lizard") was the largest predator ever to walk the Earth. This gigantic creature weighed more than an African elephant. Five complete specimens of *Tyrannosaurus* have been found around the world.

Eye

Nostril

Teeth

A MEAT-EATER'S SKULL
Allosaurus, a 39-ft (12-m) long predator from the late Jurassic/early Cretaceous Period, weighed more than a ton. Its skull could be up to 3 ft (1 m) long. As its jaws were hinged, *Allosaurus* could swallow large pieces of flesh whole.

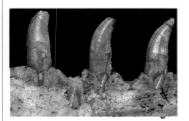

FIGHTING FOR LIFE
Tenontosaurus, a plant eater from the early Cretaceous Period, fights a pack of ferocious *Deinonychus*. This reconstructed scene may well have happened. In the United States, the fossil skeleton of a *Tenontosaurus* was found surrounded by five scattered specimens of *Deinonychus*.

TEETH AND JAWS
Theropods, such as *Megalosaurus*, had long jaws that were usually armed with sharp, serrated teeth. New teeth were ready to replace those that wore out.

Compsognathus
Coelurosaur

Oviraptor
Coelurosaur

Albertosaurus
Carnosaur

TOOLS OF EATING

The coelurosaur *Compsognathus* caught and ate prey with its hands. *Oviraptor* cracked open eggs with its beak. *Albertosaurus* had such short arms it had to tear off chunks of flesh with its powerful jaws. Scientists believe that the fish-eating *Baryonyx*, a theropod dinosaur discovered only in 1983, used the huge, hooklike claw on its hand to spear its prey.

Baryonyx
(not placed in
a group)

CUTTERS AND CHOPPERS
The shape of plant-eaters' teeth varied according to their diets. Dinosaurs that ate the hard leaves and fruit of cycads, palms and conifers had thick, peg-shaped teeth. Those that ate the leaves and fruit of softer, flowering plants had thinner, leaf-shaped teeth.

Peg-shaped tooth   Leaf-shaped tooth

| Triassic dinosaurs ate horsetail ferns as big as trees. | Jurassic dinosaurs ate pine cones and cycad fruits. | Cretaceous dinosaurs ate flowering plants such as magnolias. |

STOMACH STONES
Sauropods, such as *Saltasaurus*, had no grinding teeth. They nipped off leaves with their slender, pencil-like teeth and ground them up with stomach stones called gastroliths. These were ground together by the muscular action of the stomach and crushed tough plant material.

DINOSAUR DINNERS
New varieties of plants evolved on the Earth along with new species of dinosaurs. The plant-eating sauropods, the biggest dinosaurs of all, had to eat huge quantities of plants to provide them with enough energy.

FINGER FOOD
Othnielia, a 5-ft (1.4-m) long gazelle-like dinosaur from the late Jurassic Period, used its five-fingered hands to push aside and hold down a fern while eating it. *Othnielia* had cheek pouches to store food so the tough plant material it ate could be chewed thoroughly later on.

• A PARADE OF DINOSAURS •

Plant-eating Dinosaurs

For most of the dinosaur age, the climate was warm and moist, and plants grew in abundance. Hundreds, perhaps thousands, of species of plant-eating dinosaurs grazed on the ferns, cycads and conifers of the Triassic and Jurassic periods, then on the flowering plants of the Cretaceous Period. The bird-hipped ornithopods (the pachycephalosaurs, iguanodonts, duckbills, armored dinosaurs, and the horned dinosaurs that roamed in huge herds during the late Cretaceous Period) had special cheeks to store plants while they were busy chewing. The lizard-hipped sauropods, which included *Apatosaurus*, *Diplodocus* and *Brachiosaurus*, reached the lush vegetation at the tops of the trees with their long necks. These enormous plant eaters had large fermenting guts and stomach stones (as discussed above) that helped them digest huge amounts of plants.

TEETH AND BEAKS

Paleontologists can tell much about how a dinosaur lived from the shape of its teeth or its beak, if it had no front teeth. Giraffes' teeth are different from zebras' teeth because giraffes eat tender leaves from the tops of trees, while zebras eat tough, dry grass. In the same way, different families of dinosaurs evolved different kinds of teeth and beaks to cope with a variety of plants.

Protoceratops, one of the smaller horned dinosaurs, had a parrotlike beak for shearing off plant stems, and scissorlike teeth to slice up its food.

Camarasaurus, an 59-ft (18-m) long sauropod, had spoon-shaped cutting teeth but no grinding teeth. However, it could reach high into trees to tear away leaves.

Corythosaurus, a duckbill, tore off leaves with its horny beak, stored them in its cheek pouches, then used rows of strong interlocking teeth to grind them.

Plateosaurus, an early, long-necked giant, had leaf-shaped teeth to pluck off the leaves of soft plants such as ferns. It did not have grinding teeth.

Iguanodon grazed on tough plants such as horsetails, and used its horny beak to nip off leaves. Its rows of ridged, grinding teeth crushed the leaves into a pulp.

STRANGE BUT TRUE

Heterodontosaurus, a plant eater from the early Jurassic Period, had three kinds of teeth. In the front upper jaw it had small cutting teeth; on the lower jaw it had a horny beak. Then it had two pairs of large, fanglike teeth, with grinding teeth at the back.

Long-necked Dinosaurs

LONGEST NECK
Mamenchisaurus had the longest neck of any known animal— an amazing 36 feet (11 m). It could hardly bend its neck, but it could rear up on its hind legs to reach the tops of the highest trees.

The biggest, heaviest and longest land animals that have ever lived were the long-necked sauropod dinosaurs. These strange creatures had long tails, compact bodies, small heads, front legs that were shorter than the hind legs, and clawed first fingers or thumbs that were much larger than their other fingers (they may have used these to hook branches). In 1986, paleontologists unearthed a few bones from an enormous sauropod named *Seismosaurus* ("earthquake lizard") that may have been more than 98 ft (30 m) long. They have also discovered complete skeletons from sauropods almost as large. *Brachiosaurus*, for example, grew to 75 ft (23 m), stood 39 ft (12 m) high and weighed as much as 12 African elephants. *Brachiosaurus* and the other giants had pillarlike legs to support their great weight, but their skeletons were very light. Their bodies were shaped like giant barrels, and they carried their long tails high off the ground. *Diplodocus'* tail ended in a thin "whip;" other sauropods may have had tail clubs for self-defense.

MIGRATING HERDS
Trackways (fossil footprints) and groups of fossils indicate that many sauropods lived in herds and may have migrated to find fresh food, with the adults protecting their young from predators.

Small head
A small head and a small mouth meant *Diplodocus* had to spend a lot of time eating to nourish its huge body.

Strong but light
Struts of bone and air spaces kept *Diplodocus'* skeleton light but strong.

LONGER BUT LIGHTER
Diplodocus was longer than *Brachiosaurus*, but weighed only a third as much—partly because the skeleton of *Diplodocus* contained air spaces that reduced its weight but not its strength. The head of a *Diplodocus* was no larger than that of a horse, but its neck was 23 ft (7 m) long and its tail stretched an incredible 46 feet (14 m).

Long legs
With the help of its long front legs, this grazer could reach the tender young leaves in the treetops.

Strong legs
Diplodocus' hind legs were almost solid pillars of bone to support the weight of its intestines and tail muscles.

LONGER NECK

Brachiosaurus carried its tiny head high off the ground on the end of a 20-ft (6-m) long neck. Its front legs were almost as long as its hind legs, which gave its already long neck extra reach.

Fit for a King

In 1905, American millionaire Andrew Carnegie presented a plaster cast of *Diplodocus* to the Natural History Museum in London. He had financed the excavation of the original specimen. King Edward VII was there to unwrap the biggest present any king has ever received! Ten copies of the skeleton were sent to other museums around the world.

Whiplash
Diplodocus could injure or stun predators with the bony tip of its 46-ft (14-m) long tail.

Muscular tail
Diplodocus could not outrun a predator, but its great size and heavy, strong tail protected it.

LONG NECK

A modern giraffe, like all mammals, has only seven neck vertebrae. Sauropods, however, had between 12 and 19 neck vertebrae—all with bony struts to provide extra support.

Armored, Plated and Horned Dinosaurs

Many plant-eating dinosaurs evolved in strange ways to defend themselves against predators or to fight over mates and territories. Pachycephalosaurs, for example, had domed-shaped heads with thick, strong layers of bone. The plated and armored stegosaurs were slow-moving, small-brained ornithischians that relied on spikes and armor plating to defend themselves. The best known are *Stegosaurus*, a 30-ft (9-m) long, late Jurassic dinosaur that had one or two rows of plates along its back, and two to six pairs of long, sharp spikes at the end of its strong tail; and *Ankylosaurus*, a 33-ft (10-m) long, late Cretaceous dinosaur that was protected by hundreds of bony nodules (some of them with spiky bumps) on its back and sides and a double-headed club of bone on its tail. The ceratopians, or horned dinosaurs, were the last group of ornithischians to evolve before the dinosaurs died out at the end of the Cretaceous Period. They lived for only 20 million years or so, but spread out across North America and Asia. Ceratopians formed vast herds and used their platelike, horned heads to protect themselves and their young against predators such as *Tyrannosaurus* and *Velociraptor*.

PREDATORS BEWARE!
Styracosaurus, a 16-ft (5-m) long ceratopian, defends its young from a predator by displaying its nose horn and spiked head shield. Its spiky frill protected its neck, and it could use its nose horn to rip open a predator's belly.

BIG BUT LIGHT
Chasmosaurus' head shield was light and easy to move. It was designed more for display than defense, since this animal could easily outrun predators.

SMALL BUT STRONG
Centrosaurus, a 20-ft (6-m) long ceratopian, was a slow-moving animal that defended itself with its short, heavy head shield.

362

BODY ARMOR
Kentrosaurus, a 16-ft (5-m) long stegosaur from Africa, had seven pairs of plates from the neck to the middle of the back, and seven pairs of spikes on its back, hips and tail.

SPIKES AND SPINES
Polacanthus, a 13-ft (4-m) long nodosaur, protected its head and vital organs with a double row of vertical spines and used its strong, spiked tail for self-defense.

DISHES AND DAGGERS
Stegosaurus may have used its back plates for defense, or for heating and cooling, but its tail spikes were used for self-defense. They were fused to the bones of the tail, so *Stegosaurus* could swing its spiky tail to scare off a predator.

BUILT FOR DEFENSE

An ankylosaur *Euoplocephalus* from the late Cretaceous Period moved slowly and had a small brain. It could not hope to outwit fast, intelligent predators such as *Velociraptor*. But 20-ft (6-m) long *Euoplocephalus* was very heavily armored—even its eyelids were protected by bony shutters. It could cause serious damage with the club at the end of its 8-ft (2.5-m) long tail.

A HOLLOW CREST
A male *Parasaurolophus* could stay in touch with
other members of the herd or bellow a challenge to another
male by forcing air from its mouth up into its hollow crest,
then out through its nostrils. It must have had flaps or valves
inside the crest to stop it from hooting whenever it breathed.

• A PARADE OF DINOSAURS •

Duckbilled Dinosaurs

The duckbilled dinosaurs (hadrosaurs) had broad, ducklike beaks. They walked or ran on their hind legs, and leaned down on their shorter front legs to graze on vegetation. There were many species of duckbills; they were the most common and widespread plant-eating dinosaurs of the late Cretaceous Period. Hadrosaurs probably evolved in central Asia, but spread to Europe and North America. They had a varied diet, which meant they were able to survive as the Cretaceous climate became drier. All hadrosaurs were closely related, but they looked very different from each other. Some may have had inflatable nose sacs so they could communicate with each other by hooting. Others had hollow crests that acted like echo chambers. They could bellow or call each other by making noises that may have sounded like those made by a modern bassoon (above left).

HEAD OF THE FAMILY

Paleontologists used to believe that duckbills with different crests belonged to different species. Now they think these different-crested duckbills were members of the same species. A female *Parasaurolophus*, for example, had a medium-sized, curved crest; a young, or juvenile *Parasaurolophus* had a short, fairly straight crest; and an adult male had a long, curved crest. All used their hollow crests to produce sounds that other members of the herd would understand.

Adult
female

Adult
male

Juvenile

A DUCK'S BILL

Like all hadrosaurs, 43-ft (13-m) long *Edmontosaurus* had a toothless duckbill, covered with leathery skin, which it used to pluck leaves and fruits. It had rows of teeth in the back of its mouth, and it chewed food by moving its jaw up and down so the overlapping teeth crushed its food.

CHOPPING AND GRINDING

Seen close up, *Edmontosaurus'* tooth rows consisted of scores of tiny, leaf-shaped teeth, which acted like a cheese grater.

DID YOU KNOW?

Saurolophus, which had only a small, hornlike crest, may have produced noises by inflating a skin-covered sac on top of its nose. This would have been supported by the crest at the back of its head.

LIVING TOGETHER

Like giraffes (which eat tree leaves) and zebras (which eat low-growing plants), flat-headed and crested duckbills were able to live together without taking one another's food supply.

Discover more in The Cretaceous World

Record-breaking Dinosaurs

The dinosaurs were one of the world's most successful group of animals. They were the biggest, heaviest and longest land animals that have ever lived, and they dominated the Earth for almost 150 million years. Compared to this record, the four million years that humans have been on Earth seems like the blink of an eye. Dinosaurs were the world's strangest and most extraordinary animals. It has always been hard for people to imagine a world populated by such huge creatures: the remains of the first dinosaur ever described, 30-ft (9-m) long *Megalosaurus*, were first thought to belong to a human giant. It has also been hard for people to understand just how spectacular the dinosaurs were. *Seismosaurus*, the "earthquake lizard" and the biggest of the sauropods, may have been more than 98 ft (30 m) long. Only a few of its bones have ever been found: a 8-ft (2.4-m) long shoulder blade, taller than the biggest human giant; and a 5-ft (1.5-m) long vertebra. The ground must have quaked with each footstep from this gigantic creature.

SMALLEST
Compsognathus was one of the smallest known dinosaurs. It was only 3 ft (1 m) long, weighed just 8 lb (3.5 kg), and stood no taller than a chicken. It must have been a swift and efficient hunter. One specimen was found with the bones of a tiny lizard in its stomach cavity.

HEAVIEST
Weighing 78 tons (80 tonnes), 75-ft (23-m) long *Brachiosaurus* was as tall as a four-storey building. Its shoulders were more than 20 ft (6 m) off the ground and its humerus, or upper arm bone, was 7 ft (2 m) long. The humerus of an adult human is only about 1 ft (35 cm) long.

DID YOU KNOW?

What do a *Struthiomimus* (whose name means "ostrich-mimic") and an ostrich have in common? They can both sprint swiftly on very long slim legs (an ostrich can outrun a horse) and have long thin necks with small heads.

FASTEST
Struthiomimus, stood 7 ft (2 m) high and was 10–13 ft (3–4 m) long. It defended itself against predators by running at speeds of up to 31 miles (50 km) per hour, balancing on its long, birdlike hind legs.

LONGEST NECK
Mamenchisaurus, at 72 ft
(22 m), was almost as long as
its close relative *Diplodocus*,
but it had a fairly short tail.
Its 36-ft (11-m) long neck,
which it used to reach the tops
of tall trees, is the longest
neck of any known animal.

LONGEST
With more than half of its
total length of 89 ft (27 m) taken up by its 46-ft (14-m)
long tail, *Diplodocus* was the longest known dinosaur.
It would have used its strong, whiplike tail to defend
itself against predators such as *Allosaurus*.

BIGGEST PREDATOR
Tyrannosaurus was bigger
than any predator except
the sperm whale. It could
grow up to 46 ft (14 m)
long and was taller than
a double-decker bus.
It weighed 7 tons
(7 tonnes).

BIG, BIGGER, BIGGEST

In the 1970s and 1980s, fossil
hunters found massive bones
from sauropods even bigger than
75-ft (23-m) long *Brachiosaurus*.
Called *Supersaurus*, *Ultrasaurus*,
and *Seismosaurus*, these
incredible animals may have
been 98 ft (30 m) long! In this
photograph, paleontologist Dr.
James Jensen stands next to the
reconstructed front leg of one of
these giants. These fossils are still
being unearthed, and it may take
10–20 years to reconstruct their
skeletons. Then they will topple
the record-breakers
of today.

MOST TEETH
Anatotitan, a duckbilled
dinosaur, had about 1,000
tiny, leaf-shaped teeth
arranged in rows of 200–250
on each side of its upper and lower
jaws, all at the back of its mouth. Two
mummified fossils of this species have been
found, complete with the remains of their last
meals: pine needles, twigs, seeds and fruits.

Fossilized Clues

We rely on fossils for clues about how dinosaurs lived. But dinosaur fossils are very rare. The chances of a plant or animal becoming fossilized were low because conditions had to be just right for fossilization to occur. An animal had to be fairly big (small dinosaurs had delicate bones that were easily scattered or destroyed, or eaten by scavengers), and it had to die in the right place. If a dinosaur's body was washed into a lake, for example, silt would cover it up quite quickly and its bones were more likely to be preserved. In most cases only the bones of the dinosaurs were preserved (a few turned into minerals such as opal), but occasionally the animal was covered by sand or volcanic ash that preserved, or mummified, the body and left an impression of the texture of its skin. Sometimes, only a dinosaur's footprints or its droppings have been preserved. Paleontologists use all these clues to piece together pictures of the creatures that lived so many millions of years ago.

BACK IN TIME
The deeper a layer of rock, the older it is. The oldest and deepest rocks contain single-celled bacteria and algae. More complex plants and animals are found in the newer rocks above.

A FOSSIL IN THE MAKING
A 20-ft (6-m) long *Camptosaurus* lies at the water's edge, dead of disease or old age. The hot sun has begun to dry the body, and if scavengers do not tear it apart, it will be covered by silt and gradually fossilized. The *Coelurus* shown here are eating the insects and other animals around the carcass. Their jaws are too weak for the thick skin of *Camptosaurus*.

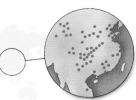

MONGOLIAN FOSSIL SITES
Mongolia, in central Asia, is covered by sand and desert today. During the Jurassic and early Cretaceous periods, Mongolia was warm and moist, with lakes and shallow seas. Many species of dinosaur lived in this ideal environment.

NORTH AMERICAN FOSSIL SITES
North America was warm and moist in the Jurassic and early Cretaceous periods. Great herds of plant eaters lived there, but they disappeared when the climate became colder and more changeable toward the end of the Cretaceous Period.

Bones That Are Not Bones

Skeletons can fossilize in different ways. In a petrified fossil (right), preserved bones that form partial or complete skeletons have outer and middle layers that have been replaced by minerals. They literally "turn to stone." A cast is formed when mud fills the hollow spaces inside bones—this occasionally happens with a dinosaur's brain or the canals of its middle ear. The bone then rots away. Sometimes fossil skulls are hollow, and scientists can make a mold of the dinosaur's brain. Very rarely, a dinosaur is mummified in dry sand that gradually hardens into rock, leaving an impression of the animal's skin.

OUT OF REACH
Beneath the surface of a lake, a dead dinosaur is safe from large scavengers. Its flesh rots away or is eaten by fish, and the skeleton remains intact.

COVER-UP
Layers of sand or silt cover the dinosaur's bones, and stop them from being washed away.

FOSSILIZATION
Trapped and flattened by layers of sediment, the dinosaur's bones are gradually replaced by minerals that are harder than the rocks around them.

FOSSIL FINDS
Millions of years later, upheavals in the Earth's crust bring the dinosaur's fossilized skeleton close to the surface, where it is exposed by the weather and erosion.

Discover more in Skeletons and Skulls

369

Skeletons and Skulls

Most of the dinosaurs we know about were much bigger than even large modern mammals. An average-sized dinosaur such as *Camptosaurus* was about 21 ft (6.5 m) long—a third longer than an African elephant. But *Camptosaurus* weighed only about 3 tons (3 tonnes)—less than half the weight of an elephant. Dinosaurs had two distinct body types: a bipedal fast-running kind such as *Hypsilophodon*, and a quadrupedal heavy type such as *Camarasaurus*. They could grow to enormous sizes because their skeletons were superbly engineered; they were very strong without being very heavy. The vertebrae of the giant sauropods were supported by struts and thin sheets of bone because they were almost hollow; solid vertebrae would have made these animals too heavy to stand upright. Most dinosaurs had holes in their skulls. Meat eaters had the largest holes of all, to accommodate the bulging and powerful jaw muscles that opened and closed their jaws.

Skull
This 5-ft (1.5-m) long, ligh built "gazelle" of the dinos world had a horny beak at front of its mouth, a fairly large brain and large open for the eyes.

Backbone
Extra ribs in front of the shoulders supported the neck muscles.

HYPSILOPHODON

Hands
Four long, clawed fingers were used to grasp plant food or to support *Hypsilophodon* as it grazed on low-growing plants.

CAMARASAURUS

Backbone
Like the steel rods of a crane, the vertebrae provided support where it was needed most.

Skull
This 59-ft (18-m) long sauropod had a small head. The large openings on top of the skull may have helped to cool the small brain.

Leg bones
Like all sauropods, *Camarasaurus* had massive, pillarlike legs to carry its great weight.

Chest
Very deep ribs supported the large stomach *Camarasaurus* needed to digest its tough plant food.

Hind feet
Camarasaurus's toes could spread out for support as it reared up to reach young leaves in the treetops.

Front feet
Five strong, clawed toes helped to support the weight of the chest, neck and head.

CERATOSAURUS
This 20-ft (6-m) long predator had a strong lower jaw and a high, narrow skull. Both had large cavities to make space for the huge jaw muscles that drove razor-sharp fangs.

OURANOSAURUS
Although its jaw muscles were weak, *Ouranosaurus* was an efficient plant feeder. As it closed its mouth, the bones of the upper jaw moved apart, breaking up food with bands of cheek teeth.

Tail
Spines on the undersides of the tail vertebrae supported muscles that helped *Hypsilophodon* carry its tail off the ground.

Leg bones
Hypsilophodon was a fast runner. As its femur was very short, the long tibia and foot could swing forward to give the dinosaur great speed.

Feet
Long, strong toes like those of an ostrich gave *Hypsilophodon* a sure footing as it sprinted away from danger.

IN THE NOSE
Corythosaurus (left) may have drawn air in through the nostrils at the front of its snout and into its hollow crest to produce sounds. *Brachiosaurus* had nostrils on the top of its head, possibly to help keep its body cool.

BUILT FOR STRENGTH
The tibia and femur of *Tyrannosaurus* were the same length, and had powerful muscles attached to them. *Tyrannosaurus* could charge at its prey with a sudden burst of energy, but its legs were not designed for a long chase.

DINOSAUR BRAINS

Dinosaurs had small brains, but this does not mean they were stupid. Brain size is not the most important factor. Brain complexity and brain size in relation to total body size are far more important. *Iguanodon's* body was as big as a bus; its brain was no bigger than a goose's egg. *Iguanodon* did not need much intelligence to find its food of leaves and fruit. *Deinonychus*, however, had to see, smell and chase fast-running animals. Its brain was the size of an apple, even though its body was smaller than a car. But the "thinking" part of a dinosaur's brain, the cerebrum, was much smaller than a mammal's cerebrum, which meant that a dinosaur could not have learned new things as easily as a monkey or a dog could today.

Rhesus monkey

Iguanodon

DID YOU KNOW?

Stegosaurus's brain was the size of a walnut. A cavity in the vertebrae above its hips may have housed a gland that produced energy-rich glycogen. This gave *Stegosaurus* a burst of speed if it needed to escape from a predator.

Discover more in Plant-eating Dinosaurs

ARMOR PLATING

Dinosaur skin, like that of living reptiles, was made up of scales, sometimes with bony lumps (called osteoderms) that provided protection against predators' teeth.

TRACKING FOSSIL FOOTPRINTS

Footprints show that many dinosaurs traveled in groups. These *Apatosaurus* prints were made by five adults moving in the same direction.

DAILY DIET

Coprolites (fossilized dung) have been found containing hard seeds, pieces of pine cones, and even plant stems.

STORIES IN STONE

Small plant eaters stick close to a herd of long-necked sauropods as it migrates across the late Jurassic landscape of North America. Sharp-clawed theropods shadow the herd, hoping to pick off a sick or injured animal.

Footprints and Other Clues

Fossilized teeth and bones tell us much about how dinosaurs looked and lived. But paleontologists also use other clues to piece together pictures of the dinosaurs' day-to-day lives. Skin impressions show that dinosaurs were protected against predators and spiky plants by a tough covering of skin. Fossil footprints, called trackways, tell us how dinosaurs moved about, and that sauropods, hadrosaurs and horned dinosaurs traveled in herds. The remains of nests show that dinosaurs built nests close to each other for protection against predators and scavengers. The fossils of eggs and even baby dinosaurs indicate how small these animals were when they hatched and how quickly they grew. The bones of adult dinosaurs give clues to their diet, injuries and the cause of their death, while fossilized dung provides information about what dinosaurs ate.

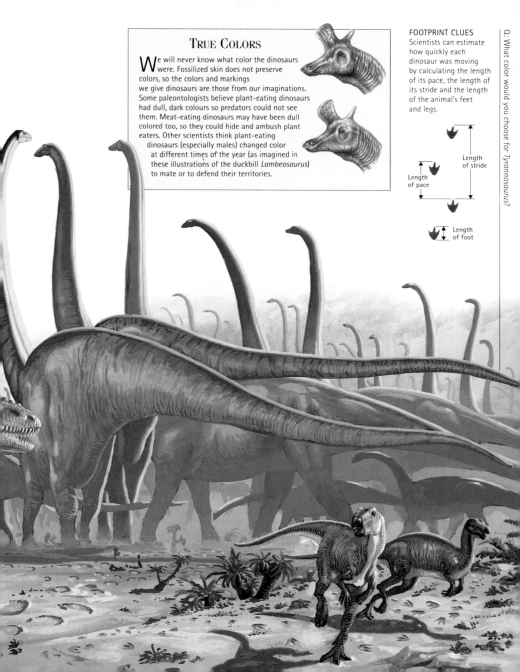

True Colors

We will never know what color the dinosaurs were. Fossilized skin does not preserve colors, so the colors and markings we give dinosaurs are those from our imaginations. Some paleontologists believe plant-eating dinosaurs had dull, dark colours so predators could not see them. Meat-eating dinosaurs may have been dull colored too, so they could hide and ambush plant eaters. Other scientists think plant-eating dinosaurs (especially males) changed color at different times of the year (as imagined in these illustrations of the duckbill *Lambeosaurus*) to mate or to defend their territories.

FOOTPRINT CLUES
Scientists can estimate how quickly each dinosaur was moving by calculating the length of its pace, the length of its stride and the length of the animal's feet and legs.

Length of stride

Length of pace

Length of foot

Q: What color would you choose for *Tyrannosaurus?*

ON THE INSIDE

Amniotic sac
A fluid-filled bag cushioned the embryo.

Chorion
This membrane provided oxygen.

Yolk sac
This provided nourishment.

Eggshell
Dinosaur young developed inside a sealed container.

A DINOSAUR NURSE
Up to 25 eggs were la
in each *Maiasaura* nes
which was a 7-ft (2-m
wide, 3-ft (1-m) deep
bowl scooped out of m
The hatchlings were
about 1½ ft
(50 cm) long.

• LIFE AS A DINOSAUR •

Raising a Family

Paleontologists used to think that dinosaurs did not look after their eggs or their young because very few dinosaur nests had been discovered. In 1978, however, Dr. John Horner found a duckbill dinosaur nesting site in North America, with dozens of nests spaced just far enough apart so that adult dinosaurs could guard their own eggs without stepping on another dinosaur's nest. He also found fossil eggshells and the fossils of 15 baby duckbills. The babies had already grown much larger than when they were born, but they had not left the nest because they were still being cared for by their parents. Dr. Horner called these dinosaurs *Maiasaura*, or "good mother lizards."

Paleontologists know that at least two meat eaters, *Troodon* and *Oviraptor*, laid eggs. Fossil eggs from the giant sauropods have been found in Europe, South America and China, but we do not know how these enormous creatures managed to lay their eggs safely.

Chicken's egg

Possible
theropod egg

Oviraptor's egg

Emu's egg

BIG BODIES, SMALL EGGS
Dinosaur eggs were very small in proportion to their bodies. Very large eggs would have very thick shells, and these could never be broken by the hatchlings.

A TERRIBLE EGG THIEF?

Many paleontologists believe that *Oviraptor*, a theropod from the late Cretaceous Period, stole eggs from the nests of other dinosaurs. Its strong jaws could have easily broken eggshells and crushed the bones of the young dinosaurs it caught with its clawed hands. The first *Oviraptor* fossil, discovered in Mongolia in 1924 with a clutch of eggs, seemed to confirm this belief. Paleontologists thought the eggs belonged to a *Protoceratops*, but new evidence has shown that the eggs did in fact belong to *Oviraptor*. The debate continues.

DID YOU KNOW?
Microscopic examination of *Maiasaura* embryos and hatchlings shows that they had very poorly developed joints in their legs. They had to be cared for by their parents. Hypsilophodons (the cousins of hadrosaurs such as *Maiasaura*), however, had strong legs and could fend for themselves as soon as they hatched.

Discover more in Duckbilled Dinosaurs

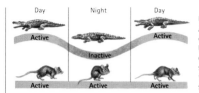

Day | Night | Day

Active | Inactive | Active

Active | Active | Active

UPS AND DOWNS
A cold-blooded reptile, such as a crocodile, must bask in the sunlight before it is warm enough to move quickly. But a warm-blooded mammal, such as a mouse, can be active all the time. Its body temperature stays the same no matter how cold it is outside.

Staying cool
Spongy skin over the sail would have allowed heat to radiate quickly. Even a small drop in the temperature of the blood would have helped *Ouranosaurus* to stay cool.

Cooling the blo
A complex syste
of small veins carri
warm blood up ir
Ouranosaurus' sa
where it was cool
before it flowe
back down ir
the bo

• LIFE AS A DINOSAUR •

Keeping Warm; Keeping Cool

Every animal needs to keep its body temperature stable. If it cannot stay warm, it will not have enough energy to move around. If it becomes too warm, its brain may overheat and its breathing and digestion will not work properly. Dinosaurs had different ways to keep their bodies at stable temperatures. Some had frills, plates, sails or spikes to help them warm or cool their blood. Some scientists believe that dinosaurs may have had divided hearts to pump blood into their brains. This advanced body structure would probably have included an internal temperature control, or warm-bloodedness. The small, energetic meat eaters may have been warm-blooded, but this does not seem to be true for large, adult dinosaurs. Their bodies had a wide surface area, which meant they were able to radiate heat quickly and maintain a stable temperature.

AIR CONDITIONING
Ouranosaurus could warm up quickly in the morning, then cool down by the afternoon by pumping blood under the skin of the spiny "sail" on its back.

HOT PLATES

Tuojiangosaurus had 15 pairs of bony plates along its back. Some paleontologists think the plates were covered by skin that was rich with blood to help the dinosaur warm up or cool down quickly.

BIVALVES

A divided heart separates blood that flows under high pressure to the body from blood that flows under low pressure to and from the lungs. Some scientists think that tall or fast-moving two-legged dinosaurs needed a high-pressure blood supply to their brains and muscles.

Low pressure   High pressure

NECKS AND TAILS

Sauropods had long necks to help them reach the treetops, and long tails to balance their long necks. Their necks and tails provided a large surface area to soak up heat from the sun or to cool them down in the middle of the day.

A CHANGE IN TEMPERATURE

Scientists have looked at dinosaur bones under a microscope, and believe these reptiles may have been both warm-blooded and cold-blooded. Dinosaurs seem to have grown quickly (like warm-blooded mammals) when they were young, then more slowly (like cold-blooded reptiles) when they became adults. But small meat eaters, such as *Dromiceiomimus* (left), were very active predators, hunting lizards and insects. They would have needed a constantly stable temperature and may have been more warm-blooded as adults than other dinosaurs.

Nostril

STRANGE BUT TRUE

Sauropods such as *Brachiosaurus* could "let off steam" when they became too hot by pumping blood through the delicate skin inside their huge nostrils. This cooled the blood so the rest of the body could then keep cool.

Discover more in What is a Dinosaur?

Down the neck
Powerful muscles pushed food down *Apatosaurus'* 20-ft (6-m) long esophag tube running from the m to the stomach.

A WIDE VARIETY
Like a duckbilled dinosaur, this rhinoceros has a wide mouth so it can eat many types of plants.

Into the mouth
Paleontologists do not know if *Apatosaurus* had a muscular tongue or used its peglike teeth to rake leaves or twigs into its mouth.

SPECIAL DIETS
Like a horned dinosaur, this gazelle chooses its food carefully, plucking leaves and fruit with its narrow mouth.

Living reptile
Crocodile teeth are designed to grip, not cut.

Large theropod
Tyrannosaurus tooth

Eating and Digesting

Different dinosaurs ate and digested their food in various ways. Scientists have learned about these dietary habits by studying dinosaur teeth and bones, analyzing dinosaur dung and observing how living animals eat and digest their food. Paleontologists have found fossils of dinosaurs that sliced and ripped meat, dinosaurs that chewed plants or ground leaves into a paste before swallowing them, and toothless dinosaurs that ate eggs. The meat eaters had sharp teeth to cut up meat, which is easier to digest than coarse plants. *Tyrannosaurus'* sharp, serrated teeth were designed so that its prey's struggles actually helped it tear off chunks of flesh. Large plant-eating dinosaurs had internal features such as stomach stones (gastroliths) to help grind and digest the large quantity of plants they ate.

Small theropod
Troodon tooth

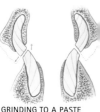

Upper jaw

Lower jaw

CUTTING DOWN TO SIZE
Styracosaurus used rows of scissorlike teeth to snip leaves into small pieces.

GRINDING TO A PASTE
Edmontosaurus used rows of grinding teeth to crush leaves into a paste.

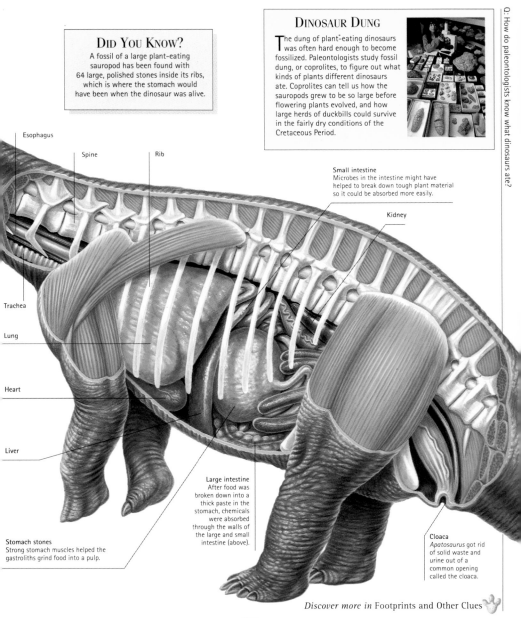

DID YOU KNOW?

A fossil of a large plant-eating sauropod has been found with 64 large, polished stones inside its ribs, which is where the stomach would have been when the dinosaur was alive.

DINOSAUR DUNG

The dung of plant-eating dinosaurs was often hard enough to become fossilized. Paleontologists study fossil dung, or coprolites, to figure out what kinds of plants different dinosaurs ate. Coprolites can tell us how the sauropods grew to be so large before flowering plants evolved, and how large herds of duckbills could survive in the fairly dry conditions of the Cretaceous Period.

Esophagus

Spine

Rib

Small intestine
Microbes in the intestine might have helped to break down tough plant material so it could be absorbed more easily.

Kidney

Trachea

Lung

Heart

Liver

Stomach stones
Strong stomach muscles helped the gastroliths grind food into a pulp.

Large intestine
After food was broken down into a thick paste in the stomach, chemicals were absorbed through the walls of the large and small intestine (above).

Cloaca
Apatosaurus got rid of solid waste and urine out of a common opening called the cloaca.

Discover more in Footprints and Other Clues

379

A SPIKY SHIELD

Triceratops' neck was a massive frill of solid bone with 3-ft (1-m) long horns that protected its neck and chest from an attack by another *Triceratops* or a predator.

BUILT LIKE A TANK

Euoplocephalus was protected by bands of armor, bony studs on the shoulders and a heavy, bony skull. It could injure a predator by lashing out with a bony club at the end of its tail.

STABBING TAIL

To defend itself against a predator, *Tuojiangosaurus* used its muscular tail, which was armed at the tip with two pairs of sharp spikes.

Attack and Defense

Many dinosaurs used their horns, spikes or armor to defend themselves. But even those without armor had their own defense weapons. *Apatosaurus* could rear up on its hind legs and crush an attacker with its front feet, or use its tail to injure a predator. Many sauropods travelled in herds, relying on safety in numbers so that only weak or sick animals would be attacked. The bird-mimic dinosaurs such as *Gallimimus* used their speed to escape, while *Pachycephalosaurus* could use its thick skull to defend itself against predators and other members of its own species. Meat eaters had speed, agility and sharp teeth for effective attack and defense. Large predators such as *Tyrannosaurus* hunted alone, and relied on a surprise rush. We will never know if dinosaurs used camouflage. Perhaps some species of plant eaters had dappled skin so they could hide from predators. Meat eaters may have used the same kind of disguise to ambush their prey.

DID YOU KNOW?

Iguanodon used its hand in many ways: for walking, for grasping food, for stripping leaves from branches and for self-defense. This peaceful plant eater could also use its thumb spike to injure or kill a predator by stabbing its neck or eyes.

MULTI-PURPOSE TAIL

Diplodocus' tail was very long. It used the tail for support when it reared up to crush a predator with its front legs or swung it like a whip to blind or stun an attacker.

THE TERRIBLE CLAW

Just as a falcon uses its razor-sharp claws to kill its prey, *Deinonychus* (whose name means "terrible claw") used the 5-in (13-cm), swivel claw on the second toe of each foot to kill its prey. It would leap into the air to kick or balance on one leg as it slashed at the skin of plant eaters. Fossils of five *Deinonychus* have been found beside the body of a *Tenontosaurus*, which suggests that the fast-moving, big-brained *Deinonychus* hunted in packs.

BATTERING RAM
Pachycephalosaurus' skeleton was designed to withstand its charging attacks against other males, or predators.

HEAD TO HEAD
Two 26-ft (8-m) long male *Pachycephalosaurus* are butting heads like mountain goats to see which will mate with a herd of females. Although protected by a solid dome of bone 10 in (25 cm) thick, one has become dizzy and is about to plummet to its death.

Why Did They Vanish?

BIG BANG
According to one theory, several volcanic eruptions produced climatic changes that wiped out the dinosaurs.

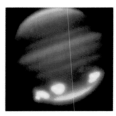

METEORITE HITS
Perhaps a giant meteorite hit the Earth, causing dust clouds, acid rain, storms and huge waves.

END OF AN ERA
When the dinosaurs died out, all large land animals disappeared. Late Cretaceous mammals were small (*Alphadon*, shown here, was only 1 ft [30 cm] long) but evolved rapidly into thousands of new species to replace the dinosaurs.

The extinction of the dinosaurs 65 million years ago was the most mysterious and dramatic disappearance of a group of animals in the history of the Earth. But the dinosaurs were not the only animals to die out. More than half of the world's animals also disappeared, including the pterosaurs and large marine reptiles. The number of species of dinosaurs had been dropping for at least eight million years, but some species were common right up to the "K/T boundary," which marks the end of the Cretaceous Period and the beginning of the Tertiary Period. Some scientists believe that a volcanic disaster or a giant meteorite wiped out the dinosaurs. Others argue that such a disaster—causing disease, rising sea levels and gradual changes in climate—would have affected all animal life. Another theory combines these thoughts: changes in weather and sea levels had already reduced the amount of land and food for dinosaurs, and they were unable to cope with a sudden disaster.

INTO THE FUTURE
Even today, habitat loss through earthquakes, storms or human activity such as clearing forests, is threatening the future of many animals.

STRANGE BUT TRUE
People have produced some weird and wonderful theories to explain why the dinosaurs disappeared. Some suggest they died of boredom, "drowned" in their own droppings, were hunted by aliens, or even committed suicide!

VICTIMS AND SURVIVORS
None of the current theories can explain why some animal groups disappeared, while others survived. Pterosaurs died out, but birds did not. Dinosaurs vanished, but small land reptiles and mammals survived. Mosasaurs, plesiosaurs and pliosaurs were wiped out, but turtles and crocodiles are still alive today.

Victims	K/T Boundary	Survivors
Dinosaurs		
Pterosaurs		
Plesiosaurs		
Ammonites		
Mammals		
Crocodiles		
Lizards and snakes		
Turtles and tortoises		
Amphibians		
Fishes		
Insects		
Birds		

FEATHER FOSSILS
The detailed impressions of feathers on this *Archaeopteryx* fossil confirm an important evolutionary link between reptiles and birds.

SCALY SURVIVORS
Crocodilians have hardly changed since the beginning of the Cretaceous Period. They have evolved slowly because they live in a stable environment.

Surviving Relatives

D inosaurs are dead, but it seems that certain dinosaur features live on in other animals. Dinosaurs and birds, for example, are very different animals but they have many characteristics in common. Scientists are now convinced that dinosaurs were the ancestors of birds. The skeleton of *Archaeopteryx*, the earliest known bird, was very similar to that of the lizard-hipped carnivorous dinosaur *Compsognathus*. Many scientists now classify *Archaeopteryx* as a small, flesh-eating dinosaur with feathers (fossilized feather shown left). Dinosaurs are also related to crocodilians, which survived the great extinction at the end of the Cretaceous Period. Crocodilians and dinosaurs have very similar skulls and common ancestors—the archosaurs. The dinosaurs disappeared, but crocodilians today are almost the same as their ancestors. Their way of life has changed little in 150 million years.

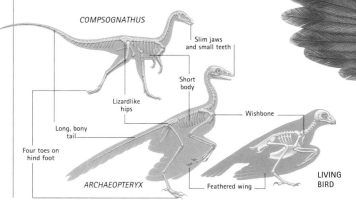

COMPSOGNATHUS

Slim jaws and small teeth

Short body

Lizardlike hips

Long, bony tail

Four toes on hind foot

ARCHAEOPTERYX

Wishbone

Feathered wing

LIVING BIRD

FROM DINOSAUR TO BIRD
Fossil records show a strong similarity between small carnivorous dinosaurs that ran upright on long, slim hind legs, *Archaeopteryx*, and living birds.

LIGHT PATH
Archaeopteryx
would fly by
flapping its broad
wings, but more
often it would
dive from its perch
onto prey such
as insects and
small reptiles.

RESEMBLING THE PAST

Some of today's birds are very similar to dinosaurs in their structure and behavior. The secretary bird of Africa rarely flies, but runs after insects, small reptiles and mammals on its hind legs—just as the dinosaur *Compsognathus* did. Baby hoatzins, from South America, use claws on the front of their wings to climb around in trees— just as *Archaeopteryx* did.

Hoatzin

Secretary bird

FAMILY TREE

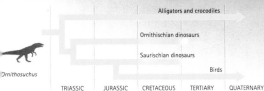

Alligators and crocodiles

Ornithischian dinosaurs

Saurischian dinosaurs

Birds

Ornithosuchus

| TRIASSIC | JURASSIC | CRETACEOUS | TERTIARY | QUATERNARY |

INGENIOUS BUT INACCURATE
In 1853, an *Iguanodon* was constructed in the Crystal Palace in London. It looked just like a giant, prehistoric iguana.

REPTILIAN HUMANS
If dinosaurs had not become extinct, would some have evolved to resemble humans?

Myths and Tall Tales

Dinosaurs have been the subjects of myths and tall tales for years. When people first began to discover dinosaur fossils, they had many imaginative theories about the creatures that had such enormous bones. The earliest description of a dinosaur fossil came from China, almost 3,000 years ago. Chinese scholars thought the fossils were dragon bones. More than 300 years ago, a *Megalosaurus* thigh bone dug up in England was believed to be the bone of an elephant, then a giant human. In 1820, a scientist thought that dinosaur trackways had been made by prehistoric giant birds. Dinosaurs died out 61 million years before humans appeared, but movies have shown them attacking people who lived in caves. In the past 50 years, however, we have begun to dispel many of the misunderstandings about these amazing animals.

...AGONS AND DINOSAURS

...en Chinese scholars
...nd dinosaur fossils, they
...gined they belonged to
...at and powerful dragons,
...ught to bring good
...une to their people.

DID YOU KNOW?

The ancient Chinese ground up dinosaur
fossils to make powerful medicines and
special magic powders. Even today, tiny
amounts of these powdered "dragon bones"
are used in some traditional
Chinese medicines.

...EEPING DINOSAURS

...rly scientists could not believe that
...osaurs walked upright on straight
...s. They thought these strange reptiles
...pt on sprawled legs.

A STONE-AGE MYTH

Television has helped to
keep myths alive by
showing humans flying on
pterosaurs, working with
dinosaurs and even
keeping them as pets.

A DINOSAUR REVIVAL

People are understandably fascinated by
dinosaurs. These diverse creatures ruled
the world for 150 million years and were
able to meet the challenges of a changing
planet. Now, dinosaurs have "reappeared"
in modern life. The box-office hit *Jurassic
Park* stars a whole cast of plant- and
meat-eating dinosaurs.
A brightly painted
reconstruction of
Allosaurus (right) might
be seen on the back of
a car. You can also buy
dinosaur balloons,
cartoons, posters,
stickers and books.

Discover more in Why Did They Vanish?

387

Allosaurus
Al-oh-sore-us:
"Different reptile"
Group: meat eater
Period: late Jurassic/early
    Cretaceous
Discovered: North America, 1877
Size: up to 39 ft (12 m)

Plateosaurus
Plat-ee-oh-sore-us:
"Flat reptile"
Group: plant eater
Period: late Triassic
Discovered: Europe, 1837
Size: 26 ft (8 m) long

Coelophysis
Seel-oh-fie-sis:
"Hollow shape"
Group: meat eater
Period: late Triassic
Discovered: North
    America, 1889
Size: 10 ft (3 m) long

Coelurus
Seel-ure-us:
"Hollow tail"
Group: meat eater
Period: late Jurassic
Discovered: North America,
    1879
Size: 7 ft (2 m) long

Euoplocephalus
You-op-loh-seff-a-lus:
"True plated head"
Group: plant eater
Period: late Cretaceous
Discovered: North America, 1910
Size: 20 ft (6 m) long

Stegosaurus
Steg-oh-sore-us:
"Roof lizard"
Group: plant eater
Period: late Jurassic
Discovered: United States,
    1877
Size: up to 30 ft (9 m)

Saltasaurus
Salt-a-sore-us:
"Salt reptile"
Group: plant eater
Period: late Cretaceous
Discovered: South
    America, 1970
Size: 39 ft (12 m) long

• THE END OF THE DINOSAURS •

Identification Parade

Dinosaurs marched across 150 million years, and represented an amazingly successful and varied group of land animals. They prospered for many times longer than human beings have. Although we will never know exactly how many kinds of dinosaurs there were, we know enough about their evolution to see their steady progress from only a few species during the Triassic Period to almost twice as many during the Jurassic Period. This was followed by an incredible "flowering" during the Cretaceous Period, when there were more species of dinosaurs than during both preceding periods. Dinosaurs have taught us many valuable lessons about evolution and about how a group of animals spread across the land, and dominated the world before disappearing. But we are left with only tantalizing clues about how dinosaurs lived.

Pachycephalosaurus
Pack-ee-seff-ah-low-sore-us:
"Thick-headed reptile"
Group: plant eater
Period: late Cretaceous
Discovered: North America, 1943
Size: up to 26 ft (8 m) long

Maiasaura
My-ah-sore-ah:
"Good mother lizard"
Group: plant eater
Period: late Cretaceous
Discovered: North America, 197
Size: up to 30 ft (9 m)

Brachiosaurus
Brak-ee-oh-sore-us:
"Arm reptile"
Group: plant eater
Period: late Jurassic
Discovered: North America, 1903
Size: up to 75 ft (23 m)

Deinonychus
Die-non-i-kus:
"Terrible claw"
Group: meat eater
Period: early Cretaceous
Discovered: North
America, 1969
Size: 10 ft (3 m) long

Hypsilophodon
Hip-sih-loh-foe-don:
"High-ridged tooth"
Group: plant eater
Period: early Cretaceous
Discovered: Europe, 1870
Size: 7 ft (2 m) long

DINOSAURS TODAY

When Richard Owen invented the name dinosaur 150 years ago, we knew of just nine species. Today we know of at least 1,000, which includes an incredible variety of plant eaters, meat eaters and egg thieves, dinosaurs with horns and crests, spikes and razor-sharp claws. We are surrounded by dinosaurs: in museums, movies and theme parks, such as this display of robot dinosaurs in Japan. Even though they disappeared 65 million years ago, dinosaurs are "alive" in our imaginations. We are still learning about them; in fact, children today know more about dinosaurs than most adults do.

Ouranosaurus
Oo-ran-oh-sore-us:
"Brave reptile"
Group: plant eater
Period: early Cretaceous
Discovered: Africa, 1976
Size: 23 ft (7 m) long

Tyrannosaurus
Tie-ran-oh-sore-us:
"Tyrant lizard"
Group: meat eater
Period: late Cretaceous
Discovered: North America, 1902
Size: up to 46 ft (14 m)

Parasaurolophus
Par-ah-sore-ol-oh-fus:
"Parallel-sided reptile"
Group: plant eater
Period: late Cretaceous
Discovered: North America, 1923
Size: 33 ft (10 m) long

Triceratops
Try-ser-ah-tops:
"Three-horned face"
Group: plant eater
Period: late Cretaceous
Discovered: North America, 1889
Size: up to 30 ft (9 m)

Struthiomimus
Strooth-ee-oh-mime-us:
"Ostrich-mimic"
Group: meat eater
Period: late Cretaceous
Discovered: North America, 1917
Size: up to 13 ft (4 m)

389

— Dinosaur Facts —

Q Could dinosaurs swim?

A Although dinosaurs were not related to the giant marine reptiles, we know that at least some species could swim, and many of the plant eaters probably grazed in swamps. Scientists were puzzled by a set of *Diplodocus* footprints that showed only the animal's front feet. Then they realised the sauropod was floating in water, pushing itself along with its front feet and steering with its back legs and tail (as above).

Q How do you become a paleontologist and dig up dinosaur fossils?

A To be a paleontologist, you need to study science, especially biology and geology, in high school and in college. You usually need a specialized research degree as well.

Q Where did dinosaurs live?

A Dinosaur fossils, and sometimes footprints, have been found on every continent, including Antarctica, which was not as cold during the Age of the Dinosaurs as it is today. Most parts of the world looked very different when the dinosaurs were alive. Slow geological changes have pushed up flat ground into steep mountains, and regions have become colder because continents have moved.

Q Did dinosaurs fly?

A No, dinosaurs could not fly, but there were some Mesozoic reptiles, such as *Pteranodon*, which could fly.

Q Did any dinosaurs eat both meat and plants?

A Paleontologists believe that some of the lizard-hipped dinosaurs, such as *Ornithomimus, Gallimimus* and *Struthiomimus,* probably ate small reptiles, mammals, insects—even other dinosaurs' eggs—as well as plants. Meat gave these gazelle-like animals the energy they needed to outrun predators. Speed was their only defense.

Q How can you tell a dinosaur's sex?

A It is very difficult to tell whether a dinosaur was male or female just from the bones. By looking at mammals, however, we can guess that male dinosaurs were generally larger than females, and it is likely that male duckbills (such as *Parasaurolophus* shown here) had larger crests. Fossils of *Pachycephalosaurus* show big differences in the size of the skull, and it seems that while both sexes had domed skulls, males had heavier heads for fighting, just like today's mountain goats.

Male

Female

Q Were dinosaurs affected by insects and parasites?

A Dinosaurs had thick, tough skins, but we are sure there were insects and ticks that bit them and sucked their blood—after all, today's crocodiles and monitor lizards are bitten by mosquitoes and blood-sucking flies. Although paleontologists have never found fossils of parasites inside dinosaur bodies, it is likely that parasites attacked dinosaurs just as they do animals today.

Q Were meat-eating dinosaurs smarter than plant eaters?

A Yes, meat-eating dinosaurs had larger brains than plant eaters, and needed intelligence to hunt or ambush large and sometimes heavily armoured prey.

Q How long could dinosaurs live?

A Paleontologists are unable to determine from fossil remains how long a dinosaur could live, but they do have some clues about how long it took dinosaurs to reach sexual maturity. Recent studies suggest that various dinosaurs, such as hadrosaurs, could breed somewhere between 5 and 12 years.

Q Why are fossil finds so exciting?

A They are incredibly rare. Some dinosaurs were the largest land animals ever to have lived on Earth, but large animals—whether they are reptiles or mammals—are not as common as small animals and their bones are therefore less likely to be found. Recently, the remains of many small dinosaurs were found in the Gobi Desert. But this was a very unusual find. Small animals can be torn apart by scavengers or eaten by insects. Their bones can be scattered by rain, or crushed by earth movements before they can become fossils. Even if these small bones are fossilized, they will be very hard to find and recognize millions of years later.

Q How many species of dinosaur were there?

A This is one question we will never be able to answer; only a few animals from any group are ever fossilized, so fossils give just a small "window" into the world of dinosaurs. About 800 species of dinosaur have been described but many of these may have been males and females from the same species and of different ages, so we probably know about only 350 genuine species of dinosaur. However, some scientists think there may have been between 1,000 and 1,300 species of dinosaur, while others estimate as many as 6,000 species.

Q Could dinosaurs sweat?

A No, their skin was scaly and did not have sweat glands, so they had other ways of keeping cool.

Q What do the names of dinosaurs mean ?

A The names of dinosaurs, like those of all animals and plants, tell us something about how each dinosaur is related to other dinosaurs. Names are made up from Latin and Greek words, and usually describe something outstanding about the animal. *Tyrannosaurus rex,* for example, means "king of the tyrant lizards;" *Corythosaurus* is "helmet lizard;" and *Protoceratops* stands for "first horned face."

Q Did prehistoric humans and dinosaurs live at the same time?

A Some movies may place humans and dinosaurs in the same prehistoric world, but humans evolved only 4 million years ago. This was 61 million years after the dinosaurs became extinct.

Under the Sea

Why is the sea blue?

What kinds of creatures live at the bottom of the ocean?

How do fish survive in the freezing temperatures of the polar seas?

Contents

Our Oceans

If you looked at the Earth from space, it would look extremely blue. This is because vast oceans cover almost two-thirds of our "blue planet." The Pacific, the Atlantic, the Indian, the Arctic and the Southern are the world's major oceans. They were formed by complex geological processes that continue to affect the Earth. The Earth is made up of seven main parts, called lithospheric plates, formed from the upper part of the Earth's mantle layer and the crust. Many millions of years ago, these parts all fit together. But nothing on Earth is fixed, and these plates are constantly moving (at about the same speed your fingernails grow) over a layer of soft, squishy rock called the asthenosphere that lies beneath the crust. When two plates move away from each other, hot melted rock, or magma, rises to fill the space and forms a new sea floor. In this way, ocean basins can grow gradually over millions of years. Five million years ago, the Red Sea was a shallow basin. Now, as the sea floor spreads, scientists think it has the makings of a new ocean.

THE BEGINNING
About 250 million years ago, there was one huge continent known as Pangaea, but before this, the real "beginning" is still shrouded in mystery.

PLATES MOVE APART
About 200 to 130 million years ago, Pangaea broke into separate pieces.

DID YOU KNOW?
Alfred Lothar Wegener, who lived between 1880 and 1930, was a German scientist. He was the first to suggest that many millions of years ago the world was one huge supercontinent.

Forces below
The core of the Earth is getting gradually hotter. When plates move apart, more magma bubbles up to the surface. As the channel of magma gets wider, it pushes against the sea floor, which buckles and forms ridges of crust. When this happens, the sea floor spreads outwards, pushing the areas of land further and further apart.

RED SEA SPREADING

The African and Arabian plates began moving apart between five and ten million years ago. As this movement continues at a rate of about 1/2 in (1 cm) a year, the basin of the Red Sea is spreading slowly. Astronaut Eugene Cernan photographed Africa and the Arabian Peninsula as *Apollo 17* traveled toward the moon in 1972. The gash you can see in the continental crust is called the Great Rift Valley. It runs from the Jordan Valley and Dead Sea in the north down through East Africa in the south, and was probably caused by the movement of the plates.

TO THE CENTER OF THE EARTH
This is a cross-section of the Earth. There are four main layers with the hot, solid inner core at the bottom. The layers become cooler as they move away from the core. Volcanic islands rise above the sea at the top.

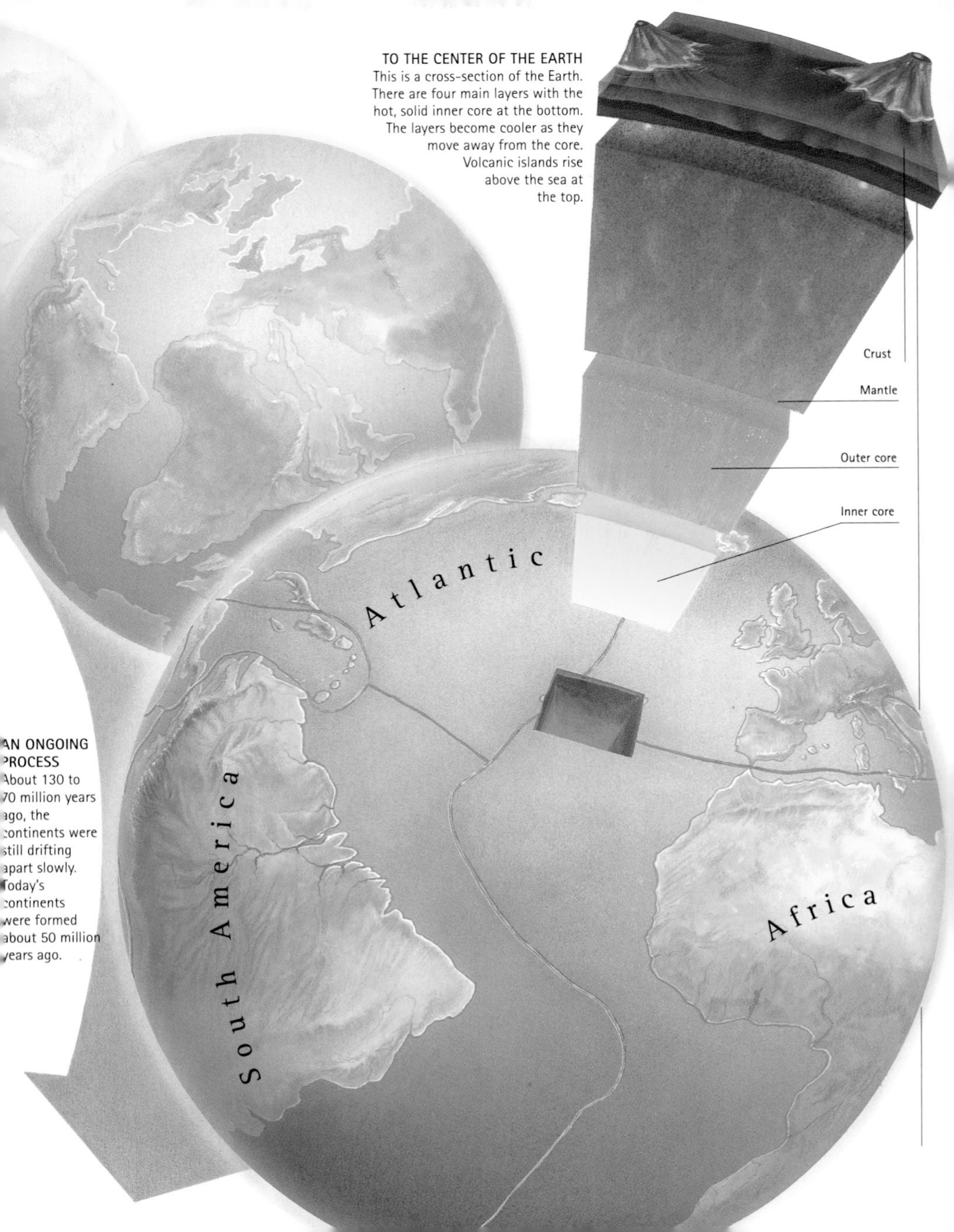

Crust

Mantle

Outer core

Inner core

Atlantic

AN ONGOING PROCESS
About 130 to 70 million years ago, the continents were still drifting apart slowly. Today's continents were formed about 50 million years ago.

South America

Africa

The Sea Floor

I f all the water in the world's oceans was sucked away, we would be able to see the amazing landscape of the sea floor. With huge mountains and deep valleys, slopes and plains, trenches and ridges, it is surprisingly similar to the landscape of dry land. Modern ships and equipment have made it possible for us to learn about this hidden area. Between 1968 and 1975, the deep-sea drilling ship *Glomar Challenge* bored more than 400 holes in the sea bed and collected rock samples to be examined. These helped scientists piece together an accurate picture of the sea floor. They were able to detail its many features, such as a shallow continental shelf that extends from the land into the sea and may once have been dry land; and a continental slope, where the continent ends and the underwater land plunges to the very depths of the sea floor. Scientists continue to chart more of this underwater land with the help of computer images of underwater land forms and maps of the sea bed.

Continental shelf
This is a shallow extension of a continent, which is covered by water. This part of the ocean is rich in marine life. Oil exploration also takes place here.

Continental slope
This is the gently sloping, submerged land near the coast that forms the side of an ocean basin.

VOYAGE TO THE DEEP
This diver looks like an underwater astronaut as he dangles from a line attached to a vessel above.

LAYING CABLE
A diver and an underwater cable layer install telephone cables on the continental shelf.

RESEARCH INSTRUMENTS
Scientists collect and analyze deep-sea specimens and other information from the ocean floor to learn how the underwater landscape was formed. They use instruments such as the bathythermograph, which measures underwater temperatures, and the fisher scoop, which gathers up small samples of sand and mud from the sea bed.

Fisher scoop

Bathythermograph

PILLOW LAVA
When hot gases and liquid bubble up to the surface of the ocean floor, they harden and turn into lava. This is pillow lava, which has become part of the sea bed near the Galapagos Islands.

398

Seamounts
Most of these underwater volcanoes remain beneath the sea. Those that rise above the surface form islands.

Guyots
These are flat-topped seamounts.

SEEING WITH SOUND

This map of the sea bed of the Great Barrier Reef in Australia shows a 19-mile (30-km) wide section of the seaward slope. It was produced by GLORIA, a mapping instrument that sends waves of sound energy down to the sea floor and records the returning echoes.

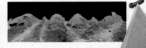

GLORIA
This instrument is attached to its "mother" ship by a conducting cable. It can reach depths of 164 ft (50 m) below the surface.

Abyssal plains
These are some of the flattest places on Earth. They spread out from the oceanic ridge to the edges of the continents.

Oceanic ridge
is a ridge that rises new sea floor wells om inside the Earth.

Oceanic trench
A long, narrow valley, or trench, usually forms next to islands or beside coastal mountain ranges.

DID YOU KNOW?

Some of the world's deepest sea trenches extend further downwards than the highest mountains on land rise upwards.

Sea Upheavals

The ocean is always moving. Its surface can change from calm and mirrorlike to wild and treacherous. Most waves at sea are caused by wind. The waves created by the gale that blow during a tropical cyclone are 46 ft (14 m) and high The largest wave known to have been caused by the win was 112 ft (34 m) high. Waves can also be created by volcanic eruptions or earthquakes under the sea. These waves are known as tsunamis (pronounced soo-nah-mees). They are wide columns of wate that reach down to the sea floor and can trav for great distances, at the speed of a jet pla across the ocean. The surface of the ocea can also be changed by colliding curren When the tide turns, the opposing currents meet and may create a whirlpool. One famous whirlpool is the fearsome Maelstrom off the c of Norway. The thunder of its crashing eddies of water can b heard 3 miles (5 km) away.

WHIRLING WINDS

A waterspout is a whirling column of air, laden with mist and spray. First cousin to the tornado, it can occur when rising warm, moist air meets cold, dry air. Sometimes schools of fish are sucked up by the fury of the spout, which can reach nearly 4 miles (6 km) into the air. Waterspouts rarely last more than 60 minutes, and while they are spectacular, they seldom cause any serious damage.

WALL OF WATER

People who live in coastal cities can be affected by sea upheavals. Imagine how frightening it would be to see an enormous wall of water rushing toward you. Your first reaction would be to run, but to where? The impact of the wave could destroy your whole city. Thousands of years ago a large part of Mauna Loa, one of the volcanic Hawaiian Islands, collapsed into the sea. This landslide produced a tsunami that traveled to the next island, Lanai, and crashed across it to a height of 918 feet (280 m). If such an event occurred today, all coastal areas in the Hawaiian Islands would be damaged. Waves of up to 98 ft (30 m) could roll into the city of Honolulu.

A DEVASTATING FORCE

A hurricane has a wind of force 12 or above on the Beaufort Scale, and it may be 400 miles (645 km) wide. This photograph of a hurricane called Elena was taken from the Space Shuttle *Discovery*.

THE BEAUFORT SCALE

This scale uses the numbers 1 to 12 to indicate the strength of wind at sea. At 0, the sea is as calm as a mirror; at 6 there is a strong breeze and large waves 10 ft (3 m) high. At 12, a hurricane is raging and the waves are more than 46 ft (14 m) high.

STORMING AWAY

This dramatically colored image of a severe storm in the Bering Sea was taken from a satellite in space.

Force 2

Force 8

Force 12

Currents and Tides

O cean currents are the massive bodies of water that travel long distances around the world. The major force that produces the currents is the wind. There are seven main ocean currents and thousands of smaller ones. They move in large, circular streams at about walking pace (1–5 knots). In the Northern Hemisphere, currents move in a clockwise direction; in the Southern Hemisphere they are counterclockwise. Winds carry the warm or cold water currents along the shorelines, affecting the climate of the various continents on the way. The Gulf Stream, for example, is a current that carries warm water from the Caribbean Sea, up the east coast of the United States and then to the west coasts of Britain and Northern Europe. Without the Gulf Stream, these areas would be much colder. Oceans are also influenced by the "pull" of the moon and the sun. This pull causes the tides. Each day the level of the sea rises and falls and then rises and falls again. Each high tide and the following low tide are about six hours apart. The difference in height between high tide and low tide is called the tidal range. The largest tidal ranges are found in bays and estuaries. The Bay of Fundy in Canada has a tidal range of 49 ft (15 m), the highest in the world. On open coasts the tidal range is usually 6–10 feet (2–3 m).

THE PULL OF THE MOON
As the moon is much closer to the Earth than the sun is, its pull is greater. The ocean waters on the side of the Earth facing the moon are pulled the most, resulting in a high tide. As the Earth itself is also pulled towards the moon, the waters on the other side of the planet form another, though slightly smaller, high tide.

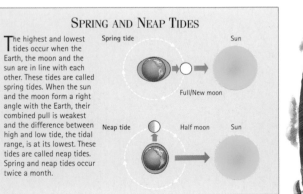

SPRING AND NEAP TIDES

The highest and lowest tides occur when the Earth, the moon and the sun are in line with each other. These tides are called spring tides. When the sun and the moon form a right angle with the Earth, their combined pull is weakest and the difference between high and low tide, the tidal range, is at its lowest. These tides are called neap tides. Spring and neap tides occur twice a month.

Spring tide

Sun

Full/New moon

Neap tide

Half moon

Sun

IN FAR-FLUNG CORNER
In 1977, Nigel Wace threw wine bottles overboard fro ship traveling between So America and Antarctica to discover how far and how ocean litter travels. Most bottles took two years to Western Australia and nea three years to reach New Zealand. Others reached s Africa, the Seychelles and Island. Because there is so litter in the oceans, Wace that today he would not t any trash into the sea, ev the sake of an experiment

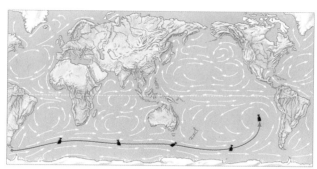

CIRCLING CURRENTS

The major currents of the world's oceans link up to make five giant loops of moving water called gyres. These circle different oceans, such as the North Atlantic, the North Pacific and the West Pacific.

MOVING OCEAN CURRENTS

In the tropics, strong winds push currents towards the equator. In the northern and southern seas, westerly winds push currents eastward. When they reach a continent, they change direction. The spin of the Earth also influences the direction of the currents: those in the northern part of the world are pushed to the right, while those in the southern part are pushed to the left. This phenomenon is called the Coriolis effect.

STRANGE BUT TRUE

When 80,000 Nike shoes were swept into the sea from a ship traveling between South Korea and Seattle, Curtis Ebbesmeyer traced their path to learn about ocean currents. The shoes began to wash up on the west coast of the United States about a year later.

River Meets Sea

MANGROVES
Mangroves thrive in fresh or salty water and many are found around the shores of river estuaries. They grow in mud that is full of water, so their roots develop above the ground and reach out to absorb oxygen.

Fresh river water and salty sea water meet in an estuary, a gateway between the river and the sea. Estuaries attract many different kinds of life. Salmon journey through them to lay their eggs in rivers before traveling back to the ocean. Newly hatched fish shelter in the beds of sea grasses that grow there. At low tide, wading birds flock to the mudflats surrounding an estuary to feed on tasty worms or scurrying crabs. People come to fish or collect shellfish and oysters. A river sometimes breaks into separate streams, or tributaries, as it reaches the sea. Mud is carried by the streams and deposited at the mouth of the river, creating a flat lowland called a delta. Because the tide floods the delta, the ground stays salty and wet all the time. Grasses grow on the marsh that forms, which makes the delta good for farming.

A SAFE PLACE
Water birds, insects, worms, shellfish, crabs, fish and plants share the safe environment of an estuary, where there is always plenty of food.

A VIEW FROM ABOVE

Fresh water from a river flows into a sheltered estuary, where it mixes with salt water from the sea.

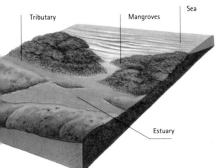

Tributary

Mangroves

Sea

Estuary

River

THE LIFE CYCLE OF A MUSSEL

Mussels begin life as larvae that swim about freely. Tiny, hairlike projections help them move in the water. As mussels grow, they develop a wedge-shaped bivalve shell, which has two sections hinged together. The shells are anchored to rocks by strands, though some species burrow into sand.

Early larva

Developing larva

Adult mussel

ARCHERFISH

These fish shoot insects with water. When the insects land in the water, the fish are ready to eat them.

CLAMS

Many kinds of clams can be eaten, but you may have difficulty finding these burrowing mollusks.

BLUEFISH

These bluefish are sometimes called tailor because their teeth cut like tailors' scissors. The young are often caught in estuaries by people who like to fish for sport.

MUD WHELKS

Mud whelks have large, spiral-shaped shells and are related to common garden snails.

GHOST NIPPERS

These small pinkish-white creatures burrow in the muddy sands and nip anyone who tries to catch them.

SEA HORSES

These unlikely looking fish swim upright, propelled by dorsal fins.

405

The Seashore

The land meets the sea at the seashore, which is the home of many animals. Hundreds of species of crabs patrol sandy seashores and hide in rockpools, searching for scraps of food. Crustaceans or mollusks have shells or other hard casing to protect them from birds, the hot sun and the pounding waves. Sand hoppers feed on rotting plants, especially seaweed that has been washed up onto the beach. Sea urchins graze on tiny animals and plants from rock and starfish feed on coral and shellfish. Certain corals provide safe shelter for other seashore animals. Some fish have also adapted to life near the shore. The weeverfish hides in the sand, ready to eat any small fish or crabs that swim nearby. Razor clams and burrowing sea anemones disappear into the sand when they have caught their prey.

Drawn in
Anemones are anchored in one place by their stalks. Their tentacles shorten when fish swim into them and pull the prey into the open mouth of the anemone.

Garibaldi
Bright orange male garibaldi seek out small crevices or overhangs in their rock-reef homes. Female garibaldi spawn with males that hold the best nest sites.

INSIDE A STARFISH

The round center of a starfish body holds the stomach. The anus is above the stomach and the mouth is below. Canals holding water, branches of nerves and intestines spread into each of the five arms. If an arm is broken off, a starfish can grow a new one in a few weeks. A starfish has tubes inside its body that pump water in and out of its many tube feet. As the water pressure builds up, the feet become longer and they bend. This action propels the starfish along. Each tube foot has a little sucker on the end, which the starfish uses to climb rocks and to open shellfish.

Water enters here

Tubes
pumping water

Tube feet

Sea otters
These live on the shores of the northern Pacific Ocean. Sea otters use their sharp teeth and strong front paws to crack open the hard shells of crabs.

Acorn barnacles
The rocky seashore is home to many acorn barnacles. They can feed only when the tide comes in and they are submerged.

Periwinkles
These rough periwinkles can be found just below the waves on rocky shores.

...elp
...is is a type of large, ...own seaweed. It provides ...od and shelter for all ...nds of sea creatures.

...ulberry whelk
...is feeds on dead ...dying animals.

...ctopus
...is has sharp ...esight and a ...rge brain.

Sea urchins
These use their long, sharp spines to defend themselves. Sometimes these spines contain a painful venom.

Suit of armor
The chiton's shell has eight plates that fit one against the other.

Coastal Seas

T he coastal seas are the richest areas of the ocean. They teem with sea life and are very popular for fishing and trawling. Most of the fish and shellfish we eat are caught in these shallow waters, which are down to 200 ft (60 m) deep. They spread out over the outer parts of continents and larger islands. Coastal sea water is alive with plankton, tiny drifting plants and animals. When blue and yellow light waves bounce back off this plankton, it makes the water look very green. Fast-swimming fish, such as yellowtails, bluefish, striped bass and some types of tuna, feed off smaller mackerels, sardines and herrings close to the coasts. Humpback whales give birth in warm coastal seas, then push their newborn calves to the surface for their first breath.

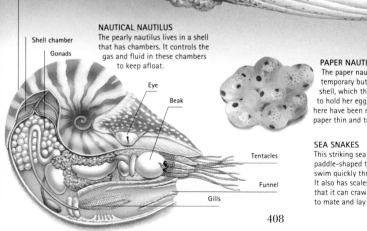

NAUTICAL NAUTILUS
The pearly nautilus lives in a shell that has chambers. It controls the gas and fluid in these chambers to keep afloat.

Shell chamber

Gonads

Eye

Beak

Tentacles

Funnel

Gills

PAPER NAUTILUS EGGS
The paper nautilus has a temporary but very beautiful shell, which the female creates to hold her eggs. The eggs shown here have been released from their paper thin and transparent case.

SEA SNAKES
This striking sea snake has a paddle-shaped tail to help it swim quickly through the water. It also has scales on its belly so that it can crawl around on land to mate and lay eggs.

408

MOTHER AND CHILD
Female humpbacks can reach 19 m (62 ft) in length. A humpback baby or calf is about one-third the size of its mother when it is born. Calves grow quickly by sucking milk from their mothers' teats.

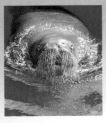

A SURFACE VIEW
This walrus poking its head through the shallow waters of the Arctic Ocean uses its sensitive whiskers to find worms, crabs and shrimp buried in the sand on the sea floor.

SOUNDING OUT

Dolphins learn about their environment, navigate and find prey by using a technique called echolocation. A dolphin searching for food will send out long- and short-range sound signals or clicks. The returning echoes tell the dolphin where prey can be found. As the dolphin closes in on the prey, it uses much shorter clicks to gain more detailed information about its target.

Click

Echo

DID YOU KNOW?
Humans have recorded the chirping sounds of male humpbacks in the breeding season, singing watery love songs to their female partners.

Coral Reefs

Brightly colored fish and thousands of other sea creatures live in the shelter of coral reefs. These marine homes grow in warm shallow seas and are built by coral animals, or polyps, with soft bodies and mouths that are ringed by stinging tentacles. The polyps construct thimble-shaped skeletons of limestone around themselves. As the polyps grow upwards, they keep dividing in two. They leave their skeletons behind them, however, and these fuse together to make a coral reef. A living mass of growing polyps always forms a film of flesh on top of the skeletons. Each polyp has many round plant cells living in its body and these cells make food from a combination of sunlight, water and carbon dioxide (a process called photosynthesis). The corals are able to catch their own food with their stinging tentacles, but most of the food they eat is made by the plant cells. Coral reefs need the food from these plant cells to grow quickly.

HIDING OUT
A clownfish lives and hides from its enemies within the tentacles of the coral reef anemone. It escapes being stung by covering itself in a layer of mucus from the anemone. The coral is fooled into thinking that the fish is part of itself.

CORAL WATCHING
Coral reefs, such as this one at Taveuni Island in the Pacific Ocean, attract snorkelers and divers from all over the world. But coral reefs are very fragile, and some are being damaged by human contact.

CORAL COMMUNITIES
Many species of coral, such as sea fan coral, hard brain coral, bubble coral and soft fire coral, grow together. They live side by side with goldfish, giant clams, surgeonfish and many other sea dwellers.

CORAL SPAWNING
When coral spawn, some release their eggs
and sperm to be fertilized in the water; others
release sperm to fertilize the egg inside the polyp.

CORAL POLYPS
These tiny coral animals form coral
colonies of different shapes and colors.
Plant cells live within the tissues of most
corals and these help the coral polyp to
produce its limestone skeleton.

Tentacles

Mouth

CROWDED HOUSE
Crustaceans, fish, sea
urchins, mollusks and
clams are some of the
many creatures that
live on a coral reef.

Butterfly fish

LEAFY SEA DRAGON
The leafy sea dragon is a type of seahorse. Its leaf-like flaps of skin help it to blend with the kelp fronds.

Camouflage

The world under the sea can be a dangerous place to live. Sea creatures often use camouflage to hide from their natural enemies. Some fish change color to match their surroundings, some take on extraordinary shapes to look like sea plants, some are almost completely transparent and are very difficult to see, while others bury themselves in the sand. Crabs are experts at disguise. Many attach algae to their bodies; others add sponges or sea squirts. The butterfly fish, shown on the left, is very clever at camouflage. Its real eyes are small and have stripes through them. But it also seems to have a large eye near its tail. These two sets of "eyes" confuse the butterfly fish's enemies. Which is the front and which is the back? An enemy does not know which way the fish will flee if attacked.

STILL AS STONE
This purple stonefish matches the coral-covered rocks on the sea floor. It has sharp spines that can inject deadly poison.

LURKING IN THE SHADOWS
Blending perfectly with the backdrop of sponges and corals, the scorpion fish waits for prey, such as fish and crustaceans, to swim close to its jaws.

EYE SPY
Some creatures bury themselves under the sand to hide from enemies. Only their large, rock-like eyeballs remain exposed.

SEE-THROUGH SHRIMP
Can you see the shrimp in this picture? It is completely transparent, except for a few glowing markings. It lives on colorful anemones.

Many sea creatures use color as a camouflage. An octopus has small, elastic bags of color in its skin. When the bags are stretched, they become dark. When the bags shrink, they are almost white. Different bags can be stretched or compressed in different parts of the body. This means an octopus can change color to match surrounding rocks.

RED ALERT
A red-and-white hawkfish camouflages itself by darting in and out of red-branched coral.

SUCKED IN
The pipefish has adapted its shape and color to match the kelp and coral that grow under the sea. It sucks in tiny animals through its small mouth.

MOBILE HOME
The hermit crab makes its home in a mollusk shell. As it grows, the crab moves out of its old home and finds a more spacious one.

ANTARCTICA

This huge, ice-covered continent around the South Pole is the coldest place on Earth. Only during the summer does the temperature ever rise above the freezing point. The ocean around Antarctica, however, teems with plants and animals—food for many seals, birds and whales.

EMPEROR PENGUINS

These are the largest and most colorful of all the penguins. They usually walk upright, but they can also toboggan over the snow, using their feet and flippers to skim along the icy surface on their chests.

AN EASY WINNER

The Weddell seal holds the seal record for deep-sea diving. It can dive to about 1,970 ft (600 m) and stay under the water for more than an hour.

• LIFE IN THE SEA •

Polar Seas

The icy seas of the polar regions are the wildest and coldest seas on Earth. The Arctic Ocean around the North Pole is covered by permanent ice and floating pack ice. It has many unique animals, such as polar bears, bearded and hooded seals and musk oxen. The Southern Ocean around the South Pole encircles the huge continent of Antarctica, which is buried beneath ice. Seals such as the crabeater, elephant and leopard seals inhabit these southern waters with 16 different kinds of penguin. Winter at the poles is long, dark and freezing. Some polar animals migrate, but most have adapted to these bitter conditions by growing special feathers or thick fur. Others have layers of fat to protect them from the cold. In summer it is light all the time, and the polar seas teem with life. Rich sea currents sweep up nutrients from the ocean depths to help the plant plankton grow. This is eaten by tiny krill, the main food for many polar creatures.

TIP OF THE ICEBERG

The Southern Ocean is filled with floating icebergs, which have broken off from the ice shelf. About 90 per cent of an iceberg is underwater, so the huge area we see above water is only the top of its immense structure.

414

FFIN
asty catch
gles from a
fin's curious bill.

ATTACK!
A hungry polar bear breaks through
the ice with its paws, snaring a baby
beluga swimming below. The bear's sharp
claws and teeth are like fishing hooks.
Scientists have learned recently that polar bears
bite or scratch a whale's blowhole so that it cannot
breathe. This makes it easier for polar bears to pull
these small whales onto the ice to eat them.

A POLE APART
In the summer, temperatures
in the Arctic rise to well
above freezing,
especially in the
coastal areas of
the bordering
continents.
Caribou
move north
to feed, and
wild flowers
bloom across
the land.

Europe

The Arctic

Canada

Greenland

415

IN QUICK PURSUIT
Killer whales are fast swimmers.
They have cone-shaped teeth to catch
and chew fish and smaller mammals.

• LIFE IN THE SEA •

Ocean Meadows

The ocean is like a giant meadow, providing food for all its creatures. The food web that operates under water is a complex system where large creatures prey on smaller creatures. Killer whales eat seals and sealions, which feed on fish and squid. Salmon enjoy small fish, which eat plankton— the tiny plants (phytoplankton) and animals (zooplankton) that float in the sunlight of the surface waters. Plankton is the basic source of food for ocean animals, and plants are the most important link in the food web. They use water, carbon dioxide and energy from sunlight to make plant food. If links in the food web are ever lost, others will take their place. Sardines once played a vital role in the food web off the coast of California. But they became scarce when too many of them were fished, and anchovies took their place.

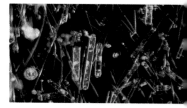

PHYTOPLANKTON
The sunlit, upper layer of the ocean teems with microscopic life, such as plant plankton, the basic food of the sea.

Uncoiled tube

Coiled tube

ZOOPLANKTON
Many kinds of microscopic animal plankton swim in the ocean. Some are the larvae of fish, which have just hatched, while others are small crustaceans, such as shrimp.

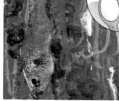

TRAILING STINGERS
Each tentacle of the Portuguese m
o' war has many stinging cells an
sac containing a coiled, barbed tu
When a fish touches the cell, the
uncoils, pierces the skin and deliv
the venomous poison.

416

SEALIONS AND SEALS
These are the natural prey of large meat-eating mammals and fish, such as whales and sharks.

PREYING ON SMALL FISH
With mouth open and sharp teeth ready, a salmon swims after a school of herring.

THE WORLD OF PLANKTON

This satellite image of the world's oceans shows where plant plankton are common. Some areas have more plankton than others and the colors on the map indicate these from the most (red), through yellow, green and blue, to the least (violet). The grey parts show where there are gaps in the information collected.

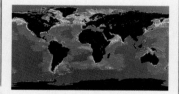

MANY LINKS
Krill are small, shrimplike creatures, which live in vast numbers in the Southern Ocean. Whales, seals and seabirds all feed on krill, and they are an important link in the food web in this part of the world.

GIANT RAY
Not all large animals in the food web eat large prey. The manta ray glides through the water, mouth agape, sieving out tiny fish and crustaceans.

TORPEDO POWER
A squid speeds through the water, its torpedo-shaped body shooting out a water jet behind it, and grabs a fish with the special suckers on the ends of its tentacles. As it is a very fast swimmer, a squid can catch prey easily.

FILTERING THROUGH
Herring feed on plankton, which they filter from the water.

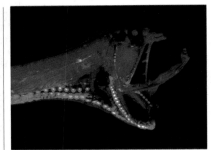

SLOANE'S VIPER
This viperfish has light organs, or photophores on its belly. Despite being only about 1 ft (30 cm) long, it has impressive jaws and teeth. It is one of the most feared of the deep-sea predators.

SWALLOWER
This fish has a hugely expandable stomach and is known as a swallower. It is able to eat fish that are longer and larger than itself.

• LIFE IN THE SEA •

Life in the Twilight Zone

Imagine the world at dusk. It is hard to see in the gloom, and shapes blur into the blackness. This is the atmosphere of the twilight zone, 656–3,280 ft (200–1,000 m) below the sunlit surface of the sea. Only blue light remains in this cold, deep-sea zone, the home of many interesting creatures that have adapted to life in this part of the ocean. Regalecus, the king of the herring, shares this murky world with lampris, a silver-spotted fish. Giant squid, which sometimes rise to the surface at night, loom in the depths with swordfish and big-eye tuna. Many of the fish in the twilight zone glow in the dark. They have bacteria that produces light—a process called bioluminescence. These animals use bioluminescence in different ways: some send out light patterns to attract mates in the darkness; several kinds of fish have bioluminescent organs on the lower half of their bodies, which they use for camouflage; others temporarily blind their predators with sudden flashes of light.

DID YOU KNOW?
Some kinds of fish and shrimp use bioluminescence to camouflage themselves. They have light organs on the lower half of their bodies that they use to blend in with light filtering from the surface. When predators look upwards, they cannot see the shape of their prey.

MOLA MOLA
This ocean sunfish has a very distinctive body shape and can be up to 10 ft (3 m) long.

KING-OF-THE-SALMON
Native Americans call the ribbonfish king-of-the-salmon. They believe it leads Pacific salmon back to the rivers to spawn when the breeding season begins.

ANGLERFISH

The female anglerfish has a luminous lure. The bulblike bait on her head contains luminescent bacteria. This attracts prey to the anglerfish, which saves energy by not having to hunt for food.

LANTERNFISH

There are huge numbers of these fish in the deep sea. They are called lanternfish because they have light organs on their heads and bodies.

COLONIAL SEA SQUIRT

The sacklike body of the sea squirt has openings through which water enters and leaves.

FLASHLIGHT FISH

This fish can be seen from a distance of 98 ft (30 m) in the dark depths of the ocean.

SQUID

Many squid live in the ocean depths. They have well-developed senses and can propel themselves quickly through the water.

VIPERFISH

The curving fangs of the small viperfish make it a dangerous predator.

SEEING IN THE DARK

Flashlight fish are found in caves at the bottom of coral reefs. They have large light organs under their eyes that contain luminous, or glowing, bacteria. The fish use these light organs to feed, and to communicate with other flashlight fish. But glowing in the dark can create problems when trying to avoid predators. The flashlight fish is able to cover the light organ with a screen of pigmented tissue, called a melanphore. This means it can turn the light on and off– just like a flashlight.

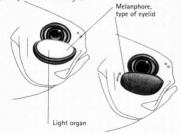

Melanphore, type of eyelid

Light organ

HATCHETFISH

These fish have light organs underneath their bodies that confuse predators swimming beneath them. Their eyes have large lenses that help them see small, glowing fish and shellfish.

SCALY DRAGONFISH

The thick, jellylike layer that covers the scales of this fish contains light organs.

Ocean Swimmers of the Dark

There are many legends about the strange inhabitants of the ocean depths. What kind of creature can survive 3,280 ft (1,000 m) below the surface of the sea— in the deepest, darkest region of the ocean? In fact, many kinds of invertebrates and fish, such as anglerfish, snipe and gulper eels and the brilliantly colored deep-sea jellyfish live here. They have all adapted to their extreme conditions, where food is scarce, in interesting ways. An anglerfish uses the long spine on its back as a glowing fishing rod to snare prey. A gulper eel has a thin, spindly body, a swollen head and jaws that are almost one-quarter the length of its body. Many ocean swimmers of the dark also have body lights (called bioluminescence), which help them find prey, and possible mates.

THE JAWS OF A GULPER E[
This black, umbrella-mou
gulper eel has huge jaws a
small teeth. Its tiny eye at the
of its snout is spying a meal, in
form of a hatchet fish, swimmi
past. Its long, tapering tail wra
itself around these pages. Follow it
the end to see the very unus
feature of a gulper e

DEEP-SEA HATCHET FISH
These silver fish have such thin bodies, you can see their bones. Their mouths point upward and their large, bulging eyes help them to see in the dim light of the ocean depths.

DEEP-SEA ANGLERFISH

The ocean depths are cold and dark and many fish, such as the anglerfish, have developed ways to live in this environment. Male anglerfish are much smaller than the females and often live permanently attached to the female, like parasites. The males follow the scent of females and mate by hooking into the female's skin and fusing with her.

TAIL LIGHT
This is a light organ at the end of a gulper's whiplike tail. It glows pink and has occasional red flashes. It may lure crustaceans and small fish to the eel's waiting jaws.

OUT OF THE DEPTHS
Creatures such as giant squid were believed to lurk in the ocean depths— waiting to attack hapless sailors.

BLOOD-RED PRAWNS
Deep-sea prawns are found in the twilight zone, but they can also live at depths of 16,000 feet (4,880 m). They are eaten by many deep-sea dwellers.

GIANT SQUID
These are the largest invertebrates in the world. They can measure up to 66 ft (20 m) in length, which includes their tentacles. They are often eaten by sperm whales.

Discover more in The Sea Floor

Life on the Ocean Floor

The ocean floor is cold, dark and still. The temperature never rises to more than just above freezing, and there is no light. This means there is little food, for plants cannot grow without energy from the sun. Deep-sea dwellers filter, sieve and sift the water and mud on the ocean floor to find tiny pieces of food that have dropped from the surface of the sea. These creatures of the deep have adapted well to their demanding environment. Some have soft, squishy bodies and large heads. They do not need strong skins and bones because there are no waves in this part of the ocean. Many are blind and move slowly through the water. Gigantic sea spiders, gutless worms and glass rope sponges are some of the unusual creatures that live in the inky blackness of the ocean floor.

Seeing in the dark
The US Navy submersible *Alvin* can carry its two crew members to a depth of 13,000 feet (3,960 m).

Eelpout
These long fish live near underwater vents and eat tube worms.

Muscling in
Mussels and giant clams live on bacteria inside their bodies.

TRIPOD FISH

The tripod fish is one of the most bizarre of the deep-sea creatures. It has three very long fins that it uses to hold itself above the ocean floor. From this position, it watches and waits patiently for unsuspecting prey. Scientists believe the tripod fish adopts the pose of a stilt-walker because it is easier to smell food in the currents above the ocean floor.

Black smokers
These mineral chimneys can be up to 33 ft (10 m) high, and occur mainly near ocean ridges. Deep-sea creatures gather around the chimneys, which blast black smoke and hot water rich in sulphur from vents at the top. These animals make their own food using the sulphur and bacteria.

Tube worms
Tube worms are found in clusters. One end of the white tube is attached to the ocean floor; a red plume, or breathing organ, emerges from the other end.

Submersibles

The ocean floor is many miles below the surface. While the safe maximum depth for scuba diving is 165 ft (50 m), the deepest parts of the ocean may be 7 miles (11 km) below the surface. The only way to reach such depths is by a submersible, a small submarine that dives from its "mother" ship. The United States submersible *Alvin* and the French vessel *Nautile* have visited the underwater site of the sunken ocean liner the *Titanic*. The crew of *Alvin* used an even smaller robot submersible, *Jason Jr.*, to probe inside places too small or too dangerous for *Alvin* to go itself. Larger submersible structures have also been used for research. The Hydrolab was launched in Florida in 1968, and for 18 years was the underwater home of scientists who observed and recorded the habits and behavior of lobsters, snapper, grouper and the hundreds of creatures living on a coral reef.

FROM THE INSIDE
The control panels at the nerve centre of the submersible *Alvin* look as complex as those on any jumbo jet or spacecraft. The crew member uses radio-controlled headphones to communicate with the "mother" ship.

DISCOVERY ON THE OCEAN FLOOR

In 1912, the luxury liner the *Titanic* struck an iceberg in the Atlantic and sank. Most of its 1,500 passengers died in the cold waters. Seventy-four years later, millions of people watched on television as the undersea craft *Alvin* and *Jason Jr.* explored this undisturbed wreck from the past.

A VIEW OF THE PAST
Divers working from *Alvin* used the robot submersible *Jason Jr.* to take this vivid picture of the *Titanic*.

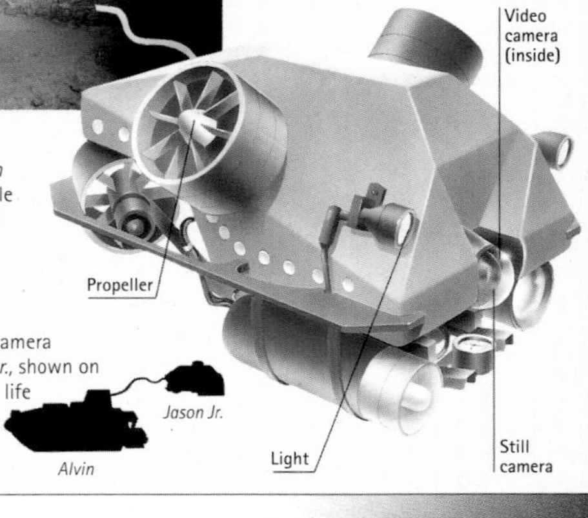

THROUGH NEW EYES
With remote-controlled camera platforms such as *Jason Jr.*, shown on the right, we can glimpse life at depths of nearly 13,120 ft (4,000 m) below the surface.

Propeller

Video camera (inside)

Jason Jr.

Alvin

Light

Still camera

E NEW FRONTIER

depths of the ocean are sterious and still. We have been ng to explore them with metal mets, diving suits, scuba gear and ng bells since the 1600s. With help of advancing technology modern submersibles, we are covering more about this tery frontier.

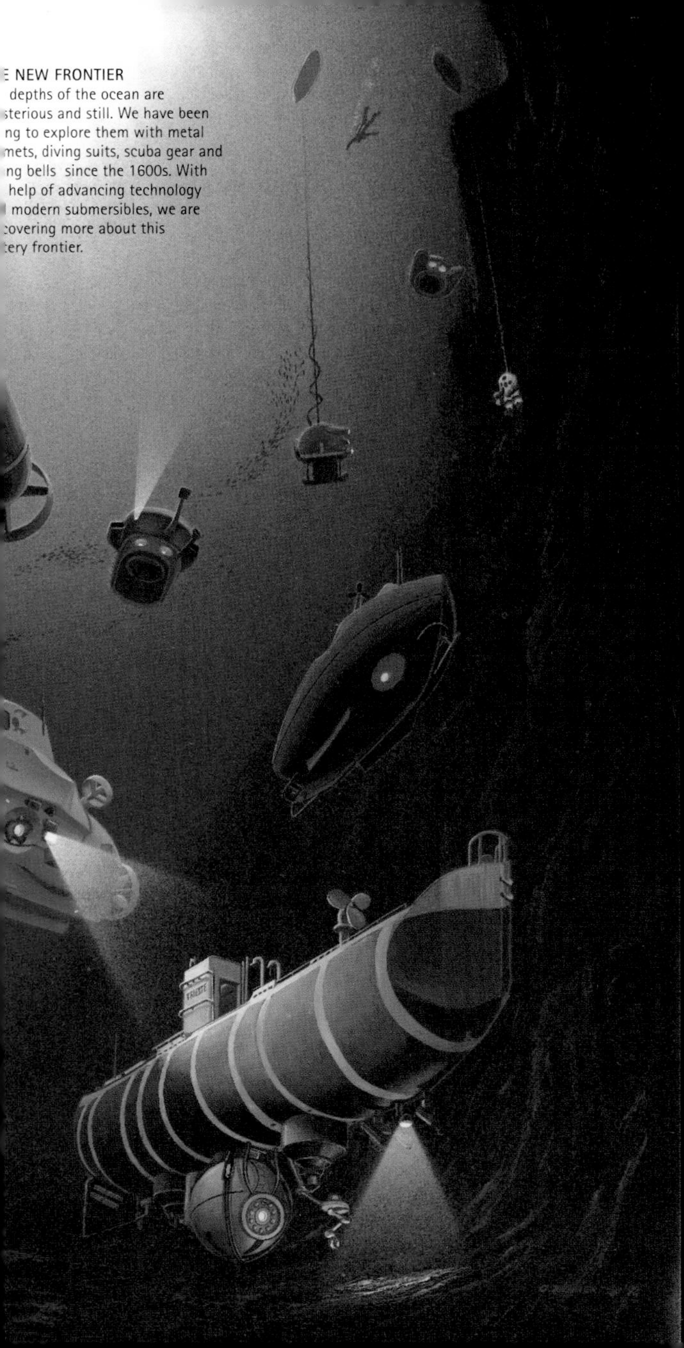

How Deep Can They Go?

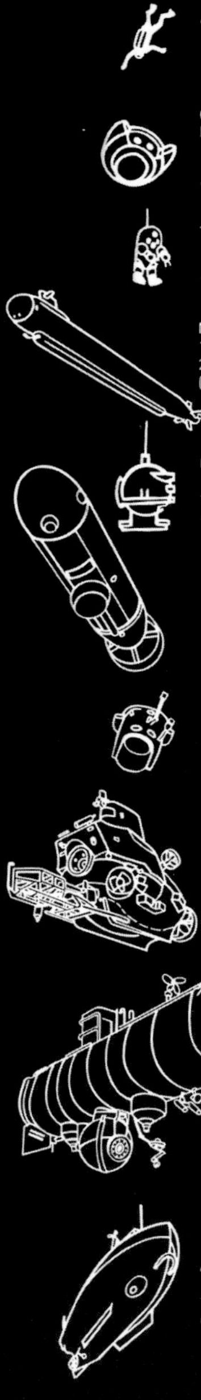

AQUALUNG
1943
165 ft
(50 m)

COUSTEAU'S DIVING SAUCER
1959
1,350 ft
(410 m)

JIM
1971
2,000 ft
(610 m)

NR-1
1969
2,300 ft
(700 m)

BATHYSPHERE
1934
3,028 ft
(925 m)

DSRV-1
1965
5,000 ft
(1,525 m)

CYANA
1959
9,800 ft
(2,990 m)

ALVIN
1964
13,000 ft
(3,960 m)

TRIESTE
1953
35,800 ft
(10,920 m)

ARCHIMÈDE
1962
36,000 ft
(10,980 m)

AN OCEAN LABORATORY
The 274-ft (83-m) *Thomas G. Thompson* is the second largest
ship in the Woods Hole Oceanographic Institution research
fleet, which is based in Massachusetts. This floating
laboratory has a permanent crew of 20 and up to 30
scientists and technicians on board for each voyage.
Thomas G. Thompson carries out research programs in
many coastal and deep-ocean areas.

KNOTTED ROPE
This square knot is used
when two ropes of
equal size have to be
joined together.

Mast
This contains the wind-measuring
instruments, lights, navigation antennas
and radar.

Staging bay
The water sampling system
is kept here.

• EXPLORING THE OCEANS •

Research Ships

The ocean covers two-thirds of the Earth's surface.
Research ships make it possible to explore some of this
enormous area. They are specially equipped so that
scientists can study deep currents and the structure of the
ocean floor; learn how the ocean interacts with the Earth's
atmosphere and how this affects climate and weather; and
how natural and human disturbances, such as burning fossil
fuels and releasing carbon dioxide into the air, affect the
oceans. These vessels carry sophisticated navigation and
communications systems, cranes and winches for their
sampling and measuring devices, special mooring cables and
tanks for live specimens. The requirements of their on-board
laboratories often change from voyage to voyage. The ships
stay in touch with their home ports by satellite.

Main lab
Samples and data are
analyzed around the
clock in the main lab.

WATER SAMPLERS
These scientists are
preparing to send
water sample bottles
to the bottom of the
ocean. Valuable
information can be
obtained by analyzing
these samples.

426

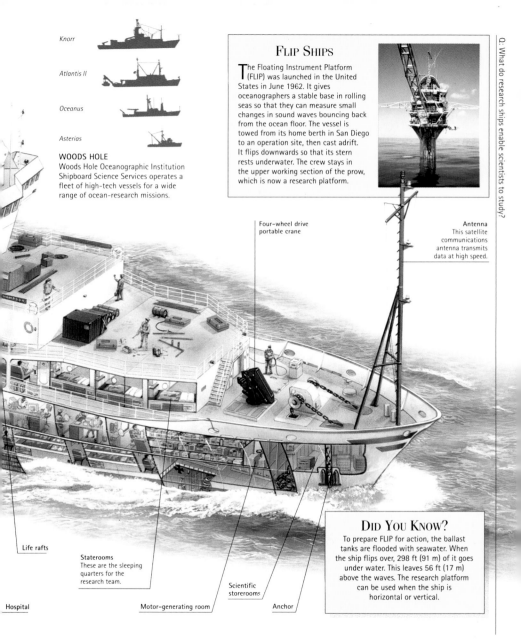

Knorr

Atlantis II

Oceanus

Asterias

WOODS HOLE
Woods Hole Oceanographic Institution Shipboard Science Services operates a fleet of high-tech vessels for a wide range of ocean-research missions.

FLIP SHIPS

The Floating Instrument Platform (FLIP) was launched in the United States in June 1962. It gives oceanographers a stable base in rolling seas so that they can measure small changes in sound waves bouncing back from the ocean floor. The vessel is towed from its home berth in San Diego to an operation site, then cast adrift. It flips downwards so that its stern rests underwater. The crew stays in the upper working section of the prow, which is now a research platform.

Q: What do research ships enable scientists to study?

Four-wheel drive portable crane

Antenna
This satellite communications antenna transmits data at high speed.

Life rafts

Staterooms
These are the sleeping quarters for the research team.

Scientific storerooms

Hospital

Motor-generating room

Anchor

DID YOU KNOW?
To prepare FLIP for action, the ballast tanks are flooded with seawater. When the ship flips over, 298 ft (91 m) of it goes under water. This leaves 56 ft (17 m) above the waves. The research platform can be used when the ship is horizontal or vertical.

Sea Legends

Early seafarers and explorers, searching for new lands, faced daily perils in unknown seas. They braved storms, icebergs, fog, hidden reefs and the unsettling calm, waiting for a flurry of wind to catch the sails. Sailors told of huge sea monsters; of mermaids and mermen; and of Neptune, the fiery god of the sea. Rumors and exaggerated tales of true and imagined sea creatures were exchanged at every port. Cartographers, drawing detailed maps of new routes and countries, even included pictures of dragon-like monsters roaring their way around the world's oceans. Many nations have legends about the sea. The ancient Greeks told stories of sirens (part woman, part bird) whose sweet songs lured mariners to their death on jagged rocks. Ulysses, one of the heroes of Greek mythology, had to put wax in his sailors' ears to stop them from jumping into the sea as they sailed past the sirens' island. He lashed himself to the mast so that he could hear their singing, but not be charmed by it.

SEA MONSTERS

Do they really exist? Or are they exaggerated versions of real sea giants, such as sawfish, narwhals or humpback whales? The octopus-like sea monster wrapping itself around this ship is said to be a kraken, a mythical creature that appears off the shores of Norway. It must seem very real to the sailors clinging desperately to the ropes on this sinking ship.

WOMEN OF THE WAVES

Mermaids often appear in legends, with long flowing tresses of hair, decorated with delicate shell combs. Stories tell of mermaids enticing humans into the sea, and drowning them in its depths.

THE LOCH NESS MONSTER

The sea is not the only water surrounded by mysteries and myths. The deep lake called Loch Ness in northern Scotland is a strange and lonely place, often shrouded by mist. Visitors claim to have seen and photographed a monster rising silently above the surface, and disappearing mysteriously. Scientists have investigated the sightings but have never found the monster. Nor have they proved that it does not exist. If you visit the lake, you can see a video of the elusive creature "Nessie."

SEA GOD

The Romans believed that Neptune was the god of the sea. He ruled the many creatures that lived below the waves.

SHOWTIME FOR NESSIE!

MONSTER ACT

This photograph is said to prove once and for all that the Loch Ness Monster really exists. But is this dark shape really a monster? Could it be a whale or a mystery submarine?

429

Where Did They Go?

GHOSTLY WATCH
On the lonely night watch, these sailors are chilled by the sight of a fully rigged phantom ship sailing silently past in the mist.

There are many ocean mysteries that have fascinated and frustrated people for hundreds of years. One region in the world that seems particularly mysterious is the Bermuda Triangle, which lies between Bermuda, Florida and Puerto Rico. Many ships and aircraft have vanished completely in the Triangle. No one has been able to explain their disappearance, and their wrecks have never been found. Strong storms, powerful currents and deep seas probably claimed any wreckage quickly. But what of the *Mary Celeste* and its missing crew? In 1872, this American ship was found floating, in seaworthy condition, in the middle of the Atlantic Ocean. There were no sailors in sight, and few clues as to where they had gone. One of the most intriguing mysteries from the past surrounds the legendary continent of Atlantis. Plato, a Greek philosopher, wrote that it sank into the Atlantic Ocean. But did it ever really exist? Many people believe the story of Atlantis was based on the Greek island of Thera, which was ruptured by volcanic explosions.

SAILING SOLO
When the *Mary Celeste* was discovered abandoned and drifting, the lifeboat and navigational instruments were missing. Did the captain order the crew to leave the ship, and with his wife and two-year-old daughter, take to the lifeboat and the endless horizon of sea?

STRANGE BUT TRUE
Did the *Mary Celeste* sail itself? The last log entry put the ship near the Azores, some 700 miles (1,130 km) and 9 days away from where it was found.

FLIGHT 19'S LAST MISSION

On 5 December 1945, the sky droned with the engine noises of five torpedo bombers on a training flight from Florida. But flying across the Bermuda Triangle, the whole squadron vanished. During the last radio contact with their base, they said they were low on fuel and might have to land in the water. Rescue crews scoured the ocean for five days. They discovered no trace of the missing men or planes.

THE LOST KINGDOM

The Greek philosopher Plato was the first to write about the lost civilization of Atlantis. He said that thousands of years ago there was a large island in the Atlantic Ocean. The temples were decorated with gold, silver, copper and ivory; the people were very wealthy and lived in magnificent buildings. But, according to Plato, the people became greedy and dishonest, and the gods decided to punish them. During one day and night, violent eruptions shook the island and it disappeared, forever, into the sea.

Plato

MAPPED OUT

A map from the seventeenth century shows Atlantis as a very large island, midway between America and the Pillars of Hercules, at the entrance to the Mediterranean Sea.

Mysteries of Migration

BABY TURTLES
These turtles make an instinctive dash for the sea after hatching in the sand. But once in the sea, they are easy targets for predators, such as sharks. Most do not survive.

Many of the animals in the world make long journeys, or migrations, each year. They move to warmer climates, to find food, or a safe place to breed and raise their young. Migrations can cover thousands of miles. Many polar seabirds migrate enormous distances, but the Arctic tern makes the longest journey of all creatures. Each year, it travels from the top to the bottom of the globe and back again— a journey of 9,300 miles (15,000 km). Whales mate and give birth in warm seas, but they migrate to polar seas to eat the huge amounts of krill they need. Marine turtles can spend more than a year building up the fat reserves they will need when they leave their feeding grounds. They journey across vast oceans to certain regions where they mate and lay their eggs. But how do marine turtles navigate over the open ocean with such accuracy? There is much about animal migration that continues to baffle scientists.

The Life Cycle of a Salmon

Salmon lay their eggs in freshwater rivers and streams. Young salmon, called alevin, hatch in gravel on the river bed and remain there for several weeks. Then they begin to swim downstream to the salty ocean, where they will feed on fish, squid and krill. This migration usually takes place at night to avoid predators. Salmon spend up to four years at sea before returning to breed in the river in which they were hatched. Some adult salmon will travel thousands of miles to reach these rivers. After breeding, the salmon die.

SALMON EGGS
Salmon hide their large yolky eggs in the gravel of river beds to keep them safe from predators. Young salmon feed on their yolk sac.

SWIMMING UPSTREAM
Leaping sockeye salmon fight their way back up the Adams River, Canada, to their home spawning grounds.

ON THE MOVE
The larvae of European eels hatch in the Sargasso Sea, in the north Atlantic Ocean. Then they swim to the mouths of freshwater rivers and streams in North America and Europe, taking two to three years to make the journey. Here they change into elvers and gradually mature into adult eels.

LOBSTER LINKS
When spiny lobsters migrate in the autumn, they form lines and march in single file across the ocean floor. Each creature stays in contact with the one in front. If an enemy appears, the lobsters back away from it and point their spiny antennae in an attack position.

Food from the Sea

People have gathered food from the sea for thousands of years. Fish and shellfish are rich in protein and essential nutrients, and people in many countries include great amounts of fish in their diet. There are different ways of taking food from the sea: fishing with a hook, line and sinker; placing baskets and pots in the sea to catch crabs, lobsters akd crayfish; setting up fish farms, where huge quantities of fish, mollusks and crustaceans are produced each year; and using fishing ships with modern equipment and techniques. These large vessels take millions of tons of fish, such as herring, tuna, cod and mackerel, from the sea every year to provide food for humans, and to turn into fish oil, animal feed and fertilizers. They find most of their catch in the waters that are close to the coast, where fish flock to find food.

TO CATCH A TUNA
Tuna are not easy to catch. They are very large and heavy, and it can take four men to land a tuna such as this on the deck of a boat. Some tuna will trail a fishing boat for a long time and then steal the bait without being caught.

A CHOICE MENU
There is an enormous variety of food from the sea: fish, octopuses, squid, eels, shrimp and many more are caught and sold to people all over the world.

Crab

FARMING OYSTERS
Many oyster farms are located in waters that are rich with microscopic algae, the natural food of oysters. The oysters are grown in trays or on sticks, and are usually harvested from 18 months to 3 years old.

NETTING THE CATCH

Large fishing fleets sometimes spend several months at sea, combing the ocean with different types of nets. A bottom or otter trawl is a large net that is towed behind a fishing boat and used to catch the many species of fish that live on the sea bed. Floats and weights keep the mouth of the trawl open so that everything in its path is scooped up. Species of fish such as anchovies are caught in a purse-seine net, which forms a large circle in the sea. When a school of fish swims into the net, it is pulled shut quickly. Fish in the open seas, such as tuna, are sometimes caught in drift nets. These are held up by floats and drift just below the surface of the water for many miles. Sea creatures such as dolphins and sea turtles are often caught in drift nets. As a result, there is now an international ban on fishing with drift nets, but some countries continue to use them.

Bottom or otter trawl

Purse seine

Drift net

THE OLD WAY
A fisherman hangs an octopus in the sun to dry. This is a traditional method of preserving food, and it is still one of the most effective.

DID YOU KNOW?

In Japan, China and other parts of Asia, cormorants are sometimes used to dive for fish. Fishermen attach a line to the birds' bodies so that they can pull them back to the boat. A ring or cord around the birds' necks stops them from swallowing the fish they catch in their mouths.

Discover more in Ocean Meadows

Oils and Minerals

Oil
A drop of heavy crude oil falls from a glass tube.

The most sought-after resources found in today's oceans are oil and natural gas. They are located offshore in many parts of the world, and new fields are being discovered all the time. Oil-rich countries sell to oil-hungry countries, and the trade in oil and gas affects the economy of the whole world. As it takes thousands of years for oil, a fossil fuel, to develop, there is a limited amount of oil in the world. When it is all gone, we will have to find other sources of energy, such as solar energy from the sun. Many useful minerals also come from the sea. Sea water is very salty and humans have extracted salt from the sea for thousands of years. Marine-based minerals form crusts, which cover parts of the ocean bottom.

Derrick
Carries the crown block and supports the weight of the drill string.

Crown block

Helicopter pad

Lifeboat

Satellite dishes

Drill pipes

Ca

HAT IS OIL?

was formed when dead plants
d animals sank to the bottom of
e ocean. The dead matter was
ried under piles of mud and
nd, which turned into rock after
llions of years. The decaying
tter was squashed and, as
e temperature and pressure
reased, it collected in the
dimentary rock as droplets of oil
d between the rock grains— just like
ponge holds water.

MINING FOR MANGANESE

Manganese is a hard, brittle metal element. It is used to make alloys, such as steel, harder and stronger. Manganese nodules are found on parts of the ocean floor. The ones shown here were dredged from the Blake Plateau in the North Atlantic Ocean, 1,378 ft (420 m) below the surface. Manganese nodules form in places where sediment builds up slowly. As each new layer of metal is added, the nodules grow bigger, sometimes joining together with other nodules. Most nodules look like small black potatoes and grow at the rate of a few millimeters every million years. Some of the world's mining companies have located rich deposits of deep-sea manganese nodules. However, mining manganese is an extremely expensive process. First, the nodules must be dredged, often in very deep waters, and transported back to shore. Then, they must be treated with chemicals to extract the manganese. At the moment, this is all too costly and the manganese nodules on the ocean floors remain largely untouched.

Revolving crane

Flare

DRILLING DEEP
Several oil wells extend at different angles through the layers of strata until they reach a pocket of oil.

Well heads
Transport oil and gas to the platform.

Processing equipment

Water level
The water level of the ocean rises and falls with the tides.

Shales and porous rocks
Water passes through the widely spaced rock grains of shale, sandstone and limestone.

Impermeable layer
A layer of dense rock forms a lid on top of the layer of oil or gas.

An oil and water mix
Oil, water and gas form pockets in the grains of porous rocks. Small amounts of oil and water mix together here.

Non-porous rocks
This layer, which is often granite, stops the oil from escaping downwards.

DRILLING FOR GOLD
An oil platform is like a huge steel and concrete hotel in the middle of the ocean. Several hundred workers can live there for weeks at a time. Most platforms stay in position for about 25 years, although one rig has survived for 60 years. Every day, these platforms pump millions of barrels of oil or "black gold," a name often given to this sticky, black, expensive liquid.

Lifeboat

CHECKING THE FOUNDATIONS
Divers must make routine checks of all the pipes and cables under an oil rig. Pounding seas constantly batter the rig and can eventually wear away or dislodge even the strongest metal framework.

The Perils of Pollution

A GIANT GARBAGE CA
Humans throw all kinds
litter into the sea, but th
garbage never goes awa

A HAZARDOUS LIFE
This seal is entangled in
carelessly discarded fish
line. Any material throw
into the sea is potentiall
harmful to sea creatures
Nets, plastic balloons an
the ring openers of soft-
cans kill many sea mamr
sea birds and fish.

Human and industrial waste has been dumped in the sea for years. People once believed that sea water could kill any lurking germs. But scientists have now discovered that sewage pumped into the sea can spread terrible diseases, such as cholera, typhus and hepatitis. If polluting material enters the food chain, it can become more and more dangerous as one creature eats another. Humans are at the end of the food chain and they can suffer the worst effects of all. In the 1950s, many people in Japan died or became paralyzed after eating fish that was contaminated with mercury from a local factory. The United Nations began to take marine pollution seriously in the 1970s, but by this time, parts of some seas were already dying. Today, oceans are still polluted by oil spills, chemicals and human waste.

STRANGE BUT TRUE
This hermit crab was found with a very unnatural shell— a plastic bucket in which it is now trapped.

SPILLING OIL

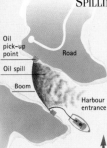

Oil pick-up point

Road

Oil spill

Boom

Harbour entrance

Wind direction

When an oil tanker spills its liquid cargo into the sea, floating booms are erected. They try to trap the oil and stop it from polluting the shoreline. The trapped oil is sucked up and stored somewhere safe. But it is not always possible to stop the oil from spreading. These workers are hosing the rocky coastline of Alaska in the huge clean-up operation that followed the *Exxon Valdez* oil spill.

BLUE-GREEN ALGAE
Clouds of marine algae, which grow when water is polluted, float near the surface of the Sea of Cortez. The algae shade the sea bottom and stop the rich seagrasses from growing. Without this source of food, fish, shellfish and worms will suffer.

THE BEGINNING
This undeveloped beach in Cyprus is already littered with trash from the ocean.

LOSING LIFE
Oil spills at sea are devastating for wildlife. When a bird's feathers are covered with oil, they are no longer waterproof. Water soaks into the unprotected feathers and the bird drowns or freezes to death.

The Future of the Oceans

Who owns the sea and who should look after it? How can we ensure that its vast resources, which we need for food, fuel and energy, are not used up completely? Will future generations be able to swim in clear, unpolluted water? If we want to protect the sea, we must manage it properly. All the continents in the world are surrounded by sea, so people from all countries must cooperate to preserve it. Important steps, such as establishing marine parks to protect endangered environments and species, have already been taken. Many nations have signed agreements to limit activities such as drift-net fishing, which can harm sea animals. But overfishing and pollution continue to threaten the sea. There is much to do to guarantee its future.

BEACHED!

Whales that swim too close to the shore may become stranded. They need water to support their bodies— without it they cannot breathe and will die. Volunteers work hard to keep this whale's skin wet until it can be floated out to sea on the high tide.

MANAGING THE OCEANS

The oceans link all the countries of the world. Different nations can manage the oceans by:

• Creating marine parks to protect marine life.

• Working out who owns particular areas of the sea and whose responsibility it is to look after it. Countries own and manage all living and non-living resources for 200 nautical miles from their low-water line. The rest of the oceans are international zones and are not controlled by any one nation.

• Placing bans or limits on some forms of drag-net fishing and whaling, both of which kill sea creatures senselessly.

• Trying to stop or control the amount and type of pollution that is pumped into the sea.

• Monitoring the seaworthiness and age of all vessels allowed to operate on the sea.

• Making sure that nuclear-powered vessels and oil tankers are not allowed anywhere near national parks, populated areas or any other sensitive areas close to the coasts.

• Ensuring that destructive animals such as the crown-of-thorns starfish are controlled and not allowed to damage heritage areas such as Australia's Great Barrier Reef.

RESPECTING NATURE

A sea bird nesting on land seems unperturbed by such close inspection. We need to protect the natural environment so that we can continue to enjoy seeing animals in their natural world.

CROWN-OF-THORNS

The crown-of-thorns starfish stays hidden during the day and comes out at night to feed on the coral that surrounds it. It eats the coral tissue and leaves nothing but a skeleton behind it. This starfish has caused great damage to reefs in the Indo-Pacific area during the last twenty years.

SELLING SEA SHELLS

Many people collect shells for their unusual shapes and colors. But these shells are the homes of many seashore animals. Their habitat is destroyed when people remove the shells from the seashore.

COMMUNITY CARE

A responsible hiker carries his trash home with him. If people leave garbage at a camping site, especially one near a river, it can eventually pollute the ocean.

Conserving the Oceans

E ach year there are 90 million more people on Earth to feed. Because the biggest increase in population is in coastal areas, more seafood is needed each year to feed the world. Sadly, most of the traditional fisheries of the oceans have either reached the limit of safe fishing or are already past that point and are now being overfished. If we want to keep the great ocean fisheries at their most productive, we must stop polluting them and also be more moderate in the numbers of fish we catch. This much-needed increase in the numbers of fish and shellfish can only happen in clean, unpolluted waters. Numbers can be further increased by opening new fisheries and by setting up fish farms in coastal lagoons and ponds, or within big nets in shallow water.

African Tilapia
Fish farming is a huge and growing industry in southeast Asia. Many local species are used, but African tilapias are very popular. Scientists have made genetic changes to the tilapia to increase dramatically the growth rate of this fish and to allow a greater number of fish crops per year.

MARINE PARKS

C oral reefs are breaking down all over the world from the effects of pollution and overfishing. To prevent this, most tropical countries are creating marine parks to help protect coral areas from further damage. Tourists can still enjoy the reefs and their fishes at these parks. The largest of these sanctuaries is the Great Barrier Reef Marine Park. It extends for 1,240 miles (2,000 km) along the coast of northeastern Australia.

Lobsters
Delicious spiny lobsters are plentiful in some southern waters. They are the basis of rich fisheries and are exported, both frozen and live, for luxury dining. But these lobsters also need to be conserved so that we can continue to enjoy them.

Tuna
The bluefin tuna is a fast and powerful swimmer. In spite of its size, it has tasty, tender flesh and is sought after for canning, cooking and eating raw. Agreements are being drawn up to restrict its fishing to allow its numbers to grow.

Cod
The Georges Bank and the Grand Banks in the northwestern Atlantic are famous for their rich cod and flounder fisheries. Exploitation, however, has resulted in the collapse of these banks and the closure of large areas. This has brought economic hardship to fishing families.

Pollution
The increase in human population has put enclosed seas at risk from pollution. The North Sea, the Mediterranean and the Baltic are examples of this. The seafood-loving nations around the Mediterranean Sea are developing the Blue Plan to reduce pollution.

Salmon
After spending years at sea, the northeast Pacific salmon swims up rivers to breed. Because many of these rivers are now silting up, they have lost their salmon. Measures are now under way to stop the silting and to restore salmon to these rivers. Salmon are also being bred artificially and grown in large offshore nets in the northern Atlantic and Pacific oceans.

Sardines and Anchovies
Sardines and anchovies live in enormous schools off the southwestern tip of Africa and in the waters off Chile and Peru in South America. These areas are rich in nutrients and give rise to blooms of plant and animal plankton on which the fish feed. There seemed to be huge numbers of sardines and anchovies when they were first caught on a large scale, but overfishing and variable weather conditions have led to a drop in their numbers.

Whales
The seas of the Antarctic teem with life: huge swarms of shrimplike krill, whales, penguins and seals. A worldwide ban on whaling, broken by only a few nations, has allowed the great whales such as the blue whale and the southern right whale to recover from extremely low numbers.

Discover more in Food from the Sea

Ocean Facts

Water makes up two-thirds of the surface of the Earth. The Southern Hemisphere is particularly wet, with four times as much water as land. With the help of technology, we are learning how the oceans were formed, how they are changing, how they are responsible for our weather and how important they are to plant and animal life.

What is the largest ocean?
The Pacific Ocean covers 65 million square miles (166 million square km) and makes up 32 per cent of the Earth's surface. It is the world's largest and deepest ocean. On average, its sea floor is 13,737 ft (4,188 m) below sea level.

What is the deepest part of the deepest ocean?
The deepest part is the Mariana Trench near the Philippines in the Pacific Ocean. It is 35,620 ft (10,860 m) below sea level. If you turned Mount Everest, the world's highest mountain, upside down in the trench, it would sink more than 1 mile (2 km) into the sea before touching the bottom.

How do fish survive in the freezing temperature of the polar regions?
As sea water freezes sooner than the blood of fish, a number of Arctic and Antarctic fish have developed an organic anti-freeze mechanism to survive in the cold waters.

Why is the sea salty?
The sea gets its salt from rocks on the sea bed and from rivers that feed into it. As the sea is evaporated by the sun, the salt level builds up.

Which oceans cover the Earth?
The Pacific, Atlantic, Indian, Southern and Arctic oceans are the five oceans that cover the Earth.

How much water do the oceans hold?
The oceans hold 48 billion cubic ft (1,358 cubic decimeters) of water.

What does the word "ocean" mean?
The word ocean comes from the Greek word "okeanos," which means river. The early Greeks thought that a river encircled the Earth.

Which is the strongest ocean current?
The Gulf Stream carries about 30 billion gallons (135 billion liters) of water every second. This is 6.5 times as much water as all the rivers in the world.

Does the ocean ever overflow?
Rain, melting ice and river water pour continually into the ocean. But the ocean never overflows because this water is always on the move. It is evaporated by the sun and turned into water vapor. The vapor then falls as rain or snow, most of which ends up back in the ocean. This is usually turned back into vapor and the whole cycle starts once again.

How did the Dead Sea get its name?
This sea is so salty that nothing can live in its water.

What is the difference between an ocean and a sea?
Seas are shallower and smaller than oceans and are partly surrounded by land.

Which sea is growing wider by 0.4 in (1 cm) each year?
The Red Sea is growing by this amount every year as the Earth's lithospheric plates move apart and the sea floor spreads.

How many kinds of shark live in the oceans?
Scientists know of 350 species of shark, most of them harmless.

What percentage of the Netherlands lies below sea level?
More than 33 per cent of the Netherlands is below sea level. Windmills control the amount of water that reaches the fields lying below the sea's surface.

If no more water was added to the oceans and evaporation continued normally, how long would it take for the oceans to dry up?
If this happened, it would take 3,000 years.

How much of the sea bed is still unexplored?
Ninety-eight per cent of the sea bed is still to be explored, but as advances in underwater technology continue, more exploration will take place.

Which is the saltiest sea on Earth?
The salt content of sea water is usually about 3.5 per cent. The Dead Sea, however, contains more than 24 per cent— nearly eight times as much!

What is the biggest fish in the ocean?
The whale shark is the largest fish. It grows up to 49 ft (15 m) in length.

How much of an iceberg do you actually see?
Nine-tenths of an iceberg is hidden under the water so you can only see one-tenth.

What is the oldest form of marine life still found in the oceans?
A form of blue-green algae has existed for some billions of years. Sharks are some of the oldest back-boned animals in the sea.

Where is the world's highest inland sea?
Lake Titicaca between Peru and Bolivia is the highest inland sea. Its surface is 12,503 ft (3,812 m) above sea level.

Which sea is the most polluted in the world?
The Mediterranean is the world's most polluted sea. More than 421 billion tons (430 billion tonnes) of pollution are poured into it each year.

Why is the sea blue?
The light that strikes the sea is either absorbed or broken up and scattered back to the surface. Blue and green wavelengths of light are scattered more than red and yellow ones, and this gives the sea its blue or green appearance.

STRANGE BUT TRUE
Some fish can change sex easily. The black-and-gold angelfish of the South Pacific live in groups of one male and up to seven females. If the male dies, the largest female turns into a male within a week or two.

Volcanoes and Earthquakes

What is a hotspot?

What is the Pacific Ring of Fire?

How do you take a volcano's temperature?

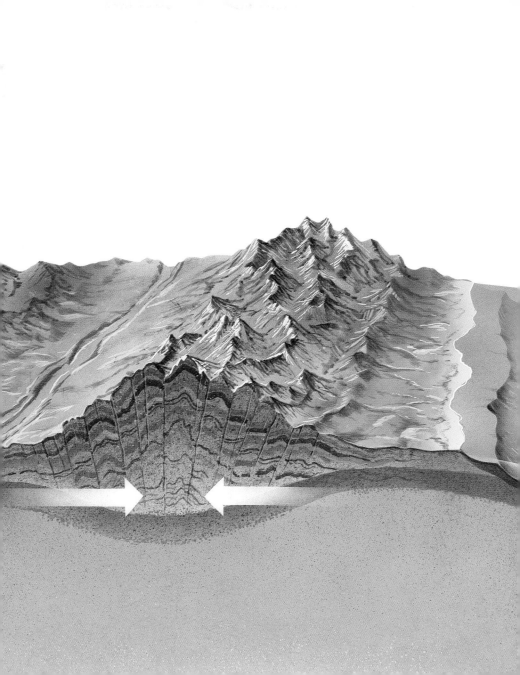

Contents

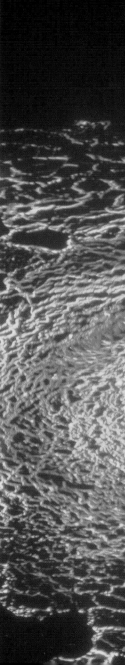

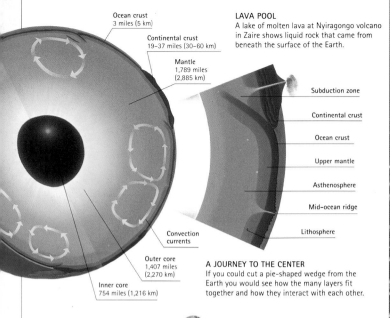

Ocean crust
3 miles (5 km)

Continental crust
19–37 miles (30–60 km)

Mantle
1,789 miles
(2,885 km)

LAVA POOL
A lake of molten lava at Nyiragongo volcano in Zaire shows liquid rock that came from beneath the surface of the Earth.

Subduction zone

Continental crust

Ocean crust

Upper mantle

Asthenosphere

Mid-ocean ridge

Convection
currents

Lithosphere

Outer core
1,407 miles
(2,270 km)

A JOURNEY TO THE CENTER
If you could cut a pie-shaped wedge from the Earth you would see how the many layers fit together and how they interact with each other.

Inner core
754 miles (1,216 km)

• THE UNSTABLE EARTH •

Fire Down Below

The Earth is made up of several layers. If you could stand at the center, 3,950 miles (6,371 km) down, you would see the solid iron inner core, which is surrounded by an outer core of liquid iron and nickel. To travel to the surface, you would pass through the solid rock of the lower mantle, then the soft, squishy area of rock called the asthenosphere. The final two layers join together to form the lithosphere, which is made up of the solid rock of the upper mantle, and the crust. The crust covers the Earth as thin apple peel covers an apple. Inside the Earth, radioactive elements decay and produce heat, and the temperature increases to an amazing 5,432°F (3,000°C) at the core. This heat provides the energy for the layers to move and interact. Melted rock called magma rises from deep within the Earth to near the surface. Some of it cools and becomes solid within the crust but some erupts on the surface as lava.

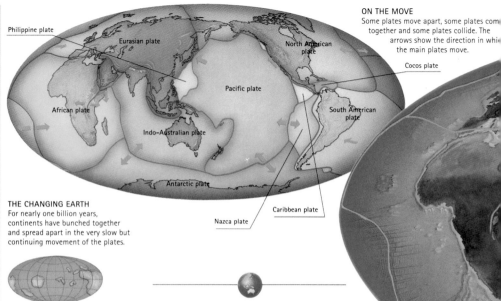

Philippine plate

Eurasian plate

North American plate

Pacific plate

Cocos plate

African plate

South American plate

Indo-Australian plate

Antarctic plate

Nazca plate

Caribbean plate

ON THE MOVE
Some plates move apart, some plates come together and some plates collide. The arrows show the direction in which the main plates move.

THE CHANGING EARTH
For nearly one billion years, continents have bunched together and spread apart in the very slow but continuing movement of the plates.

500 million years ago

325–350 million years ago

Pangaea the supercontinent
200 million years ago

Pangaea splits into
Gondwana and Laurasia
130 million years ago

Gondwana and Laurasia
65 million years ago

• THE UNSTABLE EARTH •

The Moving Continents

The Earth's outermost section, the lithosphere, is separated into seven large and several small jagged slabs called lithospheric plates, which fit together much like puzzle pieces. The crust, or top part, of each two-layered plate comes from either an ocean, a continent or a bit of both. You cannot feel it, but the plates are constantly moving. Supported by the soft, squishy material of the asthenosphere under them, plates pull and push against each other at a rate of $3/4$–8 in (2–20 cm) per year. When plates pull apart, magma from the mantle erupts and forms new ocean crust. When they move together, one plate slowly dives under the other and forms a deep ocean trench. Mountain ranges form when some plates collide. Other plates slide and scrape past each other. Most volcanoes and earthquakes occur along edges where plates meet.

ALFRED WEGENER 1880 1930
$4
REPUBLIK ÖSTERREICH

A NEW THEORY
In 1915, Alfred Wegener, a German scientist and explorer, proposed his theory of continental drift. He wrote of a huge supercontinent, Pangaea, which split apart millions of years ago. The pieces then slowly drifted to their present position. Not until the mid-1960s was the theory revised and accepted by scientists.

Energy in the form of convection currents
produced by heat in the mantle moves the
giant lithospheric plates across the surface
of the Earth. Scientists have only
a general idea of the paths
and directions these
currents take.

Mid-ocean mountains
The longest mountain range in the world
is the gently sloping mid-ocean ridge
system, which snakes along the ocean
floor at the boundaries of the plates.

STRANGE BUT TRUE

Many millions of years ago, the east
coast of South America and the west
coast of Africa fitted together as part of
the same land mass. Today, the two
continents even have similar rock,
plant and animal fossils.

Glossopteris

SLIDING BY

When some plates meet they slide past
each other in opposite directions or in
the same direction at different speeds. The
edges of the sliding plates grind when they
meet, causing a series of weblike cracks or
faults and fractures to occur. Here an
orchard changes course to follow the line
of a fault—a simple example of plate
movement. As the two plates move slowly
past each other, stress builds up in the
rocks below and an earthquake can occur.

Discover more in Fire Down Below

Ridges and Rift Valleys

The ocean crust is rugged with mountain ridges and deep rift valleys or cracks. When two plates with ocean crust move apart, magma from the mantle bubbles up to the surface to fill the rift. The magma cools and hardens and adds new strips of crust or ocean floor to the edges of the two plates. This forms what is called a spreading, or widening, ridge. The Atlantic Ocean is widening by 3/4 in (2 cm) per year. The East Pacific Rise is widening by 8 in (20 cm) per year—the fastest widening rate of an ocean floor. In 10 million years, it will be 1,240 miles (2,000 km) wider. Plates continue to move away from the spreading ridge towards other plates. When a spreading ridge fractures or breaks, earthquakes occur. Mid-ocean ridge volcanoes also form in rifts, fed by the magma from below. Over millions of years, they can grow so large that they rise above the water to form islands, such as Iceland on the North Atlantic mid-ocean ridge.

Smoking chimneys
Sulfur and other minerals deposited on the sides of the vents build natural chimneys of up to 33 feet (10 m) high.

SEA FLOOR SPREADING
New lithospheric plate is created at a spreading ridge.

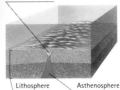

Magma chamber

Lithosphere   Asthenosphere

As two plates with ocean crust move apart, a crack or rift forms.

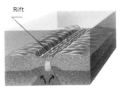

Rift

Magma from the mantle rises to fill the rift between the two plates.

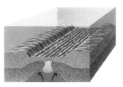

Magma cools and hardens, and adds to the edges of the plates.

BLACK SMOKERS
Volcanic hot springs or hydrothermal vents such as these were discovered in 1977 and are found along very active spreading ridges on the ocean floor. The mineral-rich water is eaten by bacteria, which is food for other vent animals such as tube worms, giant clams and eelpouts.

Circulation system
The arrows show how cold sea water seeps down through the ridge. Magma heats it to an amazing 572°F (300°C), then the water rises back up through the vent.

AN ISLAND IS BORN

In 1963, an undersea volcanic eruption created Surtsey Island, the newest land mass on Earth. Surtsey lies off the southwest coast of Iceland, a country known for its many active volcanoes. The eruption began with a large column of ash and smoke. Heat and pressure from deep within the Earth pushed part of the mid-Atlantic ridge to the surface. The island continued to grow for several months. Today, Surtsey Island measures 1 sq mile (2.6 sq km). Its dominant feature is the steep cone of the volcano.

Discover more in The Moving Continents

455

Subduction

When two plates move toward each other and meet, one plate slowly dives, or subducts, beneath the other along what is called a "subduction zone." This is an area of intense earthquake and volcanic activity caused by the movement of the two plates. There are three types of plate boundaries where subduction occurs: ocean to ocean, ocean to continent and continent to continent. The action of subduction is the same for all three types but the results are different. The area at which one plate dives beneath another creates an ocean trench, the deepest part of the ocean floor. As the down-going plate continues to sink deeper into the mantle, it mixes with hot rock and melts to form magma. Under extreme heat and pressure, this new magma mixture then forces its way back upwards to erupt violently at the surface. Compared to the gentle chain of mid-ocean ridge volcanoes, subduction volcanoes are explosive and dangerous. This is due to the presence of water and the build-up of gases dissolved in the thick and sticky magma that is produced in the process of subduction.

OCEAN TO OCEAN

When two plates with ocean crust meet, one plate subducts. When the magma rises to the surface, it forms an island arc volcano chain such as the Lesser Antilles in the East Caribbean.

Island arc volcano

Ocean crust

Magma

Subduction zone

Asthenosphere

OCEAN TO CONTINENT

When a plate with thin ocean crust meets a plate with thicker continental crust, the thinner plate subducts. Magma rises to the surface and forms a line of volcanoes such as these on the west coast of South America.

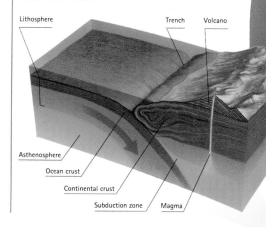

Lithosphere

Trench

Volcano

Asthenosphere

Ocean crust

Continental crust

Subduction zone

Magma

Trench   Ocean crust   Lithosphere

RING OF FIRE

The Pacific Ring of Fire is the name scientists use to describe the area of the world located around the edges of the Pacific Ocean. This is actually the boundary of the large Pacific plate, which is slowly moving and subducting under or grinding past other plates it meets. In 1994, two volcanoes, Mt. Tavurvur and Mt. Vulcan, erupted in Rabaul, Papua New Guinea. These island arc volcanoes formed at an area where the Pacific plate is subducting under the South Bismarck ocean plate.

WHERE IN THE WORLD?

This map shows the general locations in the world where one plate is subducting under another.

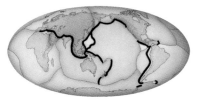

CONTINENT TO CONTINENT

When these plates move towards each other, the thin ocean part of one plate subducts but the continental part continues to push against the other plate and forms a mountain chain such as the Himalayan Mountains in central Asia.

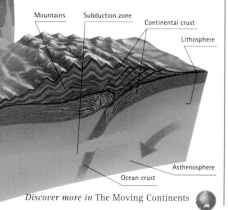

Mountains   Subduction zone   Continental crust   Lithosphere

Ocean crust   Asthenosphere

Discover more in The Moving Continents

457

North American plate

Pacific plate

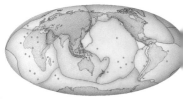

DIRECTION OF PLATES

The Pacific plate, moving northwest, has slowly carried the oldest of the Hawaiian Islands away from the hotspot and closer to the point where they will subduct under the North American plate.

• THE UNSTABLE EARTH •

Hotspots

Volcanoes are born in different ways and hotspot volcanoes, though spectacular, are often less violent than those that occur at subduction zones. Hotspot volcanoes form in the middle of plates, directly above a source of magma. Molten rock rises to the surface from deep within the Earth's mantle, pierces the plate like a blow torch and erupts in a lava flow or fountain. A hotspot stays still, but the plate keeps moving. Over millions of years this process forms a string of volcanic islands such as the Hawaiian Island chain on the Pacific plate. Hawaii's Mauna Loa and Kilauea, now active volcanoes, will gradually become dormant or cold as Hawaii moves off the hotspot. A new active volcano, such as Loihi to the southeast, might become a new island above the hotspot. The Pacific plate has carried other island volcanoes in the chain far away from the magma source.

INDIAN OCEAN VOLCANO
Piton de la Fournaise on Réunion Island is one of the most active volcanoes in the world.

KILAUEA FLOWS
The lava that erupts from hotspot volcanoes such as Kilauea in Hawaii can move at speeds of up to 62 miles (100 km) per hour.

HOTSPOT, CONTINENTAL STYLE

Yellowstone National Park, in Wyoming, has spectacular geysers and natural hot springs and is one of the most famous hotspots found on a continent. Underground water is heated by a hotspot source of magma deep within the mantle. The steam in the boiling water expands, and water and steam burst through the many cracks in the crust and erupt as geysers. Some scientists believe that one day, in the next few hundred thousand years, a major volcanic eruption could occur in the area.

...awaii
...lauea and Mauna Loa
...e both volcanoes on
...e island of Hawaii.

...ihi seamount

...SSEMBLY LINE ISLANDS
...he Hawaiian Islands on the
...acific plate formed one by
...e above a hotspot or
...agma plume.

Lithosphere

Magma plume

A SIBERIAN TALE
In Kamchatka, Siberia, there is an old story about how
a god named Tuli carries the Earth on a sled pulled
by flea-ridden dogs. Whenever the dogs stop
to scratch, the Earth shakes.

ACCORDING TO LEGEND
The ancient Greeks thought that
Hephaistos, the god of fire, lived
beneath Mt. Etna in Sicily
where he made weapons for
the gods. When he beat the
red-hot iron, fire leapt out of
the volcano above.

• THE UNSTABLE EARTH •

Myths and Legends

For thousands of years, different cultures have told
similar tales of powerful forces and superhuman
gods to explain volcanic eruptions or earthquakes.
Many myths blame these events on the anger of the gods
or evil demons that live in volcanoes and from time to time
punish their human subjects. The ancient Greeks thought that
a volcano destroyed the island of Atlantis because its people
became too wealthy and proud. The ancient Romans believed
that their god of fire, Vulcan, lived and stoked his blacksmith's
furnace in a workshop beneath the present-day island of Vulcano.
Hundreds of years ago, the Aztecs of Mexico and the people of
Nicaragua believed gods lived in the lava lakes. They sacrificed
beautiful young girls to these powerful gods.

STRANGE BUT TRUE

In 1660, little black crosses rained down on the people of Naples—proof to many that St. Januarius was looking after them. The crosses were really twinned pyroxene crystals, which the Mt. Vesuvius volcano had hurled out of its crater.

PELÉ

Pelé, the Hawaiian goddess of fire and volcanoes, supposedly lives in the crater of Kilauea volcano on Hawaii. She is thought to be responsible for the many volcanic eruptions on the island. In ancient times Pelé was greatly feared as she destroyed villages with her lava. Today she is still very much a part of Hawaiian folklore. Pelé has a terrible temper and she throws lava at anyone who speaks out against her. Pelé is also angered by anyone who steals her lava. Some people have been known to send back lava samples they have taken from the Hawaii Volcanoes National Park because of the bad luck they associate with an angry Pelé. There are also stories of lava flows avoiding the homes of people who declared loudly their trust in her. Many people claim to have seen Pelé before a volcanic eruption when she appears as a wrinkled old woman or a beautiful young girl. Others say they see her image in the glow of an eruption.

A BALANCING ACT

According to an ancient Hindu myth, the Earth is carried on the back of an elephant, which stands on a turtle that is balanced on a cobra. Whenever one moves, the Earth trembles and shakes.

461

TYPES OF VOLCANIC ERUPTION

HAWAIIAN
Large amounts of runny lava erupt and produce large, low volcanoes.

PELÉEAN
Blocks of thick, sticky lava are followed by a burning cloud of ash and gas.

STROMBOLIAN
Small, sticky lava bombs and blocks, ash, gas and glowing cinders erupt.

VULCANIAN
Violent explosions shoot out very thick lava and large lava bombs.

PLINIAN
Cinders, gas and ash erupt great distances into the air.

Volcanic Eruptions

Deep inside the Earth, magma rises upwards, gathers in pools within or below the crust and tries to get to the surface. Cracks provide escape routes, and the magma erupts as a volcano. Steam and gas form clouds of white smoke, small fragments of rock and lava blow out as volcanic ash and cinder, and small hot bombs of lava shoot out and harden. Not all lava is the same. It may be thick and sticky or thin and runny. Lava thickness, or viscosity, determines the type of volcanic eruption and the kind of rock that forms when the lava hardens. Some volcanoes are active, erupting at any time; some are dormant or cold, waiting to erupt; others are dead or extinct. Volcanoes have shaped many of the Earth's islands, mountains and plains. They have also been responsible for changing weather, burying cities and killing people who live nearby.

THE INSIDE STORY
This cross-section shows the inner workings of a volcano and what happens during an eruption.

Side vent
Under pressure, this side vent branches off from the central vent and carries lava upwards through cracks in the rocks to ooze out the side of the volcano.

WHY PEOPLE LIVE NEAR VOLCANOES

For centuries communities have grown up in the shadows of volcanoes. In Iceland, people use the energy from their island's many volcanoes to provide heat and power. Other people live near volcanoes because the soil is rich, and farmers grow crops and graze their herds on the slopes. In Indonesia more people live on the islands with active volcanoes than on the islands with none. Shown here are lush rice terraces growing on the fertile ground near the volcano Mt. Agung in Bali, Indonesia.

From the top
A white, smoke-like mixture of steam, ash and gas is blown into the air. Hard bits of lava called bombs shoot out from the top, while molten lava flows down the sides of the volcano.

Crater
This funnel-shaped opening at the top of the volcano enables lava, ash, gas and steam to erupt.

Cone
The cup-shaped cone is built up by ash and lava from a number of eruptions.

Central vent
The main vent, or chimney, rises from the magma chamber below. Magma flows up the vent to erupt on the surface as lava.

Sill
Magma does not always find an outlet to the surface. Some gathers, cools and becomes solid between two underground layers of rock.

Magma chamber
Thick, molten magma travels upward from the mantle and collects in large pockets in the crust where it mixes with gases and water. Under pressure from heat in the mantle the magma forces its way through vents to the surface.

Fissure eruption
Some magma forces its way upward through vertical cracks in the rock and erupts on the surface.

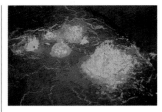

LAVA LAKES
Lava collects in a series of pools after the eruption of Pu'u O'o in Hawaii.

INTO THE SEA
Runny lava gushes from the side of a Hawaiian volcano into the sea below, where it cools.

Lava Flows

Lava is red-hot magma that erupts at the Earth's surface. A river of runny lava flows downhill from a volcano's central crater or oozes from a crack in the ground. It cools down from temperatures of up to 2,192°F (1,200°C), becomes stickier and slower-moving and often forms volcanic rock called basalt. Explosive, killer subduction volcanoes erupt thick, sticky lava that contains large amounts of silica. This cools to form rocks such as rhyolite, and different forms of volcanic glass such as obsidian. Blocked outlets or large amounts of gas or water in the lava cause violent eruptions, with lava bombs and boulders shooting out in all directions. If lava hardens with a rough, broken surface, it is called "aa". Lava that hardens with a smoother covering skin is called "pahoehoe". Pahoehoe can wrinkle to form ropes of rock. Hardened lava often cracks to form regular columns.

RIVER OF FIRE

In this Hawaiian-type eruption, the lava streams down from the volcano into an area where it burns houses and adds a new layer of volcanic rock to the ground.

Types of Lava Flow

Lava is named according to how it looks as it cools and hardens. Pillow lava is the most common form of lava found on Earth. It erupts in water especially along the mid-ocean ridge where volcanoes gently ooze pillow-shaped lumps of lava through cracks in the ocean floor. Pillow lava can also be found on dry land that was once part of the ocean floor. Pahoehoe lava is runny and very fast-flowing. The surface cools quickly and forms a thin, smooth skin with hot lava still moving underneath, which can twist and coil the surface to look like rope. Aa lava flows move more slowly and are not as hot as pahoehoe. Aa flows cool to form sharp chunks of rock, which can be as thick as 328 feet (100 m).

Pillow lava

Pahoehoe lava

Aa lava

ASH CLOUD
Ash shoots high in
the sky in explosive
subduction volcanoes.
In a pyroclastic flow,
the ash cloud drops
and speeds down
the side.

SPREADING ASH
Present-day Santorini in Greece
(indicated by the red dot) was the site
of an eruption in 1645 BC. Scientists
believe that a 18-mile (30-km) high
column of ash spread over a large part of
the east Mediterranean area (as shown).

• VOLCANOES •

Gas and Ash

As magma rises to the Earth's surface, the gases mixed in
with it expand or swell and try to escape. These gases
sometimes contain carbon dioxide and hydrogen sulphide,
which are both very harmful to humans. In runny magma, gases
have no trouble escaping and cause mild eruptions with a lava
flow. Gases trapped in thick, sticky lava build up and explode
violently. These explosive eruptions fling clouds of rock fragments
and hardened lava froth called pumice several miles into the air.
Ash is formed during the explosion when rock and lava blow
apart into millions of tiny pieces. Falling ash spreads further
and does more damage than lava flows do, although a small
sprinkling of ash can add important nutrients to the soil.
Sometimes the wind carries clouds of ash around the world,
affecting weather patterns.

COVERED IN ASH
Residents in protective masks walk down a street in
Olongapo City in the Philippines after the ash-fall
from the 1991 eruption of Mt. Pinatubo.

MAURICE AND KATIA KRAFFT

French volcanologist Maurice Krafft and his geochemist wife Katia were responsible for some of the world's most spectacular volcano photographs. They witnessed more than 150 volcanic eruptions throughout the world and wrote many books and films. Their field work often placed them in great danger, and they had to wear heat-resistant suits for close-up photography. Both died in 1991 while they were filming a pyroclastic flow from the eruption of Mt. Unzen in Japan.

PYROCLASTIC ROCKS

Small fragments of volcanic rock and frothy pumice fly into the air. Larger bombs or blocks, some the size of boulders, bounce down the side of the mountain.

ROCLASTIC FLOW

s rapidly moving avalanche
volcanic fragments and gases,
a temperature of 212° F (100° C),
rocket down the side of a volcano at
eds of up to 155 miles (250 km) per hour,
troying everything in its path.

• VOLCANOES •

In the Field

Scientists who study volcanoes are called volcanologists.
They observe the activity of a volcano so they can try
to predict when an eruption might occur. Volcanologists
often conduct field work near the craters or on the slopes of
active volcanoes, where they collect samples of lava and gas and
measure any temperature changes. They watch for an increase of
ash and fumes erupting from the crater. Minor earthquake activity
recorded on seismometers set up on a volcano's slopes can also
warn volcanologists of a possible eruption. At Kilauea volcano in
Hawaii there are observatories near the vent where scientists have
spent years recording details of its day-to-day life. A study of this
kind provides information about a particular type of volcano and
helps scientists to forecast future activity. Not all eruptions are
predictable, however, and some happen with no warning.

ROBOT VOLCANOLOGIST
This robotlike instrument called Dante
was designed to crawl inside the crater of
Mt. Erebus in Antarctica
to monitor gas and lava.

DID YOU KNOW?
Volcanologists use a special electric
thermometer called a thermocouple
to take a volcano's temperature.
Lava is so hot that a glass
thermometer would melt.

VOLCANO WORKSHOP

In 1988, after nearly 40 years of silence, Galeras volcano in Colombia showed signs of activity. An international workshop for scientists was set up there in 1993 to research and monitor the volcano. These scientists did their field work on the slopes and in the crater of Galeras. On 14 January one group was working in the crater taking measurements and samples of gases. As the group left the crater the volcano erupted, killing nine people and injuring five more. The explosion caused a 2-mile (3-km) high plume of ash and gas. The scientists had been careful but the volcano did the unexpected.

Subduction zone volcano
Galeras is 14,006-ft (4,270-m) high. The crater is 4 miles (6 km) from Pasto, a city with more than 300,000 people.

Collecting data
Scientists take gas samples from the edge of the inner crater where three men died when Galeras exploded 16 days earlier.

WORLDWIDE EFFECT
A powerful volcano can shoot
huge amounts of ash, gas and dust
upwards through the troposphere
and into the stratosphere where
strong winds carry it to all parts
of the globe.

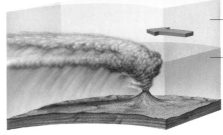

Stratosphere

Troposphere

• AFTER THE EVENT •

Under the Weather

Volcanic eruptions produce a variety of hazards and changes to the environment. After an eruption, the local area may experience months of strong winds, heavy rain and mudflows. Clouds of fine volcanic ash blown into the air affect people's breathing. The engines of aircraft flying in the area can become clogged with volcanic glass, dust and ash. Gas and ash ejected high enough into the stratosphere can travel all over the globe causing spectacular sunsets around the world. Weather patterns change in some areas, as clouds of sulphur-rich gases reflect the sun's rays back into space and the Earth below cools. This kills plants and crops and affects the animals that feed on this vegetation. In many parts of the world, volcanic twilights occur as sunlight is reduced and the temperature drops, producing long, cold winters.

FIREWORKS
Static electricity caused by colliding particles of ash and lava sparks bolts of lightning that crack in a fearsome display over an erupting volcano.

THE OZONE HOLE
This satellite picture shows the hole in the ozone layer. The hole gets bigger when damaging chemicals from volcanoes are erupted into the atmosphere.

NIGHT AT MIDDAY
The ash that fell from the 1982 eruption of Galunggung in Indonesia turned daylight skies to night.

THE YEAR WITHOUT A SUMMER

Dramatic changes in worldwide weather conditions followed the 1815 eruption of Tambora in Indonesia. Ash from the volcano shot into the stratosphere and was carried all around the world, which lowered temperatures in some countries. Summer frost and snow damaged food crops in parts of Europe and Scandinavia, causing widespread starvation. Unseasonable snowfalls also destroyed crops in the northeast section of the United States. The sky in this famous painting by British artist J.M.W. Turner shows the yellow haze caused by the volcanic dust that settled over Europe after the eruption.

DIRECTION OF FLOW
This map shows the path
of the Nevado del Ruiz
mudflow, indicated in red,
that streamed into the
Lagunella River valley
below and spread over
16 sq miles (40 sq km).

Nevado del Ruiz   Armero

MUDFLOW
In November 1985, the eruption of Nevado del Ruiz
in Colombia melted ice and snow, which caused a
devastating mudflow. Armero, 31 miles (50 km) away,
was engulfed in a 131-ft (40-m)
wall of mud and ash, which
killed more than
23,000 people.

• AFTER THE EVENT •

Mudflows and Avalanches

Mudflows and avalanches can be triggered by volcanic
eruptions and earthquakes. Explosive eruptions can leave
volcanoes covered with a layer of ash, which becomes
like thick, wet cement when mixed with water from melting ice or
thunderstorms. The resulting mudflows, called "lahars," start to move
downhill, gathering speed as they go. Stones, boulders, tree trunks and
building rubble are picked up along the way. These moving streams
of mud are often more powerful than rivers of water and can kill
thousands of people and cause enormous damage over a widespread
area before the mud sets as hard as concrete. In an avalanche, ash near
a volcano's crater can collapse and carry away part of a mountain.
Snow and rock may become airborne and travel at great speeds,
crashing from a mountain top to a valley below in minutes.

MIRACLE RESCUE
Survivors were found up to
three weeks after the eruption
of Nevado del Ruiz. Relief
workers from many parts
of the world arrived with
emergency supplies to help
the survivors. Here,
workers wash the mud
off a rescued child.

LUCKY SURVIVOR

Fewer than 3,000 people survived the mudflow from Nevado del Ruiz, which destroyed the town of Armero.

AVALANCHE!

An earthquake off the coast of Peru in 1960 triggered an avalanche from Huascaran mountain. Snow and rock fell 13,120 ft (4,000 m) and destroyed the town of Yungay six minutes later. More than 50,000 people were killed.

STEMMING THE FLOW

Japan has a large population and 10 per cent of the world's active volcanoes. It leads the way in mudflow control. Scientists use television monitors and other measuring instruments to detect volcanic activity. Check dams such as these are used around the very active Mt. Sakurajima. Steel and concrete slit dams, shown below, slow down and redirect flows of mud. Although the mudflows sometimes spill over the dams, people in danger have time to prepare or evacuate.

WHEN A CALDERA FORMS
During mild explosions, magma rises to the top of the volcano's main vent.

ERUPTING CALDERA
A cloud of ash and gas erupts from the caldera of Mt. Ngauruhoe in New Zealand.

THE NEXT STAGE
As the eruption increases in strength, the magma rapidly sinks back down to the top of the magma chamber.

THE CLIMAX
In Plinian or Peléean eruptions, the activity climaxes and magma sinks below the roof of the magma chamber, leaving an empty space where it once supported the roof.

· AFTER THE EVENT ·

Craters and Calderas

Craters are the funnel-shaped hollows or cavities that form at the openings or vents of volcanoes. The simplest craters occur on the top of cones and usually have a diameter of about $^6/_{10}$ mile (1 km) or less. Volcanoes can also form craters at the side. Small lava lakes occur when the lava is unable to escape, and it blocks the vent like a bath plug. Calderas are very large craters formed by an explosion or massive volcanic eruption. The magma chamber empties and can no longer support the weight of the volcano and the cone collapses. Calderas are often more than 3 miles (5 km) in diameter. The world's largest caldera is at Aso, Japan, and it is 14 miles (23 km) long and 10 miles (16 km) wide. When a volcano is dormant or extinct, a caldera can fill with water to form a large lake.

KILAUEA CRATER
Lava erupts from the crater of Kilauea volcano on Hawaii.

CRATER LAKES

These lakes form when the main vents of dormant or extinct volcanoes are plugged with hardened lava or other rubble. Over many years the crater gradually fills with water from rain or snow. Shown here is Crater Lake in Oregon. This lake is a caldera that formed when the summit of Mt. Mazama collapsed more than 6,600 years ago. The small cone within the caldera is called Wizard Island.

LIFE IN A CALDERA
Pinggan Village is one of the many villages within the caldera of the extinct volcano Gunung Batur, in Bali, Indonesia.

THE COLLAPSE
Once the magma support is removed, the top collapses into the magma chamber, and more eruptions can occur on the caldera floor.

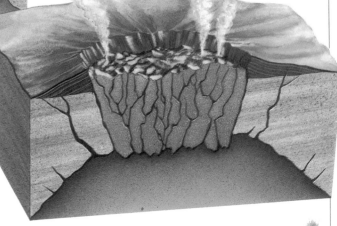

STRANGE BUT TRUE
On the Indonesian island of Flores, the volcano of Keli Mutu is well known for its different colored crater lakes. Tiwoe Noea Moeri Kooh Pai is green, Tiwoe Ata is light green and Tiwoe Ata Polo is an amazing red color.

Discover more in Volcanic Eruptions

VOLCANIC PLUG
This plug in Cameroon, West Africa, started as magma in the vent of a volcano. Over millions of years the magma cooled and hardened. The softer rocks eroded and left the plug exposed.

• AFTER THE EVENT •

Volcanic Rocks and Landforms

Deep within the Earth the heat is so intense that the red-hot rock or magma is molten. This magma rises toward the surface through cracks in the crust, then cools and hardens to form igneous rocks. When these rocks cool slowly underground within the cracks, they form intrusive igneous rocks such as granite. Intrusive rocks may appear on the surface when the surrounding softer rocks erode and expose amazing landscapes with landforms such as sills, dykes and plugs. Magma that erupts at the surface as lava and cools quickly becomes extrusive igneous rock. Runny lavas produce a rock called basalt, which in large quantities can flood an area and make basalt plateaus. Thicker, stickier lava can produce pumice, volcanic glass such as obsidian, and a light-colored rock called rhyolite.

ROCK WALL
Most volcanoes are fed by magma that forces its way up through vertical cracks in the rocks. The magma can harden underground to form a wall of rock called a dike. Erosion has exposed this dike in eastern Australia, which is called the "Breadknife."

HOT SPRINGS
Hot springs form when water seeps down through rocks and is heated by magma or hot rock from below. The water then rises up towards the surface. This Japanese macaque enjoys a warm soak in one of the hot springs in northern Japan—a volcanic area near the boundaries of the Pacific and Philippine plates.

476

DID YOU KNOW?

Diamonds originate in the mantle under extreme heat and pressure. Diamonds, such as this one embedded in volcanic rock called kimberlite, are pushed to the surface by rising magma.

USEFUL VOLCANOES

There are many uses for volcanic rocks. Small amounts of ash can add nutrients to soil. Basalt and granite are useful building materials. The mineral sulfur grows around the vents of some active volcanoes. Sulfur is mined for use in manufacturing. It is added to rubber to make it last longer, and is also an ingredient in many explosives. Here workers carry baskets full of large sulfur crystals collected from around the vent of Kawah Ijen volcano in Java, Indonesia. This sulfur will be processed and mixed with phosphate to make a type of fertilizer.

APPADOCCIA
is unusual volcanic
ndscape formed at
ppadoccia, Turkey, from lava
uptions of the now extinct
t. Erciyes. Wind and rain have eroded the
lcanic rock into pointed formations.

• EARTHQUAKES •

Surviving an Earthquake

W hen an earthquake strikes, beware of falling buildings and flying objects. To prevent building collapse and loss of life, engineers in many earthquake-prone cities follow strict rules when they repair earthquake damage or put up new structures. Many buildings are now designed to rest on reinforced concrete rafts that float when shock waves pass through. Existing buildings can be reinforced by cross-bracing walls, floors, roofs and foundations to help them withstand forces striking them from all directions. Walls and ceilings are strengthened with plywood in case of fire. Some areas have flexible gas lines that bend but do not break under pressure. Heavy furniture is bolted to walls to prevent it from flying around a room. Warning systems monitor stress in the Earth's crust, but earthquakes are still unpredictable and often much stronger than expected. In some areas, earthquake-proof buildings have collapsed.

BE PREPARED
Earthquake drills are part of the daily life of school children in Parkfield, California. Part of the San Andreas fault system lies beneath this small town.

SAFETY MEASURES
In this school, computers are bolted to tables, bookshelves and cabinets are attached to walls or fastened together. Windows are covered in transparent tape to stop them from breaking during a tremor.

WHEN THE EARTH SHAKES
An earthquake alarm is attached to the school's propane gas supply. The alarm switches off the gas automatically if a tremor above 3.5 on the Richter scale rocks the building.

TRANSAMERICA BUILDING
This rocket-shaped building in San Francisco, California, is designed to withstand an earthquake. The base is built on a concrete raft that gives extra support.

DROP!
When the teacher shouts "drop," each child crouches under the nearest desk. They link one arm around the leg of the desk to anchor it, and cover their head with both hands.

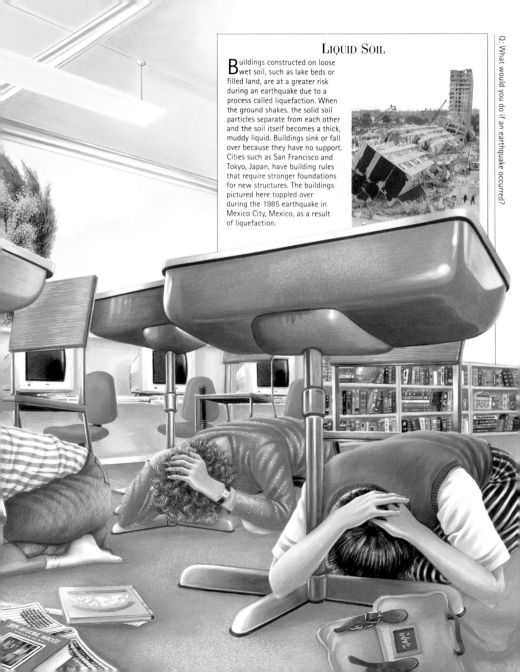

LIQUID SOIL

Buildings constructed on loose wet soil, such as lake beds or filled land, are at a greater risk during an earthquake due to a process called liquefaction. When the ground shakes, the solid soil particles separate from each other and the soil itself becomes a thick, muddy liquid. Buildings sink or fall over because they have no support. Cities such as San Francisco and Tokyo, Japan, have building rules that require stronger foundations for new structures. The buildings pictured here toppled over during the 1985 earthquake in Mexico City, Mexico, as a result of liquefaction.

Q: What would you do if an earthquake occurred?

TSUNAMI DAMAGE
Indonesian fishermen try to save what they can from their house, destroyed by one of the 12 tsunamis that struck East Java in June 1994.

• EARTHQUAKES •

Tsunamis and Floods

Tsunamis, huge killer waves, are caused by a jolt to the ocean floor from an earthquake, volcanic eruption or landslide. Unlike a surface wave, a tsunami is a whole column of water that reaches from the sea floor up to the surface. It can race across oceans for thousands of miles at speeds of up to 496 miles (800 km) per hour—as fast as a jet plane. Such a giant wave might stretch for hundreds of miles from crest to crest and yet remain unnoticed as it passes under ships. A sharp rise in the ocean floor near a coastline acts as a brake at the bottom of the wave and makes it stop and rush upwards in a towering wall of water that crashes onto land. The power of the wave batters and floods the coast, causing enormous damage and loss of life. Tsunamis occur most frequently in the Pacific area.

AS FAST AS A JET PLANE
The arcs of a tsunami, triggered by an earthquake in Alaska, spread quickly across the Pacific region. Seismic sea-wave detectors are in place throughout the Pacific area to measure the travel time of tsunamis and to warn populations in danger.

GIANT SEA WAVES

In 1992 a mild earthquake, barely noticed, hit San Juan del Sur in Nicaragua. Minutes later the peaceful harbor was drained dry as if someone had pulled a giant bath plug and let the water out. Amazed at the sight, people flocked to the harbor to look. As they stared, a giant tsunami rushed in and swept people and buildings far out to sea. This three-part illustration is an example of how the water is drained in a harbor, then builds up speed and height before rushing back to the shore.

w hours

hours

4 hours

5½ hours

8½ hours

11½ hours

14½ hours

17 hours

WAVE FORMATION
The speed of a tsunami depends on the depth of the ocean. The wave gets higher and higher as it moves towards the shallower water near land.

481

• FAMOUS VOLCANOES •

Mediterranean Eruptions

For more than two million years, earthquakes and volcanic eruptions have occurred in the area of the Mediterranean Sea along the boundary where the African plate meets the Eurasian plate. The Bay of Naples, in Italy, is the site of Mt. Vesuvius, which erupted violently in AD 79 and destroyed the towns of Herculaneum and Pompeii. Pliny the Younger wrote the very first account of an eruption after observing the event. Since then, Mt. Vesuvius has erupted numerous times. The last eruption was in 1944 but it is not known how long the volcano will remain dormant. Mt. Etna dominates eastern Sicily and is Europe's largest active volcano. It has been erupting periodically for more than 2,500 years and regularly destroys villages and farmland. People continue to settle on its fertile soil. The last major eruption of Mt. Etna occurred in 1992.

ON THEIR DOORSTEP
Mt. Vesuvius looms above
the modern city of Naples.
When will it erupt next?

DID YOU KNOW?

The 1944 eruption of Mt. Vesuvius occurred
during the Second World War. Glass-sharp
volcanic ash and rock fragments seriously
damaged aircraft engines.

RAINING ASH

People fled the town of Herculaneum during the AD 79 eruption of Mt. Vesuvius. Some ran towards the sea and escaped in boats, but many perished when a hot surge of ash and gas covered the town.

A GREEK TRAGEDY

The beautiful ancient Greek island of Thera (today called Santorini) in the Aegean Sea was destroyed by a violent volcanic eruption 3,500 years ago. The island was home to the Minoan people, a very wealthy and advanced civilization. The eruption caused huge tsunamis and ash-falls. These swept across neighboring islands such as Crete, site of the Minoan capital of Knossos, where this vase was found. What was left of Thera was covered in more than 197 ft (60 m) of ash and pumice.

Discover more in The Digs

Level of volcanic deposits at Herculaneum

Level of volcanic deposits at Pompeii

PLASTER CAST
In the 1860s, workers uncovering parts of Pompeii found holes in the volcanic rock left by the decayed bodies of the victims such as this dog. Scientists poured plaster into the holes to make models of the bodies.

• FAMOUS VOLCANOES •

The Digs

The sister cities of Pompeii and Herculaneum in Italy were destroyed when Mt. Vesuvius erupted on August 24, AD 79. Pompeii lay 5 miles (8 km) from the volcano and throughout the first afternoon and evening hot pumice, ash and rock rained down onto the crowds of fleeing people. Herculaneum, less than 3 miles (5 km) from the volcano, had only small amounts of ash-fall at first, but by midnight a pyroclastic flow of hot ash and gas followed by hot mud swept through the city, killing the residents. Early the next morning, Herculaneum was buried under 66 ft (20 m) of volcanic deposits. Another surge of ash and gas killed the remaining residents of Pompeii and buried the city under 10 ft (3 m) of volcanic deposits. Over the years archaeologists have discovered bodies, buildings and many small objects that reveal the last moments of the doomed citizens.

484

THE FIRST VOLCANOLOGIST

From 20 miles (32 km) away, Pliny the Younger observed the AD 79 eruption of Mt. Vesuvius. In AD 104 he described the event in two letters to his friend Tacitus, a writer and historian. This was the first recorded eyewitness report of a volcanic eruption. Pliny described such things as the Earth tremors that occurred before the eruption, the large amounts of ash and pumice, the low, hot ash flows, the many tidal waves and the total darkness of the sky. He also described a large column of ash shaped like a pine tree, which shot into the air. This type of volcanic eruption has since been named a "Plinian" eruption. Pictured here is a painting of a later eruption of Mt. Vesuvius showing some of the same details described by Pliny.

EVERYDAY ITEMS
Artifacts such as this glass drinking cup were found unbroken beneath the rubble.

RINGS ON HER FINGERS
Nearly 100 skeletons, including this one nicknamed "The Ring Lady," have been discovered in boatsheds and on the site of the ancient beach of Herculaneum. These people died while attempting to flee from the gas and ash of the eruption.

ROMAN COINS
These coins were found still safe inside a soldier's money belt.

HERCULANEUM TODAY
The ruins of the town lie 66 ft (20 m) beneath the modern city of Ercolano. Mt. Vesuvius can be seen in the background.

Discover more in Mediterranean Eruptions

Over England
The evening sky over London dazzled onlookers with beautiful colors. Waves raised the tides in the English Channel.

Weather changes
Volcanic dust circled the globe for several years and lowered the Earth's average temperature. Hawaiians noticed a white halo around the sun.

Trinidad
On the other side of the globe, in Trinidad, the sun appeared blue.

• FAMOUS VOLCANOES •

Krakatau

In May, 1883, ash, gas and pumice erupted from a volcano on the Indonesian island of Krakatau. The island is located in an unstable area where the Indo-Australian plate subducts under the Eurasian plate. The early rumblings from the volcano were just warm-ups before the violent explosion that blew the island apart on August 27. The boom from the explosion, one of the loudest ever recorded, was heard 2,170 miles (3,500 km) away. Clouds of dust and ash rose 50 miles (80 km) into the air, circled the globe, and created many colorful sunsets around the world. As the volcano collapsed in on itself, giant waves called tsunamis rose more than 131 ft (40 m) high. These walls of water surged into 163 villages along the coastlines of Java and Sumatra, destroying them and killing almost 36,000 villagers. Floating islands of pumice endangered ships sailing in the Indian Ocean.

NEARING THE END
This nineteenth-century engraving was based on an old photograph taken in 1883, just three month before Krakatau explode

CHILD OF KRAKATAU

When Krakatau erupted it collapsed in on itself and formed a 4-mile (6.5-km) undersea caldera. In 1927, observers noticed smoke rising from the caldera and within a year an infant island, called Anak, or Child of Krakatau, appeared. It continues to grow and is fed regularly by gas and ash during its many mild eruptions. This picture shows Anak Krakatau as it appears today.

In Calcutta
Giant waves destroyed riverboats in this Indian city.

AWAKENING GIANT

The volcanic island of Krakatau, in the Sunda Strait between the Indonesian islands of Sumatra and Java, erupted violently after more than 200 years of silence.

In Sri Lanka
Observers here reported that the sun looked green in the first few weeks after the eruption.

Krakatau

In Alice Springs
To people living in central Australia, the blasts sounded like rifle shots.

The loudest noise
The noise of the eruption was heard as far away as Madagascar.

A year later
Floating pumice from the eruption blocked some Indian Ocean shipping lanes up to a year later.

In Perth
The eruption caused a tsunami that destroyed this harbor in Australia.

Discover more in Under the Weather

Iceland

I celand is an island country that sits astride the northern Atlantic section of the mid-ocean ridge. The island provides scientists with an ideal place to study the ocean ridge above water. One part of Iceland is on the North American plate, which is moving westward, and the other part is on the Eurasian plate, which is moving eastward. As the island is slowly pulled in two, a rift, or large crack, is forming. Ravines and cliffs mark the edges of the two plates. Magma rising to the surface has created a series of central volcanoes separated by groups of fissures. As the area becomes more unstable, there is more earthquake and volcanic activity. Icelanders use the geothermal energy from their volcanoes for central heating, hot water and other electrical power.

DRAMATIC DISPLAY
Eldfell volcano gives a dramatic light show behind this church in the seaport town of Vestmannaeyjar.

AN ISLAND ERUPTION
In January, 1973, the seaport town of Vestmannaeyjar on Heimaey Island became the site of a new volcano called Eldfell. Most residents were evacuated, but for six months volunteers stayed behind to save what they could of the town.

Lava flow
Residents armed with fire hoses sprayed water on the advancing lava that threatened to take over the harbor. They saved the harbor but not before the lava flow added another 1 sq mile (2.6 sq km) of new land to the island.

DID YOU KNOW?

Iceland is the source of one-fifth of the Earth's recorded lava output. Scientists believe this is partly due to Iceland's position over an active spreading ridge and, possibly, a hotspot.

LANDSCAPE OF FIRE

In 1783, the 3-mile (5-km) long Lakagígar fissure in southern Iceland began erupting huge fountains of lava and large amounts of gas and ash. The lava flow, one of the largest ever recorded on Earth, eventually covered more than 220 sq miles (565 sq km) of land. A deadly blue haze settled over the country and spread to parts of Europe and Asia. Nobody was killed by the lava itself, but Iceland's crops were destroyed and much of the livestock starved to death. More than 10,000 people died in the famine that followed. Since then, fissures such as the one at Krafla in northeastern Iceland have continued to erupt.

The craters of Lakagígar fissure

Krafla fissure

BACKYARD VOLCANO
The crater of Eldfell glowed red as thick lava flowed down the side of the volcano and fiery ash rained down on the abandoned houses.

BURIED IN ASH
Much of the town lay beneath a thick layer of ash. Here, volunteers clear ash from rooftops to prevent the houses from collapsing.

Mt. St. Helens

The volcano Mt. St. Helens is one of 15 in the Cascade Range of the northwest United States—an area where the Juan de Fuca plate is subducting beneath the North American plate. On March 20, 1980, a string of earthquakes northwest of the mountain peak signalled the slow awakening of the volcano, which had been dormant since 1857. A week later, a small eruption shot ash and steam into the air. Groups of scientists arrived with instruments to monitor the volcano. By early May, a bulge developed on the cone. This indicated magma rising in the volcano's vent. The bulge grew bigger each day until a violent explosion, probably triggered by another earthquake, blew out the northern side of the mountain on May 18. This caused an enormous landslide that devastated an area of 234 sq miles (600 sq km) and triggered mudflows and floods.

BEFORE
In early 1980, the beautiful snow-capped peak of Mt. St. Helens was surrounded by forests and lakes.

AND AFTER
The north side of the nearly perfect cone blew apart in minutes, causing one of the largest volcanic landslides ever recorded.

PLINIAN PLUME
Minutes after the first explosion a second eruption
produced a large Plinian column of ash and gas that
rose to a height of 12 miles (20 km). This phase
of the volcanic eruption continued
for nine hours.

LIKE MATCHSTICKS
More than six million trees were uprooted or flattened
by rock blasted from the volcano. After a massive
salvage operation to clear the logs, seedlings were
planted to replace the forests.

MUDFLOWS
Thick, sticky mud caused by melting snow
and ice sped down the North Toutle River
Valley into communities below.

SWEEPING ASH

Millions of tons of ash shot 15 miles
(25 km) into the atmosphere and the
falling ash spread more than 930 miles
(1,500 km) to the east. Ash fell like black
snow in parts of Montana, Idaho, Oregon
and Washington and covered streets, cars
and buildings. Cats and dogs downwind
from the eruption turned pale grey from
the ash that floated from the sky. But ash
does not melt like snow, and it had to be
cleared. Most ended up in landfills.

CITY IN RUINS
The earthquake struck at midday when many households were
preparing their meals on hibachis—a type of open stove. As the
buildings collapsed they caught fire and flames swept
quickly through the city, killing thousands of people.
All but one section of Tokyo was damaged by
fire, and the business district was
virtually destroyed.

• FAMOUS EARTHQUAKES •

The Great Kanto Earthquake

WORLDWIDE RESPONSE
News of the devastating earthquake flashed
around the world, and many countries
rushed to Japan's aid with relief supplies.

T he Great Kanto Earthquake shook Japan on September 1,
1923. The earthquake originated beneath Sagami Bay,
Yokohama, 50 miles (80 km) south of the capital, Tokyo.
The power of the earthquake registered a massive 8.3 on the
Richter scale, and the ground shook for nearly five minutes.
A staggering 100,000 people died, and more than 300,000
buildings were destroyed. The earthquake was soon followed by
a killer tsunami, which swept people and their homes far out to
sea. More deaths were caused by the many fires that broke out
among the paper and wood houses. These building materials had
been specially chosen to make the homes safer in an earthquake,
but instead they provided fuel for the raging flames. A second
major tremor blasted the area 24 hours later, and minor
aftershocks followed in the next few days.

JAPANESE QUAKES

Japan is situated where the Philippine plate and the Pacific plate are subducting under the Eurasian plate. This makes Japan the site of frequent volcanic eruptions, earthquakes and tsunamis. People in Japan feel Earth tremors every few weeks. Cities such as Tokyo have disaster teams ready to jump into action. Many people have prepared emergency supply kits with food, water and medicine, and most take part in earthquake drills. In October, 1994, a major earthquake estimated at 7.9 on the Richter scale occurred in the ocean crust off Hokkaido, the northernmost island in Japan, causing many buildings to collapse (above). Three months later an earthquake estimated at 6.9 on the Richter scale shattered the city of Kobe. More than 5,000 people died.

REDUCED TO RUBBLE

So great was the force of the earthquake that the floor of Sagami Bay split. At the seaport of Yokohama, south of Tokyo, most buildings were destroyed as well as the harbor and port facilities.

Mexico City

An earthquake measuring 8.1 on the Richter scale struck Mexico City on September 19, 1985. As the Cocos plate subducted under the North American plate, it fractured, or cracked, 12 miles (20 km) down in the mantle. The vibrations to the ocean floor unleashed a tsunami and produced a surge of energy 1,000 times greater than an atomic bomb. The seismic shock waves travelled 217 miles (350 km) east to Mexico City. This city is built on top of a dry, sandy lake bed of soft sediment, or subsoil, which amplified the shock waves so much that many buildings collapsed. Some of the city's largest skyscrapers remained standing, but L-shaped buildings and those with large open foyers were badly damaged. The earthquake killed more than 9,000 residents, while 30,000 were injured and 95,000 were left homeless.

SHIFTING PLATES
Mexico City lies in an area
where several plates meet.

ON SHAKY GROUND
Mexico City is built on the same dry
lake bed as the old Aztec capital
of Tenochtitlan. The area is
surrounded by volcanoes and
prone to earthquakes.

SIGNS OF LIFE
Teams of rescue workers searched carefully through the rubble of destroyed buildings looking for survivors. They listened for sounds of life in the wreckage. Rescuers worked nonstop for days after the earthquake and saved more than 4,000 lives.

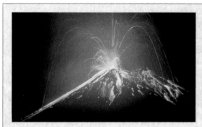

A CLASH OF FOUR PLATES
The Nazca, Cocos, South American and Caribbean plates meet and interact along the eastern section of the Pacific Ring of Fire. Plate movement triggers a large number of earthquakes and volcanoes in some areas of North America, Central America and South America. Pictured here is Arenal volcano in Costa Rica.

STRANGE BUT TRUE
A four-day-old baby boy survived for nine days buried under the rubble of a hospital. Here, the miracle baby is lifted to safety by rescue workers.

Californian Quakes

Many of the world's earthquakes occur along an edge where two lithospheric plates meet. The state of California straddles two such plates. Most of the state sits on the North American plate, which is moving very slowly. The Pacific plate, with the rest of the state, is grinding past the North American plate more quickly, and moving northwest. The grating movement of the two plates has made a weblike series of faults and cracks in the crust where earthquakes can occur. The San Andreas Fault is the most famous fault in California and slashes through the state for 682 miles (1,100 km). From time to time, the rock breaks and moves along a section of the fault, and this can trigger an earthquake. Scientists record more than 20,000 Earth tremors in California every year, although most are slight and detected only by sensitive instruments.

Sacramento

San Francisco 1906 — Oakland

Morgan Hill 1984

Loma Prieta 1989

Coalinga 1983

Par

STRANDED
Many commuters were trapped when sections of the California freeway system collapsed during the Loma Prieta earthquake in 1989.

DID YOU KNOW?
Los Angeles sits on the Pacific plate. San Francisco sits on the North American plate. Perhaps in a million years or so they will meet.

THE STREETS OF SAN FRANCISCO
A major earthquake could strike California at any time. Movement along the San Andreas fault system could cause massive destruction in cities such as San Francisco and Los Angeles. Oil refineries, chemical and atomic plants, office towers, schools, hospitals, freeways, sports arenas, amusement parks and residential areas would all be affected.

SLIPPING PLATES
This map of California shows the San Andreas and other major faults, as indicated by red lines. Labels show the sites of earthquakes that have occurred over the past 100 years.

SAN FRANCISCO 1906

On April 18, 1906, an earthquake measuring 8.3 on the Richter scale struck San Francisco. Huge buildings crumbled, and massive fires burned out of control for three days as the main water lines were destroyed. People crowded into the streets searching for relatives and shelter. The Red Cross set up emergency food lines to help feed more than 300,000 homeless. The final toll was staggering. The city center lay in ruins. More than 28,000 buildings were destroyed and nearly 1,000 people perished.

Santa Barbara 1925

San Fernando 1971

Northridge 1994

Los Angeles

Palm Springs 1986

ng Beach 1933

San Diego

NARROW ESCAPE
A home and car destroyed during the Northridge earthquake in 1994.

EARTHQUAKE TRAUMA
A survivor tearfully surveys a building damaged during the Loma Prieta earthquake of 1989.

More about Volcanic Eruptions

AD 186 Taupo, New Zealand
One of the largest volcanic eruptions in history occurred in Taupo in the North Island of New Zealand. Although quiet for more than 1,800 years, the volcano is still considered to be active.

AD 79 Mt. Vesuvius, Italy
The cities of Pompeii and Herculaneum were destroyed in AD 79 when Mt. Vesuvius erupted. Until then, people did not know that the mountain was a volcano—it had been silent for more than 300 years.

1783 Lakagigar, Iceland
Lakagigar fissure erupted one of the largest amounts of lava in history. The fissure also erupted huge amounts of ash and poisonous gases. A blue haze settled over parts of Europe. Benjamin Franklin, living in France at the time, correctly blamed the unusually cold summer on the eruption in Iceland.

1815 Tambora, Indonesia
The eruption of Tambora is considered to be the most destructive volcanic explosion ever. More than 10,000 people died during the eruption and a further 82,000 people died of disease and starvation after the event.

1991 Mt. Pinatubo, Philippines

Le Petit Parisien
SUPPLÉMENT LITTÉRAIRE ILLUSTRÉ

1902 Mt. Pelée, Martinique

1902 Mt. Pelée, Martinique
After signs of increased volcanic activity, Mt. Pelée exploded violently, destroying the beautiful city of St. Pierre. A glowing cloud of gas and ash raced down the mountain towards the city below. More than 28,000 people perished in less than a minute. The only survivor was a prisoner held in a tiny dungeon.

1980 Mt. St. Helens, United States
For people living close by, the sound from the massive explosion of Mt. St. Helens was muffled by vegetation and a huge cloud of ash and dust. People living hundreds of mi away, however, heard the explosion because the sound bounced off layers i the Earth's outer atmosphere.

1982 El Chichon, Mexico
More than 3,500 people were killed in this eruption. So much ash shot into th sky that it remained dark for 44 hours.

1991 Unzen, Japan
The 1991 eruption was predicted by scientists, and most people were evacuated in time. Many of the 38 people who perished in this explosion were geologists studying the eruption and journalists reporting it.

1991 Mt. Pinatubo, Philippines
After more than 600 years, Mt. Pinatub erupted. Large amounts of ash explode into the atmosphere and fell over a wid area. People sifting through the ash found what they believed to be diamon The rocks were actually quartz crystals formed by the hardening of magma inside the volcano.

1994 Rabaul, Papua New Guinea

1994 Rabaul, Papua New Guinea
The 1994 eruption was the sixth to occu in the past 200 years. Due to a successf evacuation there were very few deaths. The city was covered in a 3-ft (1-m) layer of ash, and large slabs of pumice filled the harbor.

More about Earthquakes

755 Lisbon, Portugal

755 Lisbon, Portugal
This wealthy merchant city was destroyed by an earthquake estimated by later seismologists to be 8.7 on the Richter scale. Buildings collapsed, tsunamis pounded the waterfront and fires burned for six days. The damage on the North African coast was so heavy that many people thought there were two earthquakes. The Lisbon earthquake was the first to be studied by scientists.

897 Assam, India
The Assam earthquake, with a magnitude of 8.7, is one of the largest ever recorded. For the first time instruments confirmed the three types of earthquake waves.

960 Santiago, Chile
A series of earthquakes killed more than 5,000 people. The surface waves produced were so powerful that they were still being recorded on seismographs 0 hours after the actual earthquake.

964 Alaska, United States
The earthquake measuring between .3 and 8.6 originated 80 miles (129 km) east of the city of Anchorage. The ground shook for nearly seven minutes. Massive damage occurred in the heavily populated south-central area, and surface waves reshaped the coastline. Large cracks opened up in the ground, and landsliding was common. Tsunamis

raced across the Pacific Ocean as far south as Antarctica.

1976 Tangshan, China
The earthquake occurred in a heavily populated area of China 37 miles (60 km) southeast of Beijing. With a magnitude of between 7.8 and 8.2, the earthquake was the most devastating to hit China in four centuries. The earthquake lasted 23 seconds but was followed by more than 125 aftershocks within 48 hours of the first tremors. The death toll was staggering. About 242,000 people were killed and more than 150,000 injured.

1988 Spitak, Armenia
With a magnitude of 6.9, the Armenian earthquake completely destroyed the town of Spitak, and nearly every building in the cities of Kirovakan and Leninakan collapsed. Thousands were trapped in the rubble. More than 25,000 people died, but miraculously, 15,000 survivors were rescued.

1989 Loma Prieta, United States
A segment of the San Andreas Fault moved and triggered a magnitude 7.1 earthquake in California. Much of the damage in the San Francisco area occurred to buildings constructed on the soft sediment of landfilled areas. Ironically, some of the landfill material used in the area was rubble cleared from the 1906 San Francisco earthquake.

1995 Kobe, Japan
More than 5,000 people died and 200,000 were left homeless in one of Japan's worst earthquakes. In 30 seconds, a devastating earthquake destroyed the city of Kobe and the surrounding villages. Broken gas mains caused fires, which swept through the streets and the tile-roofed wooden houses. Firefighters were unable to stop the flames from spreading—water mains were broken and useless. Most people were still asleep in their beds, but many early morning commuters were trapped or killed when expressways collapsed.

1988 Spitak, Armenia

Weather

Why does a tropical beach feel hotter than the Sahara Desert?

What is the coldest place on Earth?

How much water can a cloud carry?

Contents

What is Weather?

The weather affects all things on Earth. It helps to shape our landscapes and provide our food supplies. The weather influences the way we live, where we live, what we wear, the running of transportation systems and even how we feel. Extreme weather can bring storms that destroy homes, or droughts that can ruin crops. But what exactly is weather? It is the conditions that exist in the air around us at any one time: the temperature and pressure of the atmosphere, the amount of moisture it holds, and the presence or absence of wind and clouds. The weather is very hard to predict, and it can be incredibly diverse locally. One side of a mountain, for example, may be buffeted by high winds, while the other side may have no wind at all.

BURNING UP
Intense summer heat may help to ignite trees and cause dramatic fires. If these fires are fanned by high winds, they can move quickly through brushland.

BLOWN AWAY
Some of the strongest winds are associated with hurricanes. These huge tropical storms bring heavy rain and high winds.

SNOW FALLS
In cold weather, heavy falls of snow can make it difficult to move around.

FOOD PRODUCTION

Rain is very important to the production of food. When there is plenty of rain, crops grow and give good yields, and animals have plenty of water. But if it does not rain, even for just a few weeks, the effects can be disastrous. The soil can become parched and crops may wither and die. If this happens, grazing animals do not have enough food to eat and water supplies start to stagnate.

UNDER THE SUN
Vast areas become parched and dry when it does not rain for months on end.

RAINBOW
A mixture of sunlight and rain often creates this colorful sight in the sky.

FLOOD
Storm clouds bring heavy rain. Rivers can burst their banks and flood low-lying land, washing away buildings and crops.

Discover more in Global Warming

The Weather Engine

The sun fuels the world's weather. The surface of the Earth is warmed by sunlight. The tropics are heated most intensely, while the two poles receive the least heat. Only half the energy coming from the sun to the Earth is absorbed by the Earth's surface. The other half is reflected back into space or absorbed into the atmosphere. Different surfaces reflect varying amounts of heat. Bright white snow can reflect 90 percent of the sun's energy, so very little heat remains. The dark green tropical rainforests, however, absorb a large amount of energy. Temperatures on land change more than those in the oceans. These differences generate pressure patterns that cause winds to blow. They also set in motion the vast circulation of the atmosphere, which produces the world's weather and climate.

HEAT FROM THE SUN
Because the Earth is a sphere, air is warmed more at the equator than at the poles. Rays of sunlight contain certain amounts of energy. Depending on the season, rays will fall on small circular areas near the equator. At the poles, however, the rays are spread over a wider area because they hit the Earth at an angle. If the heat at the equator was not distributed by wind and water, the equator would get hotter and hotter.

DID YOU KNOW?
The amount of solar energy that reaches the Earth's atmosphere every 24 hours is similar to the amount of energy that would be released by 200 million electric power stations during the same period of time.

Thermosphere above 50 miles (80 km)	# THE ATMOSPHERE
	The atmosphere is an envelope of air that surrounds the Earth. It extends to a height of 434 miles (700 km), but there is no clear boundary as to where it ends and space begins. The atmosphere has four layers. The lowest layer is the troposphere where the air contains lots of water vapor and dust. Most of the world's weather occurs in this layer. The stratosphere has dry, warm air and this is where the ozone layer is found. The mesosphere is a colder layer and temperatures can fall to -184°F (-120°C). The thermosphere is the outer layer and the gases here are very thin. As the gases absorb ultraviolet light, the temperatures climb to as high as 3632°F (2000°C). Auroras and meteors are seen in this layer.
Mesosphere 30–50 miles (50–80 km)	
Stratosphere 6–30 miles (10–50 km)	
Troposphere 0–6 miles (0–10 km)	

MOVING WATER
The world's oceans greatly affect weather and climate. Water evaporates, which causes clouds and rain, and currents move heat from the equator to the poles.

UPS AND DOWNS
The shape of the Earth influences the weather. Mountains can deflect the wind and rain. The Himalayan mountain system has a major effect on the summer monsoon in Asia.

KEEPING CONTROL
The polar ice caps act as thermostats for the world's weather and climate. The ice and snow reflect much of the sun's energy, and any change in the area of the ice caps can affect global temperatures.

Discover more in Winds and Currents

Temperature and Humidity

I f you were standing in the Sahara Desert, the air would feel hot and dry. If you were lying on a tropical beach, it would feel hotter, even though the temperatur may be the same in both places. The reason for this difference is humidity—the amount of moisture or water vapor in the air. Humans can only tolerate a certain range of temperature and humidity. Sweating helps to keep the body cool. But if the air is very humid, water does not evaporate so easily and sweat remains on the skin. This ca be uncomfortable and makes you feel hotter. Humidity is measured with an instrument called a hygrometer. A simpl hygrometer uses two thermometers: one has a bulb that is surrounded by a wet cloth, while the other is dry. If the air is very dry, the "wet bulb" is cooled rapidly by evaporatior But if the air is very humid, little evaporation occurs and the reading of the two thermometers is almost the same.

Hot and sticky
This hygrometer shows a 90 percent humidity reading.

GROWING CONDITIONS
A desert and a rainforest often have similar air temperatures, but lush vegetation can only grow in the rainforest because the air is very moist, or humid. The heat of the desert, however, is very dry. This lack of moisture means that few plants can survive.

KEEPING COOL
In hot weather, or when we exercise, our body temperature may rise above 98.6°F (37°C). Special glands on the surface of the skin release sweat. The evaporation of this watery fluid cools our bodies.

Anders Celsius

In 1714, the German scientist Gabriel Fahrenheit invented the temperature scale. The zero point was based on the lowest point to which the mercury fell during the winter in Germany. The freezing point of water was 32°F, while the boiling point was 212°F. In 1742, the Swedish astronomer Anders Celsius proposed an alternative scale. He suggested making the freezing point of water 0°C and the boiling point of water 100°C. This scale was very useful for scientific work, and it is used more widely than Fahrenheit's scale.

Hot and dry
This hygrometer shows a humidity reading of 20 percent.

A FROZEN DESERT
Antarctica is the coldest place on Earth. Its freezing air tends to be extremely dry because very cold air holds only a small amount of water vapor.

CLOUD FORMATION
Clouds can form in many ways but they all involve warm moist air coming into contact with cooler air.

Current collision
When currents of air collide, they force each other upward.

• THE DAILY WEATHER •

What are Clouds?

Clouds are masses of water droplets and ice crystals that float in the sky. They are formed by a process that begins when warm moist air rises. As the warm air cools, it is unable to hold water vapor. Some of the water vapor condenses around dust particles and forms minute water droplets. These tiny drops make up clouds. The sky can be covered with a blanket of cloud that is formed when a mass of warm air rises above cooler air and causes the water vapor to condense. Clouds also form when warm air is forced to rise over mountains, or when warm air blows over a colder surface such as cool water. On hot days, storm clouds appear when warm moist air rises and then cools rapidly. Clouds appear to be white because the water droplets reflect light. As a cloud becomes thicker and heavier with droplets, it darkens because light cannot pass through it.

AN AERIAL VIEW
Seen from above, the tops of clouds often look like a white blanket or a field of snow.

510

Water droplets
Millions of microscopic droplets of water are needed to make one drop of rain.

THE WATER CYCLE

Water covers more than 70 percent of the Earth's surface. Warmth from the sun causes some of the water to evaporate from the surface of oceans, lakes and rivers, as well as from plants. This water vapor rises and cools, and then condenses back into water to form clouds. The water droplets fall as rain or snow, which runs into rivers and lakes and can sometimes soak into underground layers of rock. Eventually, the water returns to the oceans to complete the cycle.

Convection
On a sunny day, some patches of ground warm up more quickly than others. Bubbles of warm air form over these spots and rise into the sky. As the bubbles rise, they expand and cool. The water condenses and forms a cumulus cloud that is shaped like a dome.

In the clouds
When warm air meets a mountain range, it is forced upward. The warm air cools and banks of clouds form around the mountain peaks.

CLOUD BANK
Banks of clouds are often seen lying over mountain ranges.

Cirrus

32,800 ft (10,000 m)

Cirrocumulus

Cirrostratus

19,700 ft (6,000 m)

HIGH IN THE SKY
The three main cloud groups are based on height. High clouds are more than 19,700 ft (6,000 m); middle clouds are 6,600–19,700 ft (2,000–6,000 m); and low clouds are under 6,600 ft (2,000 m). Cumulonimbus clouds tower higher than 32,800 ft (10,000 m).

Altocumulus

Altostratus

Cumulonimbus

6,600 ft (2,000 m)

Stratocumulus

Stratus

Cumulus

Nimbostratus

Types of Cloud

No two clouds are exactly the same. Although they vary in shape and size, they can be divided broadly into two similar types: heaped, fluffy clouds; and layered clouds. Heaped clouds are formed when pockets of warm air dri upward, while layered clouds are created by moist air moving horizontally between cooler layers. Clouds are usually grouped according to how high they are above the ground. It is important identify different types of cloud because they give us information about the weather. White, puffy cumulus clouds, for example, a associated with warm sunny days. High cirrus clouds mark the approach of a weather front (an advancing mass of warm or cold air). Cirrus clouds may be followed by lower altostratus clouds and low stratus rain clouds, which cover the entire sky in a solid gray sheet.

BUBBLING SKIES
These pendulous clouds, called mammatus clouds, form below the anvil of a thundercloud. They are frequently seen with storms that produce tornadoes.

FLYING SAUCERS
These lenticular, or lens-shaped, clouds have been mistaken for flying saucers. They usually form in bands on the sheltered side of mountain ranges.

MIXED SKIES

... least five cloud types
... visible in this busy sky. In
... background, a huge pale
... mulonimbus thundercloud
... the sky. Along the lower
... ge, dark rain-bearing stratus
... uds underlie paler, fluffier
... mulus clouds. The strong,
... k streaks at the middle
... el are altostratus,
... h altocumulus
... ove and below.

VAPOR TRAILS

Some aircraft leave white vapor trails as they
fly across a clear blue sky. These "artificial
clouds" are caused when the hot exhaust gases
from the jet engines mix with the surrounding
cold air and cool rapidly. Water vapor within the
exhaust freezes and forms a trail of ice crystals.

LIGHTNING STRIK[
Lightning usually strikes the highe[
point, such as a tall building or [
isolated tree, so it is dangerous to shel[
beneath a tree during a thunderstor[
You would be much safer in a c[

• THE DAILY WEATHER •

Thunder and Lightning

O n a hot, humid summer day, strong rising convection currents of warm air form cumulus clouds that soon grow into a towering cumulonimbus cloud, or thundercloud. These black clouds are accompanied by strong winds, heavy rain, lightning and thunder, and often produce spectacular summer storms. Most lightning occurs in cumulonimbus clouds because they contain violent currents of air and a plentiful supply of super-cooled droplets of water. The intense heating of the air by lightning causes the air to expand at supersonic speed and produces a clap of thunder. Lightning and thunder occur at the same time, but as light travels faster than sound, we see the flash before we hear the thunder. We can tell how far away a storm is by timing the interval between the flash and the thunder. A three-second interval represents a distance of $^6/_{10}$ mile (1 km).

RIBBON LIGHTNING
Strong winds may cause lightning to move and give a ribbonlike effect.

CLOUD TO GROUND
Lightning can form when there is a build up of negative charges at the bottom of a cloud and the ground below is positively charged.

CLOUD TO CLOUD
Lightning may occur between a negatively charged cloud and a nearby cloud that is positively charged.

INSIDE A CLOU[
Most lightning forms within a cloud, when there[a discharge betwe[a positive and negative charge.

BALLS OF FIRE
Sometimes, lightning appears as a fiery ball. Some balls disappear quietly, while others explode. Some have even appeared to chase people! Fortunately, ball lightning is very unusual and seldom causes harm.

Rain, Hail and Snow

The water or ice that falls from a cloud is called precipitation. This may be in the form of rain, drizzle, sleet, snow or hail. The conditions within a cloud, and the temperature outside it, determine the type of precipitation that falls. One important factor is whether the cloud is high enough above the ground for the water droplets in it to turn into ice. The height at which this occurs is called the freezing level. It can be as little as 1,000 ft (300 m) or as high as 16,000 ft (5,000 m) above the ground. Snow falls from low and very cold clouds when the air temperature is around freezing, so the ice crystals can reach the ground without melting. If snow falls into air that is just above freezing, some of the crystals melt and produce a mixture of rain and snow called sleet. Dark cumulonimbus clouds bring thunderstorms, which may be accompanied by hail. A blanket of thin nimbostratus clouds produces a steady stream of rain, while low stratus clouds bring drizzle.

Rain
Rain forms when tiny water droplets collect around small ice crystals until they become heavy enough to fall.

Upper layer
The temperature here can be as low as –32°F (–40°C) and the clouds, which are spread out, are formed mainly of ice crystals.

Middle layer
Strong air currents carry ice crystals and water droplets high into the atmosphere.

Lower layer
This lower layer is close to freezing. Water vapor comes up from the ground and condenses to form a cloud.

RAINY DAYS
A low blanket of gray clouds often brings a steady downpour that can last for an hour or more. However, drizzle and light rain can last for much longer.

Hail
Hail forms around small ice crystals. As strong air currents circulate repeatedly and cause layers of ice to build up around the crystals, hailstones become larger.

Snow
Snow forms if the freezing level is below a height of 1,000 ft (300 m) above the ground, and the ice crystals do not have time to melt before they reach the ground.

STRANGE BUT TRUE
In 1953, hailstones as large as golf balls fell in Alberta, Canada. They covered an area 140 miles (225 km) by 5 miles (8 km) and killed thousands of birds.

HAIL STORM
Hail can cause great damage everywhere. This crop was ruined completely by these large hailstones.

THE SHAPE OF A SNOWFLAKE

Snowflakes are loose clusters of ice crystals usually with a flat, six-sided (hexagonal) shape. The exact shape of a snowflake depends on the temperature of the air, and no two snowflakes are the same. At very low temperatures, small needlelike crystals form, while at temperatures nearer to freezing, larger branching shapes are more common. The amount of water vapor in the air is important: at lower temperatures there is less water vapor and the crystals that form tend to be smaller.

Discover more in What are Clouds?

Fog, Frost and Ice

Clear nights with low ground temperatures often bring fog and frost, especially around dawn. The clear skies allow heat to radiate into space, and the temperature drops toward freezing. Moisture in the air condenses near the ground to form low-lying fog or mist. In the morning, the sun heats the air and the fog disperses. If the temperature is low enough, moisture in the air freezes and coats the ground, plants and other surfaces with a thin layer of frozen dew or frost. In long periods of cold, the surfaces of ponds and lakes freeze over, while dripping water freezes into icicles. Smog is a visible form of air pollution that often occurs in cities. It can be caused by the smoke from cars and huge industrial chimneys. Smog can affect everyone, but especially the health of the young, the old and those with lung problems.

COLD AND FROSTY MORNINGS
On clear nights, heat from the ground escapes back into space. Temperatures near the ground may be low enough for ice to form. Hoar frost is a coating of tiny ice crystals. If there is an icy wind, the temperature drops further and a thick coating of ice appears on exposed surfaces. This is called rime frost.

ICY FEATHERS
On winter mornings, windows are sometimes covered with beautiful patterns of ice crystals. This happens when moisture comes into contact with the cold window and is cooled to the freezing point.

TYPES OF FOG

Different conditions form different types of fog. An advection fog is produced when warm, moist air blows over a cooler surface. Radiation, or ground, fog occurs on clear nights, especially in river valleys where the ground cools quickly and moisture in the air condenses. Upslope fog is created when air is forced to rise up the side of a hill and cools, which causes moisture in the air to condense. Frontal fogs form when weather fronts, especially warm fronts, pass through a cooler area.

A WALL OF ICE
Sometimes it is so cold that ocean spray freezes, and a wall of ice forms along the shoreline.

DID YOU KNOW?

Before the invention of refrigerators, ice was cut from ponds in winter and stored in an ice house. The ice house was a pit, packed with layers of ice and straw and covered with an insulated roof. Cold air sinks, so the pit remained very cold and the ice lasted right through the summer.

GHOSTLY SHADOWS
Sometimes, the sun
projects enlarged shadows
of mountain climbers onto
low-lying clouds. This
creates a ghostly effect
called a Brocken Specter.

ROLLING ALONG
Snow rollers are created
when the wind lifts a
thin layer of snow from a
lake or field to create a
cylindrical shape.

• THE DAILY WEATHER •

Weather Wonders

COLOR OF LIGHT
Sunlight is called white
light, but it is really a mixture
of different colors. Rays of
sunlight are bent as they
pass into the raindrop.
They reflect off the
back of the drop
and bend again
as they leave.

You can often see strange effects in the sky. When
sunlight hits ice crystals or water droplets, some of the
colors of light are reflected. This creates phenomena
such as rainbows, sundogs and glories. The multicolored arc
of a rainbow stretching across the sky directly opposite the sun
is one of the most colorful sights in the sky. Rainbows occur
during isolated showers or thunderstorms, when falling rain is
illuminated by sunlight. Sundogs, or parhelia, are small suns
that appear on either side of the sun. They are created when ice
crystals bend light in high clouds. When water droplets in the
clouds reflect sunlight back toward the sun, alternating red and
blue rings—called glories—are visible beneath the sun. Colored rain
is an unusual weather wonder. Red sand carried from desert areas
by the wind can cause red rain, while soot in the air can result in
black rain. Yellow rain, caused by pollen, is very rare.

SUNDOGS
These are images that appear
to the left and right of the
sun at the same height above
the horizon. They are called
sundogs because they often
have long, white tails that
point away from the sun.

SEEING DOUBLE

Rainbows are caused by the reflection of sunlight in millions of raindrops. The sun must be behind you and fairly low for a rainbow to be visible in the sky. This is why rainbows are never seen in the middle of the day. Sometimes, if the light has been reflected twice inside each raindrop, a second fainter rainbow can be seen about 9 degrees outside the first. The colors are reversed in order, with red on the inside.

51°   42°

FALLING FROM THE SKY

An old saying, "it's raining cats and dogs," may not be as strange as it sounds. Strong storm winds can suck up quite large objects. In October 1968, during a heavy storm in Acapulco, Mexico, maggots reportedly rained down on boats in the harbor. Stories of fish and frogs falling from the sky have been told around the world for centuries. The record books also tell of worms, snails and even snakes raining on surprised people.

Natural Clues

L ong before people came to rely on weather forecasts, they looked to nature for signs that would tell them about the weather. Knowledge of the weather is important because people need to know what clothes to wear, what plants to grow, and when to harvest their crops. The livelihoods of farmers and fishermen still depend on knowing what the weather might do in the future. Farmers from the past observed the color of the sky and the way in which the behavior of animals changed with the weather patterns. Not all signs were reliable, for many were based on superstition, but some were accurate enough to help them plan ahead. This kind of weather forecasting is thousands of years old and dates back as far as the ancient Greeks. Often, information about the weather was in the form of rhymes and songs that could be passed down from generation to generation.

A NOD OF THE HEAD
When a donkey sways and nods its head, the Spanish believe that rain will soon fall from the skies.

FLYING LOW
Some people in Asia believe that rain is on the way when dragonflies hover just above the ground.

CLEAN CATS
In Germany, some believe that a cat washes itself just before a shower of rain.

FOWL WEATHER
When African guinea fowl begin to pair off and build a nest, it is a sign that rain is due to fall.

RED SKY AT NIGHT
In many parts of the world, people believe that a red sky at night indicates fine weather while a red sky in the morning means bad weather is on the way. As the red color of the sky is created only when the clouds above reflect the light of the setting sun, this is accurate only when clouds come in from the west!

BUZZING AROUND
Bees in flight, busy collecting food, are said to be a sign of fine weather.

A GLORIOUS DAY
If the flowers of the morning-glory are open, some weather watchers predict fine weather.

THE TRUTH IN THE TALE

Many natural weather clues have no scientific basis whatsoever, but there are some that prove to be surprisingly accurate. A "ring around the moon" is a fair indicator that it will rain within the next few days. The ring is actually a watery halo made up from ice crystals in cirrostratus clouds. A red sky at night is frequently followed by a fine day. African guinea fowl are able to hear the rumble of thunder hundreds of miles away, so their nesting behavior is a reliable forecast of rain. Flowers, grasshoppers and bees, however, are generally poor predictors of changes in the weather.

ALL DRIED OUT
Some people believe that if they find pine cones with their scales open, the weather will remain fine and dry.

WARMING UP
Grasshoppers tend to chirp during warm, dry weather. As the temperature increases, their chirping becomes louder and louder.

Discover more in Types of Cloud

523

Weather Myths

People have always been intrigued by the mysteries of the weather. Long before weather forecasting became a science, people tried to explain the weather by creating stories about the sun, wind and rain. They invented gods to represent the elements and myths for frightening events such as thunder and lightning. The powerful Norse god Thor, for example, was said to carry a hammer. Every time he used it in anger, thunder and lightning would strike. Some people in Asia believed that typhoons sweeping across the China Sea were caused by a monstrous bird flapping its wings. When there were droughts, people often called upon their gods to send rain. The Hopi Indians in North America performed a snake dance because they believed it would bring rain. Hopi snake priests danced around the village square with live rattlesnakes, which represented the lightning of the summer rains, in their mouths. Some cultures even made sacrifices to their gods. The Aztecs offered their children to the rain god Tlaloc to make sure there was always plenty of rain.

STOPPING THE THUNDER
In Nigeria, the Yoruba priests have special ceremonies where they hold up a staff carved with the image of their god of thunder and lightning. This is supposed to ward off thunderstorms.

THUNDERBIRDS
Some Native Americans believe that giant birds called Thunderbirds beat their wings to produce thunder. The flashing of their eyes creates lightning.

524

CHINESE
STORM GODS

[an]cient Chinese myth
[how] a thunderstorm
[cr]eated by different gods.
[Lei] Kung, the Thunder God, is helped by Tien Mu, Mother
[Ligh]tning. She produces lightning using mirrors in her hands.
[Yu-t]zu, the Master of the Rain, sprinkles water from his pot with a
[swo]rd. The Little Boy of the Clouds, Yun-tiung, piles up the clouds, while
[the] Earl of the Wind, Feng-po, releases blustery winds from a goatskin bag.

STORM SPIRIT
Kultana is an
Aboriginal spirit
from Arnhem Land,
Australia. It is linked
to the north wind
and rain.

DID YOU KNOW?

In the past, people from many
cultures interpreted the weather as
signs from the gods. Angry gods
might send lightning to strike a
person or place.

SUN WORSHIP

The sun is important in our lives—it
brings heat and light and ripens crops.
Many cultures worshipped this powerful
source of energy. In South America,
the Inca and Aztec civilizations built
temples and shrines to the sun god.
The Temple of the Sun at Teotihuacán
in Mexico is shaped like a pyramid.
A small dwelling for the god at the
top of the temple is reached by a huge
staircase. Many of the temples were
positioned so that observers could watch
the sun's passage at the summer
solstice (the longest day of the year).

History of Forecasting

The weather has been studied for thousands of years. The Greek philosopher and scientist Aristotle published the first book about weather around 350 BC. Through the centuries, farmers and sailors observed changes in the wind, the clouds and the behavior of animals, but there were no accurate instruments to measure the weather. In the sixteenth century, however, Galileo invented the thermometer. In 1644, an Italian scientist called Torricelli invented the barometer, which measures atmospheric pressure. This was followed by the invention of the hygrometer, which measures humidity, and the anemometer, a device to measure wind speed. Soon, people were able to measure the effects of the weather, and forecasting became a more exact science. With the invention of the telegraph in 1837, it became possible to transmit weather information from remote weather stations to the rest of the world. Since then, forecasting has improved steadily.

DID YOU KNOW?
In the nineteenth century, the English used cameras and giant tripods to calculate the height of clouds. Meteorologists today use laser beams.

AN EARLY THERMOMETER
One of the earliest thermometers was a glass flask with a very long, thin tube standing in it. It was filled with alcohol and the end was sealed. The alcohol inside the tube expanded as the temperature outside increased, and contracted as the temperature cooled.

WEATHER VANE
Weather vanes have been used for thousands of years to show the direction of the wind. This gilt-bronze weather vane was crafted by Vikings in the tenth century.

526

A NEW WEATHER BUREAU

In 1847, Joseph Henry, secretary of the Smithsonian Institution in the United States, established a system of meteorological observations. Telegraphic reports from weather stations all over the country were sent to the Institution. The information was analyzed each day. A large map was displayed at the Institution and a weather report sent to the *Washington Evening Post*. By 1869, more than 350 stations were sending in reports.

Measuring Weather

You can get a rough idea of the weather that is on the way just by looking at the sky and checking the direction of the wind. But to find out what is really happening, you need to use accurate instruments to measure the different weather effects. Many of these instruments are simple and can be kept in the home. You can even keep daily weather records if you wish. The most important weather readings are temperature, rainfall, the speed and direction of the wind, air pressure and humidity. Readings should be taken at the same time each day. Sometimes the hours of sunlight and the amount of cloud cover are also noted. But taking the readings is only the first stage. Before the weather forecaster can predict the weather, he or she needs to put the readings together and compare them.

YOUR OWN WEATHER STATION
A simple weather station can be set up in a garden or school. A rain gauge, placed in the open, will collect rainwater and measure rainfall. These findings can be recorded and used to calculate average rainfall.

STRANGE BUT TRUE

In 1938, just before a hurricane hit Long Island, New York, a man received a new barometer through the mail. When the instrument read "hurricane" he thought the needle was stuck, so he wrote a letter of complaint to the manufacturers. When he returned from mailing the letter, he discovered that his home had been destroyed by a hurricane.

Under Pressure

Air pressure changes with the weather. Low pressure often means rain, or even a storm, while high pressure can mean settled or fair weather. A non-liquid barometer called an "aneroid" barometer measures the effect of air pressure on a box where the air has been removed. As the air pressure outside increases, the sides of the box are pushed in and the needle moves around the dial. If the air pressure falls, the sides of the box bulge out and the needle moves in the opposite direction around the dial.

ANEMOMETER
Anemometers measure wind speed. The faster the three cups spin, the higher the wind speed. Anemometers can be connected to computers for more accurate readings.

STORM GLASS
Because mercury barometers are expensive, water-filled storm glasses were commonly used on small boats in the nineteenth century. When the water rose up the spout of the glass, sailors knew that low pressure, a sign of stormy weather, was on the way.

STEVENSON SCREEN
A thermometer and hygrometer are usually kept inside a Stevenson screen, which shields them from direct sunlight.

Q: What does a barometer measure?

Weather Watch

T
he Earth's atmosphere is a massive and constantly
moving weather machine. Weather forecasters need to
gather information about the atmosphere from all around
the world, both at the Earth's surface and at heights of up to
2,480 miles (4,000 km). There are thousands of weather stations
on land and at sea recording these changes in the atmosphere–the
changes we call weather. These observations are backed up by
balloons and aircraft that take atmospheric readings. In some places
throughout the world, automatic and manual watch stations are
found in remote places. All weather stations are required to take
readings in the same way and their reports are gathered together
for analysis by the World Meteorological Organization. Separate
national organizations obtain the information necessary for
preparing the forecasts we read or hear.

DID YOU KNOW?

Rain gauges were used in India
as long ago as 400 BC. Farmers
would place a number of small
bowls in different places to
catch rain. This helped them to
learn about patterns of rainfall.

REMOTE READINGS

Meteorologists need information
from all around the world, so there are
weather stations in some extremely
remote areas. Some stations are run by
trained observers, although automatic
weather stations are now becoming
more common.

Weather balloon
Special balloons are released high
into the atmosphere to obtain weather
readings. Miniature radio transmitters,
called radiosondes, are attached to the
balloons. They broadcast information
back to the ground.

Stevenson screen
Thermometers and
hygrometers, which record
temperature and humidity,
are kept in here.

Campbell–Stokes recorder
This monitors the hours of
sunlight in one day.

Low-level anemometer
This measures wind
speed near the ground.

Evaporation pan
This instrument traps
water and then
records the rate at
which it evaporates.

Rain gauge
This is placed in the open,
to collect and measure
rainfall over 24 hours.

Pluviograph
This automatically
records the amount of
rainfall on a chart.

A SPY

...nditions at sea are monitored by specially equipped ships and ...mote weather buoys. These buoys are towed to positions away ...m shipping lanes and anchored to the sea bed. It is important ...watch the weather far out at sea, because severe storms and ...rricanes form there.

EYE IN THE SKY

Meteorology, or the study of weather, changed dramatically in 1960, when the first weather satellites were launched into space. These satellites scan huge areas of the Earth and send back a range of measurements, as well as images of cloud cover and other weather conditions. This information enables meteorologists to plot the development and course of major events such as hurricanes, and predict the weather more accurately. By using satellite sensors that are sensitive to heat and light, meteorologists can also obtain information about the temperature of different types of clouds and the surface of the land and sea.

Meteorological satellite

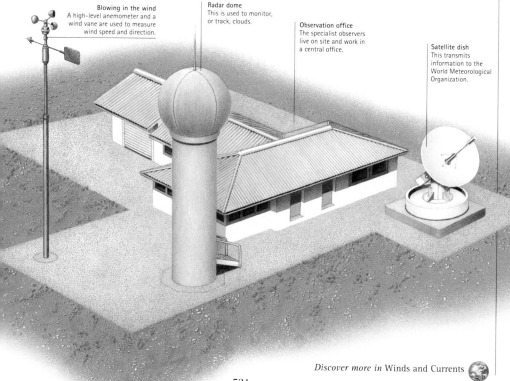

Blowing in the wind
A high-level anemometer and a wind vane are used to measure wind speed and direction.

Radar dome
This is used to monitor, or track, clouds.

Observation office
The specialist observers live on site and work in a central office.

Satellite dish
This transmits information to the World Meteorological Organization.

Discover more in Winds and Currents

Forecasting

very minute of the day and night, weather recordings from observation stations, ships, planes and satellites are received by meteorological offices all around the world. These recordings form a vast databank, from which meteorologists gather information. The system that enables this huge exchange of information is the Global Telecommunications System (GTS). The data is fed into powerful computers that enable meteorologists to prepare weather maps known as synoptic charts. Meteorologists study these charts very carefully and compare them to previous charts before they produce a weather forecast. The weather presenters we see on television use synoptic charts to prepare weather maps with simple symbols such as rain clouds and yellow suns. Weather forecasts are 85 percent accurate for the next few days. However, it is far more difficult to predict the weather for more than a week ahead.

ON THE MAP
Synoptic charts contain a wealth of information including air pressure, wind speed and direction, cloud cover, temperature and humidity. The most noticeable features on the charts are isobars. These are lines that join places of equal air pressure and are measured in hectopascals. Isobars that are close together, as they are on this map, show an area of low pressure. This usually brings wind and rain.

ON THE DRAWING BOARD
Meteorologists spend many hours preparing synoptic charts. All the different information has to be carefully plotted on the chart.

KEY TO SYMBOLS

wind symbols	cloud symbols	weather symbols		
light	clear sky	cold front	snow	rain
high	partly cloudy	warm front	fog	sleet
gale force	cloudy	occluded front		

SUPER COMPUTING POWER

Supercomputers can carry out billions of calculations every second, and are essential for the accurate prediction of weather patterns. They are programmed to simulate, or imitate, the conditions of the weather using general circulation models. General circulation models try to predict what the world's weather will be like for short periods, such as the next few hours, and longer periods, such as the next ten years.

DID YOU KNOW?

The nineteenth-century Dutch meteorologist C.H.D. Buys Ballot was the first to use a system of shadings on a weather map to indicate areas of varying air pressure. He also made the discovery that wind flows from areas of high pressure to areas of low pressure.

Winds and Currents

Winds constantly circle the Earth. They bring rain and influence temperatures. The polar easterlies, prevailing westerlies and trade winds are called prevailing winds because they cover large sections of the Earth. Small, circular wind flows are called cells. Jet streams move air between these cells high in the atmosphere and at very high speeds. Sailors have known about the patterns of wind for centuries, and many of the winds, and areas near them, were named by early sailors. The horse latitudes, for example, occur in the Atlantic Ocean. When sailing ships with cargoes of horses for the New World encountered calm, hot weather in this area, many of the horses died. The Atlantic trade winds blew trading ships between Europe and the New World, while the narrow, windless area around the equator, called the doldrums, has frustrated sailors through time. Ocean currents follow the direction of the prevailing winds and affect both the climate of the world and our daily weather.

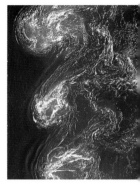

ON THE MOVE
These swirls in the ocean off the Norwegian coast are caused by currents and small whirlpools called eddies.

COMPUTER CURRENTS
Information about the oceans, including wind and temperature, are fed into computers that produce maps of ocean currents. This map shows an Antarctic current running across the bottom. The red areas indicate fast-flowing water while the blue areas are slow currents.

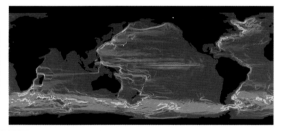

OCEAN CURRENTS

Ocean currents follow the direction of the prevailing winds. In each ocean there is a roughly circular movement of water called a gyre. Near the equator, the currents are blown toward the west, but at the poles the currents flow eastward. In this diagram it is possible to see the warm Gulf Stream. It runs up the coast of the eastern United States and then turns eastward across the Atlantic Ocean to Northern Europe. The Gulf Stream brings mild weather to parts of Northern Europe that would otherwise be much cooler.

warm currents   cool currents

Polar cell
Cold, dense air sinks and flows away from the poles and is replaced by warm air flowing in from above.

Polar jet stream
A band of air travels at high speed along the polar front.

Subtropical jet stream
A band of air travels at high speed.

Hadley cell
Warm air rises, moves away from the equator and sinks over the subtropics. Cool air flows toward the equator to replace it.

WINDS OF THE WORLD

The Earth spins as it orbits the sun. The winds do not blow in a straight line between high- and low-pressure areas, but are deflected. They bend to the right in the Northern Hemisphere and to the left in the Southern Hemisphere. This is called the Coriolis effect.

Ferrel cell
Warm, subtropical air flows toward the poles and cool, polar air flows toward the equator.

Doldrums
Low pressure area with light winds.

Trade winds
Dry winds blow from the northeast and southeast toward the equator, and replace rising, warm air.

FROM THE PAST

Knowledge of the direction of the winds around the world has improved over the last 2,000 years. This map drawn in AD 150 by Ptolemy, a Greek astronomer and geographer, shows the way many people saw the world until the sixteenth century.

Horse latitudes
A belt of high pressure is created when warm tropical air sinks to the ground. Winds blow out from this region.

Prevailing westerlies
Warm, moist winds blow toward the poles from the subtropics.

Polar easterlies
Cold winds blow from high-pressure regions over the poles

TOTAL CALM

In the past, sailing ships traveling across the equator were often becalmed in the doldrums. Sometimes they waited several weeks before the pattern of wind shifted and a breeze returned.

Discover more in The Weather Engine

World Climate

WORLD CLIMATE REGIONS
This map shows the world's major climate zones. Climate is the typical weather of a region, based on average weather conditions over a period of at least 30 years.

As the Earth is a sphere, the equator receives more heat from the sun's rays than the poles. Farther from the equator, the sun is weaker and less heat reaches the Earth's surface. The surface of the Earth is not heated equally, and this results in a pattern of winds moving the air around constantly. The intense heat of the equatorial sun causes warm, moisture-laden air to rise into the atmosphere. As this air cools, the moisture condenses and falls as rain. Warm air moves away from the equator and eventually sinks to the ground, which helps to form deserts such as the Sahara. Cool air is drawn back toward the equator to replace the rising, warm air. This sets up the circulations of air that produce the world's climates. The distribution of land and sea on the Earth, and the presence of mountain ranges, also affect climate. Coastal regions have milder climates than areas in the middle of a continent. Ocean currents influence climate as well. Northwest Europe has a mild climate because the warm waters of the Gulf Stream pass nearby.

THE SEASONS

Regular changes in weather patterns during the year are called seasons. In many parts of the world there are four seasons—spring, summer, fall and winter—while in other areas there are only two—a wet and a dry season. The Earth is tilted at an angle as it circles the sun. For six months of the year, the Northern Hemisphere is tilted toward the sun. It has long, warm, summer days while the Southern Hemisphere has short, cool winter days. For the next six months, the Northern Hemisphere is tilted away from the sun. This part of the world has winter while the Southern Hemisphere enjoys summer.

Solstice
The sun appears to stop moving south on December 21. The Southern Hemisphere has its longest day, while the Northern Hemisphere has its shortest day.

Equinox
On September 23, when the sun is over the equator, day and night are of equal length.

Solstice
On June 21, the sun appears to stop moving north. Both hemispheres experience the reverse conditions of December 21.

Equinox
On March 21, when the sun is over the equator, day and night are the same length.

POLAR ZONES

These are the coldest parts of the world. Winter temperatures fall below –58°F (–50°C).

MOUNTAIN ZONES

These high altitudes have cold climates.

TEMPERATE ZONES

These have moderate temperature ranges.

TROPICAL ZONES

These have average monthly temperatures of 80°F (27°C), and high rainfall.

DESERT ZONES

Temperatures here may range from more than 104°F (40°C) in the day to freezing at night.

DID YOU KNOW?

The world's most extreme temperature range is in Verhoyansk, northeast Siberia. Temperatures there can fall to as low as –90°F (–68°C) in winter and rise to as high as 98°F (37°C) in summer.

• CLIMATE •

Polar Zones

Climates near the North and South poles are characterized by freezing temperatures and permanent snow and ice. Polar summers are short and cold. The extreme climate is caused by lack of heat because the sun is weaker and the ice reflects much of the heat from the sun back into the atmosphere. For six months of the year, the Arctic experiences winter as the North Pole is tilted away from the sun. At the same time, Antarctica, the continent around the South Pole, enjoys a brief summer. Temperatures rise to freezing, or just above, near the coast. The pack ice drifts northward and melts in the warmer waters. Winter in the Antarctic, however, is severe. Antarctica doubles in size as the sea freezes over, and pack ice extends for hundreds of miles around the continent. Frequent blizzards and fierce winds rage across the icy surface.

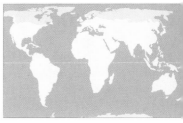

POLES APART
The Arctic is a frozen sea surrounding the North Pole, while the Antarctic is a frozen continent around the South Pole.

THE DEEP FREEZE
The Antarctic is covered in ice and snow, and the climate is bleak and hostile. Even in summer, temperatures barely reach freezing point. In spite of this, many animals live in the polar regions.

COAT OF COLORS

The fur of the Arctic fox changes color during the year. In winter, it turns from smoky gray to white to camouflage the fox against the snow.

ARCTIC DWELLERS

The Inuit (Eskimos), who live in the Arctic, have adapted well to the extreme climatic conditions.

WHITE OUT

Blizzards are strong winter snowstorms. They are particularly severe in the polar zones, where they may last for weeks at a time. Snow falls on more than 150 days of the year and is swept into huge piles by the wind. Winds are equally severe and reach speeds of more than 186 miles (300 km) per hour. The average winter temperatures plummet to -76°F (-60°C). In these extreme temperatures, unprotected human skin will freeze in seconds. People need layers of warm clothing and protective shelters to survive this bitter cold.

NEPAL
Nepal lies in the Himalayas. There is very little flat land for villages, so houses are scattered. The warm, sunny, south-facing slopes are used for farming. The north-facing slopes are usually forested. Because the steep slopes are difficult to farm, they have been gradually terraced to provide many small, level fields for farming. The higher pastures extend up to the permanent snow line.

CLINGING TO THE GROUND
The stems of alpine plants hug the ground to avoid the full force of the wind. Their leaves are small and waxy to reduce water loss. Because these plants grow only on warm days, they grow very slowly.

· CLIMATE ·

Mountain Zones

Each mountain has its own weather pattern. Within a mountain range there may be varying climatic conditions—the side of a mountain facing the wind may experience higher precipitation than the more sheltered side. Even the position of a rock or tree, creating a barrier to the wind or snow, can have an effect on the climatic conditions. The air temperature decreases by a few degrees for every few hundred yards rise in altitude. The air becomes thinner, the sky bluer and the sun's rays stronger. On the highest mountains, there is snow and ice all year round. Nothing can survive permanently on mountain peaks that are more than 23,000 ft (7,000 m) high, because fierce winds and low temperatures would freeze any living cells. Mountain weather is very changeable too. It can be bright and sunny, then stormy. Warm daytime temperatures may be followed by bitterly cold nights.

MOUNTAIN SITES
The areas highlighted above show the mountain zone around the world.

A SURE FOOTING
Mountain goats are nimble animals that ca leap from rock to rock. They are found on the highest slopes, where they are safe from predators.

540

FLYING HIGH
Strong, gusty mountain winds make flying difficult for all but the largest birds. Eagles have broad wings that are ideal for gliding. They make good use of rising air currents to soar around the mountain peaks.

SNOW FUN

Over the last 100 years, skiing has become a popular winter sport in the mountains of Europe, North America, New Zealand, Asia and Australia. The snow-covered high mountains are used as ski runs, and ski lifts carry skiers from the valleys to the slopes. But alpine environments are slowly being damaged by all the activity in these mountain areas.

SEASONAL CHANGES

Temperate regions have distinct seasons. In spring, plants begin to produce leaves and flowers and animals start to breed. This period of growth peaks in summer. As fall approaches, deciduous trees begin to drop their leaves and many animals migrate, while others prepare to hibernate. During the winter months, snow may cover the ground for weeks at a time, and the barren landscape shows little sign of activity.

• CLIMATE •

Temperate Zones

The temperate zones of the world experience a mild, moist climate dominated by cool, moist air blowing from the poles toward the tropical zones. Large swings in temperature, the distance from the equator and the varying hours of sunlight create a changeable climate with distinct seasons. The temperate zones can be divided into three regions: warm temperate between 35 and 45 degrees latitude; cool temperate between 45 and 60 degrees latitude; and cold temperate, which is experienced by regions lying in the center of continents. The majority of people live in the temperate zones, where there is an adequate supply of water for most of the year. The world's temperate grasslands are found in these zones, where huge herds of grazing animals such as buffalo once roamed. Today, farmers keep sheep and cattle, and much of the grassland has been plowed to grow crops and grains.

AROUND THE WORLD
The temperate zones lie between 35 and 60 degrees latitude, north and south of the equator.

A CHANGE OF COLOR
Many trees have adapted to the temperate seasons. They lose their leaves during the cold months and create spectacular fall scenes such as this.

BUSY BEES

Honey bees need warmth to maintain a regular body temperature. They have adapted to the conditions in temperate zones to keep up their busy way of life.

TEMPERATE CITIES

There are differences between warm-temperate and cool-temperate climates. The warm-temperate areas receive most of their rainfall in winter and have hot, dry summers. The lack of water in summer means that the vegetation is sparse and shrubby. Cool-temperate areas have cold winters with heavy snowfall and warm, humid summers. Because rain falls all year round, vegetation is plentiful.

Winter in a warm-temperate climate

Winter in a cool-temperate climate

DID YOU KNOW?

The world's climate is constantly changing. Between the fifteenth and nineteenth centuries, the River Thames in London, England froze over every year. But this has not happened for the last 160 years.

Discover more in Temperature and Humidity

Tropical Zones

Tropical zones are the warmest regions of the world. The sun is overhead for most of the year, so the climate is always hot. But there are many variations of climate within the tropical zones. Tropical wet climates are hot and humid all through the year, and have very heavy rainfall. These regions lie close to the equator and have dense tropical rainforests. Hot air, laden with moisture, rises into the atmosphere during the day. As the air cools, the water condenses to form dark clouds that bring heavy rain in the afternoons. In a tropical dry climate, a wet season is usually followed by a dry one. The wet season has heavy rain storms and hot, humid weather. The temperature can be even higher in the dry season as the days are sunny and clear. The subtropics are regions that border the tropics, and they are mostly dry.

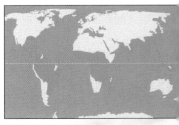

TROPICAL AND SUBTROPICAL SITES
Tropical zones lie between 30 degrees latitude north and south of the equator. Subtropical zones border these zones.

IN THE WET
When a low-pressure area develops over the land, cool, moist air from the ocean flows in. The air warms and rises as it crosses the land, and forms widespread rain clouds. The rains brought by these winds are called monsoons, and they provide 85 percent of Asia's annual rainfall.

TROPICAL DIVERSITY
In areas of South America, high temperatures and heavy rainfall support the lushest vegetation found on Earth: tropical rainforests. Many species of animal live in rainforests and feed on the fast-growing plants.

A DRY TIME
A high-pressure area over the land causes the winds to change direction. It rains out at sea and the land becomes dry.

THE SUBTROPICS

The subtropics lie to the north and south of the tropical zones. These areas do not receive as much rain as the tropics, but the temperature can be much higher. During the dry season, hot, scorching winds blow off the deserts. The ground dries and the vegetation becomes parched. As the sun moves overhead, the dry winds are replaced by hot, humid winds carrying moisture. This marks the beginning of the rainy season, which may last for several months. Zimbabwe (below) lies in a subtropical area.

Desert Zones

Deserts cover one-seventh of the Earth's land surface. They are dry regions that on average receive less than 4 in (100 mm) of rain per year. In some deserts, rain may not fall for many years. Then, quite suddenly, a storm will break and there is a huge downpour that lasts just a few hours. The absence of moisture in the air means that clouds are rare and the skies are clear for most of the year. The land is heated by the sun and daytime temperatures soar to 104°F (40°C) and above. However, the lack of cloud cover means that much of the heat radiates back into the atmosphere at night, and the air temperature plummets to almost freezing. Although they are dry and often very windy, not all deserts are hot. The cold winds that blow across the Gobi desert of central Asia produce freezing conditions, but it is still considered a desert because it has very little rain.

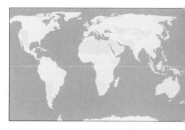

DESERT SITES
Deserts are found in subtropical areas, on the dry side of mountain ranges and in the center of large continents.

OVER THE DUNES
The strong winds in sandy deserts often create vast areas of sand dunes. The constantly shifting sand and the lack of water mean that there are few plants. Nomadic peoples often use camels as pack animals because they can survive with little water.

THE DESERT IN BLOOM

Every year, desert rains trigger the germination of thousands of plants. They grow rapidly so that they can complete their life cycle before they run out of water. A few weeks after rain has fallen, the desert is transformed into a carpet of flowers. These soon die, but their seeds lie in the ground, waiting for the next rainfall.

CREATURES OF THE DESERT

Lizards are well adapted to living in the desert. Their scaly skin enables them to retain water by cutting down evaporation. They also produce solid waste rather than liquid urine, and they can alter the color of their skin to reflect more or less heat. Desert animals have also adapted to survive. The large ears of the fennec fox enable it to lose heat from its body. The fox also has exceptional hearing and this allows it to hunt at night when temperatures are cooler. After the rains, honey pot ants collect as much nectar as they can find and give it to special ants that store the nectar in their abdomens. The ants' abdomens swell up, often to the size of grapes. During the dry months, the other ants in the colony feed off this collected honey.

Fennec fox

Honey pot ants

547

TREE RINGS
Each year, a tree grows a ring of woody material that is called an "annual ring." In warm, wet years, growth is good and the ring is wide. During years of bad weather, the ring is very narrow.

580,000 BC
Günz Ice Age

PAST ICE AGES
In the last million years, there have been four ice ages. The average temperature of the Earth during these times was 6–8 degrees below today's averages.

430,000 BC
Mindel Ice Age

A MAMMOTH EVENT
Until the Würm Ice Age, huge, elephant-like mammoths lived on the cold plains that now form Siberia. The mammoths and other giant mammals disappeared as the climate became warmer and the ice retreated. Because the ice preserved their bodies, we know that they had thick, woolly coats and huge tusks.

UNDER ICE
About two million years ago, the Earth's climate cooled and the polar ice cap expanded to cover northern Europe.

CARVED BY ICE
A glacier is a mass of ice that flows very slowly down a mountain valley. It rubs away the sides of the valley until the valley becomes a U shape.

240,000 BC
Riss Ice Age

• CLIMATIC CHANGE •

Global Freezing

The Earth's climate has changed many times in the last few million years. There were periods of severe cold, known as ice ages or glacials, when great slabs of ice inched across the land. They gouged out hollows in their path as they pushed soil and rocks ahead of them. The sea level dropped enormously as much of the water froze. Warmer times between the ice ages were called interglacials. The ice melted and the huge hollows filled with water and became lakes. Scientists learn about the different climates in the Earth's history by looking for clues in nature. Some trees have lived for thousands of years and show signs of climatic changes. Fossils also provide valuable clues about wildlife and their environment. Most evidence about past climates comes by studying sediment samples from the beds of the oceans or ice samples taken from Greenland or Antarctica.

120,000 BC
Würm Ice Age

20,000 BC
Würm Ice Age ends

HIDDEN CLUES
Geologists can break open rocks to find the fossilized imprint of plants millions of years after the sediment originally built up.

AD 1430
The Little Ice Age

THE LITTLE ICE AGE

Between 1430 and 1850, northern Europe experienced a "little ice age." It was not as severe as a full ice age, but the climate became colder, crops failed and there was widespread starvation. England experienced some of the coldest winters on record during the 1810s and 1820s. The River Thames froze over regularly and Frost Fairs, where people played games and danced, were held on its icy surface. Sometimes the weather warmed without warning. People had to flee quickly as the ice beneath them began to thaw and crack.

Discover more in Polar Zones

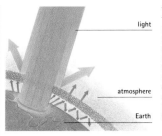

THE GREENHOUSE EFFECT
The Earth's atmosphere is like a greenhouse. It allows light from the sun to pass through it and heat the Earth's surface. Gases in the atmosphere, such as carbon dioxide, absorb the returning heat and also warm the surface. Without this greenhouse effect, the Earth would be too cold for life. But the level of carbon dioxide and other gases in the atmosphere is increasing. As more heat is absorbed by the atmosphere, the Earth becomes warmer and warmer.

• CLIMATIC CHANGE •

Global Warming

The Earth is getting warmer. Most of the hottest years during the twentieth century have occurred in the last decade. Scientists are still arguing whether this is due to the greenhouse effect or some other cause. One of the key factors in the greenhouse effect is carbon dioxide. This greenhouse gas traps heat in the Earth's atmosphere. Each year, more than 5,500 billion tons (5,100 billion tonnes) of carbon dioxide are absorbed by green plants to make food in a process called photosynthesis. This process produces oxygen, which living organisms need to breathe. However, the level of carbon dioxide in the atmosphere is increasing dramatically because of pollution, deforestation, farming methods and the burning of more fossil fuels (coal, gas and oil). Some scientists believe that the Earth's temperature will continue to rise as more carbon dioxide is released into the atmosphere.

A CHANGING WORLD
More fossil fuels are being used each year. They provide power for cars and industry, and heat homes and offices. When fossil fuels are burned, carbon dioxide is released. Cows also have a major effect on the atmosphere because they produce methane gas when they digest grass. As the number of cows increases, so does the amount of methane released.

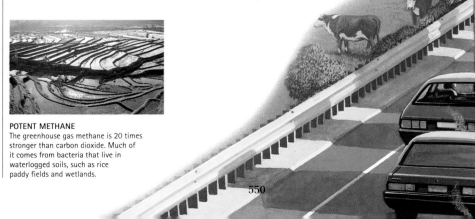

POTENT METHANE
The greenhouse gas methane is 20 times stronger than carbon dioxide. Much of it comes from bacteria that live in waterlogged soils, such as rice paddy fields and wetlands.

A Hole in the Sky

The ozone layer, which is in the upper atmosphere, shields the surface of the Earth from ultraviolet light. But scientists have discovered that the ozone layer is being attacked by manufactured chemicals called chlorofluorocarbons (CFCs), which are used in spray cans, refrigeration and air-conditioning. The blue at the center of this picture shows a hole in the ozone layer over Antarctica. This allows more ultraviolet light to reach Australia and New Zealand. In 1987, many nations around the world signed a treaty to limit the production of CFCs. This has been effective, but the damaging effects of CFCs will last for decades.

DISAPPEARING FORESTS
Trees absorb carbon dioxide and release oxygen. But forests are being cleared throughout the world. This deforestation is contributing to the increased levels of carbon dioxide in the atmosphere.

NEW LIFE
Replanting trees (reforestation) helps to reduce the greenhouse effect and fight global warming.

Discover more in Weather Watch

In the Extremes

RECORD WIND
On April 12, 1934, winds of 230 miles (371 km) per hour—the fastest surface winds ever recorded—swept across Mount Washington in New Hampshire.

TWISTING ON
A tornado that tore through Illinois and Indiana on May 26, 1917 left a track of 292 miles (471 km)—the longest ever seen.

THE HEAT IS ON
The highest temperature in the world, 136.4°F (58°C), was recorded at Al Aziziyah in Libya on September 13, 1922.

HERE COMES THE RAIN
Rain falls on Mount Wai'ale'ale in Hawaii on 350 days of the year. This creates an extraordinary average rainfall of 486 in (12,346 mm) each year.

SNOWED UNDER
Between April 14 and 15, 1921, at least 75 in (193 cm) of snow fell on Silver Lake in Colorado. This was the greatest snowfall in a 24-hour period.

ICE FROM ABOVE
The largest single hailstone to fall to the ground was recorded at Coffeyville, Kansas, on September 3, 1970. It weighed 1.67 lb (750 g) and had a diameter of 17½ inches (44 cm).

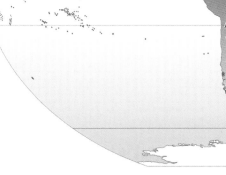

DRY AS A BONE
The driest place in the world, with an average annual rainfall of less than 1/250 in (0.1 mm) is the Atacama Desert in Chile.

RUMBLING CLOUDS
Bogor on the island of Java, Indonesia, can experience thunder on as many as 322 days each year.

HIGH PRESSURE
The highest ever barometric pressure, 1083.8 hectapascals, was recorded on December 31, 1968 in Siberia.

HERE COMES THE SUN
At the eastern end of the Sahara Desert in North Africa, the sun shines 97 percent of the possible daylight hours.

LOW PRESSURE
The lowest ever barometric pressure, 877 hectapascals, was recorded to the north of Guam in the Pacific Ocean in 1958.

DOWN THE SPOUT
On May 16, 1898, a waterspout with a height of 5,012 ft (1,528 m) and a diameter of 10 ft (3 m) was spotted off the coast of New South Wales, Australia.

COLD AS ICE
The coldest place in the world is Vostok Base in Antarctica. It has an annual average temperature of –72°F (–58.2°C). On July 21, 1983, it recorded the world's lowest temperature, –128.6°F (–89.2°C).

Stars and Planets

How did the universe begin?

Which planet is like a boiling cauldron?

Why does the tail of a comet trail through space?

Contents

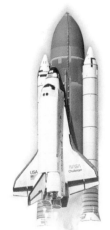

Early Astronomers

Long ago, people thought that the Earth was flat and the sky was the home of great gods. They told myths and legends to explain night and day, the changing of the seasons, and the sudden appearance of strange, "long-haired stars" (comets). The ancient Chinese, Babylonians and Egyptians were the first to record the movements of the heavenly bodies. The Greeks proved that the Earth was round and tried to figure out the order of the universe by charting the stars and planets they saw. Claudius Ptolemy, a Greek astronomer, believed that the Earth was at the center of the universe, and the Moon, the Sun, planets and stars all revolved around it. Ptolemy's view was accepted for nearly 1,500 years, but in 1543 a Polish astronomer and priest Nicolaus Copernicus suggested that the Earth and the other planets orbited the Sun. This view caused much anger and debate because people believed that the Earth was the most important planet. With the first telescopes, which were built in the 1600s, people were able to expand their view of the universe.

PTOLEMY'S PICTURE
Claudius Ptolemy pieced together a picture of the universe, but he mistakenly put Earth at the center of it. As astronomers developed specia tools, such as telescopes, they realized that many early theories about the universe were incorrect.

AN EARLY ASTRONOMER
Nicolaus Copernicus published his astronomical ideas in 1543. People were still arguing about his theories years after his death. Galileo and later astronomers helped to prove that many of his ideas were true.

LOOKING TO THE STARS
Skywatching is an ancient pastime. Our ancestors gazed at the Sun, the Moon, the bright planets, comets and meteors. The study of the sky, astronomy, has developed from people's desire to understand how these heavenly bodies relate to each other and to the Earth.

DID YOU KNOW?
More than 4,000 years ago, these giant stone slabs were placed carefully in a circle at Stonehenge in England. It seems that people may have watched and recorded the times and positions of the rising Sun and Moon from this ancient site.

SKYWATCHING
Tycho Brahe was a great sixteenth-century astronomer. In 1572, he saw a star as bright as Venus in the constellation of Cassiopeia. This strange new star was a supernova—the brightest one in 500 years.

CALENDAR OF EVENTS

The ancient Babylonians and Chinese developed the earliest calendars, based on the rising and setting of stars throughout the year. The ancient Egyptians noticed that the bright star Sirius reappeared in the eastern sky (after several months of not being visible) just before sunrise for a few days each year. As the River Nile began to flood shortly after this sighting, they arranged their calendars around the time of this event. The fifteenth-century calendar on the left is English, while the sixteenth-century calendar on the right is Danish.

Q: Why did Ptolemy place Earth at the center of the universe?

Tiger

Dog

Mouse

Horse

Cow

Rooster

EASTERN ZODIAC SIGNS
These are some of the standard astrological signs for Chinese and other eastern astrologers. They use them to define the areas where the planets travel.

Astronomy and Astrology

SIGNS FROM ABO
Ancient observ
thought they sa
patterns or figures in t
night sky. From left
right, the picture abo
shows the constellatic
of Leo, Cancer, Gem
and Taur

Early skywatchers studied the stars, kept records of the movements of the planets and compiled calendars. The night sky seemed a magical place with strange, unexplained forces and they interpreted what they saw by creating myths and legends about the gods who lived in the sky. They imagined they could see shapes in the patterns of the stars (constellations), and they named them after mythological characters, such as lions and hunters. Twelve of these constellations lie close to the yearly path of the Sun in the sky (called the ecliptic). We call this band of sky the zodiac. Astrologers believe that the heavenly bodies exert an influence on people's affairs, personalities and futures. They predict events for the different signs of the zodiac based on their observations of happenings in the sky. Astronomy, however, is the scientific study of the universe. Astronomers have learned much about the universe, but they have found no evidence that it directly affects the lives of people on Earth.

ESTERN ZODIAC SIGNS
e word "zodiac" means "circle of the
imals" in Greek. Most of the 12
nstellations of the western zodiac,
own here, are represented by animals.

CONSULTING THE STARS

Astrologers were important people in ancient society. People believed that the position of the Sun and the planets in the sky influenced their lives and that some days would be better than others for certain activities. This army general is consulting an astrologer before drawing up his battle plans. Today, some people still see an astrologer before making decisions.

The Universe

The Earth and the other planets, the stars, the galaxies, the space around them and the energy that comes from them are all part of what we call the universe. Most astronomers believe that between 8 and 16 billion years ago, all matter and energy, even space itself, were concentrated in a single point. There was a tremendous explosion—the Big Bang—and within a few minutes the basic materials of the universe, such as hydrogen and helium, came to be. These gases collected together into large bodies called galaxies. Today, the universe still seems to be expanding. Huge families, or superclusters, of galaxies are racing away from all the other clusters at incredible speeds. If the Big Bang has given them enough energy, the galaxy superclusters may keep on racing away from each other until the last star has died. But if their gravity is strong enough to slow them down, everything in the universe will eventually cascade in on itself in an event we call the Big Crunch. Then, perhaps another cycle will begin.

| The Big Bang | 100,000 years later | 1 billion years later | 8 billion years later | 13 billion years later (now) |

BIG BANG
The Big Bang took place long ago, but most of its work was accomplished in a very short time. Hydrogen was created quickly, and the galaxies began to form soon after. As stars within these galaxies exploded, the heavier elements, such as carbon (the basis of life), were formed.

A SMALL PART OF A LARGE SCHEME
We live on the Earth, just one planet in the solar system. Our solar system is part of the Milky Way, just one galaxy in a cluster of galaxies. These clusters gather into superclusters of galaxies, all of which are expanding outward.

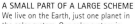

GHT SKY
e ceiling of stars we
n see on a clear night is
tiny part of the universe,
hich is immense in both
me and space.

BACK TO THE PAST

In 1965, scientists Arno Penzias and Robert Wilson were testing a radio antenna when they detected strange energy emissions. They searched for the source of these emissions and soon made a staggering discovery: the universe had a very weak level of radiation. The existence of radiation confirmed the theory of some astronomers that the Big Bang had left a cool afterglow in space. In 1978, Penzias and Wilson won the Nobel Prize in Physics for discovering this important fact about the beginning of the universe.

BIG CRUNCH

The expansion of the universe will be reversed if gravity is strong enough to pull everything together again.

Close   Closer   Closer still   The Big Crunch

Discover more in Galaxies

The planets closest to the Sun move around their orbits faster than those farther away. The Earth takes a year to complete its orbit. The planets also spin around as they orbit the Sun. The Earth spins once every 24 hours, which we call a day. Here we show the different sizes of the planets, as well as the time they take to orbit the Sun (given as a year) and to spin on their axis (given as a day).

Mercury
Year: 88 Earth days
Day: 59 Earth days

Venus
Year: 225 Earth days
Day: 243 Earth days

Earth
Year: 365.25 days
Day: 24 hours

Mars
Year: 1.9 Earth years
Day: 24.6 hours

Jupiter
Year: 11.9 Earth years
Day: 9.8 hours

DID YOU KNOW?

Pluto takes 248 years to circle the Sun and for most of that time it is the farthest planet from the Sun. But Pluto has a very oval-shaped orbit, and for 20 years of its total orbit, Pluto is actually closer to the Sun than its neighbor Neptune.

• OUR NEIGHBORHOOD •

The Solar System

Humans live on a small planet in a tiny part of a vast universe. This part of the universe is called our solar system, and it is dominated by a single brilliant star—the Sun. Our solar system is the Earth's neighborhood and the planets Mercury, Venus, Mars, Jupiter, Saturn, Uranus, Neptune and Pluto are the Earth's neighbors. They all have the same stars in the sky and orbit the same Sun. Scientists believe the solar system began about 5 billion years ago, perhaps when a nearby star exploded and caused a large cloud of dust and gas to collapse in on itself. The hot, central part of the cloud became the Sun, while some smaller pieces formed around it and became the planets. Other fragments became comets and asteroids (minor planets), which also orbit the Sun. The early solar system was a turbulent mix of hot gas and rocky debris. Comets and asteroids bombarded the planets and their moons, scarring them with craters that can still be seen today.

PLANET PATHS
The Sun is massive and has a strong gravity that pulls the planets towards it. The planets also have their own energy of motion, and without the pull of the Sun, which bends the planets' paths into orbits around it, they would fly off into space.

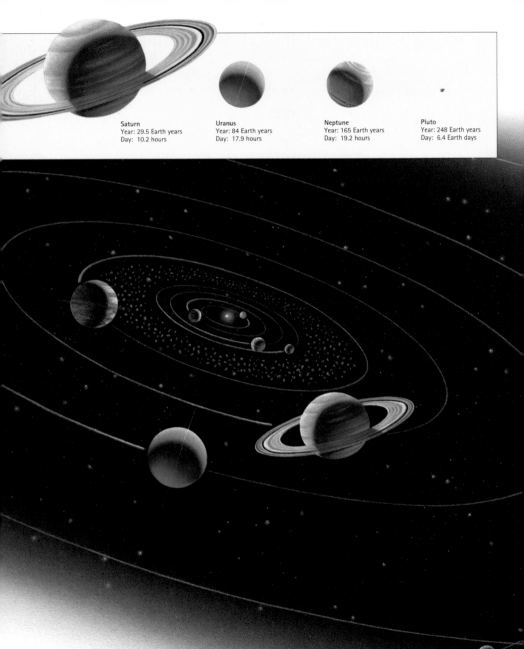

Saturn
Year: 29.5 Earth years
Day: 10.2 hours

Uranus
Year: 84 Earth years
Day: 17.9 hours

Neptune
Year: 165 Earth years
Day: 19.2 hours

Pluto
Year: 248 Earth years
Day: 6.4 Earth days

The Sun

The Sun is the center of the solar system. This enormous star gives us all the light and heat we need to grow food and keep warm. It was worshipped as the mightiest of the gods by the ancient Egyptians. The Sun, however, is not the largest star in the galaxy. It seems very big and bright because it is only 93 million miles (150 million km) away from Earth. Light from the Sun takes eight minutes to reach us; light from Sirius, the next brightest star, takes eight years! The Sun is made up of gases, mostly hydrogen, and is powered by a natural process called nuclear fusion—when atoms of hydrogen fuse, or join together, to make helium. Nuclear fusion takes place in the center, or core, of the Sun, where temperatures are around 27 million°F (15 million°C). The Sun has shone in the sky for nearly 5 billion years and scientists believe it has enough hydrogen in its core to "burn" for another 5 billion years. Then it will expand to become a red giant before shrinking to become a feeble white star.

CLOUD ACTIVITY
Clouds of gas called prominences can erupt from the Sun's surface. They are best seen during a total eclipse of the Sun—when the Moon cuts off the bright light of the photosphere.

INSIDE THE SUN
Energy is produced in the core of the Sun. It is transferred to the surface through the body of the star—the zone of radiation and convection. We can see the Sun's photosphere through the thin chromosphere and the outer atmosphere—the corona.

THE SURFACE OF THE SUN
This picture shows the boiling surface of the Sun. Cool, dark patches called sunspots lie beneath the bright spots seen here.

ENERGY BURST
Solar flares are huge eruptions that occur near sunspots. They release a massive amount of energy into space.

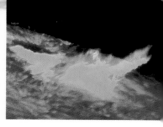

Sunspots

Core

Convective zone

Radiative zone

Photosphere

Chromosphere

RIBBONS OF LIGHT

Solar flares send charged particles from
areas around sunspots into space.
When they hit the Earth's charged upper
atmosphere near the magnetic poles, they
cause colourful dancing ribbons of light,
called auroras, or Northern or Southern
lights. Auroras appear more often when
there is heavy sunspot activity.

Mercury and Venus

For at least half a billion years after the solar system was born, the planets were battered by debris. The surface of Mercury is pockmarked with craters from this time, just as the surface of Earth must once have been. Unlike Earth, however, Mercury has no air or water to wear these craters away. As it is the closest planet to the Sun, Mercury speeds swiftly through the sky, like the winged Roman god after which it is named. But because Mercury is so close to the Sun, it is very hard to see in the night sky. Venus, however, is the brightest "star" in the morning or evening sky. Shrouded in a layer of clouds, the surface of Venus is more than four times as hot as boiling water. Even at night, the temperatures remain high. Like the Earth, Venus is heated by the Sun, but the thick canopy of clouds and carbon dioxide makes it impossible for this heat to escape. Venus is a scorching and extreme example of the greenhouse effect.

A MELTING POT

The surface of Venus is a furious mingling of elements. As a volcano belches lava, a rain of hot sulfuric acid falls from the sky onto the hot ground. Lightning strikes punctuate the chaos.

MERCURY, THE FOSSIL PLANET

Steep cliffs and craters scar the surface of Mercury. The day on Mercury is searingly hot because the planet is so close to the Sun, but the night is unbearably cold. As Mercury has no real atmosphere, impact craters that were formed nearly 4 billion years ago still dominate its ancient surface. In 1977, the *Mariner 10* spacecraft visited Mercury and took some revealing pictures of the planet, such as the one shown here. These photos gave us a bleak picture of the early history of the solar system. Comets and asteroids regularly hit Mercury and all the planets during a time we call the "age of heavy bombardment."

DID YOU KNOW?

Venus is the Roman goddess of love, and most of the features on the planet Venus are named after real or imaginary women. Two of its continents take the names of the goddesses Ishtar and Aphrodite, and a crater is named after the famous jazz singer Billie Holiday.

A RARE EVENT
If you look very closely at this time-lapse photograph, you will be able to see a small dot, which is Venus passing behind the Moon. This rare event is called an occultation and it takes place when the Moon passes in front of a planet.

BRIGHT LIGHT
As its thick clouds reflect light back into space, Venus is by far the brightest planet in the sky. However, it is visible only before dawn or after dusk for a few months each year.

Discover more in The Solar System

The Earth

We live on a small planet—the only place in the solar system where life seems to flourish. Seen from an Apollo spacecraft orbiting the Moon, the Earth is a colorful planet of green spaces, deserts, deep oceans and fields of ice. Life on Earth is possible because our planet is just the right distance from the Sun for water to exist as a liquid. If the Earth was a few million miles either closer to or farther from the Sun, it might be a boiling cauldron such as Venus, or a frozen wasteland such as Mars or the moons of Jupiter. Life is also sustained by the Earth's atmosphere—a thin layer of gas that surrounds the planet. Of all the planets in our solar system, this atmosphere is unique because it contains so much oxygen. The Earth orbits the Sun, and spins like a top once a day. This rotation and the Earth's atmosphere keep temperatures from reaching extremes, such as those on the nearby Moon.

Crust
Mantle | Outer core
Inner core

THE FOUR SEASONS
The Earth's seasons are caused by the way the Earth tilts as it orbits the Sun. Through the year, the Southern and the Northern (N) hemispheres have opposite seasons: while the Northern Hemisphere has winter the Southern Hemisphere has summer.

INSIDE THE EARTH
The solid iron inner core of the Earth is surrounded by a liquid outer core, and a soft rock mantle. The rock structures we actually see are part of the crust, which ranges in thickness from 3–43 miles (5–70 km).

THE MIDNIGHT SUN
At the equator, summer days are the same length as winter days. As you go farther north or south, the difference in length between winter and summer days becomes greater and greater. If you go far enough north or south, you will reach a place (such as Norway shown below) where on some summer days the Sun never sets.

STAR TRAILS

The Sun moves across the sky as the Earth rotates. This picture shows that the stars also appear to move to the west, but it is really because the Earth is rotating towards the east. To take a picture such as this, leave your camera well-mounted and its lens open for about half an hour. As the Earth moves east, the stars will appear to draw lines on the film.

VIEWING THE MOON
At any time, half of the sphere of the Moon is lit by the Sun. We might see just a little of the lit side (at crescent phase), most of it (in gibbous, or more than half, phase) or all of it (at full phase). How much we see depends on where the Moon is in orbit around the Earth.

HIGH AND LOW TIDES
Some places on Earth, such as the Fijian coast shown here, have extreme tidal ranges. The low tides expose much of the sea floor, while the high tides seem to sweep away the land.

GRAVITATIONAL PULL
Tides are caused by the pull of the Moon's gravity, and to a lesser extent the Sun's gravity, on the Earth's oceans.

• OUR NEIGHBORHOOD •

The Earth's Moon

People have been entranced by the Moon for centuries. The astronomer Galileo first looked through a telescope at this mysterious ball of rock in 1609. He saw its strangely uneven surface; its mountains and craters; and its dark, lava-filled basins (called "seas"), caused by collisions that rocked the Moon during the chaotic beginnings of the solar system. From the Earth, these dark markings seem to form a pattern, which people sometimes call a rabbit, a cat or even the "Man in the Moon." Astronaut Neil Armstrong became the first man on the Moon in 1969. The world watched in awe as he stepped on this airless, waterless satellite of the Earth. As the Moon moves around its endless orbit of the Earth, it seems to change shape in our sky, depending on how much of it is lit by the Sun. But we always see the same face of the Moon because it spins on its axis in the same time it takes to orbit the Earth.

STRANGE BUT TRUE

When Neil Armstrong took "one small st for a man, one giant leap for mankind," footprint he left was a permanent one. there is no air on the Moon, Armstrong footprint should last for many millions years. Eventually, tiny hits from small meteoroids will cause the footprint to fa

How the Moon came to be is a subject of great debate. The best of the current theories says that a tremendous collision, early in the Earth's history, produced a cloud of rocky debris that orbited the Earth. The debris formed clumps that heated as they collected together. The result was a new body that cooled down to become the Moon.

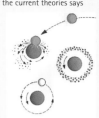

Mars

The Romans called the orange-red planet in the night sky Mars, after the god of war. Its surface is covered by rusty-red rock and dotted with huge canyons and volcanoes, polar icecaps and mountains. Phobos and Deimos, tiny moons scarred by craters, orbit the planet. Since the astronomer Schiaparelli first studied Mars in the late nineteenth century, people have wanted to believe that there was life on this planet. It is only half the size of Earth, but the planets are similar in some ways: the day on Mars is half an hour longer than ours, and it has changes in weather like our seasons. In the 1970s, space probes visited Mars, but their findings showed that the red, rocky planet is like a chillingly cold desert. Water probably lies frozen beneath the hostile ground. The atmosphere on Mars is too thin to breathe, and violent dust storms sometimes howl across its surface.

THE LARGEST OF THEM ALL
Olympus Mons is the biggest volcano in the solar system. It is as large as the American state of Arizona! Olympus Mons rises so slowly that you could climb it without being aware that you were getting higher.

INTO THE FUTURE
A spacemobile such as this may one day be used to carry scientists across the surface of Mars to collect specimens from canyons and ancient river beds.

MARS ROVER
This vehicle has been built especially for exploring the surface of Mars. Its large wheels will help it travel across the rough terrain.

COLLISIONS IN THE UNIVERSE
In July 1992, Comet Shoemaker–Levy 9
passed so close to Jupiter that it split
into 21 pieces. Two years later, the
comet fragments collided with Jupiter.
Every large telescope on Earth and in
space was poised to see the dramatic
collision and the huge, spectacular
fireballs that rose about 1,900 miles
(3,000 km) above Jupiter's clouds.

· OUR NEIGHBORHOOD ·

Jupiter

Named after the king of the Roman gods, Jupiter is the
largest planet in the solar system. It is 300 times heavier
than the Earth and more than twice as heavy as all the
other planets added together! The enormous gravity causes very
high temperatures and pressure deep inside Jupiter. This stormy
planet is cloaked by noxious gases such as hydrogen, ammonia
and methane and topped by bitterly cold, swirling cloud zones,
which change in appearance as the planet spins quickly on its
axis. A day on Jupiter is less than 10 hours long—the shortest
day in the solar system. This speedy rotation causes great winds
and wild storms. Like most of the planets, Jupiter has moons.
We know of at least 16, but there may be smaller moons
still to be found. In 1979, the *Voyager 1* space probe
discovered that Jupiter was encircled by a narrow,
faint ring made up of rocky or icy fragments.

THE MOONS OF JUPITER

Jupiter's four largest moons are very different from each other. Io, the closest of the four to Jupiter, has many volcanic vents that spew clouds of sulfur into the sky. *Voyager 1* recorded five erupting volcanoes when it visited Io in 1979. The smooth, icy surface of the next moon, Europa, is patterned with cracks that may once have been filled with water. The icy surfaces of Ganymede and Callisto, the largest moons, are marked by craters, the remains of ancient impacts.

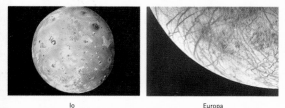

Io   Europa

AS STORMY AS EVER
Astronomers first saw Jupiter's
Great Red Spot 300 years ago.
This swirling whirlpool of gases
is a huge storm cloud that
seems to rage constantly on
this turbulent planet.

Saturn

The bright rings of Saturn are a dazzling highlight of the night sky. Ever since Dutch scientist Christiaan Huygens saw them through a telescope more than 300 years ago, astronomers have turned their sights to Saturn. From the Earth, it seems that Saturn is surrounded by three rings, but the 1981 Voyager space probe discovered that there are thousands of narrow ringlets made up of millions of icy particles. These ringlets stretch for thousands of miles into space in a paper-thin disk. The rings were formed long ago, perhaps when a moon or an asteroid came too close to Saturn and was torn apart by the strong gravity of the planet, which is the second largest in the solar system. Like Jupiter, Uranus and Neptune, Saturn is made up mainly of hydrogen and helium. It spins very quickly on its axis and is circled by bands of clouds.

Cassini's division
This has far fewer ringlets.

A LASTING IMPACT
One of Saturn's moons, Mimas, has a huge crater called Herschel. It was caused by a violent collision with a comet or an asteroid long ago, which nearly tore the little moon apart.

A ring
This is very bright where the ringlets are close together.

B ring
The color of this seems to be more solid.

STUDYING SATURN

Saturn has a smooth, yellowish tinge, which is caused by a layer of haze that surrounds the planet. Unlike Jupiter, which it resembles slightly in color, it does not seem to have any longlasting light or dark spots.

C ring
From Earth, this is seen as a faint ring.

Encke gap
This is a large gap within the A ring.

F ring
Seems to be knotted or braided.

SATURN'S MOONS

Saturn has more moons than any other planet. Eighteen have been discovered so far, but there are probably smaller moons that we have not seen yet.

FAR FROM THE SUN

Orange-colored Titan is Saturn's biggest moon. It is the only moon in the solar system with an atmosphere, which is made up mostly of nitrogen. As on Venus, this thick atmosphere hangs over Titan like a veil. Because it is so far away from the Sun, Titan is very cold and the methane on the planet is a liquid, not a gas.

579

Uranus

Uranus is the Greek god of the sky. The planet was first noticed in 1781 by Englishman William Herschel, who saw a small round object with a greenish tinge through his home-made telescope. The discovery of Uranus caused great excitement. Astronomers had previously believed that Saturn lay at the edge of the solar system. As Uranus lies twice as far from the Sun as Saturn, the known size of the solar system suddenly doubled! Uranus is nearly four times the size of the Earth, and it orbits the Sun every 84 years. Like Jupiter and Saturn, it is made up mainly of hydrogen and helium. Most of the planets in the solar system are tilted a little (the Earth is tilted at an angle of 23°, and this causes the different seasons), but Uranus is tilted completely on its side. This means that each pole has constant sunlight for 42 years. When the *Voyager 2* space probe passed Uranus in 1986, it photographed the dense clouds that cover the planet, its narrow rings and its beautiful moons.

THE MOON MIRANDA
Miranda, the smallest and most unusual of the five main moons of Uranus, looms into view in front of the planet. This photograph was taken by the *Voyager 2* space probe as it flew past Uranus in 1986.

CLOSE-UP
Miranda has a unique surface. Some astronomers believe that it may have broken apart after a collision, but then re-formed. When the pieces of the moon came back together again, its surface was buckled with deep grooves.

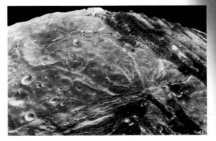

BEFORE
In the early days of the solar system, a large body may have crashed into Uranus.

AFTER
This collision tilted Uranus so that it rolls through the sky on its side.

DID YOU KNOW?

The rings of Uranus were discovered by astronomers in 1977. As Uranus passed in front of a star, they saw that the star's light flickered. They realized that rings around the planet were blocking the light of the star as they passed across it.

THE ROYAL ASTRONOMER

When William Herschel first observed Uranus, he thought he had discovered a comet or a star. His find proved to be much greater. King George III of England was so delighted with the discovery, he made Herschel his private astronomer. The king also gave Herschel the funds he needed to build larger telescopes, such as this.

Discover more in The Solar System

Neptune

Neptune is the smallest of the four gas planets and more than 2 billion miles (3 billion km) away from the Sun. Astronomers see a faint star when they view Neptune through a small telescope. This deep-blue planet is a bleak and windy place, with poisonous clouds made of methane ice crystals swirling around it. The planet's rocky core is about the size of the Earth, and is surrounded by a frozen layer of water and ammonia. Like the other gas planets, Neptune's atmosphere consists mainly of hydrogen. Neptune was discovered in 1846, but until *Voyager 2* sent pictures of it back to Earth in 1989, we understood very little about it. Now we know that Neptune has many faint rings and eight moons. The largest moon, Triton, is covered by ice and has mysterious features such as dark streaks. These could be caused by volcanoes erupting nitrogen, which becomes a liquid in Triton's intensely cold climate.

A BRIEF SPOTTING
Voyager 2 photographed this spinning storm cloud called the Great Dark Spot. Five years later, however, photographs from the Hubble Space Telescope showed that the spot had disappeared.

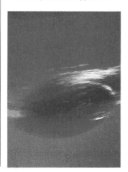

RULER OF THE SEVEN SEAS
The Romans believed that Neptune was the powerful god of the sea. His son Triton, who was half man and half fish, ruled the stormy waves with his father.

SURFACE ERUPTIONS
Triton, the Earth, Venus and Jupiter's moon Io are the only places in the solar system where there seems to be volcanic activity. But Triton's volcanoes are cold and erupt liquid nitrogen, not hot lava.

PICTURING NEPTUNE
The American space probe *Voyager 2*, shown here, was launched in 1977. Twelve years later, it reached Neptune on the distant edge of the solar system. Radio messages from the probe traveled to Earth at the speed of light.

THE DISCOVERY OF NEPTUNE

As astronomers in the nineteenth century plotted the course of the stars and planets in the solar system, they noticed that Uranus did not seem to follow its predicted orbit. Was the gravity from an undiscovered planet beyond Uranus affecting its orbit? Englishman John Couch Adams and Frenchman Urbain Le Verrier both calculated exactly where a mystery planet might lie. The German astronomer Johann Galle used their careful research, and in 1846 he

became the first person to see the new planet through his telescope.

Far left:
Urbain Le Verrier
Left: John
Couch Adams

Pluto

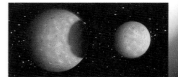

THE VIEW FROM SPACE
Pluto and Charon are very
close together. They
loom largely in
each other's
night sky.

Pluto lies in the far reaches of the solar system and is named after the Greek god of the dark underworld. This rocky planet is the smallest in the solar system and, usually, the farthest from the Sun. Pluto, however, has a strangely elongated orbit. It spends 20 years of the 248 years it takes to orbit the Sun inside the orbit of Neptune. Then it moves away and heads deeper into space. For most of Pluto's long year, the materials that make up its surface are frozen. But when Pluto moves closer to the Sun, some of these materials turn from solids into gases, and the planet has an atmosphere. Pluto was not discovered until 1930, and it has not yet been reached by a space probe. Although we know that it has a moon, called Charon, which takes about six days to circle Pluto, there is still much to learn about this distant speck in the night sky.

DID YOU KNOW?

Walt Disney, the famous American film-maker, created the droopy-eared cartoon character Pluto just a few months after the planet Pluto was found and named.

Neptune

Pluto

LOOPING THE LOOP

This diagram shows the oval-shaped orbit of Pluto around the Sun. Twice during its 248-year orbit, Pluto's path brings it closer than Neptune to the Sun.

THE VIEW FROM PLUTO

The shadow of the moon Charon falls on the icy surface of Pluto. Charon is half the size of Pluto, and Pluto is smaller than the Earth's moon.

THE SEARCH FOR THE MYSTERY PLANET

Astronomer Clyde Tombaugh (right) discovered Pluto in 1930. He had followed Percival Lowell's theories that a planet lay beyond Neptune, which could explain the irregular orbits of Neptune and Uranus. But astronomers soon realized that the discovery of Pluto did not explain this at all! Pluto was far too small to have such an effect on the planets' orbits. Some astronomers think that there is another, more massive planet farther away from Pluto. The search continues.

Comets

C omets are icy balls that sweep through the solar system. Long ago people thought these "long-haired stars," which appeared mysteriously and dramatically in the sky, were a sign that evil events were about to happen. Edmund Halley dispelled this idea in the eighteenth century by proving that comets, like all matter in the solar system, have set orbits around the Sun. Some comets pass near the Sun every few years. Others have long orbits and pass close to the Sun only once. As a comet gets closer to the Sun, its nucleus (center) begins to warm up and gives off a cloud of dust and gas called a coma. Astronomers can see the coma through a telescope because it reflects the fiery light of the Sun and becomes much larger than the Earth. As the comet journeys towards the Sun, the solar wind blows a stream of dust and gas away from the comet and the Sun. This forms the comet's tail, a spectacular streak of gas and dust that can trail for millions of miles into space.

STRANGE BUT TRUE
People in the past believed that comets brought disasters. In the fifteenth century, astrologers for the Archduke of Milan told him he had nothing to fear, except a comet. Unfortunately, a comet appeared in 1402. The archduke was seized with panic when he saw it, had some kind of attack, and died.

Gas tail
This is straight, narrow and usually fainter than the dust tail.

Coma
This envelope of gas surrounds the nucleus of the comet.

Nucleus
This is a mixture of ice and dust. It gives off a cloud of dust and gas when it is heated.

CLOSE-UP OF A COMET
The nucleus is the dirty snowball at the heart of a comet. It is so small that it cannot be seen from Earth by the naked eye. But we can see the huge coma, and the gas and dust tail (or sometimes tails) that stream behind the comet.

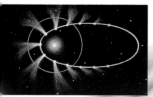

COMET'S TAIL
As a comet orbits the Sun, its tail grows and fades, but always points away from the Sun.

Dust tail
This is usually curved and is made up of gases pushed away from the Sun by the solar wind.

RETURN OF THE COMET

Halley's Comet is probably the most famous of all comets. Edmund Halley (top) was the first person to calculate that the appearance of three separate comets through the years was, in fact, the return of one comet every 76 years. The comet was named after him when he successfully predicted its return in 1758. In early times, Halley's Comet terrified those who saw it. In 1910, we had an opportunity to view the comet at close range as the Earth passed through the comet's tail. In 1986, spacecraft from different nations went out to meet Halley's Comet (bottom). The comet is now beyond the orbit of Uranus, east of the constellation of Orion. In 2062, Halley's Comet will once again brighten the sky.

COMET LEVY
Comets are often named after the people who first saw them. In 1990, Comet Levy lit the sky all night long.

587

Asteroids and Meteoroids

The solar system has many different members, the smallest of which are asteroids and meteoroids. Asteroids are small rocky bodies that never came together in the early days of the solar system to form larger planets. Most asteroids lie in the enormous space between the orbits of Mars and Jupiter, an area called the asteroid belt. Ceres, the largest of these asteroids and the first to be discovered, is almost 500 miles (800 km) wide. Most asteroids, however, are much smaller. Meteoroids are dust particles that travel along the orbital paths of comets. When a meteoroid encounters the Earth's upper atmosphere at high speed, it usually burns up and forms a bright meteor. Some people call this brief streak of light a "shooting star." Larger meteors that pierce the Earth's atmosphere and crash to the ground, making craters where they land, are called meteorites.

ASTEROID ORBITS

Not all asteroids orbit in the main belt between Mars and Jupiter (the larger planet in this picture). Two groups of asteroids called Trojans share Jupiter's orbit. Other asteroids cross the orbit of the Earth.

FLYING OBJECTS IN SPACE

On its June 1983 voyage, the space shuttle *Challenger* was hit by a tiny particle, possibly a meteoroid or a speck of paint left by a spacecraft on a previous mission. The shuttle and the small particle were traveling so fast that the impact left a small crater in the shuttle's window (below). Even the tiniest object moving at high speed is dangerous in space.

DID YOU KNOW?

In 1992, an asteroid called Toutatis passed close to Earth and astronomer Steve Ostro was able to bounce radar signals off it. From the reflection on the radar, he was able to discover that Toutatis actually looked like two asteroids close together.

LOOK OUT BELOW!

These children are standing next to one of the largest meteorites in the world. Long ago, the Inuit (Eskimos) of Cape York in Greenland worshipped this object from the sky.

MAKING ITS MARK

Astronomers calculate that large asteroids collide with the Earth every hundred thousand years or so. This crater at Gosse Bluff in the Northern Territory of Australia is the result of such a collision.

Discover more in The Solar System

Impacts in the Solar System

A bout 3.9 billion years ago, in the early days of the solar system, bright comets and asteroids orbited the Sun. These huge bodies bombarded the planets and caused enormous damage, such as the craters we can see on the Moon, Mercury and Mars, and which were once visible on Earth. Many scientists believe that the impact of a comet or an asteroid on Earth may have played some part in the extinction of the dinosaurs 65 million years ago. Impacts in the solar system caused great devastation, but it seems that they may have also made it possible for life to begin on Earth. When comets from the cool outer reaches of the solar system struck the Earth, they released carbon, hydrogen, oxygen and nitrogen into the Earth's atmosphere (these had been lost early in the Earth's history). These organic materials are essential to life forms. Life itself is based on carbon, while hydrogen and oxygen make up water (H_2O), without which plants and animals could not survive.

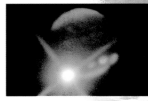

IMPACTING STILL
Major impacts still happen today, but not usually on Earth. In July 1994, Comet Shoemaker–Levy 9 collided with Jupiter and caused several brilliant explosions.

DID YOU KNOW?

Most evidence of impacts on the Earth has been worn away by erosion and the movement of the Earth's crust. The Moon, however, still shows the scars of impacts that happened several billion years ago.

IMPACTS ON EARTH
In this imagined scene, a *Tyrannosaurus* is interrupted from its meal by shattering sounds and lights as a comet hits the Earth. A major earthquake soon follows, and temperatures become as high as boiling water. A thick cloud of debris settles over the whole world, bringing months of darkness, cold and sulfuric acid rain. Many species of life eventually die in such conditions.

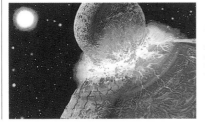

EARLY IMPACTS
Impacts in the early solar system were very common. When a huge body such as this collided with the Earth, it may have formed the Earth's Moon.

ANCIENT IMPACTS

When the Moon is near its full phase, you can see a number of dark areas. Most of these areas are huge impact basins—the lava-filled remains of ancient collisions. If you look at the Moon with a pair of binoculars or a small telescope, you will also see many craters on its surface—the results of asteroid or comet crashes.

STAGES OF A LUNAR ECLIPSE
These photographs show the progress
of a lunar eclipse, from the first bite
of the Earth's shadow on the Moon's
surface to the total phase and beyond.

• OUR NEIGHBORHOOD •

Eclipses

The Sun sends its light far into space. As light falls on the Earth and the Moon, both cast a shadow. An eclipse of the Moon (a lunar eclipse) occurs when the shadow of the Earth darkens the Moon. The Moon sometimes becomes coppery red or even brownish as the Earth's shadow marches across its surface. An eclipse of the Sun (a solar eclipse) occurs when the Moon passes in front of the Sun and blocks the light to places along a narrow strip of the Earth's surface. A strange darkness falls on the land and temperatures drop. The Moon is 400 times smaller than the Sun, but it can hide the light of such an enormous star because the Sun is so far away from the Moon. When we look at the Sun and the Moon in the sky, they appear to be almost the same size. Solar eclipses occur in cycles. One eclipse will be very similar to another that happened more than 18 years earlier, but they will not be at the same place.

CLOAKING THE SUN
Eclipses can be either partial, if only part of the Sun or Moon is covered; or total, if the whole is hidden from view. This time-lapse photograph shows the progress of a total eclipse of the Sun. The Moon takes just over an hour to cover the Sun completely. It hides the light from the Sun's surface and allows us to see the Sun's faint, ghostly corona.

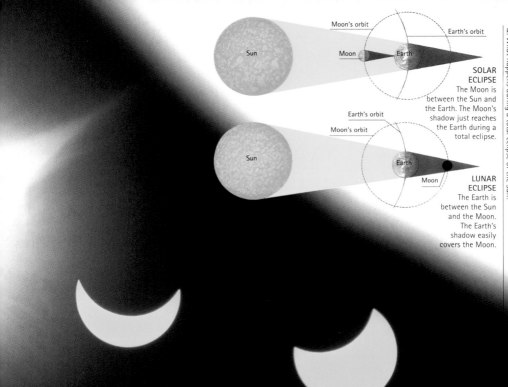

SOLAR ECLIPSE
The Moon is between the Sun and the Earth. The Moon's shadow just reaches the Earth during a total eclipse.

LUNAR ECLIPSE
The Earth is between the Sun and the Moon. The Earth's shadow easily covers the Moon.

VIEWING A SOLAR ECLIPSE

Eclipses are unforgettable sights that we would all like to see, but the Sun is very dangerous to look at without proper protection for your eyes. Permanent blindness can result from the shortest look through binoculars or telescopes. The eyepiece filters that are often supplied with small telescopes are not safe, either. The girl in this picture is safely viewing an eclipse without a telescope. With the Sun behind her, she holds a piece of paper with a hole through it. The light passes through the hole and projects an image of the eclipse onto another piece of paper in front of her.

Discover more in The Sun

593

The Life Cycle of a Star

Picture a huge, dark cloud (a nebula) in space. When a nearby star explodes, a shock wave travels through the cloud. The cloud begins to shrink and divide into even smaller swirling clouds. The center, called the protostar, gets hotter and hotter until it ignites and a new star is born. All the stars in the sky were born from clouds of gas and dust. The hottest stars are blue-white in color and burn their hydrogen fuel very quickly. The Sun, a small yellow star, burns hydrogen more steadily. Proxima Centauri, the closest star to the Sun, burns its gas very slowly and is a cool, red star. The speed at which the stars burn hydrogen determines how long they will live. Blue giants have a short life, and explode dramatically. The Sun will continue to burn for another 5 billion years. Then it will expand into a large red giant and finally shrink to a white dwarf. Proxima Centauri, however, will remain unchanged for tens of billions of years.

THE ORION NEBULA
Orion is one of the best known groups of stars (constellations) in the sky. Some 1,600 light years away and 25 light years wide, the Great Nebula in Orion is a stellar nursery, a place where new stars are being born out of interstellar gas.

White dwarf
After the planetary nebula disappears, all that remains is a small, hot, faint star.

THE CYCLE OF LIFE
The main diagram shows the different stages in the life of a star such as the Sun. This kind of star lasts for many billions of years. As it uses up its hydrogen, it begins to swell and will become, briefly, as large as the orbit of the Earth. Then it will shrink to become a white dwarf, slowly cooling for many billions of years.

Planetary nebula
Later in its life, a star slowly blows off its outer layers to form a planetary nebula that eventually disappears.

Protostar
The center of the nebula gets hotter as it shrinks, finally creating a new star.

Life of a star
Massive stars live for perhaps several hundred million years. Smaller stars last for many billions of years.

A BLACK HOLE

After a very heavy star uses up its hydrogen and explodes as a supernova, its core becomes smaller and smaller until finally it is smaller than the head of a pin. The star, however, still has gravity. This is so strong that even light from a few miles around the star cannot escape. This is called a black hole.

A SUPERNOVA
For a few days, a supernova (above left) can outshine an entire galaxy of hundreds of billions of stars. Then it becomes a tiny dot, as shown by the arrow.

THE HORSEHEAD NEBULA
A nebula is a bright or dark cloud made up of gas or dust, or sometimes both. The Horsehead Nebula is very dark and can only be seen against a background of stars or a bright nebula.

Red giant
Late in its life, a star grows to form a red giant with an enormous surface area.

Discover more in Asteroids and Meteoroids

595

• OUR UNIVERSE •

Strange Stars

S tars are giant balls of hot gas. Their range of size, color, temperature and brightness varies enormously. They can be members of a pair, triplet or a huge cluster of hundreds or thousands of stars. The color of a star indicates how hot it is: cool stars are red, hot stars are bluish. Many of the stars studied by astronomers are in pairs and orbit each other. These "binary stars" often differ in brightness and color: a dim white dwarf, for example, might orbit a red giant. Stars that make up a binary pair are usually a great distance from each other, but some are so close they almost touch. These stars are called contact binaries and as they are so close, they have to orbit each other very rapidly. The smaller star is very dense and its gravity constantly sucks hydrogen gas away from the larger star. The big star becomes distorted and turns into a distinctive teardrop shape.

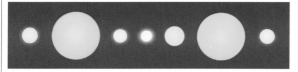

A CHANGE OF SIZE
Some stars grow bigger and smaller, as shown above. The most famous and important of these are called Cepheid variables. Their color, temperature and brightness change with their size.

QUICK FLASHES
A small, extremely dense neutron star is often all that remains of a star after it has become a supernova. It rotates in a second or less, and if we see the quick flashes we call it a pulsar.

A MEETING OF MATTERS

In this contact binary system, the large
star looks much more impressive and
powerful. But the small, dense star
has the real power. It has a stronger
gravitational pull than the big star
and is able to drag matter away and
distort the shape of the large star.

EXPLODING STARS

What happens to all the hydrogen that
the small star takes from the large
star in a binary star system? The small star
has no use for it and the hydrogen collects
in a disk. When enough hydrogen has built
up, over months, decades or possibly
centuries, it blows up in a huge nuclear
explosion. The star brightens 100 times or
more for a few days. Once the explosion
has died away, the process begins again.

Discover more in The Life Cycle of a Star

597

Galaxies

alaxies are enormous families of stars that lie scattered
across the never-ending space of the universe. Each galaxy
contains many millions of stars—a mixture of giant and
dwarf stars, old and young stars, and clusters of stars. Some
galaxies are spiral in shape, while others are elliptical (like a
flattened circle). Those that do not seem to have much of a shape
at all are called irregular galaxies. There are countless numbers of
galaxies, and they are grouped together in clusters. Our solar
system, for example, is part of the Milky Way Galaxy. This belongs
to a collection of galaxies called the Local Group, which contains
about 25 galaxies, such as the Large and Small Magellanic Clouds.
The Andromeda Galaxy, the largest member of our cluster, is so
huge we can see it in a very dark sky without a telescope. It lies
more than 2 million light years away from Earth. Light reaching
us now from the Andromeda Galaxy began its journey across
space long ago when the earliest humans lived on Earth.

NEIGHBORING GALAXY
The spiral Andromeda Galaxy is the nearest major
galaxy to the Milky Way. It contains hundreds of
billions of stars and its spiral arms are mottled
with bright and dark nebulae.

HUBBLE DEEP FIELD
This view of the universe, made by combining
a series of images, was taken by the Hubble
Space Telescope in December 1995. It shows
several hundred galaxies never seen before.

SPIRAL
The arms of a normal spiral galaxy are filled with stars and gas clouds.

BARRED SPIRAL
A barred spiral galaxy has a bar of stars across its center. The spiral arms begin at the ends of the bar.

ELLIPTICAL GALAXY
Giant elliptical galaxies are massive. This galaxy has 5 trillion stars.

IRREGULAR GALAXY
Irregular galaxies have random shapes, and they are smaller than the Milky Way.

A LIGHT FROM THE EDGE OF THE UNIVERSE

Quasars are extraordinarily powerful beacons, scattered deep in the universe. The word "quasar" stands for "quasi-stellar" (resembling a star), but quasars have far more energy than stars. A quasar called 3C-273 is several billion light years away from Earth, yet it is bright enough to be seen with a large amateur telescope. Such brilliance suggests huge size, but quasars are probably less than one light year across. Astronomers believe that a quasar is a black hole at the center of a distant galaxy, which consumes all the matter around it. The whirling matter being sucked into the hole creates an amazing source of energy and powerful "jets" of material (right), which are projected out of the galaxy's glowing core.

Discover more in The Universe

599

The Milky Way

On a clear night, the sky is speckled with thousands of stars. In fact, these are just a few of the 200 billion stars belonging to our galaxy, the Milky Way. From Earth, the thickest part of the Milky Way looks like a patchy band of white light stretching into space. But the Milky Way is actually shaped like a spiral, and is about 100,000 light years across. It has at least two major arms, made up of dusty nebulae and brilliant blue-white stars. Older yellow and red stars form the nucleus of the galaxy. As Earth lies way out on one of the arms of the galaxy, 30,000 light years from the center, it is very difficult for us to imagine what the galaxy looks like from the outside. Clouds of dust and gas also block much of our view of the middle of the galaxy. Astronomers, however, have recently determined that a huge object, possibly a black hole, lies in the center of the Milky Way.

A VIEW FROM THE UNIVERSE
The Milky Way would look like a mighty spiral of stars, gas clouds and dust if viewed from one of the distant globular clusters.

600

DID YOU KNOW?

The Milky Way is shaped like a pinwheel, but it does not rotate as one large disk. Different stars move at different speeds. The Sun, for example, takes 220 million years to complete a trip around the center of the Milky Way.

STUDYING THE MILKY WAY

Astronomer Bart Bok (below) and his scientist wife Priscilla Fairfield devoted their lives to unraveling the mysteries of the Milky Way. By careful observation, they mapped out the spiral arms of the galaxy. They also studied the great clouds that illuminate the sky in the constellations of Orion and Carina, and tried to piece together how new stars are born from these clouds.

OUTSIDE LOOKING IN
If you could look at the Milky Way from the outside, you would see a central bulge surrounded by a thin disk that contains the spiral arms.

Discover more in Galaxies

Into Space

PROBING SPACE
The Japanese space probe
Tenma looks at objects in
space, such as black holes
and supernovas, which
have much energy.

I n 1957, Russia launched the first artificial satellite, *Sputnik 1*, into orbit. The Space Age had begun. Four years later, Russian Yuri Gagarin became the first person in space, and President Kennedy declared that the United States would put a man on the Moon by the end of the decade. In 1969, the *Apollo 11* spacecraft, attached to the biggest rocket ever built, pierced the Earth's atmosphere and headed towards the Moon. Astronaut Neil Armstrong's first words and steps on the scarred surface of the Moon soon became history. In the last 30 years, we have explored and discovered much about space, the stars and the planets. Spacecraft have flown past all the planets and their moons, except Pluto on the edge of the solar system; there have been several expeditions to the Moon; and space probes have landed on both Mars and Venus. Space shuttles are sent regularly into space as workhorses. Their crews sometimes repair the many satellites orbiting the Earth, such as communication satellites, which send telephone and television signals all around the world.

LIVING IN SPACE
This is an imagined space station of the future. It is much bigger than the Soviet Mir space station, which was launched in 1986. People are aboard Mir most of the time, and the longest stay by one person so far has been a year.

LAUNCHING INTO SPACE

Space shuttles are very special spacecraft. They are
designed to be used many times, taking heavy objects,
such as space probes, around the Earth; and carrying crews
for scientific research into space. They have three parts: an
orbiter, an external tank, and two solid rocket boosters. The
first space shuttle in 1981 carried two astronauts. Today,
they can take a crew of up to eight people.

ON THE MOON
Even the simplest tasks require
great planning and patience in
the low gravity of the Moon.
This astronaut is collecting a
rock sample, which will be
examined back on Earth.

Discover more in The Earth's Moon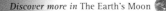

Imagined Worlds

A CITY ON MARS
In an imagined world on
Mars, a spaceship prepares
to land on the red surface of
the planet. A space base,
where people live and carry
out research, has been built
in the shelter of a deep valley.

I s there life on other planets? Astronomers and science-fiction
writers have considered this question for years. Aliens, mutant
monsters and other life forms, both menacing and friendly,
have starred in many books, films and series, such as *Star Wars*
and *Star Trek*. People all over the world regularly report sightings
of Unidentified Flying Objects (UFOs) and encounters with strange
beings from space. Is this fact or fiction? Many astronomers
believe that life-forming conditions do exist elsewhere in the
Milky Way. For many years, people looked to our solar system
and thought that Mars was the other planet most likely to
support life. Technology has now made it possible to study
Mars in detail and this idea today seems unlikely. Much of
space, however, remains unknown territory. Science-fiction
writers imagine worlds and events beyond our own.
In 1865, writer Jules Verne predicted that we
would reach the Moon. Some of our imagined
worlds may also come true.

ANYONE OUT THERE?

I n New South Wales, Australia, the
Parkes radio telescope has been
listening to the heavens for more than
30 years. But in 1995, as part of Project
Phoenix (a worldwide search for life in
outer space), the telescope examined
areas around some nearby stars for
regular signals that could come from
intelligent life. The normal levels of
radiation in the universe produce a
random noisy hiss. If a radio telescope
picks up a more orderly signal, such as
that from a radio transmission, this could
be evidence that life exists elsewhere.

WORLDS AWAY
The covers of these
science-fiction magazines
from the 1920s show strange
forms of life on Neptune
(right) and Venus (far right).

A CITY ON NEPTUNE
The complete story of this city of
the Reptile Men is told on page 144

STRANGE BUT TRUE

The distances in space are astronomical.
In order to move from one star system to
another, the makers of *Star Trek* developed the
idea of traveling at what they called warp
speed, which is many times faster than the
speed of light. Such speed would be essential
to make travel between the stars possible
within a human lifetime.

Facts and Figures

SOLAR ECLIPSES

Solar eclipses can be partial (when only a part of the Sun is blocked from the Earth's view), total (when the Sun is totally blocked from the Earth's view) or annular (when the Sun's light is still visible around the edge of the Moon).

DATE	TYPE OF ECLIPSE	AREA FROM WHICH ECLIPSE CAN BEST BE VIEWED
April 17, 1996	partial	New Zealand, Antarctica, South Pacific
October 12, 1996	partial	Greenland, Iceland, Europe, North Africa
March 8–9, 1997	total	Russia, eastern Asia, Arctic, northwest North America, Japan
September 1–2, 1997	partial	Antarctica, South Pacific, New Zealand, Australia
February 26, 1998	total	Pacific, Central America, Atlantic, West Indies
August 21–22, 1998	annular	Malaysia, Indonesia, Philippines
February 16, 1999	annular	Australia
August 11, 1999	total	Atlantic, United Kingdom, Europe, India
February 5, 2000	partial	Antarctica
July 1, 2000	partial	Southern Chile
July 31, 2000	partial	Northwest Canada, Siberia, Alaska
June 21, 2001	total	Angola, Mozambique, Zambia, Madagascar
December 14, 2001	annular	Costa Rica, Nicaragua

LUNAR ECLIPSES

Lunar eclipses can be either partial (when the Moon is only partially covered by the Earth's shadow) or total (when the Moon is totally covered by the Earth's shadow).

DATE	TYPE OF ECLIPSE	AREA FROM WHICH ECLIPSE CAN BEST BE VIEWED
April 3–4, 1996	total	Africa, South America, Europe
September 27, 1996	total	Nth America, Central America, Sth America, Europe, Africa
March 24, 1997	partial	North America, Alaska, Hawaii
September 16, 1997	total	Asia, Africa, Europe, Australasia
July 28, 1999	partial	North America
January 21, 2000	total	North and South America
July 1, 2000	partial	Southern Chile
July 16, 2000	total	Pacific Ocean, Australia, eastern Asia
January 9, 2001	total	Asia, Africa, Europe
July 5, 2001	partial	Australia, eastern Asia

SELECTED MILESTONES IN SPACE EXPLORATION

Since the mid-1950s, space has been explored by many types of spacecraft. Satellites, rockets, probes (to the Moon and between the planets) and shuttles have supplied us with a wealth of knowledge about our solar system.

October 4, 1957	September 15, 1959	April 12, 1961	December 14, 1962	July 31, 1964	July 14, 1965	March 1, 1966
Sputnik 1 (USSR) First satellite launched into space.	*Luna 2* (USSR) First rocket reached the Moon.	*Vostok 1* (USSR) Yuri Gagarin first human in space.	*Mariner 2* (USA) Flew past Venus.	*Ranger 7* (USA) Close-range photographs of Moon.	*Mariner 4* (USA) Flew past Mars.	*Venera 3* (USSR) Landed on Venus

PLANET FACTS

A comparison of the planets that make up our solar system shows the vast differences between them.

PLANET	DISTANCE FROM SUN (million miles/km)	MASS (as a fraction of Earth's mass)	DIAMETER (as a fraction of Earth's diameter)	NUMBER OF MOONS
Mercury	36 (58)	0.06	0.4	0
Venus	67 (108)	0.8	0.9	0
Earth	93 (150)	1.0	1.0	1
Mars	141 (228)	0.1	0.5	2
Jupiter	482 (778)	318	11.2	16
Saturn	885 (1,427)	95	9.4	18
Uranus	1,780 (2,871)	14.5	4.0	15
Neptune	2,788 (4,497)	17	3.9	8
Pluto	3,666 (5,913)	0.002	0.2	1

METEOR SHOWERS

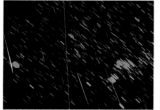

These are caused by the debris left by comets. The main annual meteor showers and their dates (which can vary by one day) are shown below. The number of meteors you see depends on the strength of the shower (sometimes as many as 50 meteors in one hour), how much moonlight is in the sky and whether you are watching them from a city or country area.

NAME OF SHOWER	DATE OF MAXIMUM ACTIVITY	COMMENT
Quadrantids	January 3	last only a few hours
Lyrids	April 22	from Comet Thatcher—produce some very bright meteors
Eta Aquarids	May 5	from Comet Halley
Delta Aquarids	July 30	a strong shower, especially with the help of the Perseids
Perseids	August 12	from Comet Swift–Tuttle
Orionids	October 22	from Comet Halley
Taurids	November 3–5	from Comet Encke—fireballs
Leonids	November 18	from Comet Tempel–Tuttle—major storm possible in 1999
Geminids	December 14	these and Perseids are the year's best showers

July 20, 1969
Apollo 11 (USA)
Humans landed on the Moon.

December 3, 1973
Pioneer 10 (USA)
Flew past Jupiter.

July 20, 1976
Viking 1 (USA)
Landed on Mars to search for life.

September 1, 1979
Pioneer 11 (USA)
Flew past Saturn.

January 24, 1986
Voyager 2 (USA)
Flew past Uranus.

March 6, 1986
Vega 1 (USSR)
Photographs of Comet Halley.

August 25, 1989
Voyager 2 (USA)
Flew past Neptune.

Glossary

Venus flytrap

Water lily

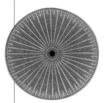

Diatom

Eucalypt flowers

Dandelion

aa Lava that hardens with a rough, broken surface.

abdomen The part of an animal's body that contains the digestive system and the organs of reproduction. In insects and spiders, the abdomen makes up the rear of the body.

abyssal plain A flat, barren area under the sea that spreads from the mid-oceanic ridge to where the continents begin.

active volcano A volcano that can erupt at any time.

adaptation A change that occurs in an animal's behavior or body to allow it to survive and reproduce in new conditions.

aerial roots Roots that absorb water from the air.

aftershock A tremor that occurs after the main shaking of an earthquake has passed.

alevin The young of salmon, which hatch in gravel on river beds.

algae Simple plants that grow in water, have no true roots, stems or leaves but do manufacture their own food through photosynthesis.

altocumulus Puffy, white clouds at mid-altitude.

altostratus A layer of clouds at mid-altitude.

alveoli Tiny air sacs in the lungs where oxygen is absorbed into the blood.

ambush When animals hide (using their own camouflage, or by concealing themselves), keep very still, then attack the surprised prey.

amphibians Vertebrate animals that can live on land and in water. They include frogs, salamanders, toads and newts. From the Greek meaning "two worlds," amphibians have moist skin and lay their eggs in water.

amphisbaenians Burrowing, legless "worm lizards" found in Southeast Asia, Europe, the United States and Africa. Their heads are similar in shape to their tails, and their name means "going both ways."

anatomy The scientific study of the body's structure.

ancestor A plant or animal from which a later form of plant or animal evolved.

anemometer An instrument that measures wind direction and speed.

angiogram A special X-ray that shows blood vessels, usually arteries.

ankylosaurs Members of a group of late Cretaceous dinosaurs that spread throughout North America and East Asia. They were heavily armored with thick plates of bone, spikes and bony nodules in the skin of their back and sides.

annuals Plants that complete their life cycle—that is, germinate, grow to maturity, disperse their seeds and die—within a single year.

Antarctic The extremely cold region at the South Pole, which is south of the Antarctic Circle.

antenna A slender organ on an animal's head that it uses to sense its surroundings. Insects have two antennae, which are often known as "feelers."

anther The part of the stamen (male reproductive organ) that produces pollen.

anticyclone A system of rotating winds spiralling out from a high pressure area. Generally associated with stable weather.

antivenin A medicine to counteract the effects of venom from snake bites and the bites or stings of other venomous animals.

antlers Bony growths from the head of deer and moose that grow and shed during the year.

aquatic Living all or most of the time in water.

arachnid An arthropod with four pairs of walking legs. Arachnids make up the class Arachnida, and include spiders, scorpions, mites and ticks.

archosaurs A major group of reptiles that includes the living crocodilians as well as the extinct dinosaurs, pterosaurs and thecodontians.

Arctic The very cold region at the North Pole, which is north of the Arctic Circle.

artery A blood vessel that carries blood away from the heart.

arthropod An animal with jointed legs and a hard exoskeleton. Arthropods make up the largest group of animals on Earth and include insects, spiders, crustaceans, centipedes and millipedes.

artiodactyl An ungulate, or hoofed mammal, that has an even number of toes. An artiodactyl has either two toes, such as camels; or four toes, such as deer, cattle, sheep, goats and giraffes.

ash Small fragments of rock and lava blown out of a volcano during an eruption.

asteroid A small, rocky body that can be as large as 600 miles (about 1,000 km) in diameter. It is sometimes called a minor planet. Many asteroids orbit in the main asteroid belt between Mars and Jupiter.

asthenosphere The soft, squishy section of the Earth's mantle.

astrology The belief that the movements of the Sun, Moon and planets affect people's personalities and lives.

astronomy The scientific study of the solar system, our galaxy and the universe.

atmosphere The layer, or envelope, of gas that surrounds a planet.

atmospheric pressure The force exerted by air on its surroundings.

atom The smallest piece that an element can be divided into and still keep its chemical properties.

atrium One of the two small, thin-walled upper chambers of the heart.

aurora A display of colored lights in the sky that makes the Earth's upper atmosphere glow. It is caused by streams of particles from the Sun and happens most around the polar regions.

avalanche A mass of snow, ice or rock that breaks off from a high ledge and slides down a steep slope, picking up more material along the way.

axis An imaginary line through the center of planets and satellites around which they rotate.

barometer An instrument for measuring atmospheric pressure.

basalt An extrusive igneous rock formed when runny lava cools and becomes solid.

basin A large, cup-shaped dent in the sea floor.

bathysphere A sphere-shaped diving vessel used by scientists to study deep-sea life.

bathythermograph A scientific instrument used to measure underwater temperatures.

Thistles

Drip tip leaf

Roses

Cactus

Conifer seeds

Garden spider

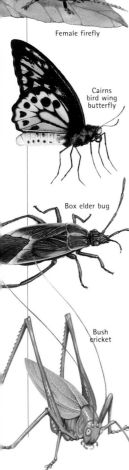

Female firefly

Cairns bird wing butterfly

Box elder bug

Bush cricket

beak The sharp, sometimes hooked bill of a bird of prey, which is used to spear, carry and tear prey.

Beaufort Scale This is used to indicate the strength of the wind at sea.

Big Bang theory The theory that the universe was formed as the result of a massive expansion of matter and energy.

Big Crunch theory The theory that the universe as we know it will collapse back in on itself and end.

bile A yellowish fluid made by the liver and stored in the gall bladder. It helps to digest fats and get rid of waste products.

binary star system A pair of stars that are bound to each other by their mutual gravity. The two stars orbit each other around a common center of gravity, which is a point between them.

bioluminescence The production of light by living organisms, such as the bacteria that live on some deep-sea fish.

bipedal Walking on two legs.

birds of prey Flesh-eating birds, such as hawks, eagles, owls and vultures.

black hole The last stage in the life of a galaxy or a massive star when they collapse and keep on collapsing until even light cannot escape from them.

black smoker A volcanic hot spring emerging from an active spreading ridge on the ocean floor.

blizzard A snowstorm with strong winds.

blowhole The nostril (can be one or two) on top of a whale's head through which it breathes.

bone A hard type of body tissue that provides strength and support for the body.

bract Modified leaf, often small but sometimes large and brightly colored,

at the base of a flower.

browser A plant-eating mammal that uses its hands or lips to pick leaves from trees and bushes (for example, koalas and giraffes) or low-growing plants (for example, the black rhino).

bulb Condensed, and usually underground, stem and leaves in which the plant's food reserves are stored.

caldera A crater usually more than 3 miles (5 km) in diameter formed by an explosion or powerful volcanic eruption.

camouflage The way an animal blends into its environment or looks like another animal in order to sneak up on prey or avoid enemies.

canine teeth The teeth between the front incisors and the side molars of mammals.

capillary The smallest type of blood vessel, which is much thinner than a hair. Substances such as oxygen and nutrients can easily pass through its very thin walls.

carapace The upper or back part of a turtle or a tortoise's shell. The bottom part is called the plastron.

carbon dioxide Gas absorbed by plants during photosynthesis and given out by plants, animals and humans during respiration.

cardiac Relating to the heart.

carnivore An animal that eats mainly meat. Most carnivorous animals are predators, or hunters, while some are both hunters and scavengers.

carnosaurs Large carnivorous, or meat-eating, theropod (saurischian) dinosaurs such as *Megalosaurus*, *Allosaurus* and *Tyrannosaurus*. Some paleontologists believe carnosaurs, which ranged from 16 ft (5 m) to 39 ft (12 m) long, were scavengers as well as predators.

carpel The female seed-bearing organ of a flowering plant, which contains the stigma (on a stalk or style) and the ovary.

cartilage A smooth, slippery, slightly soft body tissue. It covers bones where they touch in joints, and forms the framework of body parts such as the ears and nose.

cartographer A person who is specially trained to draw maps.

cell The basic unit or structure from which all plants and animals are made. Each microscopic cell has a special function or purpose.

cellulose Carbohydrate in plant cell walls that makes them strong and rigid.

Cenozoic Era This period began with the extinction of the dinosaurs 65 million years ago and is known as the Age of Mammals.

cephalothorax In spiders, other arachnids and crustaceans, a region of the body that combines the head and thorax. It is covered by a hard body case.

ceratopians Late Cretaceous horned dinosaurs that existed for 20 million years. They established themselves all over western North America and central Asia, where they lived in large herds.

ceratosaurs Medium-sized theropods distinguished by the small crests or bony horns on their noses.

cerebral Relating to the main part of the brain, the cerebrum.

chelicerae Pincerlike biting mouthparts of spiders, scorpions, ticks and mites.

chelonian A turtle or tortoise. A member of the order Chelonia, one of the four major groups of reptiles.

chitin A hard substance that gives an exoskeleton its strength.

chlorofluorocarbons (CFCs) Synthetic substances used in aerosol sprays, refrigeration, foam plastics and fire extinguishers.

chlorophyll A green pigment in special plant cells that absorbs energy from sunlight for use in photosynthesis (food making).

chloroplasts Structures within plant cells that contain the green chlorophyll.

chromosome A dark, X-shaped structure inside a cell that carries genetic information in the form of the chemical, DNA.

chromosphere A thin layer of atmosphere surrounding the Sun. It lies between the Sun's photosphere and its corona.

chyme Partly digested food that oozes from the stomach into the small intestine.

cilia Tiny hairs on cells, such as those lining the airways, which wave back and forth to move substances.

cirrocumulus High altitude, fluffy clouds.

cirrostratus A layer of high-altitude clouds.

cirrus High altitude, wispy clouds made of ice crystals.

claws Sharp, curved nails on the toes of animals that are used to catch prey, to dig and to climb.

climate The average weather conditions in a particular region over a period of at least 30 years.

cloaca The internal chamber in fish, amphibians, reptiles and birds into which the contents of the reproductive ducts and the waste ducts empty before being passed from the body.

cloud A visible mass of water droplets and ice floating in the air, formed when water condenses.

cluster A gathering of stars or galaxies

Cockroach

Mosquito

Tortoise beetle

Looper caterpillar

Queen ant

611

Pond turtle

Dwarf caiman

Baby
chameleon

Coral snake

Horned chameleon

bound together by gravity. Loosely bound groups of several hundred stars are called open clusters; tightly bound congregations of hundreds of thousands of stars are called globular clusters.

cocoon A case made of silk. Many insects use cocoons to protect themselves while they are pupae. Female spiders often spin a cocoon to protect their eggs.

coelurosaurs Small, light carnivorous saurischians. Coelurosaurs (the name means "hollow-tailed lizard") lived from the Late Triassic to the late Cretaceous Period in North America, Europe and Africa. These delicately built hunters ranged from 4-ft (1.2-m) long *Procompsognathus*, to 13-ft (4-m) long *Gallimimus*.

cold-blooded An animal that cannot keep its body at more or less the same temperature by internal means.

colony A group of animals that live, hunt and defend themselves together.

comet A body of dust and ice that orbits the Sun. As the comet nears the Sun, it boils and becomes brighter. It forms a coma of gas and dust and sometimes one or two prominent tails.

competitors Two or more animals that may fight for the same food, territory or mating partner.

complete metamorphosis A way of developing in which a young insect changes shape from an egg to a larva, to a pupa, to an adult. Beetles and butterflies develop by complete metamorphosis.

compound eye An eye that is divided into many smaller eyes, each with its own lens.

concertina locomotion A kind of movement used by some legless lizards and snakes in narrow passageways. The front of the body is extended forward,

pressed against the sides of the walls, then the rest of the body is pulled forward.

condensation When water changes from a vapor to a liquid.

cone In the retina of the eye, a type of cell that makes nerve signals when light shines on it. Cones detect colors and fine details.

conifers A group of mostly evergreen trees that produce seeds inside cones and usually have needle-shaped or scaly leaves.

conservation Looking after the Earth's resources for future generations.

constellation A group of stars that seems to make a pattern in the sky. Astronomers divide the sky into 88 constellations.

continent One of the seven main land masses of the globe: Europe, Asia, Africa, North America, South America, Australia, Antarctica.

continental drift A theory proposed by Alfred Wegener whereby the continents were once joined together as one land mass, and then, over millions of years, drifted apart.

continental shelf A flat, projecting extension of land submerged beneath a shallow sea.

continental slope The gently sloping, submerged land near the coast that forms the side of an ocean basin.

convection The upward movement of a mass of warm air, rising through cooler, denser air.

convection currents A form of motion produced by heat in the mantle. Hot rock moves up and cold rock sinks. This provides the power to move the layers of rock within the Earth and the lithospheric plates across the surface of the Earth.

convective zone An area within a star

where hot material moves upwards to cooler regions and back again, much like the movement of water when it boils.

convergent evolution The situation where different, unrelated kinds of animals in different parts of the world evolve to look similar because they live in similar ways.

coprolite A dinosaur dropping that has fossilized.

coral polyp A tube-shaped animal with a soft body and a circle of tentacles on top.

coral reef A structure that is made from the skeletons of soft-bodied coral animals or polyps, and is found in warm waters.

core The core of the Earth is its central area (both solid and liquid) composed largely of iron. The core of the Sun is its inner quarter where the temperature is high enough for nuclear fusion to occur.

Coriolis effect The deflection of winds caused by the spinning of the Earth.

corona The outermost layer of the Sun's atmosphere where the temperature is nearly 2 million°F (more than 1 million°C). The inner part of the corona can be seen during solar eclipses.

cortex The outer layer of a body part, such as the kidney, adrenal gland or brain.

crater A funnel-shaped opening at the top of a volcano. Craters usually have a diameter of 6/10 mile (1 km) or less.

crater lake The body of water that gathers in the volcano's crater when lava cools and blocks the vent.

crescent phase (for the Moon, Mercury or Venus) The part of the cycle when less than half of the face is visible from Earth.

crest A line of large, scaly spines on a lizard's neck and back.

Cretaceous Period The geological period from 145 to 65 million years ago.

crocodilian A crocodile, caiman, alligator, gharial or tomistoma. A member of the order Crocodilia.

crust The hard, outer layer of the Earth, which is closest to the surface. The crust under the continents is usually about 25 miles (40 km) thick. The crust under the oceans is only about 3 miles (5 km) thick.

crustacean An animal such as a lobster, crab or prawn that has a hard skeleton on the outside of its body.

crystal A solid substance made up of atoms, molecules or ions for example, an ice crystal made of frozen water.

cultivated Deliberately planted, tended and harvested by humans rather than growing wild.

cumulonimbus A towering, dark mass of cumulus clouds associated with thunder and lightning.

cumulus Fluffy, low-altitude clouds.

current A flow of water or air.

cycad A primitive, palmlike tree that grew in the Triassic and Jurassic periods.

cyclone A violent tropical storm, also known as a hurricane or a typhoon.

deciduous Shedding, or dropping, leaves usually in autumn, winter or dry season.

deforestation Widespread clearing of a forest.

depression A low-pressure region often associated with rain.

dermis The inner layer of skin. It contains tiny blood vessels, nerves, sweat glands, hair roots and other microscopic parts.

desert An area that receives little rain.

dewlap A flap of skin, sometimes brightly colored, on a lizard's throat.

digestion The process of breaking down

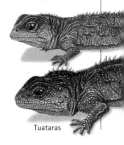

Vine snake

Tortoises

Baby alligator

Gecko foot

Tuataras

613

Sun bear

Uakari

Joey in kangaroo pouch

Fur seal with harem

Langur
monkeys

food, by physical and chemical means, into tiny pieces that are small enough to be absorbed by the body.

dinosaurs A group of reptiles that dominated Earth from the Triassic to the Cretaceous Period (245-65 million years ago). The largest land animals that ever lived, dinosaurs are more closely related to today's birds and crocodilians than they are to other living reptiles.

display A series of movements that animals use to communicate with their own kind, or with other animals. Displays often signal that an animal is ready to attack, or to mate.

diurnal Active during the day.

DNA Stands for deoxyribonucleic acid, the chemical that makes up the chromosomes inside cells. It carries the genes.

dormant Not growing but resting or waiting for more suitable growing conditions.

dormant volcano A volcano that is not currently active but could erupt again.

dorsal fin A fin on the back of some fish. It helps the fish keep its balance as it moves through the water.

drizzle Light rain, with water drops less than 1/5 in (0.5 mm) in diameter.

drone A male honeybee. Drones mate with young queens, but unlike worker bees, they do not help in collecting food or maintaining a hive.

drought A prolonged period without any rain.

dwarf star One of the large number of stars of average or less-than-average diameter and true brightness.

echolocation A system of navigation used by some animals that relies on sound rather than sight or touch. Dolphins, porpoises and many bats use echolocation to tell them where they are, where their prey is, and if anything is in their way.

ecliptic The apparent yearly path of the Sun around the sky, as seen from the Earth.

edentate A placental mammal, such as an armadillo, anteater or sloth, which belongs to the order of mammals called the Edentata.

egg sac A silk bag that some spiders spin around their eggs.

egg tooth A special scale on the tip of the upper lip of a hatchling lizard or snake. They use it to break a hole in the egg so the newborn animal can escape. The egg tooth falls off a few days after hatching.

elliptical galaxy An oval-shaped galaxy.

embryo An animal or plant in the very early stages of development. In humans, this is from three to eight weeks after fertilization.

endangered In danger of becoming extinct. A plant or animal can become endangered because of environmental changes or human activities.

endocrine Relating to hormones and the glands that make them.

enzyme A substance that speeds up (or slows down) a chemical change or reaction. Enzymes break down, or digest, the proteins in food into subunits, called amino acids.

epicenter The place on the Earth's surface that is directly above an earthquake's focus or starting point.

epidermis The outer layer of skin, made up mainly of tough, hard, dead cells.

epiphyte A plant that grows on trees and makes its own food. An epiphyte absorbs mineral salts from the surface of the tree and moisture from the air.

equator An imaginary line halfway between the North and South poles.

equinox Either of the two occasions, six months apart, when day and night are of equal length.

estuary The mouth of a river where its currents meet the ocean's tides.

evaporation A change in state from a liquid to a gas.

evergreen Having leaves all year round. An evergreen tree sheds its leaves throughout the year, instead of in a particular season, so it is never bare.

evolution The gradual change, over many generations, in plant or animal species as they adapt to new conditions or new environments.

exoskeleton A hard external skeleton, or body case, that protects an animal's body. All arthropods are protected in this way.

extinct volcano A volcano unlikely to erupt again.

extinction The complete dying out of all members of a species.

extrusive rock Lava that cools and hardens quickly on the surface.

eyelet One of the small eyes that form part of a larger compound eye. An eyelet senses light from an animal's surroundings.

fangs Long, hollow teeth in snakes and spiders that pierce flesh and inject venom.

fault A crack or break in the Earth's crust where rocks have shifted.

fertilization The joining of an egg cell and a sperm cell. This leads to the development of a new animal.

fetus An animal in the later stages of development in the womb. In humans, this is from eight weeks after fertilization to birth.

fibrous roots Roots that arise from nodes of the stem and not from a tap root.

fish A group of vertebrate animals adapted to living in water, with gills for breathing.

Koalas

fisher scoop A scientific instrument used for scooping up sand and mud samples from the sea bed. Oceanographers analyze the specimens to help them understand how the underwater landscape was formed.

flippers The broad front legs of sea turtles that act like paddles to "row" these animals through the water.

focus The place under the Earth's surface where an earthquake's shock waves start.

Pangolin

fog A dense, low cloud of water droplets lying near to the ground, which reduces visibility to less than 3,608 ft (1,100 m).

foreshock A tremor that occurs before the main shock waves of an earthquake begin.

fossil The remains or imprint of a plant or animal found in rock.

fossil fuel A fuel such as oil, coal and natural gas, which has been formed from plant or animal remains and is embedded deep within the Earth.

White rhinos

frill A collar around a frilled lizard's neck.

frost An icy coating that forms when moisture in the air freezes.

full phase (for the Moon, Mercury or Venus) The part of the cycle when all of the face is visible.

fungus An organism, neither plant nor animal, that cannot make its own food so feeds on live or dead plant

Harvest mice

Humpback whale

615

and animal tissue. Fungi break down and decompose plant and animal materials.

galaxy A large cluster of billions of stars and clouds of gas and dust, held together by gravity.

gamete Mature sex cell, either a male sperm or female egg.

gametophyte A tiny plant with male and female sex cells, or gametes. It is produced by spores, which have no sex cells.

ganglion A cluster of nerve cells that does not form part of the brain. In many invertebrates, ganglia control different parts of the body.

gas giant A large planet with a very deep atmosphere and perhaps no solid surface.

gastroliths Stomach stones swallowed by crocodilians that stay in the stomach to help crush food.

gene The part in a cell that determines an inherited characteristic, passed on from previous generations.

germination The stage in the life cycle when the stem and roots of a new plant sprout from a seed.

geyser A hot spring that boils and erupts hot water and steam.

gibbous phase (for the Moon, Mercury or Venus) The part of the cycle when more than half (but not all) of the face is visible from Earth.

gill The organ that sea-living creatures such as fish use for breathing.

glacier A slow-moving mass of ice, formed in mountains, which creeps down valleys.

gland A body part that makes a useful

product. Endocrine glands make hormones, and exocrine glands make products such as saliva and sweat.

global warming The gradual increase in the average global temperature from year to year.

Gondwana The southern supercontinent formed when Pangaea split into two, which began about 208 million years ago.

granite An intrusive igneous rock with large crystals of quartz.

gravity The force that attracts or draws one body to another.

grazer A plant-eating mammal, such as a kangaroo, horse or member of the cattle family, which feeds on grasses and plants that grow on the ground.

greenhouse effect The increase in the temperature of a planet caused when its atmosphere prevents heat from escaping.

grub An insect larva.

gyre One of the five giant loops of moving water or currents, which are driven by the wind.

habitat The place where an animal or plant naturally lives.

hadrosaurs Duckbilled dinosaurs such as *Hadrosaurus*, *Maiasaura* or *Anatotitan*. Hadrosaurs were the most common and varied plant-eating ornithopods. They evolved in central Asia during the early Cretaceous Period, and spread to Europe, North and South America.

hail Hard, icy pellets formed in cumulonimbus clouds, which are solid when they reach the ground.

haltere One of a pair of the modified back wings of a fly. They help the fly to balance during flight.

haustoria Special growths, or roots, used by parasitic plants to attach themselves to

Black widow spider

Surgeonfish

Echidna

Crocodile

Black rhino

616

a host plant and feed on its food and water supply.

heat-sensitive pit Sense organs in some snakes that detect tiny changes in temperature.

hemotoxin A kind of venom produced by venomous snakes. Hemotoxic venom (the main chemical in the venom of vipers and rattlesnakes) destroys muscle tissue.

herbivore An animal that eats only plants.

hibernation When an animal goes into a deep sleep with reduced body temperature and heart rate to survive a cold winter.

holdfast An attachment at the base of water plants such as algae that holds on to rocks. Like the rest of the plant, it absorbs water and minerals.

hooves The toes of horses, deer, antelope and related animals that are covered in thick, hard skin with sharp edges.

hormone A chemical substance that controls a process inside the body, such as growth or sexual development.

horn An outgrowth on the head of rhinoceroses, antelope and wild cattle that is used for fighting and for defense.

horsetail fern Primitive, swamp-living plants related to ferns.

host The plant on which a parasite lives and feeds.

hot spring A pool or spring that forms when water seeps down through rocks, is heated by magma or hot rock and then rises to the surface.

hotspot volcano A volcano that forms in the middle of a plate, above a source of magma.

humidity The amount of water vapor in the air.

hurricane A large tropical depression with high winds and torrential rainfall. Also called a cyclone or a typhoon.

hybrid Produced by cross-fertilizing the female cell of one plant with the male cell of a related, but different, plant.

hygrometer An instrument that measures the amount of moisture in the air.

Saltwater crocodile

ice age A cold period during which ice extends over as much as one-third of the Earth's surface.

iceberg A large, floating chunk of ice, broken off from a glacier and carried out to sea.

ichthyosaurs Short-necked, dolphin-shaped marine reptiles that lived at the same time as dinosaurs. Ichthyosaurs evolved in the Triassic Period, and ranged from 3-ft (1-m) long *Mixosaurus* to 49-ft (15-m) long *Shonisaurus*. *Ichthyosaurus* grew to 7 ft (2 m) long.

Salamander

igneous rock Rock that forms when magma cools and hardens.

iguanodonts Large, plant-eating, ornithopod dinosaurs. The 30-ft (9-m) long *Iguanodon* is its best known member.

Bear skull

ilium The main bone of the pelvis. The ilium supports the legs and is attached to the backbone.

immune Able to fight and destroy certain bacteria, viruses or other germs, so that they cannot multiply in the body and cause infectious disease.

implant An artificial part, such as a plastic blood vessel, which is put into, or onto, the body.

Lionfish

incomplete metamorphosis A way of developing in which a young insect gradually changes shape from an egg to a nymph, to an adult.

Bear prints

617

Ear canal

Teeth

Endocrine system

Blood types

Contracting biceps

inflammation The reaction of the body to infection. An inflamed area becomes red, hot, swollen and sore.

inner core The solid ball of iron and nickel at the center of the Earth.

insectivore A mammal that eats only or mainly insects or invertebrates. Some insectivorous mammals eat meat, such as frogs, lizards and mice.

insects A large group of small animals with three-part bodies, six legs, and usually two pairs of wings. It includes flies, mosquitoes, bees and ants.

insulation A layer of material that reduces the loss of heat from a body or a building.

interglacial A warm period with tropical conditions found over much of the land surface.

intrusive rock Magma that cools and hardens slowly within the crust.

invertebrates Animals that do not have a backbone. Many have soft bodies (such as worms) or a hard shell (such as insects).

irregular galaxy A galaxy with no particular structure or shape.

ischium One of the bones of the pelvis.

island arc A volcanic island chain that forms when magma rises from a subduction zone.

isobar A line on a map joining points of equal atmospheric pressure.

ivory The hard white substance that forms the main part of an elephant's tusks.

Jacobson's organ Two small sensory pits on the top part of the front of the mouth in lizards and snakes. They use this organ to analyze small molecules that they pick up from the air or ground and carry to the organ with the tongue.

Jurassic Period The period from 208 to 145 million years ago.

keratin A material found in horns and fingernails.

krill A shrimplike crustacean that lives in large numbers in Arctic waters.

lagomorph A rabbit or hare. Although lagomorphs are similar to rodents, they also have important differences. A lagomorph has hair on the soles of its feet and does not have sweat glands.

lahar A lethal mudflow often triggered by a volcano or an earthquake.

larva A young animal that looks completely different from its parents. Insect larvae change into adults by complete metamorphosis. A larva is sometimes called a grub.

lateral undulation A kind of movement used by legless lizards and snakes. Curves of the body push back against the rough ground and the animal moves forward through the curved path.

latitudes Imaginary lines drawn around the Earth parallel to the equator. Imaginary lines from one pole to the other are called longitudes.

Laurasia The northern supercontinent formed when Pangaea split into two.

lava Magma that erupts at the surface of the Earth.

lift The upward force that helps flying animals to stay in the air. Lift is produced when air flows over the wings.

light year The distance a beam of light travels through space in one year.

lightning A flash of electricity in the sky usually generated during a thunderstorm.

liquefaction A process that occurs during an earthquake when poorly consolidated or loose sand, mud and water are shaken and become liquid rather than solid. Buildings built on soil of this type can collapse because they have no support.

lithosphere The two layers of solid rock, consisting of the upper mantle and the crust, which lie above the asthenosphere.

lithospheric plates The main rigid, outer surfaces of the Earth, which are formed from the upper part of the Earth's mantle and the crust.

live-bearing Animals that do not lay eggs, but give birth to fully formed young.

lymph A clear, yellowish fluid found in body tissues. It contains water, proteins and white blood cells.

lysosome A baglike part inside a cell containing chemicals called enzymes that break down the cell's wastes.

magma Molten rock inside the Earth.

magma chamber A reservoir, or pocket, of magma in the crust.

mammal A vertebrate that is warm-blooded, suckles its young with milk and has a single bone in the lower jaw.

mandibles The biting jaws of an insect.

mantle The layer of the Earth between the crust and the outer core. The mantle has three sections: the solid lower mantle, the squishy asthenosphere and the solid upper mantle.

marine park An area of the ocean set aside as a reserve to protect endangered species and to preserve the marine environment.

marsupial A mammal that gives birth to young that are not fully developed. These young must be protected in pouches (where they feed on milk) before they can move around independently.

mass The amount of matter in a body.

medulla The inner layer of a body part, such as the adrenal gland or kidney.

melanin The body's main natural coloring substance which gives color to the hair and skin.

membrane A thin, sheetlike layer, covering or lining, such as the cell membrane around a cell, or the mucous membrane lining the nose, mouth, airways and digestive tract.

meninges Three thin coverings, or membranes, that surround and protect the brain and spinal cord.

Mercalli scale A scale that measures the intensity or amount of shaking that occurs during an earthquake. It is expressed in Roman numerals.

Mesozoic Era The Age of Reptiles that spanned the Triassic, Jurassic and Cretaceous periods. The Mesozoic Era lasted from 245 to 65 million years ago.

metamorphosis A way of developing in which an animal's body changes shape. Many invertebrates, including insects, undergo metamorphosis as they mature.

metatarsal One of the long bones (behind the toes) in the foot.

meteor A small body that causes a flash of light in the sky as it passes through the Earth's atmosphere and burns up.

meteor shower A display of a large number of meteors within a short period of time. It occurs when the Earth crosses the debris left from the orbit of a comet.

meteorite A body that has survived its fall through the atmosphere and has struck the surface of a planet or moon.

meteoroid A very small body that travels through space. If it passes through the Earth's atmosphere, it is then called a meteor.

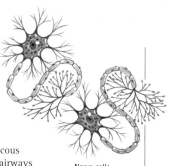

Nerve cells

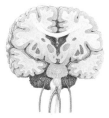

Cross section of the brain

Hinge joint

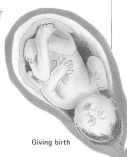

Giving birth

meteorologist A person who studies the weather.

meteorology The study of the weather.

midnight sun The name given to the Sun during summer in the Earth's polar regions when it does not set at all.

mid-ocean ridge A huge mountain range that snakes across the ocean floor at the boundaries of the plates where they move apart.

migration Birds, fish and many animals travel from one habitat to another at certain times of the year to find food or to give birth to their young.

mineral A material appearing in nature that is extracted by mining.

mineral salts Salts from metals and rocks that are present in the soil and absorbed by plant roots. Salts contain nitrogen, phosphorous, magnesium, iron, potassium, calcium and other elements.

mites Very tiny eight-legged invertebrate animals related to ticks. Many are parasites that can cause diseases in humans.

mitochondria Sausage-shaped parts inside a cell that supply it with energy for its thousands of chemical processes.

molars The side "cheek" teeth of a mammal.

mollusk An animal, such as a snail, squid or octopus, with no backbone and a soft body that can be enclosed or partly enclosed by a shell.

molt To shed an outer layer of the body. Insects molt by shedding their outer skins, while birds molt by shedding their feathers.

monotreme A primitive mammal with many features

in common with reptiles. Monotremes lay eggs. There are only three species of monotreme: the platypus and two species of echidna.

monsoon A wind that changes direction, bringing heavy rain during the wet season.

moon A natural satellite that orbits a planet.

mother ship A ship that provides supplies for one or more smaller vessels, such as submersibles.

mucus A sticky, thick substance made by the body to protect and moisten areas, such as the lining of the nose and airways.

mudflow A fast-moving stream of ash and water caused by the eruption of an explosive volcano or an earthquake.

multituberculate An extinct group of mammals that lived in the Northern Hemisphere. They looked like rodents, but were not related to any of today's mammals.

mummified Dried out by heat or wind.

muscle A part of the body that can contract or relax to produce movement. Muscle is also the name given to the tissue that makes up this body part.

navigation The science of directing the course of a ship or an aircraft.

neap tide The smallest rise and fall in tides that occurs when the sun and the moon are at right angles to the Earth.

nebula A cloudlike patch in the sky made up of gas and dust. Some nebulae are the birthplaces of stars.

nectar Sugary liquid produced in special glands in flowers to attract insects, birds and mammals as pollinators.

nephron A microscopic, blood-filtering unit inside the kidney. Each kidney contains about 1 million nephrons.

Tyrannosaurus

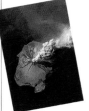
Volcano

Tuojiangosaurus

Magnolia

Horsetails

Euoplocephalus' tail

nerve A long, thin, pale, stringlike body part that carries nerve signals.

nerve cord The part of an insect's nervous system that carries signals between its body and brain.

neurotransmitter A chemical substance that carries a nerve signal across the gap between one nerve cell and the next, or between a nerve cell and a muscle.

nimbostratus A low-level, dark cloud that produces rain.

nocturnal Active at night. Nocturnal animals sleep during the day.

node Position on plant stem from which new leaves, shoots and sometimes roots grow.

normal fault A type of fault where the ground cracks as rocks are pulled apart. One side slides down to a lower level.

nuclear fusion The binding together of atomic particles to build up heavier elements. This causes a release of energy that is the source of the energy in all stars.

nucleus A cell's control center (the main part inside a cell). It contains the genes that tell the cell how to work.

nutrients Substances that are needed to maintain life.

nymph The young stage of an insect that develops by incomplete metamorphosis.

obsidian A dark, glassy volcanic rock that forms when thick, sticky lava cools rapidly.

occultation The passing of the Moon, planet or asteroid in front of a star or planet.

ocean A very large stretch of water.

ocean current A huge mass of water that travels enormous distances and mixes warm water near the equator with cold water from the polar regions.

oceanic ridge A long, narrow chain of underwater mountains formed when two of the Earth's plates meet and magma wells up to the surface to form a new sea floor.

oceanic trench A long, narrow valley under the sea that contains some of the deepest points on Earth.

oceanographer A person who studies the science of the oceans.

*Tuojiangosaurus'
tail*

oceanography The science of the features and the structure of the ocean.

ocellus A simple kind of eye with a single lens. Insects have three ocelli on the top of their head.

Parasaurolophus

omnivore A mammal that eats both plant and animal food.

opposable thumb A thumb that can reach around and touch all of the other fingers on the same hand.

Teeth of
plant–eating
dinosaurs

orbit The invisible curved path followed by one object, such as the Moon, around another object, such as the Earth.

order A major group that biologists use when classifying living things. An order is divided into smaller groups from suborders to families, to genera and finally to species.

organ A main, self-contained part of the body, such as the heart, lung, kidney, liver or brain.

ornithischians "Bird-hipped" dinosaurs. In this group the pubis pointed back and down, parallel to the ischium.

Triceratops

ornithopods "Bird-footed" ornithischian dinosaurs. This group included the pachycephalosaurs, iguanodonts, hadrosaurs and the horned, armored and plated dinosaurs.

osteoderm A lump or nodule of bone in

Pleisochelys

a reptile's skin that provides protection against predators. Most crocodilians and some lizards are protected by osteoderms as well as thick, strong skin.

outer core The liquid layer of iron and nickel surrounding the Earth's inner core.

ovipositor A tubelike organ through which female insects lay their eggs. The stings of bees and wasps are modified ovipositors.

ozone A colorless gas made up of three oxygen atoms.

ozone layer A diffuse layer of ozone molecules found high in the atmosphere. It filters out harmful ultraviolet radiation from the sun.

pachycephalosaurs Plant-eating, late Cretaceous, ornithopod dinosaurs with skulls thickened into domes of bone. Pachycephalosaurs lived in Asia and North America and ranged from 7 ft (2 m) to 15 ft (4.6 m) in length.

pack ice Ice that forms when the surface of the ocean freezes.

pahoehoe A fast-flowing lava that cools to form a smooth, ropelike surface.

paleontologist A scientist who studies ancient life, especially the fossils of plants and animals.

palp or pedipalp One of a pair of small, leglike organs on the head of insects, spiders and other arthropods, used for feeling or handling food. In spiders, the pedipalps are also used for mating.

Pangaea A supercontinent that included today's continents in one land mass.

paralyze To cause the loss of some or all parts of a body's ability to work, move and feel.

parasite An animal or plant that lives and feeds on another animal or plant, sometimes with harmful effects.

perennials Plants that continue to live and grow for several, or many, years.

perissodactyl An ungulate, or hoofed mammal, that has an odd, or uneven, number of toes. A perissodactyl has either three toes, such as tapirs and rhinos, or one toe, such as horses and their relatives.

petal The second layer in the flower. It is usually colored and attracts pollinators.

petrified Fossilized bone that has layers of bone replaced by minerals.

pharmacology The science or study of drugs, including those derived from plants, and how they act on the human body.

phases The cycle of changes, as seen from the Earth, in the shape of the Moon, Mercury and Venus as they revolve around the Earth or Sun.

pheromones Chemicals produced by animals that send a message to others of the same species.

phloem Tissue containing tubes of living cells that transport nutrients such as sugars and mineral salts from one part of the plant to another.

photophores Organs in animals, especially fish, which are able to produce light.

photosphere The Sun's visible surface from which most of the visible light radiates into space.

photosynthesis The process in which plants make their own food using carbon dioxide, water and light.

physiology The scientific study of the body's functions, especially its many chemical changes.

phytoplankton Microscopic plants (usually algae) that drift or float in water.

Scallop shells

Queen angelfish

Submersible

Emperor penguins

Black marlin tail

pillow lava Lava that erupts in water, such as along the mid-ocean ridge.

pincers The large claws of a scorpion's pedipalps.

pinnipeds Mammals such as seals, sea lions or walruses, which have evolved fan-shaped hind flippers instead of feet.

placental A mammal that does not lay eggs, or give birth to young that must be cared for in a pouch, but which nourishes the developing young inside its body with a special organ called a placenta.

plankton Tiny marine plants and animals.

plasma The pale, watery part of the blood.

plateau An area of level high ground.

plesiosaurs Large marine reptiles of the Mesozoic Era. Plesiosaurs, which ranged from 8-ft (2.3-m) long *Plesiosaurus* to 46-ft (14-m) long *Elasmosaurus*, were generally long-necked.

pliosaurs Plesiosaurs with short necks and thick, powerful bodies.

poach To hunt animals illegally. A person who does this is called a poacher.

poison A substance that causes illness or death when touched or eaten, even in very small amounts.

pollen A dustlike substance produced by male flowers or the male organs in a flower, and used in reproduction.

pollination The transfer of male pollen to the female stigma, which usually requires the help of pollinators such as the wind, insects or birds.

pores Tiny openings in the skin.

precipitation Water or ice, such as snow, sleet or rain, which falls to the ground from clouds.

predator An animal that hunts, kills and eats other animals (prey) to survive.

pregnancy The time when a baby develops in its mother's womb, or uterus. This time is also called gestation.

prehensile Grasping or gripping. Some tree-dwelling mammals have prehensile feet or tails that can be used as an extra limb to help them stay safely in a tree while feeding, climbing or sleeping.

prey An animal that is hunted, killed and eaten by other animals (predators).

primary waves The first earthquake waves to hit an area.

proboscis In insects, a long mouthpart or tongue used for feeding.

proleg A sucker-like leg in caterpillars. Prolegs disappear when a caterpillar turns into an adult butterfly or moth.

propagate To grow a new plant from the seeds, stems, rhizomes or roots of a parent plant.

prosauropods Late Triassic to early Jurassic ancestors of the long-necked sauropods. Prosauropods reached lengths of 7 ft (2.1 m) to 33 ft (10 m).

prosimian A primitive primate, such as a lemur, bushbaby, loris and tarsier.

prosthesis An artificial body part.

pterosaurs Flying reptiles, only distantly related to dinosaurs. Pterosaurs evolved during the late Triassic Period and had wingspans ranging from 11/2 ft (45 cm) to 39 ft (12 m).

pubis One of the lower bones of the pelvis.

pulsar The tiny remains of a star that rotate very fast and send out regular pulses of radio waves.

pumice A volcanic rock formed when frothy lava cools and hardens. The bubbles of air trapped inside make it so light that it can float in water.

Giant squid

Nautilus shell

Paper nautilus eggs

Spanish coins

Blue-swimmer crab

Pyroclastic rocks

Alfred Wegener

The first seismometer

Sulphur miners

Dante the robot

pupil The round or slit-shaped opening in the center of the eye. Light passes through this to the back of the eye.

purebred In plants, a plant produced when male pollen fertilizes a female stigma in the same flower, on the same plant or on a plant of the same variety and species.

pyroclastic flow A rapidly flowing hot cloud of gas and ash blown out of the mouth of a volcano.

quadrupedal Walking on four legs.

quasar A distant, starlike object with an enormous energy output many times brighter than an ordinary galaxy.

queen A female insect that begins a social insect colony. The queen is normally the only member of the colony that lays eggs.

quills Long, sharp hairs found on porcupines, echidnas and a few other mammals.

radiative zone The area of a star that contains and transfers energy to the convective zone.

radiosonde A device attached to a weather balloon released into the high atmosphere to monitor weather conditions.

rainfall The amount of rain received by a particular region over a set period.

rainforest A tropical forest that receives at least 100 in (250 cm) of rain each year and is home to a vast number of plant and animal species.

raptors Birds of prey, including hawks, eagles, owls and vultures, which eat flesh.

rectilinear locomotion A movement used by large snakes when moving slowly in a straight line.

red giant A large star with a relatively cool surface.

reflection When light bounces

off a surface.

reflex A quick, automatic reaction, done without conscious thought.

refraction The bending of light as it passes from one substance into another.

regurgitate To bring food back up from the stomach to the mouth. Many hoofed mammals use this process to break down their food into a more liquid form. This is called "chewing the cud."

renal Relating to the kidneys.

reproduction The production of offspring or new plants from two different sex cells (sexual reproduction), or by methods such as cell division that do not require sex cells (asexual reproduction).

reptiles A group of vertebrates with dry, scaly skin including lizards, snakes, turtles, crocodiles and alligators.

respiration The conversion of sugars into energy for growth, using oxygen and releasing carbon dioxide and water.

retractile claws The claws of cats that are normally protected in sheaths but spring out when the cat needs them to capture prey.

reverse fault A fault where the ground cracks as rocks are pushed together. One side slides up and over the other side to a higher level.

revolution The motion of a planetary object along its orbit.

rhizome Underground stem that looks like a root (but it is not) and grows horizontally, or parallel, to the ground. Rhizomes in some plants are food stores and in many produce new plants.

rhyolite A light-colored igneous rock formed from thick, sticky lava.

ribosome A part inside a cell that makes proteins for the cell's structural framework.

Richter scale A scale that measures the amount, or magnitude, of energy released by an earthquake. It is expressed in Arabic numbers.

ridge A long mountain.

rift The crack or valley that forms when two plates with ocean crust move apart.

Ring of Fire The area along the edges of the Pacific Ocean where many of the world's earthquakes and volcanoes occur.

ring, planetary A swarm of tiny particles of ice or dust that orbits a planet.

rival An animal competing for food, territory and mates.

rod In the retina of the eye, a type of cell that makes nerve signals when light shines on it. Rods work in dim light, but cannot detect colors and fine details.

rodents A large group of mostly small mammals including rats, mice, squirrels, hamsters and guinea pigs.

rotation The spinning of the Earth or another body in space on its own axis.

saliva The watery fluid inside the mouth that softens and moistens food and contains enzymes to begin its chemical digestion. Another name for saliva is spit.

sap The juice, made up of water, sugars and minerals, inside the stem of a plant.

sapling A young tree or shrub.

satellite A small body in space that orbits a larger one.

saurischians "Lizard-hipped" dinosaurs. In this group, the pubis pointed towards the head of the pelvis. The saurischian dinosaurs are divided into two-legged, meat-eating theropods and four-legged, plant-eating sauropods.

sauropods Large, plant-eating, saurischian dinosaurs. Sauropods evolved during the late Triassic Period, and included the largest land animals ever to have lived.

scales Distinct thick areas of a reptile's skin. Scales vary from being very small to large, and they may be smooth, keeled, spiny or granular.

scan A type of picture of the inside of the body produced by a computerized machine that builds up the image line by line.

scavenger An animal that eats carrion (dead animals)—often the remains of animals killed by predators.

scutes The horny plates that cover a chelonian's bony shell.

sea A body of water that is partly or completely enclosed by land.

seamount A large, underwater volcanic mountain that remains under the sea or rises above it to form an island.

season A weather period of the year.

secondary waves The second round of earthquake waves to hit an area.

sediment Mineral or organic matter that contains millions of tiny animals and plants, and which settles at the bottom of the sea. The layer of sediment blanketing the sea plains may be 984-1,640 ft (300-500 m) thick.

seedling A very young plant grown from a seed.

seismic activity Any of the effects, usually Earth tremors, caused by an earthquake.

seismologist A scientist who studies earthquakes.

self-pollination The transfer of male pollen to a female stigma in the same flower or in a separate flower on the same plant. Self-pollination tends to produce

Rescue workers

Plaster cast from Pompeii

The "Breadknife", Australia

Twinned pyroxene crystals

The goddess Pelé

625

Radiosonde

Seasons

Weather vane

Grasshopper

weak plants after a few generations.

sharks A group of vertebrate animals that live in water. The skeletons of sharks are made of cartilage while other fish skeletons are made of bone.

shock waves The energy that is generated by an earthquake and travels in the form of waves through the surrounding rocks.

shooting star The informal name given to a meteor when it passes through the Earth's upper atmosphere and burns up.

side-necked The way one group of chelonians draws the neck and head back under the shell by tucking the neck and head sideways under the rim of the shell.

silica A substance that appears as quartz, sand, flint and agate.

silk A strong but elastic substance produced by many insects and spiders. Silk is liquid until it leaves the animal's body.

sleet A mixture of snow and rain.

smog A fog contaminated with air pollutants, which react together in the presence of sunlight.

snow Falling ice crystals.

social Living in groups. Social animals can live in breeding pairs (a male and a female), sometimes together with their young, or in groups of thousands of animals.

solar flare A sudden, violent explosion of energy that occurs on the surface of the Sun, usually near sunspots.

solar prominence A cooler cloud of gas in the corona above the Sun's surface.

solar system The collection of planets, asteroids, comets and dust that orbits the Sun.

solar wind The invisible flow of atomic

particles that stream from the Sun's surface into space.

solitary Living alone. Solitary animals usually meet other animals of the same species during the breeding season. At other times they avoid each other's company.

solstice Either the shortest day of the year (winter solstice) or the longest day of the year (summer solstice).

species A group of animals or plants that can breed with each other and produce young that can also breed.

spectrum The rainbow colors that white light produces when it passes through a water droplet or a glass prism.

spiders A group of small invertebrate animals with eight legs. Some spiders make silk webs to catch prey; all use venom to paralyze prey.

spines Sharp structures on fish that can pierce flesh and sometimes inject venom.

spinneret An organ that spiders use to produce their silk. The spinnerets are near the tip of a spider's abdomen.

spiracle A round opening that leads into an insect's trachea, or breathing tube.

spiral galaxy A large, flat galaxy (such as the Milky Way) with arms in a spiral pattern like a pinwheel.

sporangia Cases or capsules that produce spores in plants such as mosses and ferns.

spore In plants, a reproductive cell that does not contain sex cells, or gametes, but is able to grow into a new plant called a gametophyte.

spreading ridge A place on the ocean floor where magma cools and hardens in a rift and adds new strips of crust to the plates.

spring ligament The tough tissue that

controls the retractile claws of cats. When the ligament is stretched, the claws spring out of their sheaths.

spring tide The greatest rise and fall in tides that occurs when the sun and the moon are in line with the Earth.

spurs Sharp, clawlike structures on the legs of platypuses and some birds.

stamen The male part of a flower, containing a stalk with an anther, that produces pollen.

stegosaurs Late Jurassic dinosaurs that had alternating or staggered rows of plates along their backs, and two pairs of long, sharp spikes at the end of their strong tails.

stigma The sticky tip of the stalk (style) in a flower's female reproductive organ, which receives the male pollen.

stingers Hollow structures on the tails and heads of insects and the tails of scorpions that pierce flesh and inject venom and saliva.

stolon A horizontal stem, that grows along and above the ground. New plants can grow from the nodes of the stolon where it touches the ground.

stomata Tiny holes, usually on the underside of leaves, through which gases and water vapor enter and exit.

straight-necked The way one group of chelonians draws the neck and head straight back into the shell.

stratocumulus A layer of fluffy clouds at low altitude.

stratus A layer of low, gray clouds covering the sky.

stridulate To make a sound by scraping things together. Many insects communicate by scraping their legs against their body.

strike-slip fault A fault where rocks break and a block of land moves sideways.

stylet A sharp mouthpart used for piercing plants or animals.

subduction The process of one plate slowly diving beneath another. Plate is destroyed at a subduction zone.

submersible A small submarine that is able to reach the depths of the ocean, or to probe inside places that are too small for ordinary vessels.

sunspot A cooler, darker spot on the surface of the Sun caused by the Sun's magnetic field.

supercluster A giant grouping of many clusters of galaxies. The local supercluster, for example, includes our own group of galaxies as well as many nearby clusters.

supergiant A very large star that has great mass and is extremely bright.

supernova A stage in the life of a massive star when the star collapses in on itself and then explodes.

surface waves The third and most destructive round of earthquake waves to hit an area.

sweating Evaporation of liquid from the surface of the skin, which cools the body.

synapse The junction, or join, between one nerve cell and another, with a tiny gap that the nerve signal crosses by means of chemicals.

synapsid An animal that has a single opening in the skull behind the eye socket, which is used to anchor jaw muscles.

synoptic chart A weather map showing conditions at a particular point in time.

talons The long, curved nails on the feet of birds of prey.

tap root The first seedling root that may become the main root of the plant.

temperate When an environment or

Dragonfly

Formation of a rainbow

Hygrometer

Measuring the weather

The Milky Way

Sixteenth-century calendar

Viewing a solar eclipse

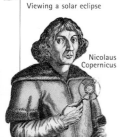
Nicolaus Copernicus

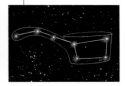
The Big Dipper

region has a warm summer and a cool winter.

temperate forests Forests growing in parts of the world, such as Europe and much of North America, where there are large seasonal differences in temperature.

temperature A measure of the amount of heat.

tendril A thin appendage on a climbing plant that coils around and clings to a support.

tentacle A slender, flexible feeler that enables an animal with no backbone to touch things.

terrestrial Living all or most of the time on land.

territory Area of land inhabited and defended by animals.

textile plant A plant with fibers that are woven into materials called textiles.

thermometer An instrument that measures the temperature.

theropods Meat-eating saurischian dinosaurs that walked on their hind legs.

thorax The middle part of an animal's body. In insects, the thorax is divided from the head by a narrow "neck." In spiders, the thorax and head make up a single unit.

throat flap A valve at the back of a crocodilian's throat that closes to stop water from entering the trachea when eating prey underwater.

thunder A rumbling shock wave created when lightning heats the air.

ticks A group of small, blood-sucking invertebrate parasites with eight legs.

tide The repeating rise and fall of the Earth's seas, caused by the pull of the moon and sun on the water.

tissue A part of an organism made up of a large number of cells that have a similar structure and function.

tornado A violent, spiraling wind that is short-lived but destructive.

trachea A breathing tube in an animal's body. In vertebrates, there is one trachea and it leads to the lungs. Insects have many small tracheae that spread throughout their body.

trackways A series of footprints that are left as an animal walks over soft ground.

transit The passage of a small body, such as a planet, in front of a larger one, such as the Sun.

transpiration The movement of water from the roots to the stem and leaves and through the open holes, or stomata, into the atmosphere.

transplant To move a natural body part, from one site in the body to another, or from one body to another.

Triassic Period The period from 245 to 208 million years ago.

Trojan asteroids Asteroids that orbit the Sun in the same orbit as Jupiter, some leading and some following the planet.

tropical Hot and often humid conditions experienced in regions close to the equator.

tropical cyclone A mass of rapidly whirling air, formed as moist, sun-heated air starts to rise and colder air takes its place.

tropical forests Forests growing in parts of the world, such as central Africa, northern South America and southeast Asia.

tsunami A gigantic, often destructive, sea wave which is triggered by an underwater earthquake or volcano.

tusks The very long teeth of elephants, warthogs, walruses and narwhals that are used in fights and in self-defense.

typhoon A violent tropical storm, also known as a hurricane or a cyclone.

ungulates Large, plant-eating mammals with hooves. They include elephants, rhinoceroses, horses, deer, antelope and wild cattle.

valve A flap or similar device that allows substances to pass through one way, but not in the opposite direction.

vapor A gaslike state of a solid or liquid.

variable star A star that varies in brightness.

vein A blood vessel that carries blood back to the heart.

venom A poisonous fluid that is transmitted by a bite or a sting.

venom duct The hollow center of a snake fang through which venom flows.

venom gland The place in an animal's body where venom is made.

venom sac The place in an animal's body where venom is stored until it is needed.

venomous Describes animals that bite or sting, and deliver chemicals that can immobilise or kill prey or predators.

ventricle One of the two large, thick-walled lower chambers of the heart.

vertebrae Bones from the back of the skull to the tail that protect the spinal column.

vertebrate An animal with a backbone. Vertebrates include fish, amphibians, reptiles, birds and mammals.

villi Tiny, finger-shaped projections in the lining of the small intestine.

volcanologist A scientist who studies volcanoes

warm-blooded An animal that can keep its internal body temperature more or less the same, regardless of the outside temperature.

waterspout A whirling column of air that hangs down from the bottom of some clouds. It occurs when warm, moist, rising air meets cold, dry air.

weather The atmospheric conditions experienced at a particular place or time.

weather satellite An orbiting instrument that monitors atmospheric conditions and transmits the information back to Earth.

web A silk structure made by many spiders to catch prey.

whirlpool A whirling, circular movement of water created when the tide turns and the opposing currents meet.

white dwarf A small, hot star near the end of its life.

wind A mass of air that moves from one place to another.

worker A social insect that collects food and tends a colony's young, but which usually cannot reproduce.

xenarthran Another scientific name for a member of the order Edentata.

X-rays Invisible rays that pass through most body tissues, but not through hard, dense parts, such as bone.

xylem Tissue containing tubes of dead cells that carry water and mineral salts up from the roots of plants, through the stem, to the leaves.

zodiac An imaginary band around the sky of 12 constellations through which the Sun, Moon, and planets appear to move.

zooplankton Tiny plant-eating sea creatures that eat phytoplankton and which are in turn eaten by small meat-eating creatures.

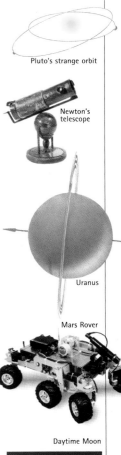

Pluto's strange orbit

Newton's telescope

Uranus

Mars Rover

Daytime Moon

Index

Page numbers in *italics* indicate
illustrations and photos

A

acupuncture 286
air pressure 510, 529, 553
Albertosaurus 357, *357*
algae 28–9, 342
   bloom 28, *28*, 439, *439*
alligators 252, *252*
Allosaurus 347, *353*, 356, 387, *388*
alpine plants 48–9, *48–9*, 540, *540*
Alvin 422, 424, *424–5*
amphibians 124, 127, 342
amphisbaenians 152–3, *152–3*
   heads 153, *153*
anatomy
   chelonian 128, *128–9*
   crocodilian 137
   insect 72–5, *72–5*, 77, 78, 95
   lizard 144–5, 151, *151*
   plant 18, *18–19*
   primates 196
   snake 160–1, 163
   spider 108, *108–9*
   study of 286–8
Anatotitan 367
Andromeda Galaxy 598, *598–9*
anemometer 526, 529, *530, 531*
anemones 266–7, *266–7*, 406, *406*
anglerfish *419*, 420, 421, *421*
Ankylosaurus 362
annuals 36
Antarctica 414, *414*, 509, 538, 553
anteaters 192–3, *192–3*
antennae 76, *76*
antlers 216–17, 234–5
ants 100–1, *100–1*, 233
   driver *275*
   honey pot 547, *547*

stinging 260–1
   weaver *275*
Apatosaurus 345, 358, 372,
   378–9, 380
apes 202–3, *202–3*
Archaeopteryx 348, 353, 384, *385*
archerfish *405*
Arctic 415, *415*, 538, *538–9*
   tern 432
   tundra 48–9
arteries 292–3
arthropods 73
artificial body parts 334–5, *334–5*
ash, volcanic 466, *466*, 470,
   472, 491
asteroids 564, 588–9, *588–9*
   Ceres 588
asthma 295
astrology 560–1, *560–1*
astronomy 558–9, *558–9*
Atlantis 430–1
atmosphere 507, 570
auroras 567, *567*
avalanches 472–3, *472–3*
aye-ayes 199, *199*

B

bacteria 322
Bactrosaurus 355, 355
balance 313
barnacles 407, *407*
barometer 529
barracudas 241, *241*
Baryonyx 357, 357
bathythermograph 398, *398*
bats 194, *194–5*
bears 210–11, *210–11*, 248–9,
   248–9
   claws 241, *241*
Beaufort Scale 401
beavers 218, *218–19*

bees 74, *74–5*, 96, 100–1, *100–1*,
   260–1, 542
   dancing *274*
   killer 274, *274*
Bermuda Triangle 430–1
Big Bang theory 562
Big Crunch theory 562–3
bile 300
biodiversity 63
bioluminescence 418
birds
   evolution from dinosaurs 347,
      384–5
   prey 250–1, *250–1*
black hole 595, *595*
blizzards 539, *539*
blood transfusions 293
blood types 293
blood vessels 292–3, *292–3*
body language 325
bones 302–5, *302–5*, 330
   broken 304–5, *304–5*
   marrow 305, *305*
botanists 16
Brachiosaurus 353, 353, 358,
   360–1, *361*, 366, 367, *371*,
   377, *388–9*
Brahe, Tycho 559
brain 316–17, *316–17*
Brocken Specter 520, *520*
bugs 104–5, *104–5*
bulls 239, *239*
butterflies 98–9, *98–9*

C

cactus 44–5, *44–5*
calderas 474–5, *474–5*
calendars 559, *559*
Camarasaurus 358, 370, *370–1*
camouflage
   insects 84, 98

E

F

G

H

Credits

ILLUSTRATORS

Susanna Addario; Mike Atkinson/Garden Studio; Graham Back; Kenn Backhaus; Alistair Barnard; Andrew Beckett/Garden Studio; André Boos; Anne Bowman; Gregory Bridges; Rod Burchett; Sam Burgess; Martin Camm; Lynette R. Cook; Wendy De Pauuw; Simone End; Christer Eriksson; Alan Ewart ; Nick Farmer/Brihton Illustration; Rod Ferring; John Foerster/Foerster Illustration, Inc; Giuliano Fornari; Chris Forsey; Sian Frances/Garden Studio; John Francis/Bernard Thornton Artists, UK; Jon Gittoes; Mike Golding; Mike Gorman; Ray Grinaway; Lorraine Hannay; Tim Harrison; Tim Hayward/Bernard Thornton Artists, UK; Adam Hook/ Bernard Thornton Artists, UK; Richard Hook/ Bernard Thornton Artists, UK ; Robert Hynes; Janet Jones; Roger Kent/ Garden Studio; Peter Kesteven/Garden Studio; David Kirshner; Frank Knight; Mike Lamble; Robyn Latimer; Alex Lavroff; Dr. Levent Efe/CMI; Jillian B. Luff; John Mac/Folio; David Mackay ; Martin Macrae/Folio; Iain McKellar ; James McKinnon; Peter Mennim; David Moore/Linden Artists; Colin Newman/Bernard Thornton Artists, UK; Paul Newman; Kevin O'Donnell; Nicola Oram ; Darren Pattenden/Garden Studio; R. Spencer Phippen; Jane Pickering/Linden Artists; Evert Ploeg; Marilyn Pride; Tony Pyrzakowski; Oliver Rennert; John Richards; Ken Rinkel; Andrew Robinson/Garden Studio; Trevor Ruth; Claudia Saraceni; Michael Saunders; Peter Schouten; Rod Scott; Stephen Seymour/ Bernard Thornton Artists, UK; Christine Shafner/K.E. Sweeney Illustration; Ray Sim; Kevin Stead; Kate Sweeney/K.E. Sweeney Illustration; Bernard Tate; Steve Trevaskis; Thomas Trojer; Rod Westblade; Steve Weston/Linden Artists; Simon Williams/Garden Studio; Melissa Wilton; Ann Winterbotham.

PHOTOGRAPHS

(t = top, c = center, b = bottom, l = left, r = right, i = icon
ADL=Ad-Libitum (S. Bowey); AM=Australian Museum; APL=Australian Picture Library; ARDEA=Ardea, London; AUS=Auscape International; AUST=Austral international; BCL=Bruce Coleman Limited; BIO=Bio-photo Associates; E=Esther Beaton; GC=The Granger Collection; IB=The Image Bank; MEPL=Mary Evans Picture Library; MP=Minden Pictures; M&PF=Michael and Patricia Fodgen; PR=Photo Researchers, Inc; MW=Mantis Wildlife Films; NHM=The Natural History Museum, London; OSF=Oxford Scientific Films; PEP=Planet Earth Pictures; STO=Stock Photos; TPL=photolibrary.com; TSA=Tom Stack & Associates.

16 cl AUS. 17 cr ADL; tc BIO; tcr BIO. 18 tr TPL; cl PEP (M. Mattock); tl PEP (A. Mounter). 20 br BIO; cl BCL (E. Pott). 21 cr APL (MP); bc TPL; br TPL. 22 bcl AUS (J.P. Ferrero); bl AUS (J.P. Ferrero). 23 cl BCL (K. Taylor); br Natural Science Photos (J. Burgess). 24 c MW (D. Clyne); cr TPL (SPL). 26 cl OSF (S. Stammers). 27 tr AUS (W. Lawler); tc Lochman Transparencies (E. Boogaard). 28 cl AUS (R. Morrison). 29 cr BCL (J. Burton); tr OSF (G.I. Bernard); tc OSF (London Scientific Films). 30 tr AUS (J.P. Ferrero). 31 tl BCL (H. Reinhard); tc BCL (K. Taylor); tr Heino Lepp; cr PEP (D. Phillips). 32 cr MW (G. Carruthers); tr PEP (J. Lythgoe). 34 cl Bill Bachman; bl OSF (R.A. Tyrrell). 34/35 c ADL. 36 bl AUS (T. De Roy). 37 tr PEP (N. Garbutt); br PEP (Joyce Photographics). 38 tr BIO; cl BCL (A. Davies). 39 cr BCL (S. Prato); tr PEP (A. Bartschi); tl PEP (L. Tackett). 40 c AUS; bc The Bridgeman Art Library (Wallace Collection, London). 41 tr Heather Angel; br MW (J. Frazier); tc STO (R. Hemingway). 42 cl STO (D. Noble). 43 bl Bill Bachman; cl STO (P. Steel); br Wildlight (P. Quirk). 44 c Gerald Cubitt. 45 c Heather Angel; tl BCL (E. Pott). 46 tr APL (A. Jones). 47 bl PEP (J Eastcott/Y. Momatiuk); tl PEP (P. Oxford). 48 bl Hedgehog House New Zealand (C. Monteath). 49 c AUS (J.P. Ferrero); tr Hedgehog House New Zealand (S. Novak). 50 tr AUS (J.P. Ferrero); c PEP (W.M. Smithey). 51 tr BCL (N. De Vore); bl STO (O. Rogge). 52 tr OSF (L. & T. Bomford/Survival Anglia); bl Royal Botanic Gardens, Sydney (J. Sainty). 54 cl STO (B. Bachman). 55 bc Heather Angel; bl APL (L. Meier); cl OSF (R. Singh). 54/55 t Wildlight (P. Quirk). 56 tcl AUST (F. Monaco/Rex Features); c TPL (A. Evrard); cl Photographie Bulloz. 57 tl OSF (E. Parker); c TPL (S. Fraser/SPL). 58 cl BCL (T.O. Hansen); tl North Wind Picture Archives. 59 cl TPL (G. Tompkinson/SPL); tr STO (L. Nelson). 60 bc STO (L.

Nelson); cl STO (O. Rogge). 61 cr British Textile Technology Group, Leeds, UK. 62 bl The Fairfax Photo Library (Taylor); TPL (SPL). 63 br AUS; bc BIO; tr TPL (D. Parker/SPL); cr Wave Productions (O. Strewe). 70 tr NHM Picture Library (NHM); bl NHM Picture Library (NHM); br OSF (D. Shale); tl Charles Palek. 72 br TPL (D. Scharf/SPL). 73 tl AUS (K. Atkinson); br OSF (G.I. Bernard). 74 br Nature Focus (AM); bl TPL (Nuridsany & Perennou/SPL). 75 cr MW (D. Clyne); tc NHM Picture Library (NHM); tr Nature Focus (AM); tl TPL (A. Syred/SPL); bl PEP (S. Hopkin). 76 bc PEP (J. Lythgoe); br PEP (J. Lythgoe). 77 b CSIRO Division of Entomology (Melbourne University Press); tr TPL (D. Scharf/SPL). 78 tl AUS (P. Goetgheluck P.H.O.N.E.); c NHPA (A. Bannister); bcr TPL (Dr J. Burgess/SPL); br TPL (Nuridsany & Perennou/SPL); bl TPL (Nuridsany & Perennou/SPL); bcl TPL (D. Scharf/SPL). 79 tr OSF (London Scientific Films). 80 bc AUST (H. Pfletschinger/Camera Press); tl BCL (J. Burton); br PEP (B. Kenney). 81 tl OSF (S. Camazine); tr Premaphotos Wildlife (K.G. Preston-Mafham). 82 bl BCL (J. Burton); c TPL (SPL); cl PEP (D. Maitland). 83 bl BCL (K. Taylor). 84 cl BCL (K. Taylor); tl TPL (Nuridsany & Perennou/SPL); bl Premaphotos Wildlife (K.G. Preston-Mafham). 85 cr OSF (D. Fox); tl TPL (J. H. Robinson); tr PEP (B. Kenney). 86 tl NHPA (A. Bannister); cl OSF (G.I. Bernard); bl Premaphotos Wildlife (K.G. Preston-Mafham). 87 tcr AUS (C.A. Henley); bcr AUS (R. Morrison); tr BCL (K. Taylor); br BCL (K. Taylor); tl PEP (K. Lucas). 88 l MW (D. Clyne); tr TPL (C. Cooper). 89 tl BCL (G. Dore). 90 bl Kathie Atkinson; cl MW (D. Clyne). 91 bl AUS (A. & J. Six); c BCL (Dr S. Prato). 92 bl AUS (R. Morrison); br BCL (Dr E. Pott). 93 tr BCL (J. Brackenbury). 94 bl ARDEA (J. Daniels); tr TPL (Dr J. Burgess/SPL). 95 br AUS (P. Goetgheluck P.H.O.N.E.); bl AUST (H. Pfletschinger/Camera Press); tl OSF (London Scientific Films); tcr Terra Australis Photo Agency (E. Beaton). 96 c BCL (Dr F. Sauer); br NHPA (S. Dalton). 98 br ARDEA (A. Warren); tr TPL (A. Pasieka/SPL); c Premaphotos Wildlife (K.G. Preston-Mafham). 99 br Dr Hans Bänziger; bl PEP (G. du Feu). 100 c AUS (J. Cancalosi); tl AUST (R. Amann/Sygma); bl PEP (S. Hopkin). 101 tr MW (D. Clyne); tl OSF (J.A.L. Cooke). 102 cl NHPA (G.I. Bernard); bc TPL (M. Dohrm/SPL); c Premaphotos Wildlife (K.G. Preston-Mafham). 103 tr TPL (Dr J. Burgess/SPL); br Terra Australis Photo Agency (E. Beaton). 104 tl AUS (J.P. Ferrero); cl Ellis Nature Photography; bl TPL (D. Scharf/SPL); c TPL (G. du Feu). 105 bl BCL (J. Cancalosi); br BCL (K. Taylor); tr MW (D. Clyne). 106 cr ARDEA (I.R. Beames); r CSIRO Division of Entomology (J. Green); bc PEP (J. Downer); tr PEP (J. & G. Lythgoe). 107 tc MEPL; tl OSF (J.A.L. Cooke). 106/107 c AUS (Helio/Van Ingen). 108 br AUST (D. Heuclin/SIPA Press); cl BCL (F. Labhardt); tr BCL (A. Stillwell). 109 tl Kathie Atkinson. 110 cr AUS (J.P. Ferrero); br APL (M. Moffett/MP); bl BCL (Dr F. Sauer); tr PEP (S. Hopkin). 111 br BCL (J. Burton). 112 bc BCL (K. Taylor); cl OSF (D. Fox); bl OSF (A. Ramage). 113 r OSF (G.I. Bernard). 114 tl Kathie Atkinson; br BCL (R.P. Carr); tc Pavel German; bl NHPA (G.I. Bernard); bc OSF (J.A.L. Cooke); cl Premaphotos Wildlife (K.G. Preston-Mafham). 115 br BCL (F. Prenzel). 116 cr AUS (P. Goetgheluck P.H.O.N.E.); bl BCL (J. Burton); tr BCL (A. Stillwell); br MW (J. Frazier). 117 tl OSF (J.A.L. Cooke). 118 bl AUS (J. Six); tl BCL (Dr F. Sauer). 119 bc AUS (J.P. Ferrero); cl AUS (P. Goetgheluck P.H.O.N.E.); tl AUS (P. Goetgheluck P.H.O.N.E.); cr AUS (G. Threlfo). 124 cl AUS (U. Hirsch); tr IB (N.J. Dennis). 125 tc TSA (T. Kitchin). 126 tl OSF; cr TSA (K. Schafer). 127 bl OSF (M. Fogden). 128 cl ARDEA (H.D. Dossenbach); tr TSA (T. Kitchin). 129 tl BCL (H. Reinhard); tc PEP (D.P. Maitland); cr TSA (M. Clay); tr TSA (K.T. Givens). 130 c ARDEA (W. Weisser); bc North Wind Picture Archives. 131 cl AUS (T. de Roy). 132 cl BCL (A.J. Stevens); bl IB (J. Blossom). 133 tl BCL (S. Nielsen). 135 tl Kathie Atkinson; cr PEP (M. Conlin). 136 bc M&PF. 137 c BCL (Jeff Foot Productions); bc IB (N.J. Dennis). 138 cl APL (S. Osolinski). 139 tr BCL (A. Deane); tl PEP (R. de la Harpe). 140 bl OSF (K. Westerskov). 141 bl Michael Schneider (*New Zealand Geographic*); tr South Australian Museum (S.C. Donnellan). 142 cr BCL (J. Burton). 143 c M&PF; tl IB (D. Heuclin). 144 tl BCL (J. Visser); br Pavel German; bl PEP (M. Conlin). 146 bl BCL (A.J. Stevens). 147 cr Pavel German; tc IB (D. Heuclin); tl IB (D. Heuclin). 148 c M&PF; cr PEP (M. Clay). 149 br Kathie Atkinson; tr IB (D. Heuclin). 150 c ARDEA (F. Gohier); br IB (D. Heuclin). 151 bl M&PF. 152 tl John

Visser. 153 cr John Visser; tr John Visser; tr Thomas A. Wiewandt. 154 br BCL (J. Visser). 155 br AUS (Ferrero/Labat); tr M&PF; bl IB (S. Dalton). 157 cr Kathie Atkinson; cl M&PF; c TSA (J. McDonald). 158 bl IB (J.H. Carmichael, Jr.). 159 c ARDEA (T. Willock); bc APL (G. Bell); bc TSA (M. Bacon); tl TSA (J. McDonald); cr Thomas A. Wiewandt. 160 cl BCL (C. Zuber); t IB (H. Palo Jr.). 161 tc TSA (D.G. Barker). 162 cl M&PF; bcl M&PF; tcl M&PF. 163 cl TSA (J. McDonald). 164 tr Pavel German; bl IB (J.H. Carmichael, Jr.). 165 c AUST (Shooting Star/A. Sirdofsky). 166 tc NHPA (A. Bannister); br IB (H. and V. Ingen). 167 bl BCL (G. McCarthy). 168 tr Ocean Earth Images (K. Aitken). 169 tl M&PF. 170 tr ARDEA (P. Morris); cl OSF (M. Fogden). 171 tl BCL (A.J. Stevens); tc M&PF; tr TSA (K.T. Givens). 170/171 b M&PF. 172 tr BCL (C.B. and D.W. Frith); cr PEP (J.D. Watt); bl Oliver Strewe (Wave Productions). 173 tr Heather Angel; tc Aurora (J. Azel); cr AUST (Sipa Press); br NHPA (D. Heuclin). 172/173 c OSF (F. Schneidermeyer). 179 tr AUS (Jacana); tcr BCL (H. Reinhard); tl IB (J. van Os); cr TSA (B. Parker). 180 tl TSA (R. Planck). 181 cr NHPA (H. Ausloos). 182 tr AM. 184 bc APL (MP/F. Nicklin); tl BCL (G. Zielser). 185 tr TPL (N. Fobes/TSI); br PEP (R. Coomber). 187 tl AUS (T. De Roy); tc AUS (Ferrero/Labat); tr BCL (R. Williams). 188 tcr AUS (D. Parer & E. Parer-Cook). 189 br Kathie Atkinson; bc AUS (J.P. Ferrero); tl Mitchell Library, State Library of New South Wales. 190 bc AUS (D. Parer & E. Parer-Cook); tl APL (ZEFA). 191 tr AUS (D. Parer & E. Parer-Cook). 192 tl BCL (J. Burton); br BCL (F.J. Erize). 193 tc ARDEA (P. Morris); tr TSA (D. Holden Bailey). 194 bc Merlin D. Tuttle/Bat Conservation International; tl Merlin D. Tuttle/Bat Conservation International. 197 br AUS (J.P. Ferrero). 198 tl APL (MP); br BCL (K. Wothe). 199 bl BCL (K. Wothe). 200 bc NHPA (K. Schafer). 201 tr BCL (F. Bruemmer); br TSA (A. Wolfe/TSI). 202 tr BCL (P. Davey). 203 br Magnum (M. Nichols); tc NHPA (A. Williams). 204 c ARDEA (B. Arthus); tr NHPA (M. Wendler). 205 tc International Photographic Library. 207 b AUS (J. Sauvanet); tl BCL (R. Williams); tr TSA (B. von Hoffmann); tr NHPA (A. Bannister); br NHPA (G. Lacz). 208 tr ARDEA (J.P. Ferrero); cl PEP (A. Dragesco). 209 tc TPL (K. Schafer/TSI). 210 tl AUS (J. Cancalosi); tcl IB (P. McCormick). 211 tr AUS (J.P. Ferrero); tr TSA (B. von Hoffmann). 210/211 c Images of Nature (T. Mangelsen). 212 tcl PEP (K. Scholey). 213 tr NHPA (N.J. Dennis). 214 cl BCL (G. Cubitt). 215 tl BCL (D. & M. Plage); tr NHPA (A. Bannister). 216 c BCL (F. Bruemmer). 217 tr BCL (J. Shaw). 219 tc BCL (Jeff Foot Productions). 220 tcl APL (ZEFA); tl APL (ZEFA). 221 tr APL (MP); tc TPL (A. Wolfe/TSI). 222 bl PEP (J.D. Watt). 224 bl TSA (D. Watts). 225 tcr BCL (H. Reinhard); tr TSA (D. Holden Bailey). 226 tl AUS (A. Henley); bl TSA (E. Robinson); tr TSA (D. Tackett). 227 br AUS (Ferrero/Labat); tc AUS (Jacana/PR/M.D. Tuttle). 230 ti AM (H. Pinelli); ci PR (K. Lucas). 231 tl AM (H. Pinelli); ci EB; bi MW (D. Clyne). 232 b AUS (Y. Gillon/Jacana); i AM (H. Pinelli); t PR (D.P. Maitland). 234 i PR (K. Lucas). 235 b BCL Ltd (E. Pott); tl MEPL; tr MP (M. Moshin). 236 cr MEPL; tr MEPL; i PR (K. Lucas). 237 b BCL Ltd (M.P. Kahl); i MW (D. Clyne). 238 tr AUS (Ferrero-Labat); c APL (Corbis Bettmann); i PR (K. Lucas). 239 TPL (Hulton-Deutsch). 240 tr APL (R. Grunzinski/ Agence Vandystadt); tl EB; c MEPL; br PEP (G. du Feu); bl Smithsonian Institution NMNH (C. Clark). 241 tl AM (C. Bento); tr AM (C. Bento). 242 tl AUS (J. Foott); b BCL Ltd (J. Burton). 243 tr AM (C. Bento); cr AM (C. Bento); br AM (C. Bento). 244 cl AUS (Y. Arthus Bertrand). 245 i EB; cr Comstock, Inc (G. Lepp); tr MEPL. 246 t MEPL; bl PEP (R. Mathews). 249 cr ADL; t IB (J. Van Os); bl OSF (N. Rosing). 250 bl AUS (N. Birks); t MEPL; cl PEP (N. Greaves). 251 br AM (C. Bento). 252 br AUS (Ferrero-Labat); cr MP (F. Lanting). 253 i EB. 254 l MEPL. 255 cr APL (G. Bell); tr Lansdowne Publishing; t PEP (R. Cook). 256 bl AUS (Mammi-France/Jacana); i AM (H. Pinelli); tl AM (H. Angel); tr MW (D. Clyne); bc Project Advertising; cl TSA (D. Watts). 258 bl AUS (M.W. Gillam); i AM (M. Tinsley); tl AUS (M. Tinsley); i AM (H. Pinelli); r APL (Zefa). 259 tl AUS (C.A. Henley). 260 i AM (H. Pinelli); t BCL Ltd (F. Sauer). 261 tr MW (J. Frazier); tc OSF (G.J. Bernard); tl PEP (G. du Feu); b PEP (D.P. Maitland). 262 i AM (H. Pinelli). 263 i AM (H. Pinelli); tr APL (A. Tolhurst); br BCL Ltd (A. Stillwell); b OSF (S. Camazine); r PEP (K. Lucas). 264 i AM (H. Pinelli). 265 i AM (H. Pinelli); tr PR (A. Power); br PEP (G. Douwma). 266 i AM (H. Pinelli); bl PEP (N. Coleman). 267 t PEP (P. Scoones); tr PEP (P. Scoones). 266/267 AUS (K. Atkinson). 268 bl AUS (Y. Arthus Bertrand); i EB. 269 r OSF (J. Aldenhaven). 270 l AM (C. Bento); tl AM (W. Peckover/National Photo Index); i EB; b BCL Ltd (J. Dermid). 271 cr AUS (K. Atkinson); bc AUS (J.P. Ferrero); c AUS (J.P. Ferrero); br APL (Orion Press). 272 l AUS (J.M. La Roque); i EB. 273 b AUS (E. & P. Bauer); br AUS (E. & P. Bauer); r AUS (D. Parer & E. Parer-Cook); tr AUS (D. Parer & E. Parer-Cook). 274 j EB. 275 r APL (J. Carnemolla); j

MW (D. Clyne) 276 i MW (D. Clyne); l OSF (J.H. Robinson); bl STO (Phototake); tr TSA (D.M. Dennis). 277 r APL (Zefa); tr TPL (J. Burgess/SPL). 276/277 c AUS (Ferrero-Labat). 278 bl AM (H. Pinelli); tc APL (T. Stoddart); bc EB; tl EB; i MW (D. Clyne). 279 br AUS (J.P. Ferrero); b EB; bl EB; tr STO (L. Nelson). 281 tl AUS (J. Cancalosi); tr AUS (T. De Roy); bl AUS (Ferrero-Labat); br APL (Zefa). 286 tl The Bodleian Library, Oxford (MS. Ashmole 399); tr GC; bl The Science & Society Picture Library (The Science Museum). 287 tl AKG, London (Naturhistorisches Museum, Vienna/E. Lessing); tr GC. 288 tl The Bridgeman Art Library (Museum of the History of Science, Oxford); bcl TPL (GJLP-CNRI/SPL); bl PR (Dept. of Energy); tcl Rainbow (B. Stanton); cl STO (The Stock Market/H. Sochurek). 289 tr MEPL. 290 bl AUST (T. Bauer); cl The British Museum; tl TPL (SPL). 291 br ADL (Royal North Shore Hospital, Sydney). 293 The Bodleian Library, Oxford (MS. Ashmole 399, fol. 19r); tcr Medical Images, Inc (B. Slaven); tr TPL (Hulton Deutsch). 294 The Bodleian Library, Oxford (MS. Ashmole 399, fol. 20r); cl TPL (P. Motta/SPL); bl TPL (SPL). 295 tr TPL (D. Scharf/SPL). 297 tr PR (K. Eward/Science Source). 298 tc TPL (P. Motta/SPL). 299 br TPL (H. Michler/SPL); tr TPL (J. Mills). 300 bc Medical Images, Inc (H. Sochurek). 301 br Rainbow (H. Morgan). 302 cl STO (The Stock Market/H. Sochurek). 303 cr TPL (BIO). 304 tcl TPL (J. Durham/ SPL); tc TPL (P. Motta/SPL). 305 tc John Watney Photo Library; bc TPL (A. Kage/SPL); br TPL (SPL); tl TPL. 307 tcr BIO; br Melbourne Muscular Dystrophy Association of Victoria (Neurology Department, Royal Children's Hospital); c TPL (M. King); bcr PR (M. Abbey/Science Source); tr PR (M. Abbey/Science Source). 308 c TPL (D. Scharf/SPL); 309 tr APL (West Stock). 308/309 c TPL (S. Terry/SPL). 310 tr BIO; bl TPL (B. Longcore); cl PR (D. Wong). 311 tr ADL; bc IB (D. de Lossy). 313 tc TPL (SPL); bc Sport The Library (D. McNamara). 314 cl TPL (H. Michler/SPL); tl PR (Omikron). 316 tl TPL (J. Mazziotta/ SPL); tc TPL (M. Phelps & J. Mazziotta/SPL); cl PR (S. Camazine/B. Camazine). 318 tl APL (Bettman). 319 tc TPL (N. Kedersha/SPL). 320 tr IB (C. Navajas); cl TPL (A. Pasieka/SPL); tl STO (Mug Shots). 321 br TPL (M. Clarke/SPL). 322 tc AUST (H. Pfletschinger/ Camera Press); tr International Photo Library (Superstock); cl TPL (SPL). 323 tc AUS (S. Wilby & C. Ciantar); br TPL (NIBSC/SPL). 322/323 c STO (D. Kunkel/Phototake). 324 bc ADL; tl Sally Greenhill. 325 tr Peter Arnold, Inc (L. Dwight); tc Rainbow (D. McCoy). 326 c AUS (Ferrero/Labat); tl AUST (Rex Features); cl APL (MP). 327 cr AUS (E. & P. Bauer); tl APL (MP); bc Rainbow (D. McCoy). 328 tl Dr. John Tyler. 329 bl Dr. John Tyler; bcl Image Select/Ann Ronan; ci Image Select/Ann Ronan. 330 tr BIO; cl GC; tcr TPL (P. Motta & S. Makabe/ SPL); tl TPL (D. Phillips); tcl TPL. 331 tl Petit Format (Guigoz); br Rainbow (C. Dittmann). 330/331 c Lennart Nilsson. 332 bc Petit Format (A. Chaumat); bl Petit Format (A. Chaumat); br Petit Format (A. Chaumat); tl TPL (Hulton Deutsch). 333 bc Petit Format (A. Chaumat); bl Petit Format (A. Chaumat); br Petit Format (A. Chaumat); tl PR (F. Grehan). 334 br ADL; c ADL; tr AUST (Sygma/I. Wyman); cr Cochlear Ltd, Australia; bl Peter Arnold, Inc (Siu); cl TPL (PR/C. Bjornberg); tcr TPL (TSI/Med. Illus. SBHA). 335 bl ADL; tcl ADL (Sydney Artificial Eyes); bc AUST (Sipa-Press/F. Durand); tcr The Bridgeman Art Library (Christie's, London); tr The Bridgeman Art Library (London Library, St. James's Square); tl MEPL; r Otto Bock; c TPL (C. Priest/ SPL). 342 cl Coo-ee Picture Library (R. Ryan). 347 tc ARDEA (M.D. England); tr NHM; tl TSA (J. Cancalosi). 349 tr NHM. 350 bl University of Chicago Hospitals. 356 bl Matrix (NHM/L. Psihoyos). 358 c NHM; tl NHM. 361 c NHM. 360/361 b NHM. 364 cl ADL. 367 cr Matrix (L. Psihoyos). 369 tc TPL (SPL/S. Stammers). 371 cr American Museum of Natural History (Neg. No. 35423/A.E. Anderson). 372 tcl ARDEA (F. Gohier); tc AUST (Keystone); cl NHM; tl NHM. 374 bl NHM. 375 t ADL. 378 c AM (C. Bento); bl NHM; tcl Natural History Photographic Agency (P. Johnson); tl PEP (W. Dennis). 379 tr Matrix (L. Psihoyos). 382 cl APL (NASA/Reuters); tl IB (Image Makers). 383 tr IB (J. Hunter). 384 tc Berlin Museum für Naturkunde (P. Wellnhofer); tl Matrix (Humboldt Museum, Berlin/ L. Psihoyos); cl PEP (P. Chapman). 385 br AUS (Ferrero/Labat); bcr STO (Animals Animals). 386 cl Image Select (Ann Ronan Picture Library); bl David Norman. 387 br APL (P. Menzel); bl Everett Collection; bcr Matrix (L. Psihoyos). 389 tr Matrix (L. Psihoyos). 390 bl ARDEA (F. Gohier). 394 t AM (H. Pinelli); c AM (H. Pinelli). 395 c AM (H. Pinelli); b ADL. 396 i AM (H. Pinelli); br PR (NASA/SPL); cr TPL (SPL). 398 i AM (H. Pinelli); tl Images Unlimited Inc (C. Nicklin); bl PR (J. R. Factor); br PEP (R. Hessler); c PEP (F. Schulke). 399 James Cook University (D. Johnson). 400 i AM (H. Pinelli). 401 tl MEPL (PR); bl TPL (SPL); cl TPL (SPL). 402 i AM (H. Pinelli); tl TPL (J. Sanford/SPL). 403 cr ADL. 404 i AM (H. Pinelli). 405 cl BCL Ltd (K. Taylor); tr Survival Anglia (J. Foott). 406 i AM

639